To my parents

This book has been published with the assistance
of a grant from Ómnium Cultural

Contents

Acknowledgements

I would not have embarked upon such an ambitious undertaking as a comprehensive study of contemporary Catalonia, let alone been able to bring it to completion, without the help of many people. Josep Garcia Reyes, formerly responsible for North American affairs with the Generalitat, first encouraged me to undertake the project and has maintained an interest throughout its development. Josep Millàs, of Òmnium Cultural, provided a publication advance which made the project possible but at the same time left me free to develop the book as I felt appropriate.

Close to 90 public officials, scholars, and experts, mainly in Catalonia, generously agreed to be interviewed, in some cases on more than one occasion. Several people read and commented on various sections of the manuscript: Robert Agranoff, Cesaero Aguilera de Prat, Miquel Caminal, Miren Etxezarreta, Mireya Folch-Serra, Enric Fossas, Salvador Giner, Michael Keating, Ferran Requejo, Jordi Sanchez, Miquel Strubell, and Josep Soler. I am especially grateful to Xavier Arbos, who read almost the whole manuscript. Finally, Shaudin Melgar Foraster edited the text with an eye to correcting the use of Catalan. Enrique Duran Cordova corrected the Castilian, as well as preparing the bibliography. David Cashaback prepared transcripts from the tapes of a large number of interviews. Needless to say, I alone am responsible for all remaining errors.

At Oxford University Press, Ric Kitowski enthusiastically supported the project in its early stages. Subsequently, Laura MacLeod and Phyllis Wilson guided the production of the book. Finally, I was most fortunate to have Freya Godard as editor. As with a previous book of mine, she consistently sought to maintain the highest of editorial standards. During the final stages of the book's production, as I became preoccupied with my new responsibilities at Glendon College, I frequently tried the patience of these people. I am most grateful that they persevered and brought the project to fruition.

Throughout the whole enterprise my wife, Susan Chapman, supported my efforts while fully sharing my new-found enthusiasm for Catalonia and Spain. By dedicating this book to my parents I wish to thank my mother, who first encouraged my intellectual endeavours so many years ago, to honour the memory of my father, who took such interest in them, and to thank my stepfather, who has shared in my more recent pursuits.

Introduction

Catalonia is not well known in the English-speaking world. North Americans, in particular, often confuse it with the Basque Country, another part of Spain that is more frequently in the headlines, and assume incorrectly that Catalonia has an active terrorist movement.

And yet Catalonia's long history as a distinct entity goes back to the late 900s. During the Middle Ages, when it was among the most advanced of European societies, Catalans fashioned a set of covenants that pre-dated the Magna Carta and established one of Europe's first parliaments. And Catalonia was a major trading centre; indeed, it dominated much of the western Mediterranean, both economically and politically.

After centuries of economic and political decline, Catalonia once again became a major economic force in the early 1800s and has remained one ever since. Along with the Basque Country, it brought Spain into the industrial age. Catalonia continues to be an important site of economic innovation and a net exporter of goods to the rest of Spain. Indeed, it leads most of Spain both in general economic activity, as measured by such indices as gross domestic product, and individual well-being, as measured by personal wealth and standard of living.

Moreover, Catalonia has produced cultural figures who are known throughout the Western world. The painter Salvador Dalí and the muralist Joan Miró were both Catalans, as was the architect Antoni Gaudí. Pablo Picasso was not a Catalan by birth or adoption, but he spent his formative Blue Period in Barcelona, Catalonia's capital. The cellist Pablo Casals was a Catalan, as are the outstanding opera singers José (Josep in Catalan) Carreras and Victoria de Los Angeles (dels Angels in Catalan). Yet few North Americans recognize them as Catalans; at best they are thought of as Spaniards.

If Catalonia and Catalans are not well known on their own terms, it is not because their society is inward-looking and out of touch with the larger world. Historically Catalonia has participated fully in European cultural and economic movements, as the prominence of its artists and performers clearly demonstrates. Indeed, Catalans like to see themselves as the most European of Spaniards and can make a good case to that effect.

Nor do Catalans lack any clear sense of themselves as a distinct entity. For a century now, Catalonia's cultural and political leaders, and much of its population, have shared the belief that Catalonia constitutes a nation. Indeed, it does have most of the earmarks of a nation: a language and culture, a long history of distinct institutions, a strong sense of common history, and such symbols of nationhood as a flag and a national anthem.

The reason Catalonia is so little known lies in politics. Simply put, through most of the last few centuries Catalonia has not existed as a political entity within Spain. Indeed, especially in its early years, the Franco regime systematically sought to eliminate public use of the Catalan language in a campaign that has been aptly called 'cultural genocide'. Since Spain's transition to democracy, Catalonia has enjoyed the status of one of Spain's 17 autonomous communities, but even this new arrangement falls short of federalism. In other words, Catalonia is a striking case of a 'nation without a state'.

It is perhaps for this reason that there is no comprehensive study of Catalonia available in English. This book corrects that state of affairs by providing an overview of Catalonia's political, cultural, economic, and social life, with particular emphasis upon the last few decades.

But there are other reasons for a book on contemporary Catalonia than merely filling a gap in the social-science literature. Catalonia poses in an especially interesting fashion many key issues of contemporary debate.

For instance, there has been much discussion of whether nations are willed into existence by historical forces or are merely the artifacts or creations of intellectuals who have deliberately 'constructed' them. Clearly, the emergence of a Catalan nation was the work of intellectual and political élites who, towards the end of the nineteenth century, began to make the argument that Catalonia was indeed a nation and to identify the characteristics and qualities that made it so. But once the idea had been formulated and disseminated, it took hold quite rapidly among people who saw themselves as Catalans and set strong enough roots to survive the best efforts of the Franco regime to eradicate it. This was possible only because Catalonia had already existed as a distinct entity for so many centuries and did indeed have many of the qualities associated with a nation.

Catalonia also offers important insight into the debate over whether nations, especially nations that exist within larger nation-states, are necessarily 'ethnic' in nature with membership restricted to people who share, or at least claim to share, a common historical descent. From the outset Catalan nationalists have tended to define the nation in terms, not of ethnicity or descent, but of language and culture. Membership in the nation is open, in principle, to all who adopt the Catalan language and culture, whatever their origins. Although some Catalan nationalists have tried periodically to define the nation ethnically, especially when confronted by large numbers of newcomers, on each occasion the dominant nationalist leaders have rejected such claims. We will examine a variety of explanations for the strength of this 'civic' view of nationalism.

At the same time, Catalonia challenges the common image of nations without states as economically backward or dependent 'peripheries'. For Catalonia, along with the Basque Country, has historically been the economic core of Spain. Yet despite its economic strength, Catalonia, unlike the Basque Country, has never had a significant movement for political independence. Instead, Catalan nationalists have usually attempted to obtain some form of political autonomy within

Spain. Yet, even a federal state with a clear constitutional basis may be long in coming.

Still, Catalonia demonstrates that nations without states can be remarkably successful. Some of Catalonia's greatest achievements, such as its economic resurgence and cultural renaissance in the nineteenth century or its economic boom in the 1950s, occurred precisely at times when it had no political institutions whatsoever. To a considerable extent, economic growth and, in particular, the good works of an indigenous bourgeoisie, provided the wherewithal to survive, indeed to prosper, without a state.

For some observers, Catalonia points the way to the future as well: with globalization, state structures have become obsolete, as have notions of political sovereignty. For advocates of the 'region state' Catalonia is a perfect example of what can be accomplished by open and dynamic regional economies. Yet there are continuing pressures to develop an autonomous Catalan state, at least within a federal framework. There is a need for development policies and employment strategies to offset Catalonia's disadvantages as an economic region. Globalization is also presenting Catalonia's linguistic and cultural distinctiveness with new challenges that, according to many Catalans, can be met only through political action.

Finally, Catalonia's relationship with the rest of Spain offers important insights into the politics of 'multinational states'. There are many states in the Western world that contain such 'internal nations'—one thinks of Belgium, Canada, and the United Kingdom—and all of them are wrestling with the complications of having two or more nations within the same state. Upon becoming a democratic state, Spain tested the possibilities of asymmetry as a formula for reconciling the demands of Catalonia and the two other 'historic nations' (the Basque Country and Galicia) for autonomy with the commitment of the rest of Spain to a strong central state. And Spain has tried to handle the linguistic aspirations of its historic nations through a formula of 'co-officiality'. In contemporary Catalonia nationalists have proposed creative models for a confederal Spain.

Catalonia offers important insights into other areas than the dynamics of states without nations. The Catalan language, for instance, has demonstrated remarkable resilience. Despite the concerted effort of the Franco regime to suppress the language, not only did Catalan survive as a spoken language but in the 1960s there was an outpouring of books and other writings in Catalan. With the transition to democracy and the creation of the Generalitat, an autonomous government with a role in education, there has been a prodigious increase in the number of Catalans able to read and write in Catalan, including the children of Spanish-speakers. Yet the case of Catalonia clearly demonstrates that knowledge of a language does not in itself guarantee it will be used, for in many spheres, the use of Catalan remains limited. It is far from certain that a language can survive under such conditions.

Finally, Catalonia offers the instance of an especially rich 'civil society'. Historically, Catalans took pride in the number, scope, and dynamism of their social, cultural, and philanthropic associations. Rooted in centuries-old traditions of political participation by Catalan burghers and middle classes, civil society seemed to be far stronger in Catalonia than in the rest of Spain. It helped to compensate for the absence of a state. Yet the decline of the indigenous bourgeoisie that underwrote much of this associational activity, coupled with the accelerating need for various forms of social services, have forced these associations to become dependent upon the Generalitat. Catalan civil society is no longer freestanding. Indeed, the Catalan case suggests that this may no longer be possible anywhere today despite the claims of neo-liberal theorists. In short, there are a multitude of reasons to study Catalonia.

Chapter 1 provides an overview of Catalan history up to the twentieth century. In particular, it demonstrates how this history offered an especially rich base on which nationalists could construct the idea of a Catalan nation. Chapter 2 describes the processes through which intellectual and political élites finally did develop the idea of a Catalan nation. It traces the struggles to give political form to the Catalan nation and then shows how they came to an abrupt halt with the victory of Franco's forces in 1939.

The subsequent chapters examine in detail the effort, in the wake of the Franco regime, to 'reconstruct' the Catalan nation in the midst of political, social, and economic change. So profound were these changes that national reconstruction could not mean simply re-establishing the nation that had existed before. In any event, Catalonia was in the hands of a new leadership whose religious faith and economic and social conservatism led it to reject key elements of the nationalist project that had guided Catalonia in the 1930s. National reconstruction had to be a quite different project.

Chapter 3, which examines the transition to Spanish democracy, shows how the negotiations for a new constitution afforded Catalonia the opportunity to restore a certain degree of political autonomy. At the same time, it shows how the outcome of these negotiations reflects fundamental divisions over the nature of Spain. The many contradictions and ambiguities that appear in the constitution are themselves the result of these divisions. Chapter 4 explores the effort to secure Catalonia's autonomy within this new political order. It shows that, largely through parliamentary dealings, Catalonia has been able to secure an important degree of autonomy that extends over most of the areas of greatest concern to Catalan nationalists. Yet even by the standards of federalism, Catalonia remains a nation without a state.

Turning to political economy, Chapter 5 shows how Catalonia has maintained its status as a core region of the Spanish economy, with concomitant economic dynamism and relative affluence, but under very different terms from those of mid-century Spain. Chapter 6, which examines Catalonia's society, argues that in these terms the reconstructed Catalan nation is fundamentally different from what existed in pre-Franco times.

Focusing upon the Catalan language, Chapter 7 explores how constitutional structures, political economy, and the composition of Catalonia's population jointly shaped the Generalitat's attempts to reinforce or 'normalize' the Catalan language. It analyses two successive laws and assesses their effects. Chapter 8, which examines identity in Catalonia, shows that many Catalans share the basic tenets of contemporary Catalan nationalism, but also that other Catalans, especially those whose mother tongue is Spanish or Castilian, reject these ideas outright.

Finally, Chapter 9 draws some general conclusions from the study and compares Catalonia and other minority nations or nations without states.

Chapter 1

The Historical Roots of Nationhood

It goes without saying that the idea of a Catalan nation did not simply emerge spontaneously or through the mysterious workings of some hidden forces. Like all conceptions of nation, that of the Catalan nation was 'constructed' or 'imagined'. But the idea of a Catalan nation must be especially compelling to have been so tenacious as to resist even the determined efforts of the Franco regime to stamp it out.

In fact, the intellectuals and thinkers who gave birth to the Catalan nation in the late nineteenth century did have unusually powerful materials to work with. Simply put, they gave 'national' form to a cultural, social, and even political reality that had existed for many centuries, indeed since the late 900s. Moreover, this historical entity has some remarkable accomplishments and achievements to its credit. Given such a long and illustrious past, it is not difficult to see why so many contemporary Catalans remain committed to obtaining recognition of their nation.

The Catalan Language

At the centre of all claims for Catalan nationhood is language. The Catalan language serves to distinguish Catalonia from all other would-be nations, including the Spanish one. To varying degrees, it is shared by all presumed members of the nation; and it has been the basis of important national achievements, including a rich literature.

Indirect testimony to the centrality of language to Catalonia's status as a nation lies in the periodic attempts of the Spanish authorities to eradicate it. The most dramatic instance, of course, is the Franco regime, which, dedicated to the integrity of the Spanish nation and having a morbid fear of Catalan nationalism, systematically prohibited any public use of the Catalan language. It was not the first such attempt, just the most draconian. Yet even it failed in the face of the determination of Catalan nationalists to save this essential feature of Catalan nationhood.

Contrary to a widespread assumption among Spanish nationalists, as well as many foreigners, Catalan is not simply a dialect of the Spanish language or Castilian but is generally recognized by linguists to constitute a language of its own: Catalan and Castilian are not mutually intelligible, Catalan is not derived historically from Castilian, it has its own grammatical system and lexicon, and it has a centuries-old literature.[1] Indeed, in linguistic terms it is closer to French and Italian, which are also derived from late Latin, than to Castilian.[2]

Historically, Catalan emerged in the same way as the other Romance languages. After the Romans completed their conquest of the 'Catalan Lands' in 197 BC, their imperial language, Latin, began to mix with the vernacular, and out of this process developed a new language with Latin structure but a vocabulary drawn largely from the local vernacular. The Latin from which Catalan emerged was more modern and popular than the one on which Castilian was based.[3] Moreover, according to some analysts, Catalan bears a closer relationship to Latin than does Castilian since, as a Mediterranean region, Catalonia underwent a longer and more intense 'romanization'.[4] And during the Middle Ages, the fact that Catalonia was closely linked to the south of modern-day France meant that Catalan could develop along lines similar to Languedoc, sheltered from the influence of Castilian.[5] In the fifteenth century, when Castilian finally did begin to exert an influence in Catalonia, thanks to changed geopolitical circumstances, Catalan was already well formed.

Indeed, in the past some linguists even argued that Catalan should be seen as a Gallo-Romance language rather than an Iberian one, but this position has fallen out of favour. Although the Latin from which Catalan emerged is close to the Latin of Gaul, its morphology clearly places it in the Ibero-Romance group.[6]

Catalan emerged as a written language during the tenth and eleventh centuries.[7] In the twelfth century it began to appear in religious and juridical texts and was widely used in commerce.[8] By the thirteenth century it had become the main administrative language[9] of the region and had emerged as an important literary language, thanks in particular to the philosopher and story-teller Ramon Lull, who broke with tradition to write on philosophy in Catalan rather than Latin. Similarly, Arnau de Vilanova (who, in the thirteenth century, wrote his medical texts in Latin) wrote his theological works in Catalan.[10]

The subsequent two centuries were a golden age of Catalan literature, featuring among many the Valencian writer Joanot Martorell, whose *Tirant lo Blanc* was judged by Cervantes to be 'the best book of its kind in the world'.[11] During this period, owing to Catalonia's economic and political ascendancy, Catalan spread to other parts of the Mediterranean. It became the official language of Sardinia in 1323, remaining so until the end of the eighteenth century. In Sicily it was regularly used in public assemblies, along with Sicilian and Latin, until the end of the fifteenth century.[12]

When Catalonia's economic and political fortunes declined over the subsequent centuries, so did Catalan literary production: the sixteenth, seventeenth, and eighteenth centuries did not produce one figure of note.[13] Indeed, during the seventeenth century, which began with the open suppression of Catalan under the Bourbons, the majority of Catalan intellectuals wrote in Castilian. None the less, Catalan survived as an oral language, as well as the language of non-literary texts and personal correspondence.[14]

With the second half of the nineteenth century came the Renaixença, a remarkable revival of Catalan as a language of literary creation. The manifesto for the Renaixença was Joaquim Rubió i Ors preface, written in 1841, to an anthology of poetry in which he called for Catalonia to recover its cultural, although not political, independence.[15] Instrumental in spurring on this revival was the Jocs florals (Floral games), which were established in 1859. Based upon fourteenth-century poetry contests and history pageants, the Jocs florals served not only to present Catalan literature to a public audience but to make it known on the European cultural scene. They also launched an effort, which was to extend over several decades, to standardize the spelling of Catalan.[16] Though the Renaixença began with poetry, it soon extended to all forms of literature and to every other field of cultural activity.

In the early twentieth century modern Catalan was finally standardized through the creation of a language academy, the Institut d'Estudis Catalans, in 1907 and the publication of a dictionary and other reference works by the linguist Pompeu Fabra.[17] Catalan was also used in the new mass media: by 1900 there were six Catalan-language newspapers in Catalonia, compared to 18 in Castilian.[18] There was a large growth in the number of books published in Catalan, including translations of foreign classics. And various attempts were made to teach Catalan to the general public, although only during the 1930s was it the language of public instruction.

During the Franco period Catalan was systematically suppressed but still survived as a popular language, but since then Catalonia's government (the Generalitat) has made a priority of restoring or 'normalizing' Catalan's status and making it the common language of all Catalan residents. By 1996 it was understood by 95 per cent of Catalonia's six million residents and spoken by over 75 per cent.[19] Catalan is also understood by about 2.8 million people in Valencia and 560,000 in the Balearic Islands.[20] Beyond that, it is the official language of Andorra and is spoken by a small number of people in Sardinia. In total, about 6.5 million people speak Catalan and about 9 million understand it. To be sure, if more stringent standards are used, the figures are considerably smaller: in 1996, only 72.4 per cent of Catalonia's residents could read Catalan and only 45.8 per cent could write it.[21] It also appears that Catalan is the normal language of family life for only a little more than half of Catalonia's residents, the rest of whom use Castilian.[22]

Though Catalan continues to face serious obstacles and has suffered periods of sustained persecution, it is still the primary or secondary language of a critical mass of people. The numbers that speak Catalan are roughly similar to those that speak such other European languages as Danish, Norwegian, or Swedish.[23] Moreover, it continues to be an important medium of cultural creation and thus provides a strong base for claims of Catalan nationhood.

Emergence of Catalonia as a Distinct Entity

The long historical existence of the Catalan language and its notable achievements as a medium of literary expression reflect something more profound: the presence and support of a distinct social entity. Ultimately, nationalists are able to trace the existence of Catalonia itself into the distant past; by some accounts it has existed for over a thousand years.

Starting with the founding of the coastal city of Empúries by the Greeks in about 600 BC, Catalonia underwent a long series of invasions, most of which involved lengthy occupations. The Romans arrived in 218 BC and began the processes of romanization that were to leave such an indelible mark not only on language but on many other aspects of life in the Catalan lands. With the collapse of the Roman Empire, Catalonia was settled by the Visigoths, whose kingdom survived until the beginning of the eighth century. Then, like the rest of the Iberian peninsula, Catalonia fell under the control of the Moors.

By AD 790, Charlemagne had succeeded in expelling the Moors from a borderland south of the Pyrenees, known as the *Marca Hispanica* (Hispanic March), thus creating the embryo of Catalonia. Then in 801 Charlemagne's son freed Barcelona from the Moors as he attempted to push his empire farther to the south. Thanks to the decline of the Frankish monarchy, in 878 Count Wilfred the Hairy was able to unite under his rule five of the nine earldoms (including Barcelona) that made up the Hispanic March. Under the terms of his will, Barcelona and two other earldoms remained united, forming the nucleus of Catalonia.

When the Moors returned and attacked Barcelona in 985, the Frankish monarchy provided no assistance and the city was destroyed. In response, the Count of Barcelona, Borell II, broke off his ties of vassalage with the French monarch in 988. It is to that year that nationalists date the creation of Catalonia as a political entity, claiming that Catalonia is no less than a 'millennial country'.[24] Apparently the term 'Catalan' was not actually used to denote the population of the area until the end of the eleventh century and beginning of the twelfth.[25] Be that as it may, Catalonia as an autonomous political entity was already in existence.

A Distinct Social Entity

Beyond a long historical existence, the case for Catalan nationhood is also based on a distinctiveness that goes far beyond language. Here too, there is much to support such claims.

In its origins, Catalonia was a profoundly feudal society. In this, according to many scholars, it differed from the rest of the Iberian peninsula, where feudalism was 'deficient' and imperfect.[26] In fact, Catalonia was one of the very first feudal societies. In 1070 the Count of Barcelona, Ramon Berenguer I, succeeded in making the competing counts his vassals and thus creating the Catalan feudal state. So Catalonia became a feudal state at the same time as the Norman state was created in England.[27]

According to some scholars, these distinctively feudal beginnings set Catalonia on a different course from the rest of the peninsula, including Castile. The feudal structures spawned a network of contractual relations among noblemen, clergy, peasants, and burghers through which each sector enjoyed certain areas of freedom. Thus, in a process very similar to what was taking place in England, Catalonia developed an elaborate structure of covenants, contracts, and, ultimately, a feudal constitution. Indeed, the Catalan Usatges was adopted in 1150, well before the English Magna Carta. Among the laws it proclaimed was legal equality between 'men of honour' (burghers) and the nobility.

By many accounts, this system of covenants and law implanted a world view, dubbed *pactisme*, that has become an enduring trait of Catalan society. Under normal conditions, it is argued, the legal and political life of Catalonia has been governed by *pactist* assumptions: rules emerge from contracts that parties make of their own accord, and social life in general should be based upon bargaining and accommodation rather than force or domination. In effect, 'contractualism became an essential component of the Catalan way of life and the institutionalized life of the people.'[28]

This *pactisme* helps to explain why Catalonia developed one of Europe's first parliaments—by some accounts the very first.[29] During the thirteenth century regular assemblies were held to give advice to the Catalan monarch. Called the Corts and embodying the assumption that the relationship between the monarch and his subjects should be based on negotiation, they provided representation for three 'estates': the nobility, the clergy, and the burghers as represented by the heads of the municipal councils. By the end of the century the monarch needed the consent of the Corts to approve laws or collect revenue, and in the mid-fourteenth century the Corts established a standing committee, called the Diputació del General, or Generalitat, which negotiated with the king the sums of money he was to receive. By the beginning of the fifteenth century, the Generalitat had become a political body designed to maintain control over the monarchy.[30]

To be sure, these developments should not be equated with democracy. Representation within the Corts was limited to a few. None the less, especially for the times, they did represent major innovations in the institutional limitation of the monarch's authority.

According to many scholars, both *pactisme* and parliamentarianism differentiated Catalonia clearly from the rest of the Iberian peninsula.[31] The parallels with Catalonia lie elsewhere, particularly in England. Nor should this be surprising, for just as England and Catalonia were arguably the first feudal structures in Europe, so they can be said to have become the most highly developed ones.[32]

But the argument goes further. Catalonia's distinctively feudal origins are also used to explain how Catalonia ultimately could be an important site of commercial and then industrial capitalism. Catalonia's Mediterranean setting supported the development of commerce but its elaborate feudal structures enabled a class of merchants to develop, and, of course, contractualism was the ideal framework for commercial dealings. At a later point contractualism enabled Catalonia's *menestralia*, a middle class composed of artisans, shopkeepers, and workshop owners, to provide an indigenous leadership for Catalonia's early transition to industrial capitalism.[33]

Once again Catalonia followed a different path from the rest of the peninsula. Indeed, Castile's transition to capitalism was late and difficult. And once again the parallel with England is especially striking. As Salvador Giner has put it, the greater 'Europeanness' that Catalonia has always displayed compared to the rest of the Iberian peninsula has less to do with its geographic proximity to France than the 'Europeanness' of its beginnings, as a feudal society, with all that implied for its subsequent development.[34]

Importance as an Economic and Political Power

Beyond tracing a distinctiveness in origins and history, especially in relation to the rest of the Iberian peninsula, Catalan nationalists look to the past for evidence of great achievements that can be a source of pride but that also, perhaps, might offer some promise for future attainments. The legal and political innovations that we have already noted can certainly serve that purpose. But there is much more. In particular, Catalan nationalists can point to the fact that during the late Middle Ages Catalonia was a major economic and political power, dominating much of the western Mediterranean. This golden age long preceded Castile's emergence as a major force.

Catalonia began by building up links with its neighbours and potential rivals. In 1112 it gained predominance over Languedoc and Provence; in 1137, through a dynastic marriage, it established a confederation with Aragon, a likely competitor. Formally based upon equality between the two parties, but with Catalonia as the dominant one, the confederation left the two entities intact but bestowed the titles of King of Aragon and Count of Barcelona on the same person.

During the reign of Jaume I (1213–1276), Catalan merchants became increasingly active in trade, not just with the Italian maritime republics but with the North African coast and the East. Initially, the trade may have been limited to such items as contraband and slaves, but it appears that with time Catalonia became an important supplier of goods to other parts of the peninsula, to which it sold spices, fine fabrics, sugar, paper, and other luxury goods from the Mediterranean and the Orient. It exported wine, dried fruits, leather, furs, and shipbuilding materials.[35]

By the mid-twelfth century some Catalans had acquired a great deal of wealth. Indeed, whether individually or collectively, wealthy 'citizens' financed the construction of ships used by the king himself. Nine citizens financed the conquest of neighbouring Tortosa, held by the Moors.[36] At the same time, the king supported Catalan shipping interests by giving them first right to ship goods waiting in the port of Barcelona and a monopoly over the shipment of Catalan wines.[37] In medieval Catalonia, merchant capital and the sovereign worked closely together.[38]

Linked to this commercial expansion was the development of a system of consuls to represent Catalan interests. Between 1260 and 1290, Catalan consuls were established in Alexandria, Pisa, and Seville, as well as in the North African towns of Tunis and Bougie (now known as Bejaïa). By the end of the fourteenth century, Catalonia had 42 such consuls. These posts, which were often filled by members of Barcelona's great families, carried great prestige.[39]

Catalonia also became an innovator in maritime law; indeed the Consolat de Mar is the oldest known body of such law. Widely applied in the Mediterranean, it was one of the bases from which international mercantile law developed.[40]

Catalonia's ascendancy in the Mediterranean was based not just on trade but on control of territory as well, largely through conquest. Together Catalonia and Aragon conquered the neighbouring Muslim-controlled territories of Lleida and Tortosa. In the thirteenth century Jaume I conquered Majorca, which was held by the Muslims; a joint Catalan-Aragonese campaign took Valencia from the Muslims; and Peter the Great conquered Sicily in 1282. Corsica was conquered in 1298. Through mercenaries, the Catalan-Aragonese confederation even seized control of the Greek duchies of Athens and Neopàtria in 1379. In 1323 Catalonia conquered Sardinia, and finally, in 1443, Alfons IV conquered Naples. In addition, Catalonia held territory on the other side of the Pyrenees, including Roussillon and Cerdagne.

In the end, Catalonia controlled a major share of Mediterranean territory. By and large, these annexed territories were granted a degree of autonomy and their own institutions, while sovereignty resided with the Catalan-Aragonese monarch.[41] But Catalonia's overseas holdings exceeded its means, and ultimately led in the fifteenth century to a clash between the Catalan monarch and the bourgeoisie.[42]

Catalonia's achievements during this golden age were truly remarkable by any standard. The volume of trade through Catalonia as a whole, including Valencia and Majorca, rivalled that of Venice or Genoa.[43] Equally noteworthy were the flowering of Catalan poetry and other forms of literature and the early development of the Corts, maritime law, and system of overseas consuls. The Corts emerged, moreover, not through agitation, let alone revolution as in England and France, but through *pactisme* and 'spontaneous collaboration'[44] among the king, the cities, the Church, and even the nobility. This institution speaks to a remarkable cohesion around the monarchy.

An especially striking assessment of this period is found in the monumental study by the French historian Pierre Vilar. Despite his evident sympathy for Catalonia, which was the essential focus of his long professional life, Vilar was frequently sceptical of the claims of Catalan nationalist historians, especially those of the past. Yet, when it came to the golden age, he openly recognized Catalonia's pre-modernity; he even considered that Catalonia had come close to being a nation-state:

Between 1250 and 1350, the Catalan principality was perhaps the European country to which it would be the least inexact or risky to use such seemingly anachronistic terms as political and economic imperialism or 'nation-state'.[45]

The fundamental conditions for a nation had been there since the thirteenth century:

language, territory, economic life, psychological make-up, cultural community, even the preoccupation with 'the market', 'the school where a bourgeoisie learns about nationalism'. Ten documents prove that this is indeed the dominant concern, with the result that the Catalan merchant class wanted its own.[46]

Surviving Adversity

One can only imagine what the outcome would have been if Catalonia had continued along that path. Certainly, there is more than enough here to stimulate nationalist fantasies. But, of course, this did not happen; instead, Catalan nationalists have had to seek a far different kind of inspiration from the next two centuries: evidence of the ability of Catalonia to survive in the face of severe adversity, including loss of its political autonomy and outright suppression of its language.

Economic and Social Decline

In large part, Catalonia's decline stemmed from internal conditions. A series of plagues took their toll, starting with the Black Death of 1348[47] and continuing at regular intervals through the fifteenth century.[48] At the middle of the fourteenth century almost all 100 members of Barcelona's city council, Consell de Cent, succumbed to the plague.[49] Then the peasants abandoned the countryside, partly because of the plague, and agricultural production began to fall.[50] Thus, in 1333, a famine took 10,000 lives in Barcelona.[51] There was even a series of earthquakes in the fifteenth century.[52]

As a result during the second part of the fourteenth century and into the fifteenth the population of Catalonia declined dramatically. The population of Barcelona fell from 50,000 in 1340 to 20,000 in 1477. By the end of the fifteenth century Catalonia's population had fallen to half of what it had been 150 years earlier.[53]

This decline intensified the contradictions within Catalonia's feudal structures. In the countryside, the serfs began to rebel against these structures, prompted in part by their desire to occupy lands that had been abandoned by others through death or migration to the cities.[54] In Barcelona a party representing the more popular elements demanded the right to participate in the city government; the Corts and the Generalitat called on the king to resist these demands. In addition, Catalonia's public finances were strained by the combination of population decline and the heavy costs of maintaining its overseas territories.[55] In 1410, for the first time in five centuries, the Catalan dynasty underwent a succession crisis.

Anti-Jewish sentiments developed, and pogroms were conducted in 1348 and 1391.[56] And devaluations of the Catalan currency, the *florin*, spurred popular unrest.[57] Catalonia's remarkable social solidarity was fast disappearing.[58]

In the end, the Generalitat led an uprising against King Joan II, and Catalonia was engulfed in civil war from 1462 to 1472.[59] Though the king finally prevailed, his victory carried a fateful price, for during the war, in an effort to secure outside support, he had pledged his son in marriage to Isabelle of Castile. In 1469 the two dynasties were joined and Catalonia fell into Castile's orbit.

Under the new arrangement Catalonia maintained its self-government, but it lost all control over foreign policy and, as a subordinate part of the Spanish empire, it was not allowed to trade with the American colonies, the new source of European wealth. Moreover, Catalonia's established economic base, Mediterranean trade, was collapsing; a Turkish-French alliance blocked the route to the East.[60]

According to Vilar, there was a multitude of ways in which Catalonia, like several foreign powers, might still have been able to acquire some of the riches of the Americas. But it no longer had the capital and resources necessary to pursue them, given the demographic and economic losses it had suffered.[61] In effect, the changed geopolitical circumstances simply reinforced Catalonia's decline. Conversely, once Catalonia was able to refashion itself, it experienced such a remarkable economic renewal that it obtained the right to trade with the Americas.

Centralization under the Spanish State

During the sixteenth and seventeenth centuries, Catalonia retained a certain degree of formal political autonomy. It maintained its own currency, customs, and tax system, and Catalan remained the official language. But the monarchs now lived in Madrid, and they summoned the Catalan Corts less and less. Finally, after 1632 the Corts did not meet at all—until 1701. The king's authority was represented by a viceroy for Catalonia.

Limited as this autonomy may have been, it did spare Catalonia the worst effects of an economic decline affecting Spain in general. In relative terms, Catalonia was prosperous and was therefore the natural target of a central government facing an acute fiscal crisis. The Corts and the Consell de Cent resisted these pressures as best they could. At the same time, the Catalan peasantry became aroused against the presence, and behaviour, of large numbers of Spanish troops (Catalans were excluded from the army) and the expense of maintaining them.[62]

In 1640, under the leadership of the Generalitat, the Catalan peasantry rose in revolt; the viceroy was assassinated and Catalonia declared its independence. (Catalonia's present-day national anthem—'Song of the Reapers'—originated during this insurrection.) Thanks to the assistance of the king of France, the Catalans were able to hold off the Spanish troops, but in 1651 Spain and France signed a treaty under which Catalonia lost its independence, although maintaining its formal autonomy vis-à-vis Castile. And, eight years later, Catalonia lost the two Catalan regions of Rossillon and Cerdagne to France.

Upon assuming the Spanish throne in 1701, Philip V, a Bourbon, had summoned the Corts to Madrid and had sworn to uphold Catalonia's laws. But Catalans remained suspicious of his intentions, and in 1705 a revolt broke out; the Archduke Charles of Austria, who had been a pretender to the throne, was declared king of the Catalans. For a while the rebels had English support but ultimately were abandoned to the joint action of French and Spanish troops. Barcelona surrendered on 11 September 1714. (The eleventh of September is now Catalonia's national holiday.[63])

In 1716, Philip V proclaimed the Nueva Planta decree, by which Catalonia's political institutions—the Corts, the Generalitat, Consell de Cent, and the other town councils—were all abolished; councillors, appointed by the king for life, were to head the local councils. Catalan was suppressed, and Spanish became the language of the courts, local administration, and the schools. Catalonia was subjected to higher taxes than Castile, as the Spanish monarchy sought to eliminate its deficit.[64] Thus, in the name of Bourbon absolutism and the supremacy of Castile, seven centuries of Catalan self-government had been ended and the Catalan language was put under severe threat. Catalonia's descent from its golden age was complete.

Cultural Persistence

The Spanish state's plans for the future of Catalan were made clear in secret instructions to its municipal officials: they were to favour Castilian through measures of which the citizens would not be aware.[65] None the less, the measures did produce a reaction. Beyond instances of armed resistance, there were various forms of passive resistance. Appeals were also made to the international community. And books were published in Catalan, including Baldiri Reixac's *Instruccions per l'ensenyança dels minyons* (Instructions for teaching youth) (1749) and Josep Pau Ballot's *Gramàtica i apologia de la llengua catalana* (Grammar and defence of the Catalan language) (1815).[66]

Still, despite the apparent determination of its leaders, the Spanish state probably lacked the means to succeed in its assimilationist project. Salvador Giner argues that the state was too cumbersome and inefficient to undertake the kinds of reforms that were necessary. And it lacked a Jacobin conception of the polity that would waive aside cultural particularities in the interests of equality and universalism.[67] Thus, Carlos III may have decreed in 1768–71 that all primary and secondary schooling should be Castilian,[68] but it was not until the second half of the nineteenth century that the Spanish government was able to establish a state school system; even then, the system remained unfunded and largely ineffective. Nor could the government establish a universal military service, for evasion and desertion was rampant among the lower classes, and the upper classes could obtain exemptions.[69] In any case, with a population that was largely illiterate, restrictions on the literary use of Catalan were largely irrelevant; as Woolard notes, literary decline need not imply linguistic decline.[70]

If the Spanish state had been capable of modernization, Catalonia's linguistic and cultural distinctiveness would have been much more vulnerable, perhaps going the way of the Catalan-speaking regions of southern France. Instead, Catalonia was able to persist as a culturally distinct entity, albeit with its language absent from formal political institutions.

Economic Dynamism

In fact, Catalonia did more than persist. Through the rest of the eighteenth century, despite the loss of its political autonomy, it actually underwent a major economic recovery. Its population increased dramatically, even if it did not double as early historians claimed.[71] Its countryside was repopulated. Catalonia joined the world market and was more than ready when the ban on trade with the rest of the empire was finally lifted in 1778; it even had an industrial revolution.

This surprising economic recovery came from within. The increase in population created a local market. Agricultural surpluses fuelled the development of a wool industry. The production of paper surged, partly for the American market. Most spectacular was the industrialization of textiles, involving equipment similar to what was being used at the same time in England.[72]

Thus, the consequences of 1714 were not all negative, for integration with Spain gave Catalonia full access to the Spanish market.[73] As Catalonia's political institutions were eliminated, so was the Catalan aristocracy, either disappearing outright or being absorbed into the Spanish nobility. Other archaic institutions, such as monopolistic guilds, also lost ground. As a result, other class forces were able to come to the fore.[74] Peasants and farmers, the *pagesia*, were free to operate on their own; landowning (not outright but by indefinite assignment) was very widespread in eighteenth-century Catalonia.[75] And the *menestralia*, made up of artisans, shopkeepers, and workshop owners, were no longer shackled by the guilds. Ultimately, they led Catalonia into industrial capitalism.[76]

The Nineteenth Century: Economic and Cultural Renaissance

With the nineteenth century the full effect of all these changes came into play. Thus, after three centuries of persistence under adversity and oppression, history offers a new theme for Catalan nationalists: the achievements of an industrial economy, coupled with a cultural renaissance. Once again, then, Catalan history tells a story of great undertakings.

An Industrial Economy

The century started out badly, with the invasion by Napoleon's troops. Factories were destroyed, and Catalonia's commercial and industrial development was halted. But once the war was over, Catalonia was able to resume its economic ascent; indeed, it entered into a period of full-scale industrialization that was to make it the economic leader of all Spain.[77]

Catalonia's index of industrial production tripled between 1840 and 1860. At the centre of this remarkable development was the textile industry, based in particular on cotton, which by 1860 had captured 80 per cent of the Spanish textile market.[78] By mid-century Catalonia had become the fourth-largest producer of cotton goods in the world after England, France, and the United States.[79] In the years 1860 to 1870, two Catalan cities, Sabadell and Terrassa, were responsible for 60 per cent of Spain's wool production.[80]

Some textile companies used water power for their sewing machines, but the true industrial revolution lay in the organization of workers in a manufacturing system marked by hierarchy, specialization, and strict control. In 1832, a large factory in Barcelona, the first to use steam power and the mule jenny, employed 700 workers and had a foundry and metalwork plant to make its own modern sewing machines.[81] Technological innovations were adopted with remarkable speed. Mechanized spindles, for example, of which there had been none in 1841, numbered 96,328 in 1859 and 437,054 in 1857.[82]

Spain's first railway was built in 1848, linking Barcelona and Mataró; Barcelona was linked to Valencia in 1867 and to the French border in 1878. Moreover, unlike the railways in the rest of Spain, these were built by local interests.[83]

Mechanization and industrialization required the support of financial institutions. The Bank of Barcelona, founded by Manuel Girona in 1844, played a critical role as a commercial bank and an issuer of bank notes until the government prevented it from doing so. A savings bank, la Caixa d'Estalvis de Barcelona, was created in 1844. Trust companies were established, including the Societat Catalana General de Crèdit and the Crèdit Mobiliari Barcelonès. And the Barcelona stock exchange was created in 1851, although it was largely ignored by the industrial enterprises.[84] In 1876 the Banco Hispano-Colonial was formed, grouping together Catalan and Cuban financial, industrial, and commercial interests.

Underpinning these changes was the emergence of an industrial bourgeoisie and great family fortunes. Some of the new industrialists were of humble origin, coming from the *menestralia*; others were descended from Barcelona's leading citizens of the past, the 'honest burghers'. There were even some members of the old landed aristocracy.[85] Collectively, they represented a powerful new force that was to dominate the next few decades in Catalan history.

At the same time an urban working class was developing and was organizing rapidly; the first union appeared in 1840 among workers in the cotton industry. Other unions followed in other sectors, and in June 1841 a confederation of unions was formed. With industrialization had come an industrial society.

Cultural Revival

The nineteenth century was a time not just of economic renewal but of cultural renewal as well; indeed, the two are quite closely related. At the centre was the

Renaixença, which began with the revival of Catalan poetry but sought the renewal of Catalan in all forms of literary creation. In effect, it hoped to reclaim the illustrious literature of Catalonia's medieval golden age.

The revival of the fourteenth-century poetry contests, the Jocs florals, was an ideal means of doing this. Intended to demonstrate that Catalan was still the basis of a great national literature, these events brought members of the Catalan literary élite together to recite works written in an archaic Catalan and expressing romantic and patriotic sentiments. The number of entries grew from 39 in 1859 to 466 in 1875.[86]

Restoring Catalan was an ambitious goal, for over the centuries, especially under Spanish rule, it had virtually disappeared as a written language. The literary Catalan that had survived was a medieval, archaic language, and few Catalans were able to write in it. And, unlike Castilian, it did not have standard rules for spelling and usage. It is no surprise, then, that the Renaixença began with poetry rather than prose; in fact, most of the founders of the Renaixença doubted that Catalan could become a 'normal' everyday language.[87]

But restoring Catalan was only part of the cultural renaissance that took hold of nineteenth-century Catalonia. The Renaixença involved all areas of the humanities: theatre flourished, first in Castilian but then in Catalan. Scottish and German philosophical movements were applied to the Catalonian renaissance. In particular, Francesc-Xavier Llorens i Barba drew upon Herder's notion of a *Volksgeist* to argue that every people, including the Catalans, has its own spirit, expressed through its distinctive culture.[88] The Renaixença also spread quickly to the countryside, which was thought to have remained closer to Catalonia's traditions than had the cities. Indeed, in one interpretation the Renaixença was a reaction against the forces of modernization. None the less, the movement also appealed to urban leaders for its glorification of a distinct Catalan identity.[89]

Coupled with this surge in distinctive cultural expression was the construction of splendid new buildings and the futuristic development of Eixample, an area of Barcelona beyond the old walled city. An opera house, the Gran Teatre del Liceu, was completed in 1847. The joint-stock corporation that built the Liceu financed construction by selling the house's boxes, for as much as 15,000 pesetas a year, to Barcelona's leading families.[90] After a fire broke out in 1861, a subscription fund was opened and the Liceu was restored in rapid order without any government funding.[91]

Underlying these cultural achievements was the active support of the new Catalan bourgeoisie and the upper-middle classes, who took pride in Barcelona's new prominence as a cultural centre and in Catalonia itself.

Modernisme

By the late 1880s, the inherent conservatism of the Renaixença had produced a new movement—*modernisme*—which dominated the period 1890–1910. Reacting against the Renaixença's obsession with the past and the authentic Catalan self, the *modernistas* drew much of their inspiration from their contemporaries in France and Germany.[92]

While *modernisme* extended over a variety of areas, its greatest achievements were in architecture. The towering figure of *modernisme* was Antoni Gaudí, whose deep religious faith set him apart from the secularism of most of *modernisme*'s practitioners. His most dramatic creation is Sagrada Família, a yet-to-be-completed church that juts up on Barcelona's skyline. Other Gaudí creations, such as Parc Güell, Casa Milà, and Casa Batlló, have also become Barcelona landmarks. All of them reflect Gaudí's creative genius. Nor was Gaudí alone. Lluís Domènec i Montaner, responsible for the spectacular Palau de la Música Catalana, has also been called a genius.[93]

Under *modernisme*, painting and sculpture underwent a revival. The leading figures were Santiago Rusinyol and Ramon Casas, who were well abreast of developments in Paris and sought to link Barcelona with them. At the same time, Pablo Picasso moved from Malaga to Barcelona in 1895, at the age of 20, and stayed there until 1904. It was in Barcelona that he began his artistic career, with his Blue Period.

In music, the choral society Orfeó Català, was created in 1891. Housed in the Palau de la Música Catalana, the Orfeó was intended to perform not only works of international composers but also Catalan popular music. The example of the Orfeó led to the creation of 145 choral societies throughout Catalonia; it also inspired the creation of the rival Societat Coral Catalunya Nova by Enric Morera, who believed that the Orfeó had become too attuned to bourgeois tastes, as opposed to those of the common Catalans.[94]

In *moderniste* literature, the most prominent writers were the poets, and among them the most celebrated is Joan Maragall. His belief that Catalonia had to save itself from Spain's cultural and political decadence was most dramatically expressed in his famous 'Oda a l'Espanya', which he wrote after Spain lost the remnants of its empire in 1898. Maragall's solution was for Catalonia to 'Europeanize itself'. He complemented his own work with translations of Goethe, thus embodying *modernisme*'s attachment to the rest of Europe.[95]

Conclusions

By the end of the nineteenth century, history had given Catalans more than enough material to formulate a compelling idea of a Catalan nation. Beyond Catalonia's distant origins as a distinct political entity, the historical development of a rich Catalan literature and culture and the pioneering creation of such institutions as their parliament, there is the fact that in the late Middle Ages Catalonia had become a major economic and political power. The virtual prototype of a nation-state, it was one of the most advanced societies in Europe. The Spanish state appeared as an adversary seeking to eliminate Catalonia's bases of national distinctiveness by suppressing the Catalan language and abolishing Catalonia's distinct political institutions. On two occasions, the state suppressed attempts by

Catalonia to win its independence. The tragedy of Catalonia's failure to fulfill its early promise is partially offset by its success in enduring political and economic adversity. In the nineteenth century Catalonia emerged as Spain's first industrial centre and became the site of remarkable cultural creativity, starting in poetry but extending over all domains. Barcelona itself became the site of startling architectural innovations that attracted attention throughout Europe.

All the conditions were present for a powerful nationalism: the glories and pre-modern maturity of a medieval golden age; political and linguistic suppression; failed declarations of independence; and an economic and cultural dynamism that left most of Spain far behind.

The reality, however, may have been more complex. The seeds of the decline of the medieval golden age probably lay within Catalonia itself. During the nineteenth century the Spanish state did not have the capacity to pursue its assimilationist plans. And Catalonia's new industries had trouble competing on international markets and became increasingly dependent on Spanish protectionism. Still, the builders of national myths were free to ignore such complexities.

Another factor that boded well for a Catalan nationalism was the loyalty of the population to the Catalan language and their Catalan identity. Especially in recent centuries, the Catalans, both peasants and artisans, have repeatedly rallied in defence of Catalonia against foreign powers, particularly Spain, as in the War of Separation (1640–51) and the War of Succession (1705–14). The fact that both of those wars ended in crushing defeat does not seem to have destroyed this popular loyalty to Catalonia; rather it seems to have strengthened it.

Still, despite the presence of all these conditions for a strong Catalan nationalism, the construction of an explicit idea of a Catalan nation and the mobilization of Catalans around it entail complex intellectual and political processes.

Chapter 2

The Rise of Catalan Nationalism

In Catalonia, as elsewhere, the emergence of nationalism as a full-blown political movement involved several stages. Before there could be an explicit idea of a Catalan *nation* there had to be an idea of *Catalonia* and its historical distinctiveness. The elaboration of such an idea and the celebration of it took up a good part of the nineteenth century in a movement called, appropriately, 'Catalanism'. Once Catalanism had taken root, the next step was to define a political framework for Catalonia and a strategy for securing it. Naturally, this process became infused with debates over not only what would be the most appropriate political structures for Catalonia but what social and economic policies these structures should pursue. As it happened, all this took place at a time when Catalonia was struggling with the contradictions of industrial capitalism; indeed, class relations were becoming highly polarized. It was one thing to celebrate Catalonia's historical glories and cultural distinctiveness; it was quite another to define a contemporary strategy for the Catalan nation.

In short, there was nothing inevitable in the emergence of Catalan nationalism as a viable political movement. The process was long and laborious, and at each stage differences over not only the nature of the nation but social and economic questions threatened to overwhelm it. Happily for the nationalist cause, periodic repression by the Spanish state served to restore an otherwise fragile unity.

The Rise of Catalanism

By reviving the Catalan literary tradition, the Renaixença created a new sense of pride in Catalonia and its historical achievements. The publication in 1841 of Joaquim Rubió i Ors's call for cultural independence and his declaration that Spain was no longer the 'fatherland' of Catalans inspired an outpouring of poetry and other literary forms that celebrated Catalonia and launched an effort to reclaim the Catalan language after decades of suppression by the Spanish government.

Although the movement profoundly shaped Catalonia's intellectual and cultural élite, this new Catalanist spirit was not restricted to 'high' literary circles. The Catalan populace was also caught up in the movement: after all, Catalan was their only language. Unlike the literati, who resorted to Castilian in their early defences of Catalan, the working classes had little knowledge of Castilian, and they flocked to the Catalan-language plays that Frederic Soler wrote under a pseudonym. With titles like *El castell dels tres dragons* (The castle of the three dragons) and *L'esquella de la torratxa* (The balcony bell), these popular dramas strengthened the collective consciousness of being Catalan. His work in turn inspired many young writers to write popular plays, which, though they did not receive critical acclaim, had a strong following. Some of the Renaixença literary leaders criticized the popular Catalan, full of Castellanisms, that was used in these plays, but their supporters replied that this was the language of the people, unlike the archaic and incomprehensible Catalan used by the critics. In short, the popular response to the Renaixença was sufficiently strong to dislodge the movement somewhat from the literary purism of its founders.[1]

Another aspect of the Renaixença that had a strong popular appeal was the choral concert of traditional Catalan songs. Among the many choirs that were formed, the most prominent was L'Orfeó Català, which performed Joan Maragall's 'Cant de la senyera', a famous celebration of Catalan identity. The *sardana*, a Catalan folk dance, was revived during this same period.[2]

The use and celebration of the Catalan language in a wide variety of cultural forums stimulated a new pride and sense of identity among not just the literary élite but most of Catalan society. What may have started as the exercise of an intellectual élite quickly acquired a popular dimension as well. And, while it remained pro-Spanish in its political allegiances, the new Catalan bourgeoisie was quite prepared to finance many of the literary festivals and drama and musical productions, finding in them confirmation of this class's own greatness.[3]

Still, if this cultural revival of the second half the nineteenth century instilled a strong collective consciousness in most Catalans, the question remained as to how this should be translated into the political realm. What form should a *political* Catalanism take?

Political Catalanism

The first political manifestation of the new Catalan consciousness was the response of Catalans to a new movement on the Spanish political scene, Federal Republicanism. Though the intellectual leader of the movement, Francesc Pi i Margall, was a Catalan, he and his colleagues framed federalism in terms of universalism and democracy rather than cultural particularism.[4] None the less, in the 1869 election, when universal male suffrage was adopted for the first time, Catalonia gave majority support, 28 of 37 seats, to Federal Republicanism and was the only part of Spain to do so. Clearly, whatever may have been the formal rationale for Republican Federalism, many Catalans saw its promise of self-government as a vehicle for realizing their own distinctive aspirations.[5] Federalism also became linked with several other movements—republicanism, radicalism, anti-clericalism, and progressivism. Thus, it put down deep popular roots in Catalonia.[6]

The First Spanish Republic was declared on 9 March 1873, after the abdication of Amadeus of Savoy, but the Republican Federalists' plans for a new Spanish federation were not to be fully achieved. The Republic never adopted a constitution; in any event, by some accounts the draft that was under discussion did not amount to federalism.[7] In late 1874, amidst turmoil in many parts of Spain, the Spanish army overthrew the new regime and the Spanish monarchy was restored. Catalonia did not obtain its self-government. In early 1873 the government of Barcelona province had considered proclaiming a Catalan state to initiate the federalization of Spain, but was dissuaded from doing so. Although the restoration of the monarchy was strongly supported by the Catalan bourgeoisie, Republican Federalism remained important as a political force in Catalonia.

The Transition to Nationalism

Federalism provided the framework within which a leading Catalan, Valentí Almirall, attempted to draw together the several groups that had coalesced around Catalanism. But he tried to do so by reformulating their established positions in his own terms.

Almirall and the Centre Català

Almirall had long been a major figure in the Republican Federalism movement. In 1869 he had been active in the *pacte de Tortosa,* an assembly seeking to establish a federal structure patterned after the Catalan-Aragonese Confederation. But, as this would suggest, his brand of federalism was rooted more in local traditions than was the federalism of the Spanish party and its Catalan leader Pi i Margall.[8] In 1882 he broke with Pi's group and founded a new association, Centre Català, to promote his vision of political Catalanism.

Though Almirall did not share the traditionalism of the Renaixença, he was very much committed to strengthening the Catalan language. In 1879 he established the first Catalan-language daily newspaper, the *Diari Català,* and the defence and standardization of Catalan was to be a major concern of the Catalanist Congress that he convened in 1880.

At the same time, Almirall sought to draw the Catalan bourgeoisie into political Catalanism by making the defence of Catalan economic interests one of its themes. Here, he had much to work with. The Catalan bourgeoisie was certainly aware that it had economic interests that were distinctively Catalan. Catalan industry was having great difficulty competing on world markets: it had to import coal, and labour was relatively costly, owing in particular to the price of bread. English textile production was alleged to be 90 per cent cheaper than Catalonia's. Railways were built to the Catalan interior in order to reach promising coal sites and to reduce the cost of importing Castilian grain, but the coal did not materialize and the railway companies went bankrupt.[9] Finally, with the financial crisis of 1866, the Catalan bourgeoisie ended its quest to enter world markets and turned to a campaign for protection against foreign producers on the Spanish market and what, after the liberation of South America, remained of the Spanish empire: Cuba, Puerto Rico, and the Philippines. But this too was to prove frustrating.

Catalonia was the main industrial centre of Spain; the only other one was the Basque Country. Elsewhere in Spain the predominant economic interests, especially peasant and landholding ones, saw no benefit in protectionism. Nor was the Spanish state well disposed towards Catalonia's particular concerns, linked as the state was to the landed aristocracy and to merchant and financial capital.[10] Indeed, there were few Catalans in the government: among the 900 ministers in Spanish governments between 1833 and 1901, only 25, or 2.7 per cent, were Catalan.[11] And Catalonia's economic superiority over most of Spain had fostered among Castilian intellectual and professional circles an anti-Catalanism that was not unlike anti-semitism.[12]

Almirall's first attempt to put together his synthesis of the different strands of Catalanism was the First Catalanist Congress in 1880. There, he was hampered by the refusal of the Catalan literary leaders to engage in political action; indeed, they abandoned the congress. None the less, the congress passed several resolutions that did serve Almirall's purposes. It agreed to establish an Acadèmia de la Llengua Catalana to standardize the Catalan language, and it adopted a policy of defending the Catalan civil law against the intention of the Spanish government to impose a Código Civil based on Castilian law. In addition, plans were made to create a body to co-ordinate the many different Catalanist organizations; in the end this was the Centre Català, which was founded in 1882 and which was able to draw in the cultural faction that had dissented in 1880.[13]

A Second Catalanist Congress, held in 1883, endorsed the principle that the Catalan language should have co-official status (together with Spanish) in Catalonia; defended Catalan civil law; proclaimed that Catalonia as a political entity should have pre-eminence over the Spanish government's provincial administrative divisions; called upon the Spanish government to adopt a protectionist economic policy; and condemned the participation of Catalans in Spain's general political parties. Clearly, Almirall had succeeded in turning Catalanism into a coherent political movement.[14]

In addition, in 1885, Almirall and the Centre Català were able to obtain the assent of a broad range of groups to a statement of grievances, known as the Memorial de Greuges and addressed to the Spanish king, Alfonso XII. The document denounced Castile's oppression of Catalonia and called for harmonization of the interests and aspirations of the different regions of Spain. At the same time, it sought to defend the Catalan textile industry by decrying the Spanish government's renewed interest in free trade and expressed concern that the Catalan civil law might be abolished. On this basis, it secured the support both of the major organizations of the Catalan bourgeoisie, such as Foment del Treball Nacional, and of the cultural organizations, such as Consistori dels Jocs Florals, as well as a number of Catalan jurists. Though received with apparent sympathy by the Spanish monarch, the document was treated quite differently by the Spanish government. None the less, it constituted an impressive coalescence of the various strands of Catalanism.

Ultimately, however, it proved impossible to maintain within the same political organization the cultural revivalists of the Renaixença, the progressives of Republican Federalism, and members and supporters of the Catalan bourgeosie. The Catalan industrialists, still harbouring visions of *catalanizing* Spain and its politics, were not prepared to abandon their allegiance to Spain; nor could they abide Almirall's denunciation of the Barcelona Universal Exhibition of 1888 as an acceptance of the restoration of the Spanish monarchy. Moreover, their loyalty to the Spanish regime was reinforced in 1891 when the government adopted protectionism. Yet leftists in the Centre found Almirall and his party too moderate on social questions, and many republicans distrusted his Catalanism.[15] The literary traditionalists were also uncomfortable with Almirall's political Catalanism, and in 1887 they left the Centre to form the Lliga de Catalunya, which gathered young emerging leaders around a more conservative brand of Catalanism. The Lliga's leader, the architect Domènec i Montaner, was one of the chief planners of the Barcelona Exposition that Almirall had denounced. The Centre Català was finally dissolved in the mid-1890s, unable to retain the support of the Catalan nationalist left.[16]

The Bases de Manresa and the Birth of Catalan Nationalism

In 1889 the Lliga de Catalunya, in collaboration with a university student organization, Centre Escolar Català, launched a campaign to save Catalan civil law. In the end, the Spanish government relented. This successful effort provided the momentum for the establishment of a new confederation of Catalanist organizations, Unió Catalanista, which largely succeeded in drawing together the various forces of Catalanism and overcoming the schism of 1887.[17]

The first draft statute for a Catalan self-government, known as the *Bases de Manresa*, emerged in 1892 from a Unió assembly in Manresa, north of Barcelona. The Catalan government would have jurisdiction over public safety, taxation, the issuing of currency, education, civil and criminal law, and a regional political force. Catalan would be the only official language in Catalonia, public office would be reserved for Catalans (whether by birth or 'naturalization'), and there would be no appeals beyond Catalan courts. Belying charges that the document was 'separatist', the *Bases*'s first section was devoted to outlining the exclusive responsibilities of a reorganized Spanish government, with a continuing role for a monarch. But clearly the *Bases* did outline very substantial powers for the new Catalan government.[18]

The *Bases* was of great historical significance. Not only did it offer the first detailed outline of a Catalan government, but its notion of a Catalan government was derived from an explicit Catalan nationalism. The sense of Catalonia as a distinct nation, as opposed to a region, is clearly reflected in such provisions as the restriction of public office to Catalans. In effect, the *Bases*, and the Lliga and Unió from which it sprang, represented the transition from Catalanism to modern Catalan nationalism.[19] This was to become more evident in later years, when Prat de la Riba, one of the young founders of the Lliga and the dominant figure in Catalan politics in future years, wrote his *La nacionalitat catalana*. The fundamentally nationalist thrust of the Lliga helps to explain the scission from the centre through which it had been created. For the Centre Català had emerged from Republican Federalism, albeit with the Catalanist focus of Almirall. Almirall's charge that the Lliga was 'separatist' was clearly off the mark, but it did reflect a rueful recognition that the Lliga sprang from different, distinctly nationalist, roots.

At the same time, the *Bases de Manresa* seemed to suggest that this nascent nationalism was moving in a distinctly conservative direction. Unlike the Spanish parliament, Catalonia's was to be organized along corporatist lines rather than on the basis of universal suffrage.[20] For that matter, Catalonia's constitution 'will retain the expansive character of our ancient laws' ('mantindrà el temperament expansiu de nostra llegislació antiga') while responding to 'new requirements' ('les noves necessitats').[21]

Prat de la Riba: Formalizing Catalan Nationalism

The emergence of coherent Catalan nationalism was confirmed in 1895 by the publication of *Compendi de Doctrina Catalanista*, a sort of Catalanist catechism jointly written by Prat de la Riba and Pere Muntanyola. While using the term 'fatherland' rather than 'nation', it held that Catalonia was the only 'fatherland' of Catalans; Spain was simply their 'state'. Over 100,000 copies of the book were printed.

Finally, in 1906 Prat de la Riba published his *La nacionalitat catalana*, in which the term 'nation' figured prominently. He distinguished carefully between nation and state, arguing that, unlike states, nations are 'natural' phenomena: 'Catalonia is a nation' because it contains the constituent elements of a nation: 'a collective spirit, a Catalan soul, which was able to create a Catalan language, Catalan law, and Catalan art.' Thus, on the assumption that 'a cada nació, un Estat', Catalonia must have its own state. But this must be squared with 'la unitat política d'Espanya'. The solution for Prat de la Riba was 'l'Estat compost' or a federation. The book was to have a profound effect on the development of Catalan nationalism.[22]

The Consolidation of Conservative Nationalism

By the end of the nineteenth century the elements of a Catalan nationalism were in place. As Joan Culla notes,[23] over the preceding three decades the symbolic and mythological components of a Catalan nationalism had been settled upon. A song memorializing the 1640 rebellion, 'Els segadors' (The song of the reapers), had been designated a national anthem. The date of the fall of Barcelona to Philip V, 11 September 1714, had become Catalonia's national holiday. A series of figures from the distant past had been designated national heroes. The Memorial de Greuges and the *Bases de Manresa* had provided the elements of a nationalist doctrine. What remained was the creation of a distinctly nationalist political party, with a clearly defined social base; this was about to come.

Despite its continuing allegiance to Spain, the bourgeoisie was profoundly affected by the loss of Spain's two remaining colonies in 1898. Some of them had had major holdings in Cuba, and 60 per cent of Catalonia's exports had gone there.[24] More important, the loss of these possessions appeared to be the ultimate proof of Spain's inherent decadence and inevitable slide from the world stage. Indeed, Joan Maragall spoke for many Catalans in his famous lament, 'Adéu Espanya', which decried Spain's moral decline and failure to reform itself: 'You have lost everything—you have nothing. Spain, Spain, come back to yourself!'[25]

Catalan conservative forces were ready to give a chance to a new Spanish conservative government, formed under Francisco Silvela. But in the end, despite initial sympathy, the government rejected such measures as making Barcelona a free port or giving it financial autonomy. Indeed, the government raised taxes to pay off its war debt. For some Catalan manufacturers, this confirmed that Catalan interests could not be served within the established Spanish parties.[26]

The Lliga regionalista

In order to capitalize on this shift in bourgeois attitudes, a group of Unió Catalanista militants, including Prat de la Riba, left to found a new party, which, just before the 1901 general election, merged with the union Regionalista, founded by the Fomento del Trabajo Nacional. The result was the Lliga Regionalista de Catalunya. The party avoided the terms 'national' and 'nationalist' for fear of alienating potential supporters. But, as the presence of Prat de la Riba would suggest, the party's ideology was indeed nationalist.[27] At the same time, though the new party claimed to unite all the forces of Catalanism, it was dominated by the industrial bourgeoisie, along with important commercial elements.[28] Indeed its successful candidates in the 1901 election included the presidents of Fomento del Trabajo *Nacional*, the Lliga de Defensa Comercial i Industrial, and the Sociedad Económica de Amigos del País. A second faction was composed of lawyers and notaries, who had an obvious stake in the defence of the Catalan civil law and who controlled the Commisió d'Acció Política, the Lliga's strategic centre.[29] Uniting the leadership of the Lliga was a fundamentally conservative world view that saw society as composed of corporate entities, in which privilege was quite appropriate, and that viewed with suspicion such ideas as popular sovereignty and democratic equality.[30] For its part, the Unió Catalanista became a base for leftist nationalists before it finally dissolved.

In 1906 almost all political forces did come together in the defence of Catalonia; this was the doing of the Spanish government. An anti-militaristic caricature in a

Catalan satirical magazine, Cu-cut! had led furious army officers and cadets to assault the offices of both Cu-cut! and La Veu de Catalunya, the Lliga Regionalista's organ. Rather than punish the responsible officers, the Spanish government proceeded to table a bill, Ley de Jurisdicciones, under which any offence against the unity of the fatherland or the army would come under military jurisdiction. In effect, the law reflected the strongly anti-Catalan feelings in the Spanish capital, and threatened Catalanism. The result was a vast mobilization of Catalan political forces, including many republicans, in Solidaritat Catalana, which swept the 1907 provincial and general elections.

However, a year later the republican members left the coalition. Their initial adherance to Solidaritat had paved the way for another faction of republicans, led by Alejandro Lerroux, to mobilize around an openly anti-Catalanist platform that appealed to workers, especially immigrants, through populist attacks on the Catalan bourgeoisie. The word *Lerrouxism* persists in contemporary Catalonia as a term for populist, anti-Catalan demagoguery.

Two years later, Catalonia's steadily building class conflict exploded. In response to an extension of military conscription, anarchists and syndicalists declared a general strike. The imposition of martial law triggered five days of savage violence, which came to be known as *setmana tràgica* (tragic week). For its part, the Lliga regionalista firmly supported the Spanish government's harsh suppression of the uprising.[31] The events dealt a final blow to Solidaritat Catalana, but they also prompted the Spanish government to develop a plan for autonomous administrative bodies[32] that led to Catalonia's first actual experience with self-government.

The Mancomunitat: Catalonia's First Self-government
Four years passed before the scheme came to pass, because of changes in the Spanish government and divisions within the Spanish parties over the idea. But, finally, on 6 April 1914, the four Catalan provinces were granted a commonwealth or Mancomunitat. Although the enabling law applied to the country as a whole, only in Catalonia was it put into effect with the creation of a regional commonwealth.

The Lliga regionalista dominated the new body. Prat de la Riba was elected the first president; on his death in August 1917, Josep Puig i Cadafalch, also from the Lliga, was elected. An assembly was composed of all the deputies from the diputacions of the four Catalan provinces; a council, with two members from each province, acted as the government. The Lliga regionalista had only about one-third of the seats in the assembly and required the support of other parties to govern, but it dominated the council. Its position was strengthened by the fact that it controlled the Barcelona city council throughout this period.[33]

The Mancomunitat was in fact a purely administrative arrangement, but the Catalanists sought to make the most of it with a wide range of innovative measures. Able to secure loans, it embarked on a modernization of Catalonia's

infrastructure through the construction of roads and railways and the electrifica-
tion of the Catalan countryside.[34] The Association for the Protection of Catalan
Teaching was created to oversee Catalan-language private schools and to publish
textbooks.

Noucentisme

The *Mancomunitat* established a close relationship with Catalan artists and intellectuals through an ambitious cultural policy that was based on its ideology of
Noucentisme or 'nine-hundred-ism' (for the new century). The Noucentiste
movement, which was active between 1906 and 1923, produced several major
figures, including a number of poets, of whom the most important was Josep
Carner. Another important writer was Eugeni d'Ors, who published under the
pseudonym Xénius.[35]

As Conversi argues, Noucentisme was like *modernisme*, the movement it supplanted in about 1906, in that it too was Catalanist, Europeanist, social-reformist,
and anti-traditionalist, although it was not anti-conservative. But unlike *modernisme*, Noucentisme had an institutional base in the Mancomunitat.[36]

As president of the Barcelona Diputació, Prat de la Riba had already created the
Institut d'Estudis Catalans (IEC) in 1907, with Eugeni d'Ors as its director. Under
the Mancomunitat the IEC flourished, enlisting Pompeu Fabra to pursue the standardization of Catalan. In 1914, a national library was created, along with a
system of public libraries. The Mancomunitat subsidized Catalan-language publishers and periodicals. And in 1918–19, it adopted almost unanimously the
Missatge i bases de l'autonomia, which drew upon Woodrow Wilson's Fourteen
Points to demand sovereignty for Catalonia in internal matters while remaining
part of Spain.[37]

All this came to an end in the mid-1920s, under the Spanish dictator General
Miguel Primo de Rivera. The Lliga regionalista, already weakened through the
creation by dissidents of Acció Catalana in 1922, had not supported the general's
1923 coup, but President Puig i Cadafalch had believed that the new government
might be accommodating. Instead, it quickly banned the public use of the Catalan
language, the display of the Catalan flag on public buildings, and, in a foretaste
of Franco's policies, the use of Catalan on street signs and store signs.[38] One
hundred and fifty Catalan nationalist organizations were suppressed, as was the
Association for the Protection of Teaching in Catalan. Despite all this, the Catalan
industrial bourgeoisie continued to support the dictator. Finally, in 1925 Primo de
Rivera abolished the Mancomunitat.[39]

Debating the Social Origins of Catalanism

The abolition of the Mancomunitat marked the end of the first phase of Catalan
nationalism. During this phase, under the leadership of the Lliga, the movement
became more and more conservative and increasingly aligned with the interests
of the Catalan bourgeoisie. This relationship between the nationalist movement

and the Catalan bourgeoisie has in fact been the basis of one interpretation of the social origins of Catalan nationalism, which has generated considerable debate among students of Catalan nationalism.

In Pierre Vilar's analysis, first presented in the 1960s, this bourgeoisie was itself fully responsible for Catalan nationalism, which was a direct reflection of its interest and preoccupations.[40] As 'a class that wants to have a state' ('une classe qui aspire à disposer d'un État'), it had initially attempted to bring the Spanish state and all of Spain into conformity with its vision of a bourgeois state and a bourgeois economy. Thus, for the Catalan bourgeoisie and its associated intellectuals, the 'nation' was Spain. The bourgeoisie tried to persuade the Spanish state to adopt the protectionist policies needed by the 'national' market. Only when it became clear that they would be excluded from the Spanish state and would not obtain the policies they wanted and when the final loss of colonies had demonstrated the fundamental decadence of the Spanish state did the Catalan bourgeoisie turn to Catalan nationalism, trying to secure on a regional basis the state that it had not been able to secure on a Spanish one.

> It is only because the Catalan industrial bourgeoisie, in its effort to conquer the Spanish market, succeeded neither in getting control of the State nor in identifying in leading opinion its interests with those of Spain as a whole, that Catalonia, the little 'fatherland', finally became the 'national' base for pursuing its class needs, a smaller but more reliable one.[41]

But 'the workers' movement is *continuously* . . . absent from the Catalanist movement' during the period, 1885–1917, when Catalan nationalism took form:

> The peasants and middle classes, which were unorganized, played a *subordinate* political role. The responsibility for 'Catalanism' belonged essentially to the upper-middle classes, which were dominated by the employer groups and organized politically around a party, Cambó's [the Lliga].[42] (italics in original)

In the 1970s, a more polemical version of this argument appeared in a book by Jordi Solé Tura,[43] who analysed the writings of Prat de la Riba to show how this nationalism was closely wedded to the interests of the Catalan bourgeoisie. That was not hard to do. Not only did Prat de la Riba want the political autonomy of the Catalan nation to be used to strengthen Catalonia's economic competitiveness, but he drew on patriotism in appealing to the working class to accept its subordinate position. And he was even prepared to co-operate with the Spanish conservatives in Madrid in order to contain the influence of anarchism among Catalan workers.[44]

Yet this is not a satisfactory explanation of the rise of Catalanism and Catalan nationalism. Clearly, the Catalan bourgeoisie's support was heavily guided by its class interests; only this can explain the wide fluctuations in its support of the Catalan cause. But it is surely simplistic to reduce the Catalanist and nationalist movements themselves to the self-interest of this class alone. Long before the Catalan bourgeoisie finally overcame its hesitations and supported the conservative nationalism of the Lliga, Catalanism was an established force, not just in literary and intellectual circles but in the lower classes as well and in the workers' movement.[45]

Most of the intellectual and literary leaders of the Renaixença were not from the bourgeoisie themselves. And we have seen that there is ample evidence of popular support for Catalanism. The Renaixença involved a surge in enthusiasm for popular Catalan-language drama and performances of Catalan music. Though the workers' groups used Castilian for their written propaganda, they conducted their meetings exclusively in Catalan. The Catalan choral societies of the late nineteenth century were often made up largely of workers and were conceived as a means of mobilizing them to improve their condition as workers.[46] Similarly, strong popular Catalanism helps to explain the unusually strong electoral support that the federal republicans received in Catalonia in 1869 and other manifestations of political Catalanism.

Prat de la Riba may have provided the first formal theory of Catalan nationalism, situating it within a fundamentally conservative world view. But his theory was to be one among many. Indeed, by the 1930s Catalan nationalism had entered a new phase, in which it was dominated by republican and socialist formulations and was thus able to draw upon the long-established Catalanism of the working classes, as well as the early precursors of republican and socialist nationalism.

The Struggles of Leftist Nationalism

During the first two decades of the twentieth century, various political forces tried to advance a more progressive version of Catalanism and, especially, to weaken the dominance of the conservative Lliga regionalista. But they were hindered by infighting and schisms, which were a reflection not only of their political weakness but of the broader forces of class conflict and ideological polarization that dominated Catalonia during this period. And they were still haunted by the failure of their great opportunity during the First Republic.

In 1906 a group of republican dissidents from the newly formed Lliga regionalista established the Centre Nacionalista Republicà, which was dedicated to 'nationalism, democracy, and a republic'. While it attracted notable figures from the Catalan literati, it had little political impact. The Partit Federal Català called for the Constitució de l'Estat Català dins la Federació Espanyola (Constitution of the Catalan state in the Spanish federation), but with little effect. In 1910 an attempt was made to unite leftist parties through the Unió Federal Nacionalista Republicana, which declared, 'We intend to work for the recognition of the Catalan nationality' as part of 'the federal union in the Spanish State.'[47] But the new group apparently alienated its potential voters in 1914 when it entered into an alliance with the radicals, who were still associated with *lerrouxiste* anti-Catalanism.[48] The party was soon dissolved. In 1917 a Partit Republicà Català was formed, seeking to link republican federalism with a synthesis of Catalanism and concern for the working class. It too was to have little influence.

As Roger Masgrau argues, several factors hampered these efforts to develop an electorally viable leftist Catalanism: Lerroux's populist attacks on Catalanism, an inability to dislodge the middle class from its reliance on the Lliga regionalista, and the inroads made among Catalan workers by revolutionary ideologies, especially anarchism and syndicalism, which delegitimized electoral strategies.[49] Indeed, this polarization led to the death of one of the most promising leftist nationalists, Francesc Layret, who was assassinated in 1920.

The situation changed during Primo de Rivera's dictatorship. As in the past, repression by the Spanish government merely served to reinforce the identification with Catalonia and its language. In fact, the publication of books in Catalan increased, as did the number of Catalan newspapers. The regime tolerated these publications as long as they were censored, but for Catalans, reading in Catalan was itself a form of passive resistance.[50]

By refusing to collaborate with the dictatorship, the Lliga regionalista retained some credibility as a defender of Catalonia's interests, but its moderation did not match the radicalization of public opinion that was occurring, thanks to the dictatorship. For that matter, the Lliga had already been weakened by the defection in 1922 of many of its leading members to the nationalist republican Acció Catalana. Moreover, support was growing for a radically different option, the explicitly separatist and leftist Estat Català, which had been formed in 1922 under Francesc Macià, a former Spanish army colonel who had been converted to the nationalist cause through his participation in Solidaritat Catalana. In November 1926, Macià actually led a 'liberation' expedition from France, but this was stopped by the French police. Macià's subsequent trial in Paris drew international attention to the Catalan cause. Few Catalans were ready to support insurgency, but Macià's status as champion of Catalan nationalism was greatly enhanced.

In January 1930, Primo de Rivera resigned and the new Spanish government started to restore Catalonia's lost rights. In light of this, the Lliga regionalista formally departed from Prat de la Riba's nationalist doctrines and committed itself to regionalism, driven by its conservatism to support the existing regime even though this alienated radical Catalanist opinion. Ultimately, it joined the new government.[51] Thus, a familiar pattern appears once again, as the conservative nationalists place the defence of their world view and class interests above the defence of the Catalan nation.

Repeatedly, the Lliga's conservatism had undermined its collaboration with republican forces in the defence of Catalan interests. Its participation in Solidaritat Catalan had collapsed when the Lliga refused to abandon corporatist representation for popular sovereignty. The Lliga's participation in an Assembly of Parliamentarians, which it helped launch in 1917, was compromised by the Lliga's decision to join a new Spanish government several months later. As Siobhan Harty demonstrates, such tactical collaboration between Catalan republicans and the nationalists of the Lliga was compromised by the fundamental difference in world views. Whereas the republicans were committed to establishing popular sovereignty, egalitarianism, and universal rights, the Lliga conservatives remained deeply attached to corporatist political structures and the defence of privilege.[52]

This time, however, Catalan republicans resolved to work with their fellow republicans in the rest of Spain. In August 1930, representatives of three Catalan parties, two factions of the republican Acció Catalana, and the Estat Català, attended a meeting with the six Spanish republican and socialist parties. The resulting San Sebastian Pact committed them to overthrow the monarchy, by revolutionary means if necessary. Beyond that, according to the Catalan participants at least, all parties agreed to recognize Catalonia's distinct personality and to obtain approval by referendum in Catalonia for a Catalan statute of autonomy. Only the parts of the statute that defined the division of powers between the Catalan and Spanish governments would be submitted for approval to the Spanish constituent Cortes.[53] Thus the document did not recognize any right to sovereignty; in signing the pact, Estat Català had renounced its commitment to independence; the groundwork was laid for a coming together of left-wing nationalist forces.

In March 1931, a union of Estat Català and the Partit Republicà Català created the Esquerra Republicana de Catalunya (ERC). Acció Catalana had been reunited and renamed Partit Catalanista Republicà (PCR). The ERC and PCR prepared for the coming municipal elections by drawing up joint lists for all of Catalonia, except Barcelona, where the two parties would run independently. In the April 1931 municipal elections, the ERC was the big winner. In Barcelona, it won 25 seats, whereas the Lliga regionalista won only 12 and the PCR none at all.

At last, after so many failed attempts, leftist and centre-leftist Catalan nationalists had broken the hold of conservatism, Catalan nationalism, and the Lliga. In the process, Catalan nationalism entered a new era, during which the dominant form drew its inspiration from republican sources.[54] The bearer of this new republican nationalism, the ERC, was to dominate Catalan politics through the 1930s until the victory of Franco.

Catalan Nationalism and the Second Republic

On 14 April, after learning that the republicans had been victorious in all the Spanish provincial capitals, an ERC politician, Lluís Companys, proclaimed the Catalan Republic from the Barcelona city hall balcony. Upon his arrival the head of the ERC, Francesc Macià, went considerably further by proclaiming that the Catalan Republic was a member state of 'the Federation of Iberian Republics'. Despite Macià's separatist past, his declaration of Catalonia's status in a non-existent federation was apparently intended simply to ensure that the new Spanish Republic would indeed be federal.[55] A few hours later the Spanish Republic was declared in Madrid and the king went into exile.

Three days later, after meeting in Madrid with officials of the provisional Republican government, Macià agreed to renounce his declaration of the Catalan

Republic in exchange for the creation of a regional government to be called by the historic term of Generalitat. It was agreed that the Generalitat would draw up a statute of autonomy, which, upon approval by the municipal governments and a popular referendum, would be submitted to the Spanish Cortes. A provisional Generalitat government was established under ERC leadership with representation from other parties, although not the Lliga. The ERC's new dominance in Catalan politics was confirmed by a resounding victory in the June 1931 elections to the constituent Cortes in Madrid.

A draft statute of autonomy (the *Projecte de Núria*) was drawn up in rapid order and approved by 99 per cent in a popular referendum on 2 August 1931.[56] As to be expected, it referred to Catalonia as an autonomous state of the Spanish Federal Republic and proclaimed that the Generalitat represented the sovereignty of the Catalan people. However, such ideas had little support among the Spanish republicans and socialists who were to dominate the government of the Second Republic. Prompted by the firm opposition of their socialist allies to the idea of federalism, the Spanish republicans advocated an 'integral state', which would be unitary in nature but in which the Spanish parliament could grant regional autonomy. Thus, the new Spanish constitution adopted on 9 December 1931 was not based on federalism. And in the following months, Spanish public opinion and such distinguished scholars as José Ortega y Gassset mobilized around the ideal of the 'integral state' and against Catalonia's demands.[57]

This was all reflected in the terms of the Catalan statute of autonomy, which was finally adopted on 9 September 1932. Under the statute of autonomy, the Catalan language was given co-official status with Castilian and the Generalitat was granted exclusive jurisdiction over Catalan civil law and local internal administration. It was to be responsible for law and order, the administration of justice, and public works. In some other areas, such as insurance and labour matters, the Generalitat was to have administrative responsibility but no legislative powers. But the statute of autonomy reduced the fiscal autonomy envisaged in the Generalitat's draft, leaving only a few direct taxes. And education remained with the Spanish state; under Article 50 of the constitution, Castilian was supposed to be the language of instruction. The central government could take over the Catalan high courts and forces of public order should it judge this necessary. Moreover, in an effort to preclude any consolidation of the Paisos catalans, the new constitution forbade any links among regional units.[58]

In November 1932, elections were held for the new Catalan parliament, and the ERC's dominance was strongly confirmed with 52 of 75 seats. In a short-lived revival, the Lliga secured 16 seats. The socialists did poorly: the Spanish socialist party, the PSOE, won no seats at all, while the Unió socialista de Catalunya, which was closely allied with the ERC, won five.

Clearly, Catalan nationalism had undergone a remarkable transformation, and a new version, rooted in republican and leftist forces, had become dominant. Through the 1930s, Catalonia was the only area of Spain to be thoroughly republican, with parliamentary democracy an established part of its political culture. Elsewhere, republicanism and its opponents struggled for control.[59] The ERC was to retain control of the Generalitat until the end of the Second Republic. Upon his death in 1933, the first Catalan president, Francesc Macià, was succeeded by Lluís Companys, who remained in office until Franco's troops occupied Catalonia in February 1939.

The Generalitat and the Second Republic

During its seven years of existence, the Generalitat introduced a substantial number of reforms, reflecting its version of Catalan nationalism. It adopted progressive measures in such areas as education, municipal government, the rights of farmers, and the legal rights of women, including the right to abortion.[60] However, its progress in implementing these reforms was limited by the resources and powers available to it.

In the case of education the Generalitat was able to innovate with experimental pilot projects such as the l'Institut-Escola and les Escoles del Mar.[61] However, its overall impact on education was small because the Spanish state retained control over the existing system of elementary and secondary schools; the Generalitat could only try to set up parallel institutions with its limited resources. Thus, the full Catalanization of the school system did not take place. A decree of the Spanish state did guarantee that Catalan could be taught in all of Catalonia's schools, but implementation was limited not only by a shortage of Catalan-speaking teachers but by a lack of will on the part of the state.[62]

Still, during these years there was a surge in Catalan cultural activity. The number of books published in Catalan went from 308 in 1930 to 865 in 1936 and Catalan-language newspapers grew from 10 in 1927 to 25 in 1933, although newspaper readership was greater in Castilian than Catalan. Catalan was prominent in radio broadcasting: Ràdio Associació de Catalunya broadcasted entirely in Catalan, and Ràdio Barcelona broadcasted three-quarters of its programming in Catalan.[63]

The Generalitat did undertake some dramatic measures at the end of its tenure, that is, after 1936, when the necessity of fighting Franco not only gave it a pretext for exceeding its constitutional powers but caused the ERC to allow anarchist and Marxist forces to take the dominant role within the Generalitat. Thus, on 24 October 1936, the Generalitat passed a decree collectivizing larger firms while protecting small property. And with a Consell de l'Escola Nova Unificada it aggressively pursued the Catalanization and modernization of education.[64] However, these measures were to be short-lived.

Challenges to Leftist, Republican Nationalism

Throughout its time in office, the ERC was confronted and substantially hindered by challenges from several quarters. In Catalonia itself, the Catalan bourgeoisie saw a clear threat in the Generalitat's leftist policies and was prepared to use all means available to defend its interests, even if this meant compromising

Catalonia's autonomy. Thus, in 1934 a struggle broke out over the rights of tenant farmers in Catalonia's wine-growing region. Under the *Llei de Contractes de Conreu* (Law of agricultural contracts), tenants who had farmed the land for 18 years were entitled to buy it at a set price; those who had planted their own vines could acquire the land at its value before the vines were planted. Clearly, this was a major piece of social reform, since about 70,000 farmers could have become landowners. The Catalan parliament passed the law in the spring of 1934, but by that time the Lliga regionalista (now known as Lliga catalana) had withdrawn from the parliament, claiming that it had been the victim of political violence and compromising the Generalitat's legitimacy in the process.

The struggle spread beyond Catalonia itself as the landowners looked to the Spanish government to bring the Generalitat into line. The landowners enlisted the Lliga in challenging the constitutionality of the law. The Spanish government, which was in the hands of radicals who had defeated the Spanish left in the 1933 elections, was pressured by the rightist CEDA (Confederación Española de Derechas Autónomas) to hand the matter over to the predominantly right-wing constitutional court. It did so, and the court proceeded to strike down the law in its entirety. The Companys government tried to find a workable compromise, but in the resulting polarization between farmers and landowners both the ERC and the Lliga had difficulty controlling their respective clients.

To compound matters, in October 1934, the Samper government fell and was replaced by one headed by none other than the anti-Catalanist Alejandro Lerroux, and containing members of CEDA. Thus, the Generalitat was confronted with a Spanish government formed of left- and right-wing forces that had in common a deep antipathy to Catalan nationalism. Fearing that Catalonia's autonomy was in mortal danger, Lluís Companys, now the Catalan president, responded by pro-claiming a 'Catalan state within the Spanish Federal Republic.' Within 10 hours, the Spanish army had forced the Catalan government to capitulate. Moreover, the Spanish government used Companys' proclamation as justification for suspend-ing the Catalan statute of autonomy and closing parliament. Members of the Catalan government were sentenced to 30 years' hard labour, and a state of emer-gency was declared. Not only was the *Llei de Contractes* repealed, but 1,400 appli-cations were filed to evict tenant farmers. The Lliga initially protested the suspension of the statute of autonomy but then agreed to co-operate with the new bodies set up in Catalonia by the Spanish state.[65] Now that Catalan autonomy and Catalan nationalism were linked to a leftist project, the Catalan bourgeoisie was quite prepared to support Catalonia's ostensible enemies if its class interests so dictated.

In the 1936 Spanish elections, however, the Catalan Front d'Esquerres (Left-wing front), dominated by ERC and republican candidates, won all of the Catalan constituencies, securing 59 per cent of votes as compared with the 41 per cent won by the Lliga-dominated Front d'Ordre. The left was also triumphant elsewhere in Spain, although not to the same extent. With a new Spanish government,

Catalonia's statute of autonomy was restored and amnesty declared. In fact, the Lliga returned to the Catalan parliament and championed the legality of the republic.

None the less, the experience showed the vulnerability of Catalan autonomy and the leftist nationalist project if the Catalan bourgeoisie and the Lliga saw their interests in danger. As in the past, they were prepared to sacrifice Catalan autonomy and call on class allies in the rest of Spain to defend their vision of the proper social and economic order within Catalonia.

As it happened, the ERC and its leftist nationalist project were also attacked by the revolutionary and anarchist left in Catalonia. Several factors may explain why anarchism should have become such a powerful force in Barcelona. In part, it may have to do with the intransigence of the Catalan bourgeoisie, whose enterprises remained largely familistic in structure and resistant to the new forms of ownership, mergers, and takeovers that would usher in advanced capitalism. Within these familistic structures, there was no place for collective bargaining and other more conventional methods for dealing with employees. In fact, the Catalan bourgeoisie was strikingly unenlightened in its dealings with workers.[66] For its part, the Spanish state's relative hostility to Catalan economic interests made it reluctant to intervene in Catalonia's labour struggles until they had become so deep as to threaten the Spanish state itself. Then it intervened with brutal repression, ensuring that workers would be convinced that revolutionary action was the only means available to them.[67] Finally, Catalan nationalism may help to explain the particular strength of anarchism in Barcelona, for anarchism offered the prospect of a radical decentralization of power from Madrid.[68]

Revolutionary anarchism had been building for decades in Catalonia. Frightened by it, the Catalan bourgeoisie had supported counter-organizations, such as the Sindicat Lliure. The intense conflict between the revolutionary and bourgeois organizations had engendered spirals of violence and assassination throughout the first three decades of the twentieth century. By 1930 the anarchist CNT (Confederación Nacional del Trabajo) had become the primary force among Catalan workers. One of its factions, the FAI (Federación Anarchista Ibérica) preached revolutionary violence and contributed to a wave of bombings and assassinations during the summer of 1931. The Generalitat had responded with police repression.[69]

As Salvador Giner argues, a distinctly Catalan version of anarchism had been emerging. This anarchical syndicalism eschewed violent revolution, as represented by the FAI, and coupled notions of self-management by workers with an openness to collective bargaining. Yet the ERC, which was led by middle-class radicals, refused to recognize these tendencies, harassing all anarchists instead.[70] For their part, the anarchists and the CNT tended to dismiss as inconsequential the ERC's brand of leftist nationalism and its struggle for autonomy. In January 1932, after an unsuccesssful anarchist insurrection, the ERC broke totally with the CNT. Thus, when Companys proclaimed the Catalan state in October 1934, the CNT remained largely on the sidelines, to the satisfaction of the Generalitat.[71] This all changed after the restoration of the Catalan statute of autonomy in 1936.

During the first few months after the restoration of autonomy, Catalonia's political life was relatively peaceful—Catalonia has been described as a virtual 'oasis' in the class conflict that was marking the rest of Spain. None the less, the outbreak of civil war was profoundly destabilizing, and, confronted with the need to mobilize a defence against Franco's troops, the Generalitat became dependent on all potential allies in Catalonia. On 19 July 1936, the day after an uprising of officers in Morocco had launched the Spanish Civil War in the defence of both the unity of Spain and the social order, troops marched to the centre of Barcelona. The Civil Guard, loyal to the Generalitat and the Republic, was able to prevail but arguably would not have succeeded without the efforts of a large number of citizen soldiers, essentially anarchists, whom the Generalitat had armed to help defeat the uprising.[72] Moreover, on 19 July anarchists stole 30,000 rifles from an artillery depot. In effect, the anarchists had become an important armed presence in Barcelona, perhaps the most important one, and Companys had no choice but to come to terms with them.[73]

Initially, the anarchist leaders were placed on a new central committee (Comité Central de Milícies Antifeixistes). However, on 26 September, the anarchists entered the government along with two Marxist organizations, the Partit Socialista Unificat de Catalunya (PSUC), which was linked to the Communist International, and the Partit Obrer d'Unificació Marxista (POUM), a Trotskyite organization. Clearly, the Companys government had felt obliged to move far from its original republican, leftist base. The anarchists and Marxists now held the majority in the Generalitat.

At last, the full range of working-class and leftist organizations had mobilized around Catalanism. This alliance came too late to save Catalan democracy, if that had ever been a possibility, and it was to be riven with conflicts. But the reconciliation between Catalanism and leftism, including some Marxist forms, was a major development that was to persist into the Franco years.[74]

The newly constituted Generalitat was plagued by struggles for power among the new arrivals. In December 1936 the PSUC succeeded in having the POUM excluded from the government, given its denunciation of purges by the Soviet government, which had been the only major power to help the republicans in their struggle against Franco. In May 1937 an attempt by the police, under direction from the PSUC police commissioner for Catalonia, to take over the CNT-controlled Barcelona telephone company provoked a spontaneous anarchist revolt, which, while denounced by the anarchist leaders, was supported by the POUM.[75] In order to restore order, Companys had to allow the Spanish government to resume control over public order in Catalonia. A new Catalan government was formed, composed solely of the ERC and the PSUC, but it was to be plagued by conflict between these two parties.

Unable to act coherently because of these internal struggles, the Generalitat saw its power flow back to the Spanish Republican government. Indeed, in October

1937 the government transferred its headquarters to Barcelona.[76] Apparently this was done partly to bring the Catalan government into line; in particular, the communists in the Republican government were strongly centralist and had no patience with Catalonia's autonomist ambitions. The Republican government took permanent control of public order in Catalonia, placed Catalonia's war industry directly under military authority, and tried to place Catalonia's courts under military control as well. Defence of Catalan autonomy was branded as treason against the Republic.[77] In April 1938, Companys declared in a letter to the Republican president that 'the Generalitat has been turned into an empty shell' ('la Generalitat ha quedat convertida en una institució sense relleu').[78] But when the ERC objected to this state of affairs in August 1938, the PSUC sided with the Republican government. The ERC was effectively isolated in its defence of the Generalitat's autonomy.[79]

By the late 1930s the Generalitat had been gravely weakened by the actions of both its enemies and its ostensible allies, inside and outside Catalonia. The ERC did succeed in obtaining a measure of autonomy for Catalonia and in using that autonomy to advance a republican, leftist brand of Catalan nationalism. In the process, it was able to bring about an impressive array of progressive measures, especially during its early years. And it had been able to seize the nationalist mantle from its former, profoundly conservative, champions. The result was a much more coherent form of Catalan nationalism than that of the Lliga, with its highly tentative pursuit of regional autonomy. However, this form of nationalism was also one that could propel the Catalan bourgeoisie into full alliance with powerful anti-Catalanist forces in the rest of Spain. The repression of 1934–5, with the collusion of Catalan conservatives and the Lliga, was a clear foretaste of what was to come. Nor, despite its clear progressivism, could the ERC and leftist nationalism count on the support all of the forces that were arrayed against Catalan conservatives and the bourgeoisie. The support of revolutionary leftists and anarchists for the ERC and the Generalitat was at best tactical and often brought with it debilitating power struggles. Beyond that, the anti-clerical excesses and violence of the anarchists and other forces discredited the Generalitat with which they were associated and caused some Catalans to turn against Catalanism itself.[80]

The Generalitat persisted until the end of the Second Republic, with the ERC at the helm. But the intense class polarization of the late 1930s largely drained the Generalitat of political legitimacy in Catalonia and hindered its effort to assert any real authority. And the Generalitat's ability to exercise authority was further hindered by its ostensible allies in the Spanish Republican government, who had lost all patience with notions of Catalan autonomy. Finally, on 16 February 1939, Franco's troups entered Barcelona. The Republican government and the Generalitat had already crossed the border into France, joining a mass of civilians and retreating soldiers. With the creation of Pétain's government in southern France, Franco required extradition of the Republican leaders. Over Pétain's objections, the Gestapo handed over a number of them, including Companys, who was executed in Barcelona on 15 October 1940.

Catalan Nationalism under the Franco Regime

The Catalan leadership that went into exile, largely in France and Mexico, was demoralized and badly divided, and different factions blamed each other for the disaster. In the wake of the defeat, hostility between the ERC and the PSUC prevented Companys from forming a government-in-exile. Indeed, some leaders argued that the legal continuity of Catalonia's Second Republic statute of autonomy should be abandoned altogether since it had been undermined by the centralism of the last Republican government and, in any event, there was no hope that it could be restored. It would be better to form new movements able to embrace all Catalans.[81] Finally, after the Allied victory in 1945, a government-in-exile was formed under Josep Irla, who, as speaker of the Catalan parliament in 1938, was Companys' legal successor as president. But it became clear that the Allies had no interest in taking up the Catalan cause; in fact, with the rise of the Cold War, they were looking for an accommodation with Franco. The exiles lost hope for a restoration, at least in the near future, and became increasingly estranged from their compatriots in Catalonia.

During the 1940s some Catalan groups took up arms against the Franco regime. After the failure of an armed invasion through the Pyrenees in 1944, the effort changed to guerrilla actions, mostly by anarchists and communists. But the sabotage, holdups, kidnappings, and even assassinations (13 between 1943 and 1953) received little popular support and had no effect on the Franco regime. By the early 1950s they had largely come to an end, having been judged ineffective.[82] It was difficult to see how Catalonia could regain its autonomy without the active support of the major powers, and that clearly was not forthcoming.

The Franco Regime and 'Cultural Genocide'

Thanks to the massive flight from Catalonia at the end of the Civil War, as well as the imprisonment and death of some who stayed on, Catalonia no longer had a clearly defined leadership. Most of the major political and intellectual figures of the Catalan Republic were gone. In six days alone, between 1 and 6 May 1939, 266 people had been executed by war councils.[83] Estimates of the number of permanent exiles vary from 60,000[84] to 100,000,[85] out of a population of about 3 million.[86]

Moreover, upon assuming power, the Franco regime was determined to put an end once and for all to the 'Catalan problem'. From the outset, defence of the unity of the Spanish nation had been a driving preoccupation of the fascists. This had been one of the justifications for the initial military uprising in July 1936; throughout the military there had been alarm over the inroads of regional 'separatism'. And the integrity of the nation was an obsession for the Falange that dominated the Franco regime in its early years.

Upon its first arrival on Catalan soil, on 5 April 1938, the Franco dictatorship eliminated Catalonia's statute of autonomy.[87] A law dated 9 February 1939 made it retroactively illegal to belong not only to the republican and leftist political parties but even to various sport and cultural organizations as well.[88] At the same time, executions continued, involving in particular members of the ERC, the CNT, and the Unió de Rabassaires (a tenant-farmer association). Over the period 1938–53, 3,800 people were executed as a result of military tribunal sentences.[89]

In a process that has been aptly labelled 'cultural genocide' by Salvador Giner and other scholars,[90] the new government set about to eliminate not only the expression of the Catalan identity but also the language and institutions upon which the identity was based. The Catalan flag and anthem were outlawed, and patriotic monuments were destroyed. The public use of Catalan was banned, and Catalan-language signs and notices were removed. Public employees were forbidden to use Catalan either in public buildings or outside. Catalan culture was banned as a subject at the University of Barcelona, and cultural institutions such as the Institut d'Estudis Catalans were closed. Teachers suspected of Catalanist sympathies were transferred elsewhere and were replaced by teachers from other regions of Spain, who, having no knowledge of Catalan language and culture, could be counted upon to advance the cause of assimilation. Signs were erected on trains and in other public places inciting people to 'Speak Spanish! Speak the Language of the Empire!' Mail was censored, and correspondence in Catalan was destroyed. Catalan could not be used in the civil register; Catalan first names were banned and Catalan family names were transcribed in Castilian.[91]

Even if fascism and the Falange had little support in Catalonia, the Franco regime could count on the active co-operation of members of the Catalan bourgeoisie. Many of them came from the old Lliga. If some were disquieted by the Franco regime's anti-Catalanist policies, they were still caught up in the shock they had experienced in 1936, when revolutionary anarchism seemed to be in control of Barcelona.[92] Most were handsomely rewarded for their support of the regime.

Little was left of the political and intellectual leadership that had guided Catalonia through its Republican phase of the 1930s. Its numbers had been radically reduced through exile, imprisonment, and execution. And the implacable opposition of the Franco regime, especially in its early years, to any expression of Catalan nationality ensured that the surviving members of that leadership could exercise no public role in Catalonia. Not only had the Catalonia of the Second Republic been eliminated, but Catalonia itself was fading from view.

Artistic Exiles

The collapse of the Second Republic also cost Catalonia some towering artistic figures. Born in Barcelona in 1893, Joan Miró had emerged as a major surrealist painter by the 1920s. During a period in Paris he produced one-man shows with the surrealists there. Miró had returned to Barcelona by the end of the decade, but in 1936, with the outbreak of the Civil War, he settled in Paris and stayed there until 1940, when he fled the Germans for Mallorca, where he remained for the rest of his life.

Salavador Dalí was born in 1904 in Figueres, in the foothills of the Pyrenees. After a period in Madrid he held his first one-man show in Barcelona, in 1925. By the late 1920s he had become internationally famous as one of the leaders of surrealism. With the outbreak of the Second World War he fled to the United States, where he stayed until 1948. He went back to Catalonia periodically over the subsequent decades and finally died in his hometown.[93]

The internationally famous cellist Pablo Casals moved to France after the Civil War and refused to visit Spain as long as Franco was in power. In 1956, he moved to Puerto Rico, where he died in 1973.

New Leaders with a New Nationalism

With time, new leaders did emerge in Catalonia. But they understood Catalonia in very different terms. Many of the young new leaders had grown up within the institutions of the Catalan Church, and for them, Republican Catalonia was eradicably tarnished by anti-clericalism. Indeed, they tended to hold this anti-clericalism responsible for the débâcle. Thus rather than seeking to restore the Catalonia of the 1930s, they denied any continuity with it and reached back to an older, more rural and traditional Catalonia. Once again, then, Catalan nationalism underwent a major transformation as it was defined in terms of the experience and world view of a different generation of Catalans.

The first stirring of a renewed Catalanism occurred within the Church. Although most of the Catalan upper clergy identified firmly with the Franco regime, some did not. Two notable exceptions were Vidal i Barraquer, the exiled archbishop of Tarragona, who had refused to support Franco during the Civil War, and Canon Carles Cardó, who attacked the regime's subordination of the Church. Moreover, the Church was sufficiently powerful that some Catalans could use it as a sanctuary in which to affirm their identity.[94]

The first such opportunity was a ceremony in 1947 to enthrone the Virgin of Montserrat. Before a gathering of 70,000, Catalan was used once again in public; the Catalan flag was displayed from a high mountain peak. In the mid-1950s, a new distinctly Catholic version of Catalanism emerged among young Catalan students and the leadership of the Catholic scout movement, with the superior of the Montserrat Benedictine abbey as their spiritual leader. In 1954, they founded Crist i Catalunya (CC). In 1959, one of the most militant CC members, Jordi Pujol, led a public campaign against the pro-Franco editor of the Barcelona newspaper, La Vanguardia, for a slur against Catalans and their language, and was associated with the singing of a forbidden patriotic song at a concert attended by Francoist dignitaries. For his part in these events, plus circulation of a pamphlet about Franco, Pujol was sentenced to seven years' imprisonment.[95]

Out of this experience, Pujol emerged as leader of a breakaway faction of the CC which, rejecting the pro-labour orientation of the CC majority, focused its energies upon restoring the Catalan nation and building up a Catalan infrastructure. At the same time, emboldened by Pope John XXIII's 1963 Pacem in terris encyclical, which condemned the repression of national minorities, clerical figures began to support Catalanism more openly. The abbey of Montserrat became the centre of this movement: in an article in Le Monde, its superior, Aureli Escarré, denounced the Franco regime's violation of fundamental Christian principles.[96]

Through these processes Catalan nationalism moved in a radically different direction. Profoundly different from the nationalism of the 1930s, this new phase was also much more spiritual and traditionalist than the earlier conservative nationalism of Prat de la Riba and the Lliga.

The Left: A Structured Opposition

Although the primary vehicle of 1930 nationalism, the ERC, had virtually disappeared, its sometime partner, the PSUC, did survive under the Franco regime. Joan Comorera continued to lead the party, ensuring that it maintained its Catalanist leanings. However, this stance earned it the enmity of the Spanish Communist Party (PCE), which, in 1948, removed Comorera from power, accusing him of Titoist tendencies. Henceforth, the PCE held the PSUC in check. None the less, the party continued to represent a type of Catalanism, even after it began to absorb some of the massive wave of immigrants from southern Spain who entered Catalonia in the 1950s. Its tight organizational structure, as befits a Communist organization, served the PSUC well in providing a clandestine opposition to the Franco regime.

The Catalan socialists were less effective organizationally, but they were able to maintain themselves as a distinctly Catalan movement, eschewing any formal relationship with the Spanish socialist party (PSOE) until after the death of Franco. The Franco years also saw the radical decline of the old anarchist CNT, and the rise of two union organizations, the Communist Comisiones Obreras (CCOO) and the socialist Unió General de Treballadors (UGT).

Thus, despite the determined efforts of the Franco regime to eliminate both the expression of Catalan nationalism and the national characteristics upon which this nationalism was based, Catalan nationalism persisted. But it took a new form, sheltered by the Church, which was the one Catalan institution the Franco regime could not suppress. And it was strengthened by the Communists and other left-wing forces that had always been uneasy with the Republican nationalism of the 1930s. Though they had even less in common with the new Catholic nationalists, the Franco regime made them allies.

Conclusion

Compared to other self-proclaimed nations, Catalonia came rather late to nationalism. For all intents and purposes, Catalan intellectual and political leaders did not claim the status of 'nation' until the end of the nineteenth century. And it was only in 1906, with the writings of Prat de la Riba, they had had a formal elaboration of Catalonia's credentials for nationhood. Yet, once the claim had been made, it stuck. The assumption of Catalonia's nationhood has guided Catalan politics ever since. Even the attempted 'cultural genocide' of the Franco regime could not put an end to it.

The fact of the matter is that Catalan nationalists had a great deal to work with. They could claim that Catalonia had existed as a political entity since the late 900s. They could point to the glories of a medieval empire, the early development of parliamentary institutions, and the persistence of a rich literary tradition based on a distinct language. Catalonia's historical role as Spain's primary site of economic innovation and development provided a strong basis for feeling not only distinct from, but superior to, the rest of Spain, and resentful of Madrid's political dominance. There was more than enough to sustain a strong sense of nationhood.

Over the first six decades of its existence Catalan nationalism took radically different forms. The first phase, culminating in the conservative nationalism of the Lliga, was followed by a second phase, dominated by Republicanism and socialism, only to be followed by a strongly spiritualist nationalism that rejected much of Republican Catalonia. Time and again differences in world views and class interests broke through any national solidarity. The Catalan bourgeoisie repeatedly abandoned Republican nationalists in favour of its class allies in Madrid, and during the 1930s, the PSUC broke with the ERC nationalists out of solidarity with its Communist brothers and allies. The celebration of the Catalan nation and the formulation of strategies to advance its interests were never free of other concerns, least of all those of class.

None the less, as Joan Culla argues, during the first decades of the twentieth century, Catalanist political culture steadily took root throughout Catalan society. Typically, Catalan nationalism was tied to specific classes and milieux, usually the Lliga. But there were many times when all Catalan social forces were united in defence of the nation: Solidaritat Catalana, the campaign for the Mancomunitat, the campaign at the end of the First World War, and the reaction to the Primo de Rivera dictatorship. The Mancomunitat was itself instrumental in the spread of a Catalanist political culture. As a result, in the 1930s, the nationalist symbols, doctrines, and values were accepted by all political forces in Catalonia.[97] By the same token, through the creation of the Generalitat and the democratization of political life, the regions and localities within Catalonia were integrated and local attachments weakened in favour of a national identity.[98]

Through it all, however, Catalan nationalists were never able to establish a satisfactory relationship with the rest of Spain. The Lliga conservatives came closest, but the anti-Catalanism of their class ally, Primo de Rivera, put an end to their greatest achievement—the Mancomunitat. The relationship between the Catalan Republicans of the ERC and their Republican allies in Madrid was always difficult, beginning with Macià's ill-fated proclamation of a Catalan Republic and ending with Spanish Republicans' takeover of Barcelona.

All these contradictions were to come to the surface when Spain finally began its transition to democracy and Catalonia began its process of national reconstruction.

Chapter 3

The Transition to Democracy

Despite the best efforts of the Franco regime, Catalonia was still intact when Franco finally died on 20 November 1975. Catalonia had managed to retain its cultural distinctiveness, especially its language, and many Catalans remained convinced that they were a nation. The old leaders of the Second Republic may have disappeared, whether through repression, exile, or old age, but during the Franco period new ones had emerged who were more than prepared to lead Catalonia into the new era that would come with Spain's transition to democracy. There should have been no surprise, then, that Catalan nationalism returned in full force to challenge the assumptions of Spain's political élites, for Catalan nationalism, though it had been suppressed, had never disappeared.

The Contradictions of 'National Reconstruction'

Yet it was no simple matter to chart the new course for the Catalan nation. As in the past, Catalan nationalists held radically different social and economic visions. While some still adhered to the social democratic or socialist vision of the Catalan nation that had held sway during the Second Republic, and remained loyal to the ERC leadership that had controlled, if only nominally, the Generalitat, others had acquired their conception of Catalonia and Catalan nationalism through the institutions of the Church and Catholic social movements. For them, the nationalist leadership of the 1930s had no appeal whatsoever. Instead, they drew their inspiration from earlier decades, when the Lliga and other conservative forces dominated Catalan nationalism, as well as from Catalonia's distant historical past. Still other elements of the Franco resistance were linked to Communist forces and, as such, had their own critical reading of Catalonia's experience in the 1930s.

For many, then, restoring the Catalan nation did not necessarily mean returning to the pre-Franco days when Catalonia had first regained its autonomy. The conception of the nation that guided the 1930s Generalitat was a fiercely contested one. To that extent, 'reconstructing' the Catalan nation would have to mean constructing something quite new and different, however much it might be legitimized through the evocation of a recent or distant Catalan past.

In any event, more had changed in Catalonia than the ideological perspectives of its presumed leaders. Over the Franco decades, Catalonia had itself changed in at least two ways that were both fundamental and irrevocable.

First, by the 1970s the traditional Catalan bourgeoisie had virtually disappeared. During the late nineteenth century this class had helped to underwrite the emergence of the Renaixença and Catalanism, and ultimately had become closely linked to Catalan nationalism itself in its conservative form. Beyond that, its largesse had supported a rich complex of social and cultural institutions. It is because of strong civil society that Catalonia has been able to persist as a 'nation without a state'. Without a strong bourgeoisie, this formula would be highly problematic and the need for a strong Catalan Generalitat would be correspondingly greater.

Second, the Franco years had seen a profound and unprecedented change in the composition of Catalan society. From 1951 to 1970, about 1.16 million immigrants came to Catalonia,[1] primarily from Andalusia.[2] In 1961–5 alone there were over 400,000 immigrants.[3] By 1970, immigrants represented 47.4 per cent of the population of Catalonia.[4] Whereas previous waves of immigrants to Catalonia had tended to speak Catalan or closely related languages such as Occitan, most of the new immigrants spoke only Castilian. The integration of such large numbers of immigrants would be a massive challenge for any society. Indeed, few societies have undergone such a change. Yet this happened at a time when, thanks to the Franco regime, Catalan society was in no position to assume such a task. Coming to Catalonia in search of work, these Castilian-speakers had no particular attraction to the Catalan language, and, of course, there were no opportunities for formal instruction in it.

Beyond that, the Franco regime had conducted a systematic campaign to eliminate the language of Catalonia, and indeed any sign of national distinctiveness. The Francoists had a special hatred for Catalonia, believing that Catalan nationalism and separatism were one and the same. The Falangists even appealed to anti-semitism by claiming that Companys and leaders of the Lliga were secret Jews. In fact, in their resolve to eliminate the Catalan threat once and for all, some Francoists talked of reducing Catalonia to an agrarian economy and moving its industries to other parts of Spain.[5] Believing that use of Catalan was synonymous with separatism the Francoists acted in a concerted fashion to eliminate the public expression of the language.

After the war, and especially in the 1960s, the Franco regime did relax somewhat its enforcement of these laws. Books were published again in Catalan, with annual production reaching 650 in 1967;[6] some lectures and conferences took place in universities; Catalan was taught once again in private institutions; and major historical research on Catalonia was conducted in Catalan.[7] Indeed, during the 1940s and 1950s a new generation of writers in Catalan emerged, and in the 1960s Catalan reappeared on the radio and was given a marginal role on television.[8] But this revival was largely restricted to the intelligentsia. The Franco regime's suppression of Catalan continued to have a deep effect within Catalan society as a whole. Since there was no public instruction in Catalan, many educated Catalans who spoke the language in private could not read or write it. And Catalan remained prohibited in public institutions, although there was some support of Catalan cultural activities by local and municipal institutions.[9] Many of the Catalan cultural and intellectual leaders who had left Spain at the end of the 1930s were still in exile. And some members of the Barcelona bourgeoisie had adopted Castilian in their private lives, returning to the aristocratic practices they had followed before the 1930s.[10]

In short, the end of the Franco regime opened up great opportunities. Catalonia could at last secure the political autonomy that it had so briefly enjoyed during the 1930s and could go about 'reconstructing' the Catalan nation after decades of suppression. But the tasks to be faced were little short of staggering. Moreover, any project of 'national reconstruction' was bound not only to be opposed elsewhere in Spain but to be contested in Catalonia by supporters of opposing projects.

Restoring the Generalitat

Long before Franco's death, pressure had begun to build in Catalonia to restore the Generalitat. In 1971 the Assemblea de Catalunya was created to unite opposition forces; its slogan was 'freedom, amnesty, and statute of autonomy'. In 1975 the Consell de Forces Polítiques, uniting all Catalonia's political parties, was formed to demand the creation of a provisional Generalitat. Upon Franco's death the Spanish government sought to head off the movement by offering to establish a Consejo General de Cataluña, similar to the Mancomunitat, but the proposal fell on deaf ears.[11]

By 1975 the campaign for a Catalan Generalitat had an added twist. Some political forces were demanding that the Generalitat be established with Joseph Tarradellas as its president. Tarradellas, who was an exile living in France, had been a member of Macià's government in the early 1930s. He had been designated president in 1954 at a gathering in Mexico City of Catalan parliamentarians in exile but, declaring that his only goal was to return to Catalonia as president of a restored Generalitat, refused to establish a government-in-exile.

In his late seventies and rooted in the Second Republic, Tarradellas represented a different political generation and a different ideology than the nationalist leadership that had come of political age under the Franco regime. Thus, he clashed with nationalists in Catalonia, including members of Òmnium cultural and the Assemblea de Catalunya. In particular he clashed with Jordi Pujol, whom he distrusted, and with the PSUC, whose leader flatly declared that he did not believe in Tarradellas' plans.[12] For that matter, he was not well known by the general Catalan public.

But Tarradellas prevailed. A Comissió Pro Retorna del President Tarradellas was formed in late 1976; by March it had collected 20,000 signatures on a petition.[13] Demonstrations were organized on behalf of autonomy; one such gathering at

Sant Boi on 11 September 1976 was attended by 100,000 people. In the Spanish general elections held in June 1977, nationalist forces dominated the Catalan vote. The parties committed to autonomy won 80 per cent of the popular vote in Catalonia, 37 of 47 seats in the lower house, and 15 of 16 in the Senate.

In principle, restoring the Generalitat under Tarradellas would be a radical move since it would establish a continuity with the Generalitat of the Second Republic. By restoring precisely what the Franco regime had destroyed, it would constitute a sharp break with the regime itself. Nevertheless in July 1977, Spanish president Adolfo Suárez agreed to precisely this arrangement. Dismayed by his party's poor showing in the June election, Suárez had resolved to meet the Catalans' evident desire for autonomy, but he preferred to hand power over to Tarradellas rather than to the Catalan socialists.[14] Accordingly, on 19 September 1977 a decree established a provisional autonomous Catalan government and on 24 October 1977, the Generalitat was indeed restored and Tarradellas was sworn in as president of the Generalitat.

Tarradellas formed a provisional government containing all parties represented in the Cortes. But without any agreement about the terms of Catalonia's autonomy, the Generalitat was an empty shell.[15] It had to rely on the resources of the Diputacio de Barcelona, of which Tarradellas was also president. It was further handicapped by the need to maintain consensus among the several different parties represented in it. However, by incarnating the ideal of a head of state, Tarradellas gave a certain credibility to the new Generalitat. More fundamentally, by rooting the new Generalitat in that of the Second Republic, Tarradellas and his associates achieved the only total break with the established regime that was to occur during Spain's transition to democracy. To that extent, Catalonia had indeed obtained recognition of its distinctiveness within Spain.

Catalonia's Place in a Democratic Spain

Breaking with the Franco Regime

Re-establishing the Generalitat was one thing; defining its place within Spain was another. In restoring the Generalitat, the Suárez government had not restored the statute of autonomy of 1932. For that matter, the constitution was still that of the Franco regime. The terms of the Generalitat's autonomy would have to be defined in a new statute of autonomy which, in turn, had to await the adoption of a new Spanish constitution.

Among democratic forces in Spain, there was a general consensus that Catalonia would have to be granted some degree of autonomy. Indeed, they applied the same reasoning to Spain's two other 'historic nations', the Basque Country and Galicia. Beyond whatever sympathy they felt for the claims of these three 'nations'—and some felt none whatsoever—there was a practical necessity: to have any hope of prevailing they needed the support of the three sets of nationalists. Like it or not, and many Spaniards didn't, the goals of democratization and Catalonian autonomy were intimately linked.

The form and extent of that autonomy were to be dealt with in the new constitution. But what form would this constitution take? Would it represent a total break with the Franco regime, or would it emerge through an adaptation or reform of the existing legal order? This had had some bearing on Catalonia's role in any constitutional negotiations. If it was to be a break from the existing regime, there was a greater chance that Catalonia as a distinct entity would be a party in the negotiations. Indeed, Tarradellas, as president of the restored Generalitat, expected to be in charge of negotiations for Catalonia.

A total break was a distinct possibility, as it had been in Portugal, where four years after the death of the dictator Salazar in 1970, a military coup ushered in a period of political turmoil.[16] The Franco regime was indeed vulnerable. The Church had withdrawn its support. The new industrial bourgeoisie that had emerged under Franco saw the dictatorship as a hindrance to its plans for Spain's economic integration with Europe. Much of the middle class was committed to democracy. Spain was already sufficiently secularized to render the Franco regime anachronistic.[17]

Moreover, almost all democratic leaders were calling openly for a formal break. In October 1976, the opposition parties formed a Platform of Democratic Organizations, calling for a 'democratic break': a new provisional government ('government of democratic consensus') would be established and a constituent process launched in which all the fundamentals of political authority, including the monarchy, would come into question. For this purpose, a 'constituent assembly' would be elected.[18]

The old ruling class, however, still controlled the Spanish state and much of the ideological apparatus, and it could call on the loyalty of the army and much of the civil bureaucracy.[19] Thus, a debate raged within the Spanish government as to how far it should go in meeting the demands for political change.[20]

As Franco had planned, upon his death Juan Carlos, son of Don Juan, was crowned king. During his illness the previous year, Franco had already transferred powers to Juan Carlos provisionally. Arias Navarro, who remained prime minister, tried to resist pressures to democratize the regime but, failing to do so, resigned on 1 July 1977. Juan Carlos chose as his new prime minister a relative unknown, Adolfo Suárez, who, despite his firm roots in the Franco regime,[21] quickly embraced the cause of democratization. The forces for change were to be contained through a reform of the existing legal order. Popular support for the newly restored monarchy was to be secured by restoring democracy; Spain was to be a constitutional monarchy.[22]

Within two weeks of coming to office, the Suárez government announced a program of political reform. A bill to reform political institutions would be debated and passed by the existing Cortes (parliament) and submitted to a referendum; then the government would call upon the opposition forces to take part in free elections; finally, the newly elected parliament would formulate a law of constitutional reform that would be submitted to Spaniards in a second referendum.[23]

The government obtained passage of its political reform act, which created a bicameral parliament based on universal suffrage, and, in December 1976, it submitted the law to a referendum. The coalition of opposition parties campaigning for democracy did not participate in the referendum campaign, either taking no position on the proposition or urging voters to abstain.[24] They were offended by the Suárez government's attempt to define and manage the process through which Spain was to become democratic. They were formally committed to *ruptura*, or a democratic break. But the government's proposal was approved by an overwhelming majority of voters, including 69 per cent of Catalan voters.[25]

Confronted with the Suárez government's democratization program and the legitimacy it had won in the referendum, the leading opposition forces recognized that they had to settle for a *ruptura pactada*, or 'negotiated break'. In many cases their commitment to a democratic break had been pro forma anyway.[26] The result was not even a break but reform.

The opposition parties all participated in the general election called by the Suárez government for 15 June 1977. Despite the strong showing by the democratic socialists (PSOE) under Felipe González, Suárez's UCD won the largest number of seats and Suárez remained prime minister. So Spain's transition to democracy continued to be led by a party that was controlled by reconstructed Francoists, albeit containing some moderate anti-Francoists.[27]

Negotiating Catalonia's New Status
To the extent that the demands of Catalan nationalists were to be addressed, it would be not as part of the construction of a totally new Spanish political order but as part of changes to existing institutions negotiated among the members of the parliament, including both reconstructed and unreconstructed Francoists. Although Catalan nationalists would participate in these negotiations, the negotiations would be among political parties rather than territorial entities such as regions, let alone nations or nationalities. Catalonia would be represented by Catalan members of the Spanish parliament, rather than the Assemblea de Catalunya.[28]

Moreover, the negotiations necessarily would be dominated by the basic assumption, shared by all of Spain's major political parties and by most Spaniards, of Spain's integrity as a nation. Any concession of autonomy to Catalonia would have to be closely bound by this fundamental understanding of Spain.

Beyond that, most Spaniards rejected the very idea of federalism, which might otherwise seem to be the logical means of accommodating demands for autonomy. Spain's nineteenth-century experiment with federalism, the First Republic, was generally regarded as disastrous, and federalism was unacceptable not just to the right but to much of the Spanish political spectrum. And there was apprehension over dismantling the central administration, with its relative efficiency, in favour of some unknown alternative.[29]

To be sure, Catalonia might look to the two other 'historic nations' as allies in its campaign for autonomy. But Catalan nationalists had no natural affinity with the more ethnically based Basque nationalism, let alone the Basque terrorist movement. By the same token, concessions to Basque nationalists that Spanish political élites might feel necessary in order to undercut Basque terrorism would not be automatically applied to Catalonia as well. And Galicia, the other historic nation, remained firmly under the control of Francoists. Yet, for all intents and purposes, there was no compelling desire for autonomy elsewhere than among these three historic nations.

Coupled with this commitment of most participants to the integrity of the Spanish nation was the fact that Catalonia, the Basque Country, and Galicia together represented only 28 per cent of the Spanish population.[30] Even though in the case of Catalonia and the Basque Country this demographic inferiority was partially offset by economic superiority, the historic nations remained very much minority players in the negotiations over the future of Spain.

As was to be expected, the designing of a new constitution was a lengthy process. Two days after the 1977 election, the Catalan parliamentarians met to form the Assemblea de Parlamentaris Catalans and, as such, called for autonomy and restoration of the Generalitat, along with amnesty for political prisoners and exiles and the legalization of all political parties. The socialist leader, Joan Roventós, called for recognition of the right to autonomy of 'all the nationalities and regions in the Spanish state'. That was a far cry from 1931 when Francesc Macià proclaimed the existence of a Catalan Republic within a non-existent Iberian federal republic. In effect, it was a deliberate effort to avoid the errors of the 1930s: this time Catalonia would secure its autonomy in an orderly fashion once a new constitution had been adopted.[31] At the same time, this position put the parliamentarians on a different path from Tarradellas, who wanted a restored Generalitat under his presidency to be in charge of negotiations.

Soon after the 1977 election, the Congreso de los Diputados, the lower chamber of the Cortes, established a constitutional committee of 36 members. In July 1977, a drafting committee was formed with seven members, of whom two were Catalans: Miquel Roca Junyent, of the nationalist CDC, and Jordi Solé Tura, of the Catalan Communist Party (PSUC). Yet another Catalan, Eduardo Martín Toval, was charged by the socialists with drafting the section on autonomy.[32]

After extended deliberations, the committee, in the summer of 1978, submitted a draft constitution to the Congreso, which duly approved it. The document was in turn debated in the Senate, where it was approved after some significant amendments. The two versions were then reconciled. Finally, on 31 October 1978, a common text was approved by overwhelming majorities in both houses of parliament, including all but one of the Catalan nationalists.[33]

The terms of the agreement clearly reflect the balance of forces within the Cortes. Thus, the new constitution responds to the demand for recognition by Catalonia and the two other historic nations. But it does so in terms carefully framed so as not to offend Spanish nationalism; there is no clear recognition of a multinational Spain. And it responds to demands from some regions in Spain that any concession to the historic nations also be available to them. The combined effect of these two constraints was to minimize any distinction between the historic nations and the rest of Spain.

For the nationalist leaders, Catalonia, the Basque Country, and Galicia had every right to be regarded as nations. Yet for most Spaniards the term could only apply to Spain as a whole; there was no question of viewing Spain as 'multinational'. Apparently the socialists were at first prepared to refer to Catalonia and the Basque Country as 'nations', but a Francoist committee member, Manuel Fraga, objected vigorously. As a compromise, the Catalan Roca proposed the term 'nationality', which was supported by most, but not all, committee members, including those from Suárez's UCD. The historical nations would be called 'nationalities', and as such would be given a right to autonomy. But when news of this agreement was leaked to the press, public opinion mobilized rapidly against any such recognition of a multinational Spain. Ultimately, negotiations among Suárez, Jordi Pujol, and Santiago Carrillo, leader of the Spanish Communists, resulted in a new wording.[34] The constitution would indeed 'recognize and guarantee the right to autonomy of the nationalities and regions' of which Spain is composed, but this provision was to be preceded by the statement, 'the Constitution is based on the indissoluble unity of the Spanish Nation, the common and indivisible country of all Spaniards'.[35]

When the draft constitution was presented to the Cortes, this question was the subject of prolonged debates. (It was also debated at length among Spanish academics.[36]) Manuel Fraga denounced the provisions, declaring that 'nationality' had the same meaning as 'nation'. A party colleague declared that to constitutionalize 'nationality' could lead to the national disintegration of Spain.[37] A Basque nationalist, however, rejected the formulation as too weak and proposed that the constitution should instead recognize the 'multinational character of the Spanish state',[38] along with the right to self-determination of the nations and regions that make it up. Other Basque nationalists and some Catalans made the same argument.[39] But for the most part, Catalan nationalists supported the constitutional committee's formulation as the best available and joined in the overwhelming rejection of any amendments.[40]

Beyond using 'nationalities' to refer to the historic nations, the new constitution also refrains from naming these nationalities.[41] Instead it equates them with all the other parts of Spain by granting the right of autonomy not only to 'nationalities' but to the 'regions' that make up the rest of Spain.[42] It also refers to them all as 'autonomous communities'.

As for the demands of nationalists for recognition of their national languages, the constitution does stipulate that autonomous communities (not just the historical nations) may declare 'other Spanish languages' to be official. But they cannot be the *exclusive* official language; Castilian also must be an official language of the autonomous communities. Nor do such languages have any status within the Spanish state. In another clear expression of Spanish nationalism,

Article 3 begins with the declaration that 'Castilian is the official Spanish language of the State. All Spaniards have the duty to know it and the right to use it.'[43] A Catalan senator had proposed that the same obligation should apply to co-official languages declared by autonomous communities: residents should know and use them as well. But his proposal was ignored. There was some objection in the Cortes to calling Spain's official language 'Castilian' rather than simply 'Spanish'. As at the committee stage, the Catalans had to insist on the term 'Castilian', so that Catalan, as well as Basque and Galician, would have at least some legitimacy in Spain.[44]

Similarly, Article 4, which designates the Spanish flag, allows autonomous communities to recognize their own flags and ensigns but stipulates that they 'shall be used together with the flag of Spain' on public buildings and in official ceremonies.

Another provision was clearly aimed at putting an end to the longstanding dream of Catalan nationalists of uniting the Països Catalans (Catalan Countries) by combining the autonomous communities of Catalonia, Valencia, and the Balearic Islands.[45] Section 145 states: 'Under no circumstances shall the federation of Autonomous Communities be allowed.'[46] (Catalan and Basque nationalists had objected to no avail to this reiteration of a provision from the republican constitution of 1931.[47]) For good measure, the constitution declares that agreements among autonomous communities that are not provided for in their statutes of autonomy would require the consent of the Cortes.[48]

By the same token, while the Senate is designated as 'the House of territorial representation',[49] this representation is based, not on the autonomous communities, let alone the historical nations, but on the much smaller administrative unit of the province, each of which is entitled to four senators.[50] The autonomous communities are each to appoint one additional senator, plus one senator for every million inhabitants.[51] But this constitutes a small minority of total senators (47 of 255 in the current Senate).[52]

Turning to the actual degree of autonomy to be exercised by the autonomous communities, the constitution drafters were confronted with the extreme heterogeneity of the ACs, if they were to extend over all Spain. The 17 units that ultimately became ACs ranged from the three historic nations to regions that had no previous existence at all, such as Cantabria and La Rioja, which culturally and historically had been part of Castile, and Madrid, which was detached from Castile to become a new autonomous community.[53] All three are composed of a single province.[54] Clearly, these 17 ACs did not share the same desire, need, or even capacity for autonomy.

By linking the historic nations with all manner of regions, and calling them all 'autonomous communities', the drafters had avoided having to recognize the national distinctness of Catalonia, the Basque Country, and Galicia. Yet, as a result, entities that were manifestly different had to be treated the same way. Moreover, other regions were encouraged to imitate the aspirations of the historic nations and thus to intensify the decentralizing pressures that leading participants in the constitutional negotiations had tried to avoid in the first place.

Two means were adopted to accommodate this extreme diversity. First, it was agreed that the terms of autonomy would be tailored to each autonomous community. Within each would-be AC, an assembly of local politicians and members of the Cortes Generales would draw up a statute of autonomy that would establish territorial boundaries, internal political institutions, and the powers to be assumed. This would, in turn, be enacted into law by the Cortes Generales.[55] Any change to the statute would require approval of AC institutions as spelled out in the statute, as well as a popular referendum, and the consent of the Cortes Generales.[56]

Second, there would be two ways of achieving autonomy. Under a special transitional provision, the three historic nations (territories that had approved statutes by referendum in the 1930s) were to be allowed to present their draft statutes of autonomy immediately, upon approval by their 'pre-autonomous' political bodies.[57] All other entities were to assume autonomy on a slow track, spelled out in Articles 143 and 148: after having established themselves as ACs, they would have to wait five years before, through an amendment to their statutes, they could move beyond a minimal set of responsibilities. However, in response to complaints of special treatment for the historical nations, the drafters added a further provision that blurred the distinction between the two tracks. Under Article 151, an AC did not have to wait for five years if it obtained majority votes in a referendum in each of its provinces.[58]

Yet, if Catalonia had the right to draw up the terms of its autonomy, subject to approval by the Congreso, and along with the Basque Country and Galicia could enjoy a 'fast track' to securing the full extent of powers available to an autonomous community, just how significant was the autonomy it might hope to gain?

Apparently, the Spanish socialists had proposed a classic federal model under which some jurisdictions would remain exclusive to the Spanish state and others would be exclusive to the autonomous communities. This proposal was rejected by Suárez's UCD precisely because it was federal. It was also rejected by Roca, the nationalist colleague of Pujol's, who feared that it would place all units on the same footing and thus dilute the distinction between the three historical nations and the rest of Spain. Accordingly, the constitutional committee agreed to distinguish responsibilities in terms not of exclusive jurisdictions but of stages: legislation, legislative development, and implementation.[59]

Article 149 does designate jurisdictions that are exclusive to the Spanish state. As is to be expected, the list of exclusive jurisdictions is generous, including such matters as citizenship, international relations, defence, administration of justice, some aspects of law, customs, the monetary system, and economic planning. The state is also given the right to impose basic laws with respect to health, social security, and education. Ultimately, 31 powers are defined as exclusive to the Spanish state.[60] But it is difficult to locate areas that are exclusive to the ACs. As one analyst observes, the Spanish system is not based on 'a strict material division but in most cases state and AACC have jurisdiction on the same issue (legislation/execution) or the issue is divided according to certain criteria (for instance, waters or transport).'[61]

In addition, the constitution allows little by way of independent fiscal resources to the ACs. It specifies that 'the primary power to raise taxes is vested exclusively in the State by law.'[62] Thus, the ACs may impose taxes only 'in accordance with the Constitution and the law'.[63] Only the Basque Country and Navarre have independent taxing power. In recognition of the medieval notion of *fueros*, or local charters, the constitution grants these two ACs *exclusive* taxing power.[64] But for Catalonia and the other ACs, the lack of any independent taxing power can only mean the lack of any fiscal autonomy.

The autonomy that the new constitution guaranteed to Catalonia was very limited. Indeed, whether or not Spain is a federation is a matter of debate.[65] The scope of legislative powers afforded to ACs tends to be circumscribed by Madrid's responsibility for basic laws that set the framework for potential AC actions. The absence of any independent taxing power in all but two ACs is crucial. The power to amend the constitution is fully in the hands of the Cortes Generales, with the possibility of a popular referendum; the ACs have no constitutional right to be involved.[66] Those would all seem to be persuasive reasons against classifying the Spanish constitution as 'federal', with perhaps an exception for the Basque provinces and Navarre, given their 'confederal' fiscal powers.

Other arguments are less compelling. For instance, some detractors place stock in the fact that the framers of the constitution did not explicitly agree that it is to be federal or that the 17 ACs did not have a prior existence and did not establish the new system as a contract among themselves.[67] Yet the primary criterion should be the nature of the new system defined in the constitution. Also of less significance is the fact that Article 2 explicitly denies any right of secession to the ACs. Federal states have, of course, been known to block secession by one of their units.[68] Still, the deficiencies of the ACs' exclusive powers and their absence from amendment processes would seem to be sufficient reasons to disqualify the Spanish constitution as laying the basis for a federation. Indeed, Spanish scholars tended to view the new constitution as creating a new form of state, a 'regional state', which is to be distinguished from the federal state as well as the unitary state.[69]

Beyond all that, many Catalan nationalists had wanted constitutional recognition of Catalonia's right to self-determination. And rather than 'autonomy' for Catalonia, they had wanted 'sovereignty', albeit the partial sovereignty of a federal system. Clearly, the new constitution fell short of nationalist objectives.

Whatever its limitations, the constitution did offer a framework within which Catalonia could finally achieve some autonomy. Moreover, the memory of past conflicts had disposed most Catalan leaders to be pragmatic and to accept the terms that were offered.[70] Thus, the new constitution was approved by all the Catalan members of the Cortes Generales except Heribert Barrera, who abstained, and was supported by most Catalan nationalists in general, although not Barrera's party, the Esquerra Republicana, which urged the voters to abstain.[71] In a referendum it was approved by 90.5 per cent of Catalan voters.[72] In Spain as a whole it was approved by 87.9 per cent.[73] The new constitution was signed into law by the king on 27 December 1978. The following year, an election was called under the new constitution; Suárez's UCD won the largest number of seats and continued in control of the Spanish government.

Catalonia's Statute of Autonomy

With the constitution in place, Catalan nationalists then turned to negotiation of the specific terms of Catalonia's powers and prerogatives, its statute of autonomy. Thanks to delays on the part of the Suárez government, but perhaps also to a disinclination of Tarradellas to see the end of his term as president,[74] negotiation of the state of autonomy was a lengthy process.[75]

In June 1978, Catalan members of the Cortes formed a 20-member committee to draw up a new law, which became known as the Statute of Sau, after the site of the committee's first meeting on 1 August.[76] (Tarradellas had declared that there was no room in the Generalitat for the deliberations.[77]) One bone of contention was the status of the Catalan language. Initially, the nationalists proposed recognition of a right to use Catalan and the obligation to know it, effectively using the same formula with which the constitution recognized Castilian. This idea was dropped in the face of leftist concern that the provision would discriminate against Catalans from elsewhere in Spain. Yet, language recognizing the co-officiality of Catalan and Castilian had to be modified, in light of mobilization of nationalist forces, to include a mandate for the Generalitat to secure the full equality of Catalan with Castilian. Another source of contention was Catalonia's fiscal powers. Ramon Trias Fargas, a nationalist leader, tried to secure the exclusive right to collect taxes, with subsequent transfers to the Spanish state, along the lines enjoyed by the Basques. But he deferred to the firm opposition of socialists.[78]

Finally, on 29 December, the same day as the new constitution came into effect, the assembly of Catalan parliamentarians approved a draft statute and submitted it to a committee composed of Catalan and Spanish members of the Congreso. Suárez involved himself personally in the negotiations. His party, the UCD, presented 59 motions of objection to the proposal. He summoned the Catalan leaders to individual meetings. His ministers each engaged the committee in long discussions, some of which lasted all night. The debate continued for several months, with major conflicts over such questions as the status of the Catalan language, the persistence of provinces (which the Catalans wanted abolished), the power to establish a Catalan-controlled television channel, and the electoral system.[79] In April 1978, a 250,000-person demonstration was organized in Barcelona to express impatience with the delays. Evenually a number of amendments were adopted, and on 13 August the Constitutional Commission of the Congreso approved a final version of the text.

The opening sections of the statute clearly reflect the premises and claims of mainstream Catalan nationalism. The preamble, which alludes to Catalonia's past history as a political entity, declares that 'in regaining their democratic freedom' the people of Catalonia are 'recovering' self-government. At the same time, in recognition of Catalonia's continuing membership in Spain, the claim that the statute expresses the 'the collective identity' of Catalonia is coupled with the declaration that this identity is expressed in 'free solidarity' with the nationalities and regions of Spain and that this solidarity 'is the guarantee of the genuine unity of all the peoples of Spain'; in effect, there is no contradiction between Catalan identity and Spanish identity. Another provision proclaims a long Catalan tradition of 'respect for the fundamental rights and public freedoms of individuals and peoples' and expresses the wish to create a 'forward-looking democratic society'. In short, the preamble presents Catalonia's autonomy as a renewal with a historical tradition that is at the same time compatible both with being part of Spain and with modern ideals of freedom and democracy.[80]

A preliminary section delineates several basic features of the new political regime that Catalonia, 'as a nationality',[81] is establishing. In keeping with the proclaimed solidarity with the rest of Spain and national tradition of pluralism, Catalan citizenship, 'the political status of Catalans', belongs to all Spanish citizens residing in Catalonia.[82] Another provision describes the Catalan flag.[83] In addition, the statute declares that 'Catalan is the official language of Catalonia' but is careful to add 'as is Castilian',[84] lest there be any thought that Catalan should have some superior status. Indeed, the Generalitat is obliged to guarantee 'normal and official use of both languages' and to create 'those conditions which shall make possible their full equality with regard to the duties and rights of the citizens of Catalonia.'[85]

The statute has two main sections: one establishes the terms of Catalonia's autonomy and the Generalitat's jurisdictions; the other describes the political institutions that make up the Generalitat. Two additional sections define the Generalitat's sources of revenue and the procedure for amending the statute.

As one might expect, given the terms of the constitution, the exclusive jurisdictions claimed for the Generalitat are relatively few, consisting mainly of organization of the Generalitat itself, Catalan civil law, culture, research, local government, tourism, public works, roads and highways, fishing, co-operatives, youth foundations and associations, and guardianship of minors.[86] Many of these functions are in fact qualified by references to superior powers of the Spanish state.[87]

At the same time, the statute contains a substantial list of shared jurisdictions, areas in which the Generalitat acts within terms that are set by the state.[88] Thus, in the case of education the Generalitat has full jurisdiction over regulation and administration but within the framework of organic laws of the state which, under the constitution, has authority to regulate 'the conditions relative to the obtaining, issuing and standardization of academic degrees and professional qualifications.'[89] Similarly, with respect to health and social security, the Generalitat has responsibility 'to develop and implement the basic legislation of the State.'[90] And the Generalitat can regulate mass media 'within the framework of the basic laws of the State'.[91] By the same token, the Generalitat has 'sole jurisdiction' over a variety of economic matters, including economic planning but 'in accordance with the bases and planning of the general economic activity and monetary policy of the State'.[92] With respect to the administration of justice, the Generalitat exercises powers that are recognized or assigned to it by the state under its organic laws of the Judiciary and General Council of the Judiciary.[93] The Generalitat can establish an autonomous police force to protect property and persons and maintain law and order within the AC, while recognizing the state's exclusive responsibility for public safety.[94] Finally, the Generalitat is given responsibility for implementing state legislation in such areas as prisons, labour affairs, ports, and copyrights.[95] In most areas, then, Catalonia's autonomy is closely circumscribed by the basic laws and policies of the Spanish state. Indeed, to cite one scholar, 'it has been extremely difficult to delimit clearly Catalonia's and the state's power spheres.'[96]

As for the political institution of Catalonia, the Generalitat, the statute follows the requirements set out in the constitution and establishes a parliament, the office of president, and the Executive Council.[97] The parliament is elected by universal suffrage, on the basis of proportional representation, at intervals of up to four years; the president is selected by parliament from among its members; and the members of the Executive Council, each of whom heads a department, are appointed and removed by the president. In principle, the Generalitat constitutes a parliamentary system since the parliament selects the head of government, who must retain its confidence to remain in power. None the less, it has 'presidential' overtones. As president of the Generalitat as a whole, the president resembles a head of state. Indeed, as the representative of the Spanish state in Catalonia, he must promulgate parliament's laws on behalf of the king. Beyond that, the current occupant of the presidency has assumed a charismatic role within the Catalan party system.[98]

The statute provides for the creation of three additional institutions: an ombudsman ('Síndic de Greuges'),[99] a national audit office (Sindicatura de Comptes) responsible for auditing public sector accounts,[100] and 'a body of a consultative nature' (which became known as the Consell Consultiu) whose opinion may be sought regarding the conformity with the statute of bills before the Catalan parliament and which must pronounce on appeals of unconstitutionality before parliament or the Catalan government can take them to the Spanish Constitutional Court.[101]

Finally, an amendment to the statute, which can be initiated by the Catalan government, or parliament, or the Spanish Cortes Generales, requires two-thirds majority approval in the parliament, approval by the Cortes Generales through an organic law, and approval in a referendum. If the subject matter does not affect relations between Catalonia and the state, approval by the Cortes Generales may be postponed until after the referendum (with the Cortes's consent) but cannot be circumvented.[102]

In some significant respects, the final version of the statute of autonomy fell short of the original draft submitted by the Assembly of Parliamentarians of Catalonia: 'In the arduous negotiations in Madrid, the Catalan parliamentarians had to make numerous concessions'.[103] In the nationalist interpretation, these changes meant that the statute did not achieve the full degree of autonomy allowed under the constitution. Whereas the original draft had called for '*exclusive* control in matters of education at all levels, in accordance with the Constitution and the present Statute [emphasis added]',[104] the final version states that 'it is *fully* within the jurisdiction of the Generalitat to regulate and administer education in all its scope, levels, degrees, kinds and specialities, *within the area of its jurisdiction* without prejudicing the provisions of article 27 of the Constitution and organic laws. . . . [emphasis added]'[105] The transfer to the Generalitat of jurisdiction over public order was dropped. The Generalitat did not get control over appointments to the High Court of Justice of Catalonia, and the state's provincial *diputacions* and civil governors were not eliminated. In addition, the post of Delegate of the Central Government in Catalonia was added.[106] Because of these changes, Balcells says 'it was not possible to consider the 1979 Statute as more favourable to Catalonia than that of 1932, which all the Catalanist parties had considered inadequate in 1977.'[107]

Whereas Catalan socialists were unqualified in their satisfaction with the result, nationalists gave more nuanced reasons for supporting it. For Jordi Pujol, 'The statute we are going to vote on is not the one we would have drawn up, but it is a good statute'.[108] Tarradellas, who had been excluded from the negotiations, made his dissatisfaction known,[109] although in the end he called for a Yes vote.[110] Compared to the repression of the Franco years, the statute of autonomy marked a dramatic reversal in Catalonia's status. That is why it had the support of all but two Catalan parliamentarians.[111]

When the document was submitted to Catalans in a referendum on 25 October it was approved by a majority of 88.1 per cent. Still, the fact that only 59.6 per cent of those eligible voted may reflect some disappointment with the terms of autonomy and the influence of radical nationalists who counselled abstention.[112] The Congreso and the Senate ratified the document on 29 November and 12 December respectively. Finally, on 18 December the king gave his sanction; it was the first statute of autonomy to become law.

Conclusions

The death of Franco ushered in an era of profound change for Spain, including Catalonia. Through a 'negotiated break' (*ruptura pactada*) a new constitution was adopted that explicitly recognized the existence of 'nationalities' within Spain. In the process, Catalonia got back its Generalitat, which had been suppressed for two and a half centuries. And the Generalitat was granted new powers by a statute of autonomy.

Yet, as the constitutional debates clearly revealed, even though most of Spain's political élites may have been committed to reform and democracy, they were badly divided over the place of Catalonia and the other 'historic nations' in the new Spain. The new constitution did not resolve these differences; at best, it merely diffused them. Thus, the historic nations were equated with all the other areas of Spain through a common term, 'autonomous communities'. Nationalities and regions were to have the 'right to autonomy', but the definition of this auton-omy was ambiguous. Moreover, even by a generous reading it did not provide the basis for a federal relationship, nor had there been any agreement among the constitution-makers that it should. And the constitution certainly did not include any acceptance of the claims of nationalists in Catalonia, or in the Basque Country and Galicia, that Spain was fundamentally multinational. The constitu-tion made that clear by asserting the integrity of the Spanish nation and making Castilian the only official languge of the Spanish state.

All of this is faithfully reflected in Catalonia's statute of autonomy. While the opening sections give clear expression to Catalan nationalism and the historical importance of the Generalitat to the Catalan 'nationality', the autonomy to be exercised by the Generalitat is defined very narrowly.

In short, the 1978 constitution left some major contradictions for the new Spanish democracy.

Political Leadership in the New Catalonia

With the statute of autonomy enacted, Catalonia was at last able to elect its own parliament. But who was to lead Catalonia and in what direction? The negotia-tions over the constitution and then the statute had revealed sharp differences between the explicitly nationalist forces, as represented by Jordi Pujol and Christian democrats, and the Catalan left, composed of socialists and the Communists, on such matters as Catalonia's proper place in Spain and the status of the Catalan language. Of course, the two camps also differed on the social and economic policies that might be pursued by a restored Catalan Generalitat. The election was called for 20 March 1980; the outcome was to set the course of Catalan politics for at least the next two decades.

The 1980 Election

The socialists were widely expected to win the election. After all, in the 1977 elec-tions to the Spanish parliament a coalition of socialist forces had won 15 of the 47 Catalan seats and 28.4 per cent of the Catalan votes. Their ostensible allies, the Communist PSUC, had won 9 seats and 18 per cent of the popular vote. Thus, between them the two leftist parties held a majority of the Catalan seats in the lower chamber of parliament. In the 1979 parliamentary elections, the Partit socialistes de Catalunya, which had been formed in 1978,[113] had won 29.2 per cent of the popular vote and 17 seats; the PSUC had won 17.1 per cent and 8 seats.

But when it came time to elect a *Catalan* parliament, the socialists did not do as well. The PSC won 33 seats and only 22.3 per cent of the popular vote. The PSUC won 25 seats and 18.7 per cent of the popular vote. The largest number of seats, 43, and the largest popular vote, 27.7 per cent, were won by the nationalist coalition Convergència i Unió, led by Jordi Pujol, which brought together Pujol's Convergència Democràtica de Catalunya (CDC) and Unió Democràtica (Unió), a Christian Democratic party formed in 1931. The two parties shared a commitment to a moderate Catalan nationalism combined with centrist social and economic policies.

Various reasons have been cited for the surprisingly poor socialist performance. The PSC had been formed just two years earlier from several socialist formations and was still marked by internal divisions. The PSC leader, Joan Roventós, ran a weak campaign and was no match for Pujol.[114] By the same token, the socialist triumph in the 1977 elections had been favoured by the popularity in Catalonia of the charismatic PSOE leader, Felipe González. As well, the euphoria that marked the end of Francoism was at its height and favoured the more radical form of change represented by the socialists; by 1980, it had dissipated.[115] In 1980 the PSC was not as effective as the PSOE had been in mobilizing the vote of Catalans of immigrant origin;[116] at the same time, by de-emphasizing nationalist themes it weakened its appeal to native Catalans, causing them to go to the Esquerra Republicana de Catalunya or the CiU.[117]

Whatever the reasons, the CiU formed the first government of the restored Generalitat. It was able to do so thanks to the support of both Suárez's UCD (which had won 10.6 per cent of the votes and 18 seats) and the Esquerra Republicana de Catalunya (8.9 per cent and 14 seats).[118]

The question 'Who speaks for Catalonia?' had been answered. But there was nothing inevitable about this answer. With a different leader[119] and more favourable conditions, the socialists might have won the largest number of seats. Faced with such a showing, the ERC might have supported the socialists instead of the CiU. Indeed, for a party with such strong social democratic credentials, the socialists might well have been a more logical choice; certainly, the ERC was widely criticized for opting for the centrist CiU. None the less, having captured power, the CiU was able to keep it election after election after election. The die of Catalan politics had been cast for years to come.

The Catalan Party System
CiU
In the next election, held in 1984, the CiU was able to draw upon its time in power to secure an absolute majority of 72 seats and 46.6 per cent of the popular vote. It was also able to keep its parliamentary majority in the following two elections, in 1988 and 1992. In 1995, the CiU fell eight seats short of a majority but was still able to form the government. In the most recent election, in 1999, the CiU fell to 56 seats, 12 short of a majority. This time, to form the government it had to draw upon the support of the Catalan section of Partido Popular, the party of the Spanish president, José Aznar. None the less, the fact remains that the CiU, and Jordi Pujol have emerged victorious from six elections and have been able to exercise unbroken control of the Generalitat for two decades.

As for popular vote, the CiU averaged 46.1 per cent of the popular vote in the three elections of 1984, 1988, and 1992 but fell to 40.9 per cent in 1995. In 1999 it fell to 37.7 per cent. Indeed, the CiU's popular vote was less than the PSC's 37.9 per cent, even though the CiU won four more seats.

PSC

In the Catalan elections for the Catalan Generalitat, the Partit dels Socialistes de Catalunya (PSC), has had trouble exceeding 30 per cent of the popular vote. In the five elections before the most recent one in 1999, the PSC won an average of 26.3 per cent of the popular vote. In the 1999 election, it made an important break-through, securing 37.9 per cent of the vote. Even then, however, it was not in a position to form the government. With 52 seats it still did not have an absolute majority, even if the two other parties likely to support it, Iniciativa per Catalunya and Esquerra Republicana de Catalunya, had done so.[120]

On the other hand, when it comes to elections to the Spanish parliament, the PSC has always had the largest popular vote in Catalonia and largest number of Catalan seats. Over the last 7 elections the PSC has averaged 37 per cent of the popular vote. In 1993, the CiU was able to narrow the gap between itself and the PSC in the Spanish parliament, winning 17 seats to the PSC's 18 and 31.8 per cent of the popular vote, compared to 34.9 per cent for the PSC. But in the 1996 election the CiU won only 16 seats to PSC's 19 and was a full 10 percentage points behind in the popular vote (29.6 to 39.3 per cent). In the 2000 election, the CiU won 15 seats and 28.8 per cent of the popular vote; the PSC won 16 seats and 34.1 per cent of the popular vote.

Over the period 1966–2000 the CiU's 16 seats were of great strategic importance to the Aznar government, and the consequent negotiations for CiU support cast Pujol in the role of kingmaker, vastly heightening the CiU's visibility in the Spanish parliament. But this tended to conceal the underlying fact that in purely numerical terms the PSC can make a better claim to speak for Catalonia. By the same token, in the Catalan municipal elections held in April 1979 the PSC won control of Barcelona—and has held it ever since.

In short, autonomic elections have quite a different dynamic than other ones. This is partly because many recent immigrants from the rest of Spain support the PSC in Spanish elections but do not vote at all in autonomic elections, perhaps because they are alienated from Catalonia and Catalan nationalism or because autonomic politics seem inconsequential to them. The fact is, though, that many voters support the PSC in Spanish elections but the CiU in autonomic elections. Needless to say, there has been some dispute among analysts over the relative importance of each factor.[121]

Whatever the cause, despite the presence and electoral viability within Catalonia of several different parties, Catalan politics is not really competitive at all. Since the 1980s there has been no change of party in either the Generalitat or the Barcelona municipal council. In the words of two analysts, Catalonia's party system is based on 'sphere separation' in which each party exercises 'continuous control of distinct resources'.[122] Similarly, the unbroken dominance of the PSC in the Barcelona city council and in the Spanish parliament underscores the limits to the power of Catalan nationalism and the CiU over Catalan politics.

PSUC/IC

Through the Franco years, the Partit Socialista Unificat de Catalunya (PSUC) remained one of the most coherent forces for resistance. But after it had won 18.7 per cent of the popular vote and 25 seats in the 1980 Catalan election, its electoral support fell drastically. In the 1984 election, it received only 5.6 per cent of the vote and six seats. The party itself was wracked by debates over Eurocommunism and the continuing role of Marxist theory.

In 1987 the PSUC was supplanted by Initiativa de Catalunya, which was founded under the leadership of Rafael Ribó and which drew most its members from the PSUC. Though the new party forged an alliance with the Greens, it lost some of the former PSUC supporters to the Catalan socialist party. Thus, the IC has not been able to obtain the level of support that its predecessor received in 1980. Over the three elections between 1988 and 1995, the IC averaged a popular vote of 8.0 per cent, for nine seats. In 1999 the IC fell to three seats and 2.5 per cent of the popular vote, partly because of the impact of a rival party created by the Spanish Izquierda Unida of Julio Anguita.

ERC

Suppressed during the Franco regime, the Esquerra Republicana de Catalunya was legalized after the 1977 Spanish elections. It has had a checkered career under the new autonomous community. After supporting the CiU's bid to form a government in 1980, the ERC gave it its support once again after the 1984 election, despite the fact that the CiU had secured an absolute majority. In return, the ERC received a cabinet position, which it kept until 1987.

This close association with the CiU alienated ERC supporters and appears to have contributed to the ERC's decline in electoral support. In 1980, the party received 8.9 per cent of the popular vote and 14 seats; by 1988, it had slipped to 4.1 per cent and six seats. Ultimately, internal dissension led to a radicalization of the party. In December 1989, under a new leader, the party was formally committed to independence. With this new policy, the ERC increased its membership and somewhat improved its electoral performance: in 1995 it rose to 9.5 per cent of the vote, for 13 seats. Still, in the wake of a disappointing showing in the 1996 Spanish general elections, where it won only one seat, renewed dissension led to the exodus of some members to form a new PI. The party, with Josep-Lluís Carod-Rovira as its new leader, sought to place itself more clearly on the left.[123] In the 1999 Catalan elections, the ERC slipped slightly, to 8.7 per cent of the vote and 12 seats. Not surprisingly, given its strong nationalism, the ERC draws its support almost exclusively from voters who were born in Catalonia.[124]

The Unión de Centro Democrático (UCD) was founded in 1977 as a coalition of Spanish centrists, including some Francoists under the leadership of Adolfo Suárez, then prime minister.[125] Initially, it attracted some moderate Catalan nationalists, but they eventually gravitated to the CiU. It disappeared after the 1982 Spanish elections; its successor, the Centre Democrático y Social (CDS), did not run in Catalan elections. Thus, in Catalonia the role of opposing socialism from the base of Spanish nationalism fell to the PP and the Spanish right.

AP/PP

Leaders of the Franco regime, especially Manuel Fraga, were prominent in the creation of Alianza Popular, which was a coalition of the forces of the Spanish right. In 1989 it was supplanted by the Partido Popular. The Catalan PP has tried to draw support from members of the Catalan bourgeoisie who, like PP leader Aleix Vidal-Cuadras, are strongly Spanish in orientation and unsympathetic to Catalan nationalism.[126] At the same time, especially under the leadership of Alberto Fernández, the party has made a strong appeal to Catalans of immigrant descent who are also uneasy with Catalan nationalism.

From a low in 1980 of 2.4 per cent of the popular vote for Solidaritat Catalana, which is supported by the AP, the right-wing parties improved their fortunes substantially in 1995, when the PP reached a high of 13.1 per cent and 17 seats. In the 1999 election, the PP fell to 9.5 per cent and 12 seats. Not surprisingly, PP supporters tend to define themselves as primarily or exclusively Spanish and to place themselves on the ideological right. Support is stronger among voters who are older and better educated and who were born outside Catalonia, but is not restricted to them.[127]

Like the CiU, Catalonia's two other nationalist parties, the ERC and IC, have also tended to do worse in Spanish elections than in Catalan elections. In the 2000 Congreso elections, the ERC received only 5.6 per cent of the vote and one seat. The IC secured 3.6 per cent of the vote and one seat. Even if their support is combined with the CiU's, the nationalist vote was still a minority one, 38 per cent, and nationalists held only 17 of the 46 Catalan seats. Beyond the PSC vote, a full 22.8 per cent of Catalan votes and 12 seats were won by the Partido Popular, which of course has no affinity whatsoever with the Catalan nationalist cause. Indeed, during the 1996 election the Catalan PP ran a strongly anti-nationalist campaign. In short, despite the prominence of the CiU, the Catalan representation in the Congreso is virtually the reverse of that of the Catalan parliament, where nationalist forces are in such ascendance. Catalan discourse is decidedly different in the two parliaments.

None the less, in Catalonia, power has remained in CiU hands ever since 1980 and the presidency has been occupied by Jordi Pujol. As a result, Catalan nationalism, in moderate form, has maintained a clear dominance over Catalan politics and has guided Catalonia's relations with the rest of Spain. All of this has ensured that the contradictions between Catalonia and Spain that the drafters of the new constitution were unable to resolve will surface once again in the new Spanish democracy.

Chapter 4

Securing Catalonia's Autonomy

Although the new Spanish constitution and Catalonia's statute of autonomy set out the broad contours of the autonomy available to Catalonia, obtaining this autonomy was a different matter. Some sectors of Spain's élites, especially in the military and among the surviving Francoists, had no patience with these documents and feared they would lead to the disintegration of the Spanish nation. Other Spanish leaders, who were firmly committed to the new democratic regime, were still uncomfortable with the aspirations of Catalonia and the other historic nations and could be counted upon to minimize the opportunities available to the new autonomous communities. Among much of the Spanish public, there was continuing resentment of the claims of the historic nations for distinctive status. For those reasons Catalonia's leaders would have to struggle very hard if Catalonia was to be able to enjoy its promised autonomy.

The CiU and Moderate Catalan Nationalism

For the last two decades the decisions about the strategies to be pursued in this struggle to exercise Catalan autonomy have been largely determined by the Generalitat's CiU leadership. To a very considerable extent the defining force has been Jordi Pujol himself, who, through both a charismatic political style and his length of time in office, has come to personify Catalonia not only to Catalans but to most Spaniards as well. His political world view, which has profoundly shaped Catalonia's existence as an autonomous community, has made the 'national' question a continuing issue in Catalan politics and has positioned the CiU in a way that so far has put its competitors at a distinct disadvantage. Pujol's world view has been able to do this in large part because it resonates so clearly with the views held by most moderate Catalan nationalists.

Pujol and his coalition have placed nationalism front and centre in their appeals to Catalans for support: 'The CDC defines itself above all as a Catalan nationalist party. The CDC takes the political recognition of the personality of the Catalan people as a fundamental, basic and non-negotiable part of its program.'[1] Within this nationalism Catalan identity and the notion of a distinct culture are central: 'Catalonia possesses a differentiated identity based on language, culture, social cohesion, collective consciousness, common project and country pride, opposing absorption and homogenizing policies.'[2] But this identity and culture are not tied to ethnic or racial descent; they can be assumed by all residents of Catalonia. In a characteristic (and widely quoted) statement, Pujol has written: 'Everyone who lives and works in Catalonia and has the wish to be so and feels tied to this land, is Catalan.' And he was quick to add that 'the majority of people who work and live in Catalonia want sooner or later to be Catalan.'[3]

While freely referring to Catalonia as a country and a nation, Pujol and the CiU strongly supported continued membership in Spain, albeit a reconstituted Spain. In a major address in Madrid soon after first assuming the presidency, Pujol emphasized:

> The first conclusion is the existence of a Catalan reality, based mainly on language, culture, historic awareness, feelings, and a particular conception of Spain. . . . But neither Catalonia nor Catalanism nor the Catalan language is the product of an anti-Spanish machination. . . . A second concrete fact is the clear inclusion of this reality in a combined Spain, and the desire to take part in Spain, economically, politically and ideologically.[4]

In 1989, he declared: 'We are a nation without a state. We belong to the Spanish state but have no secessionist ambitions.'[5]

Indeed, in 1983 Pujol's deputy, Miquel Roca, was given the mandate of establishing a new centrist party, el Partido Reformista Democrático. Linked to the CiU, it would run candidates in the rest of Spain. It represented an effort to 'contribute to the reconstruction of centrist forces in Spain'[6] or, in effect, to 'Catalanize Spain', thus echoing the late-nineteenth-century aspirations of Catalonia's industrial bourgeoisie. Not surprisingly, the attempt met with little success in the 1986 Spanish election; no candidates were elected other than those of the CiU and the PNB, and the idea was soon abandoned.

Until very recently Pujol and the CiU managed to avoid defining their 'particular conception of Spain' in any detail. But Pujol has never hesitated to declare the existing autonomous community arrangement to be insufficient: 'We accepted the generalization of an autonomous system that did not respond to the Spanish or to the Catalan situation.'[7]

At the same time, Pujol and the CDC regularly evoke the need for Catalonia to deal freely with the rest of Europe. They argue that Catalonia's personality cannot be expressed within Spain alone since Catalonia has much stronger historical links with Europe than does the rest of Spain: 'For historical and cultural reasons and by political vocation, Catalonia is the most European country in Spain.'[8]

These ideas were vividly expressed in a widely quoted statement that Pujol made in March of 1985 when visiting the ancient capital of the Carolingian empire:

> Catalonia was born as a people and a nation 1,200 years ago, as a frontier area on Charlemagne's empire. We formed the Spanish March, the outpost of the empire to the south, the outpost . . . of Europe to the south. . . . In a certain way we remain the descendants of Charlemagne. . . . And at this moment, when Spain is joining with the European Economic Community, I wanted to come, in the name of my country, to express our joy, here in our ancient capital. Our joy in returning home.[9]

Of course, the statement also demonstrates the tendency of Pujol and many Catalan nationalists to reach far back into history to justify their claims, to frame arguments in terms of Catalonia's long and distinctive existence as a nation, and perhaps to engage in a bit of hyperbole in the process. To be sure, the two main Spanish parties, the socialist PSOE and the conservative Partido Popular, also tend to read history in ways that support their own Spanish nationalism.

In this case Pujol is echoing a tradition among Catalan leaders of stressing Catalonia's 'Europeanness' and concomitant distinctiveness from the rest of Spain. For moderate nationalists, such as Pujol, Catalonia's European roots need not prevent it from remaining within Spain. They do, however, require that Catalonia have the means to maintain a direct relationship with Europe independently of Madrid. Here too, however, Pujol has been loath to define the terms of this relationship with any great precision.

In social and economic policy, the CiU has placed itself squarely in the liberal camp. The social democratic intimations that were evident in the CDC's program in its early years have effectively disappeared: the Unió has always defined itself in Christian democratic terms.[10] Thus, the 1982 CDC program flatly declared, 'With the exception of some very concrete cases, public enterprise is not justified because it is less efficient than private enterprise.' The remedy to unemployment lies in reducing public spending, improving competitiveness, encouraging savings, and maintaining company profits.[11]

In effect, Pujol and the CDC have offered a contemporary version of the nationalism that characterized the Catalan bourgeoisie at the end of the nineteenth century. In constructing his historical arguments, Pujol tends to focus on the distant past, skipping over the events of the 1930s, when Catalan nationalism was shaped by leftist forces, such as the Esquerra republicana, with their working-class bases and readiness to seize autonomy through unconstitutional measures.

As we have seen, Pujol and other CDC leaders were influenced by their involvement with Catholic action organizations and the boy scout movement in the 1960s. Their Catalan nationalism and opposition to the Franco regime was expressed in these terms rather than any direct continuity with the 1930s Catalan nationalists. Similarly, the membership of the party has from the beginning come predominantly from the Catalan petite bourgeoisie and middle classes.[12] Pujol had been an executive with the ill-fated Banca Catalana before founding the party in 1974.

Obtaining Autonomy within Spain

As one would expect, the political world view of Pujol and his colleagues has been faithfully reflected in Catalonia's relations with the rest of Spain, and especially Madrid, over the last 20 years. The Generalitat has been unremitting in its vigorous expression of Catalan nationalism, but this has been a moderate nationalism focused on using the opportunities available under the new constitution and Catalonia's statute of autonomy. From the Generalitat there has been no talk of independence, or veiled threats that independence might become a goal if specific objectives within Spain are not met. Bargaining rather than confrontation has been the order of the day.

In this version of Catalan nationalism, there are two crucial issues: the powers to be exercised by Catalonia vis-à-vis Madrid and the extent to which Catalonia, as a historic nation, has a distinct place in the Spanish polity. The constitution and the statute of autonomy create possibilities for Catalonia, but the extent to which these possibilities are realized depends heavily on Madrid.

For instance, the Spanish state effectively decides what fiscal resources autonomous communities are to have to pursue their objectives, and under what conditions. Under the constitution, ACs (with the exception of the Basque Country and Navarre) are limited to a 15 per cent supplement to Madrid's taxes plus whatever taxes that have been 'ceded' by Madrid. Similarly, in many areas the stringency of the Spanish parliament's basic laws determine the degree to which ACs have any real discretion. Thus, any AC, including historic nations, cannot simply rely on the constitution and its statute to enjoy full autonomy. It is dependent upon the readiness of Madrid to enable it to exploit fully the opportunities available under its statute of autonomy.

Similarly, since the constitution does not explicitly recognize Catalonia's nationhood, the distinctiveness of Catalonia's place in Spain lies mainly in whether it assumes responsibilities that are not held by the 14 odd regions. Yet, as we have seen, under the constitution no powers or prerogatives are explicitly reserved for the three historic nations. The only distinction has to do with the pace at which the ACs can assume them. Thus, once again, much depends on how Madrid chooses to act in its dealings with the other ACs.

Under those conditions, much depends on bargaining between political leaders over the roles to be exercised by their respective jurisdictions. The difficulty is that, with both its monopoly of taxing powers and the importance of its basic laws, Madrid would seem to have most of the chips in any such bargaining.

Of course, one way for an AC to compensate for this would be to threaten to withdraw from the system unless Madrid accommodated its demands. Arguably, some of the Basque Country's achievements show the effects of such a threat. But in Catalonia's case the CiU leadership has consistently refrained from making such threats and would have had difficulty doing so given the low level of public support for independence.

Another way of strengthening Catalonia's hand in its dealings with Madrid would be to create broad 'common fronts' internally. That is, the various parties in the Catalan parliament would formally unite behind a common set of demands. Negotiations would be between Catalonia and the Spanish state. Such a strategy has indeed been proposed by leaders of the CDC's partner, the Unió, especially Joan Rigol.[13] It has also been endorsed by Rafael Ribó of the IC.[14] But Pujol has rejected it.[15] Presumably, this was seen as endangering the claim of Pujol and the CDC to the mantle of nationalist leadership.

Pursuing Autonomy: The Reliance on Parliamentary Politics
Instead, the Pujol government has preferred to advance its goals by bargaining with party leaders in the Spanish parliament. Rather than the construction of formal coalitions, the dealings have been limited to establishing certain policies as the quid pro quo for enabling one party or the other to form the Spanish government. In effect, they constitute 'indirect' coalitions. They have involved not only the CiU but the Basque nationalist party (PNV) as well. The two parties have seen little interest in joining a 'direct' coalition and rejected the offer when it was made by the PSOE in 1993. For their part, Spanish parties that lack a parliamentary majority have had little choice but to establish 'indirect' coalitions with the two nationalist parties.[16]

Such arrangements have been greatly favoured by the party standings in the Spanish parliament. At regular intervals no party has had an absolute majority in the Cortes. This has had the effect of heightening vastly the significance of the CiU's presence in the Cortes. Even if Pujol and the CiU control less than half of the Catalan seats, at times their support has enabled a party to take or to keep control of the Spanish government.

All three parties that have formed governments in post-Franco Spain have had to look to the CiU for support in the Spanish parliament. The UCD of Adolfo Suárez fell well short of a majority in 1977, requiring the support of a good number of opposition members to govern, but in 1979 it came much closer and was able to keep power thanks to the CiU alone. Felipe González's PSOE enjoyed majorities during its first 11 years in power but failed to get one in 1993; however, it stayed in office with the support of the CiU. And the current government, of the Partido Popular under José María Aznar, was elected in 1996 with 20 seats fewer than it needed to form a government and signed a formal agreement with Pujol and the CiU, along with the Basque PNV and the Coalición Canaria. In 2000, however, the PP won an absolute majority.

During the periods when this strategy could be followed, it was clearly effective in helping Catalonia to exploit the opportunities available to it under the constitution and its statute of autonomy; indeed, by 1982 Catalonia had acquired 80 per cent of the powers available to it under the statute.[17] The Generalitat now plays major roles in several areas. It has responsibility for the provision of public education and health and social services. It has established its own police force, the Mossos d'Esquadra. In 1983, it re-established Catalan as a language of public administration and made Catalan the effective language of primary education. Catalonia now receives 30 per cent of income tax revenues. It is consulted, along with the other ACs, regarding the positions that Spain will take in the European Community, it has a large network of offices in cities around the world to promote trade and investment, and it has the right to maintain an information office in Brussels.

Yet these achievements have their limits, which reflect the strategy that the Generalitat has pursued. First, much of the progress that Catalonia has made in its capacity to exercise its autonomy, especially in ways that go beyond that of the other ACs, has been made because the Spanish governing party has been in a minority position and has needed to enter into deals to obtain parliamentary support. There is no permanent guarantee for these arrangements; in principle, they could be modified or even revoked. Indeed, the PSOE has recently discussed a proposal that contains the notion of a two-way street (*doble vía*) under which powers that have devolved to the ACs might return to Madrid.[18]

By the same token, there is no guarantee that Spain will have minority governments; in fact the PSOE did obtain clear majorities in three different elections. The PP, which won a minority of seats in 1996, was able to secure an absolute majority in 2000. Beyond that, leaders of the PSOE and PP have proposed from time to time that the electoral system be changed so as to reduce the parliamentary weight of third parties.[19]

Besides, the powers available under Catalonia's statute of autonomy are in any event quite modest and are highly circumscribed by Madrid's constitutional responsibility for 'general interests'.

Finally, however much Catalonia's autonomy has been enhanced, it has not achieved recognition of its underlying claim to national status within a multinational Spain. All of the three parties that have controlled the post-Franco Spanish government, the UCD, PSOE, and PP, have acted in ways that directly countered this claim.

In short, the contradictions that divided Catalan nationalists and most other Spanish political leaders when they initially negotiated the constitution and the statute of autonomy have never been resolved. While the constitution was being drafted, they were circumvented by defining the question, not as one of a multinational Spain, but of nationalities and regions, extending throughout Spain, whose needs could be addressed within the common framework of statutes of autonomy. In recent decades the contradictions have been circumvented by being recast as a matter of inter-parliamentary bargaining and of the necessity, in order to form a government, of the main Spanish parties to enter into bargains with other parliamentary parties that happen to be nationalist. Of course, one reason these nationalist parties have a significant parliamentary presence is that the major parties are unable or unwilling to accommodate the claims of Catalonia and the Basque Country.

All of this can be seen by examining in some detail the relations between Catalonia and each of the three Spanish governments: UCD, PSOE, and PP.

The UCD Government of Adolfo Suárez

With their roots in the Franco regime, Suárez and his UCD could not have been well disposed to the claims of Catalan nationalists. However, their reformism and commitment to a negotiated reform (*reforma pactada*) had led them to fashion an accommodation with the Catalans, even at the price of losing such prominent members as Manuel Fraga. Moreover, on social and economic questions the UCD's centrism did find a certain affinity with Pujol and the CiU. After the 1979 election, in which it fell three seats short of a majority, the UCD was able to count on the support of the CiU members. By the same token, the UCD supported Pujol in 1980 in his bid to form the first Catalan government.

In 1981, however, the UCD government had second thoughts about the accommodations it had engineered with Catalonia and the other historic nations. Not only were Catalonia and the Basque Country pursuing a very broad interpretation of the terms of their statutes of autonomy, but one of the regions (Andalusia) had succeeded in breaking out of the slow-track category so as to get the same treatment.[20] Moreover, the gradual acquisition by the other regions of their own statutes of autonomy was becoming a complicated process. All of this was enough to trouble the UCD's vision of a united Spanish nation. Also, in the wake of an abortive coup, the government was anxious to placate the Spanish military. Reasserting the integrity of the Spanish nation was clearly important to the military, which bitterly opposed any movement to a federal Spain. But the UCD found that the PSOE was a willing ally in its campaign to 'harmonize' the autonomy process.

Accordingly, on 13 March 1981, the Spanish parliament was presented with an Organic Law for the Harmonization of the Process of Self-Government (the LOAPA). (By this time, Adolfo Suárez had been replaced as president by Calvo Sotelo.) In the name of harmonization, the Act would take back powers granted in the statutes of autonomy that had already been approved for Catalonia and the other ACs. Moreover, it required AC parliaments to have their laws ratified by the central government.[21] Beyond that, it reaffirmed Spanish nationalism with measures dealing with such matters as the treatment of the Spanish flag, the use and teaching of Castilian in the autonomous communities, the use of the terms 'national' and 'nation', and the requirement that holders of public office swear allegiance to the constitution.[22]

In Catalonia the bill was opposed through the mobilization of 1,300 different organizations by la Crida (Appeal for Solidarity in Defence of the Catalan

Language, Culture and Nation) culminating in a large demonstration in Barcelona. (La Crida was also triggered by a manifesto of Catalan intellectuals and civil servants defending Spanish-language rights in Catalonia).[23] The harmonization law was supported by the PSC members of the Spanish parliament, albeit with great reluctance.[24] None the less, it received the votes of most PSOE members. The constitutionality of the law was challenged by the Spanish Communist Party and the various nationalist parties.[25]

In short, during the UCD years there still was no consensus about the shape that the Spanish system should take. The CiU's presence in the Spanish parliament was no defence against a minority government that could enlist the support of other parties in order to assert a vision in accord with traditional Spanish nationalism.

The PSOE Government of Felipe González

With the coming to power of the PSOE in 1982, the CiU's votes no longer mattered. For the next 11 years, the PSOE ruled with clear parliamentary majorities. Nor was the PSOE necessarily sympathetic to the aspirations of Catalonia and the Basque Country. After all, it had voted in favour of the LOAPA.

In August 1983, several months after the PSOE had taken power, the Constitutional Court determined that 14 of the provisions of the harmonization bill were unconstitutional. Nonetheless, the González government continued to pursue the underlying objective of the law: to rein in the more ambitious ACs, such as Catalonia. Indeed, its approach to relations with Catalonia and the ACs was heavily shaped by the arguments of the Comisión de Expertos,[26] which was the same body that had inspired the harmonization bill.

The González government had a variety of means available to it. Some important provisions of the LOAPA survived the court challenge, such as limits on the size of AC governments.[27] Also, some of the proscribed provisions of the harmonization bill had already been agreed to by ACs whose statutes of autonomy were being negotiated while the law was before the court; they remained in effect.[28] In any event, the González government could rein in the ACs by means of the basic laws (*leyes de bases*) that are its prerogative under the constitution. Indeed, the Constitutional Court had noted in its judgment on the LOAPA that the Spanish state did not really need the law since it could achieve the same objective through the basic laws.[29]

Thus, invoking its responsibility for 'general interests', the González government passed laws to set standards and to intervene in areas of AC responsibility such as education, health care, economic development, and tourism. The claims of ACs such as Catalonia that they had final authority over the powers listed in their statutes of autonomy were effectively negated. All of this was confirmed in repeated decisions of the Constitutional Court.[30]

At the same time, beyond generally constraining the ACs, the González government acted in various ways to reduce the distinctiveness of Catalonia and the

Basque Country within the Spanish order and, in the process, countered the claim of Catalonia and the two other historic nations that they should enjoy a special status.

One strategy was to extend to other ACs the arrangements enjoyed by Catalonia and the Basque Country. In 1982, special laws—Leyes Orgánicas de Transferencias—gave Valencia and the Canary Islands additional powers that brought them closer to what had been obtained by the three historic nations under the original fast track, and by Andalusia, through its referendum in 1981. As a result, responsibility for education was assumed by Andalusia, the Canaries, and Valencia, and responsibility for health was assumed by Andalusia and Valencia (the Canaries and Galicia were slated to assume it later). In the case of health, combining four ACs with the Basque Country and Catalonia served the government's purposes well. While helping these four additional ACs to take on health care, Madrid retained important controls over these activities. It was more manageable for Madrid to deal with these six ACs collectively than it would have been to deal with the Basque Country and Catalonia alone.[31]

To be sure, the González government's efforts to reduce the distinctiveness of Catalonia and the Basque Country went in tandem with the desire of leaders of some other ACs to obtain the same advantages as the historic nations. After all, the statute of autonomy of Andalusia, which was passed in 1981, declares Andalusia to be nothing less than a 'nationality'. Valencia put a similar declaration in its statute of autonomy. In 1996, the Cortes approved amendments to the statutes of Aragon and the Canary Islands declaring them to be nationalities as well.[32]

Finally, the González government supported a constitutional challenge to the Linguistic Normalization Act that the Catalan parliament passed in 1983. This measure was the centrepiece of the Pujol government's effort to use the powers of the Generalitat on behalf of its nation-building project. Eventually, in 1994, the Constitutional Court upheld the law.[33]

Through its years as a majority government the PSOE displayed in a variety of ways its unease with any thorough-going notion of a federal Spain, least of all one in which distinctive roles would be assumed by the historic nations. This did not mean that the concessions that had been made to Catalonia and the two other historic nations could not be extended to other ACs; in fact the government's antipathy to those claims made it quite disposed to extend past concessions. In 1992 the PSOE entered into a pact with the Partido Popular that transferred functions such as employment counselling, job training, and education to the 10 ACs that had previously assumed the fewest responsibilities.[34] Under the terms of a 1993 agreement, the only areas where these 10 ACs would have less responsibility than others would be health and social security and maintenance of a distinct police force (as in the case of Catalonia and the Basque Country).[35] However, Catalonia and the Basque Country did not approve the pact. Along with Galicia, they demanded additional functions (as defined in their statutes of autonomy) as well as the abolition of the position of provincial governor.

In short, the González government was prepared to extend to the other ACs powers that had already been given to such ACs as Catalonia, but not to contemplate the new round of devolution sought by Catalans, including even Catalan socialists. The government made this clear in 1987 when the Catalan socialists (PSC) demanded that the PSOE formally embrace the transformation of Spain into a federation and that the González government undertake further decentralization.[36] The government's position was that any further decentralization should be delayed. A PSOE congress adopted the PSC proposals in January 1988 but abided by the government's position that any new decentralization should be delayed, to the frustration of the PSC.[37]

In the election of June 1993, the González government lost its parliamentary majority—and the CiU acquired new leverage in parliament. Indeed, the CiU was instrumental in keeping the government in power. Rejecting offers to enter into a formal coalition with the government, Pujol and the CiU instead made their continued support dependent on talks about a new round of devolution. In fact, a confidential document prepared by the CiU went beyond that and called for recognition of Spain as a multinational state. It even proposed that the Catalan Generalitat should bypass the Spanish prime minister and government to deal directly with the monarch.[38]

The González government was not disposed to such notions as direct dealings with the monarch. Thus, talks between Pujol and González dealt with more prosaic matters such as measures that Catalonia claimed had been granted in its statute of autonomy, including the creation of a regional police force and exclusive control of transportation (such as railways, highways, and ports) in Catalonia. Pujol also called for removal of the Spanish government's provincial governors and regional government delegates.[39]

As a result of these negotiations, the González government did propose to downgrade the power of the civil governors, and to call them simply 'governors', as well as to transfer new functions to the ACs, including responsibility for police in the case of Catalonia.[40] Also, in response to Catalonia's fiscal demands, the government adopted the principle of 'fiscal co-responsibility': that is, ACs would be entitled to a proportion of income tax receipts. The amount that was set, 15 per cent, fell well below Catalonia's objective of 30 to 40 per cent, let alone its initial demand for the right to collect all taxes, as in the Basque Country and Navarre. None the less, the ACs, including Catalonia, would, for the first time, be collecting income tax.[41] Finally, in the Senate a Comisión General de Autonomías was established to institutionalize relations between the ACs and the Spanish government. In 1995, the Senate even formed a committee to devise schemes to make the Senate truly representative of Spain's territorial units.[42]

It can also be argued that because of its minority status in 1993 the González government was less vigorous than it might have been in pursuing its contention that the Catalan government was not enforcing bilingualism in parochial schools.[43] In taxation arrangements, however, the government continued to resist claims that Spain was a multinational state. In framing its proposals for further devolution the government was careful to do so in ways that were not limited to the three historic nations, let alone Catalonia by itself. Thus, in drawing up a list of functions that might be delegated, a special government commission designated as recipients not just Catalonia, the Basque Country, and Galicia but Andalusia as well, while noting that eventually the functions should go to the Canaries, Navarre, and Valencia.[44]

The PP Government of José María Aznar

In a new election, in March 1996, the PSOE lost to the Partido Popular, which won the largest number of seats but fell short of a majority. During the election campaign, PP leaders had called for an absolute majority, precisely to avoid the necessity of having to work with the Catalan and Basque nationalist parties. For that matter, Catalan nationalists had regularly expressed their aversion to collaborating with the PP. But when Aznar was left with no other choice, he began bilateral negotiations with Jordi Pujol and his Basque counterpart. The negotiations were long and laborious but resulted in formal agreements, called 'pacto de investidura y gobernabilidad' (pact of investiture and governance), as to the terms under which the nationalist parties would give their support. For the first time, the Catalan right and Spanish right had fashioned a formal alliance; it was indeed a historic event.

These formal agreements, it should be stressed, were negotiated between party leaders in the Spanish parliament rather than between Madrid and the Basque and Catalan governments. To be sure, the Catalan president, Jordi Pujol, negotiated his agreement directly with President Aznar, as did his Basque counterpart, but the agreement itself reads as an agreement between the PP and the CiU. The terms of the agreements were not debated, let alone approved, by the Catalan and Basque parliaments. Thus, they have no guarantee other than party fortunes in the Spanish parliament.

In the immediate aftermath of the election, prominent members of the CiU had insisted that any agreement with the PP had to contain explicit recognition of Catalonia's nationhood.[45] Indeed, there was considerable opposition to the very idea of an agreement with the PP, given its longstanding hostility to Catalan nationalism, and 10 members of the CDC's executive committee opposed it.[46]

The CiU-PP pact effectively avoided the issue of Catalonia's national status. Indeed, most of the provisions apply to all the ACs rather than Catalonia alone. The preamble justifies the agreement primarily in terms of the need to create employment, modernize the Spanish state, and ensure that Spain meets the conditions for participating in the European monetary union. Only towards the end does it refer to 'the development and consolidation of the state of the autonomous communities'.[47]

With over 70 paragraphs, the agreement covered a wide range of matters. The proportion of income tax received by the ACs was raised to a maximum of 30 per cent, depending on each AC's responsibilities and spending levels, and funding for health and some other services was improved. The PP undertook to enhance the ability of ACs to act within the areas designated in their statutes of autonomy. The civil governors would be replaced by sub-delegates of the Spanish state's delegate-generals and would be career civil servants. Highway tolls would be reduced. ACs would be involved in the formulation of Spanish positions on European Union matters, and their representatives could sit on committees and in working groups of the European Commission. The PP would honour Catalonia's agreement with the González government regarding Catalonia's police force and would negotiate the transfer of responsibilities associated with this, and Catalonia would assume responsibilities linked to national manpower programs and the management of ports.

The PP also signed agreements with the nationalist parties of the Canary Islands and Basque Country. (Arguably, these agreements contained more benefits for the ACs than did the CiU's agreement.[48]) In addition, in May 1996 the Senate established a committee to design plans to transform the Senate into a body representing territorial units as well as to enhance use of the languages of the nationalities.[49]

Not only did the PP's agreement with the CiU effectively ignore the question of Catalonia's claims to national status, but in its activities as a government the PP displayed a pronounced insensitivity to Catalan nationalists. As unqualified expressions of conservative Spanish nationalism, several of its actions provoked strong resistance among the PP's ostensible parliamentary allies, the CiU and the Basque Country's PNV.

In the fall of 1997, the PP's minister of education announced his government's intention to establish uniformity in the teaching of history, geography, language, and Castilian literature throughout Spain. Jordi Pujol was quick to denounce such a policy.[50] He was joined in this by most other Catalan parties and by Catalan unions and other associations. Similar responses came from the Basque government.[51] Yet, while offering to substitute 'common' for 'unitary', the minister of education pointed out that the Spanish state has the constitutional power to establish minimum standards in education.[52] Subsequently, the Education Ministry announced that inspectors would ensure that the new requirements are met.[53] Ultimately, the measure was dropped, not through a change of heart by the PP government, but by the passage of a resolution, supported by all other parties in the Congreso, that called upon the government to withdraw the proposal and prepare a new one in consultation with the ACs.[54] The parliamentary defeat was a major embarrassment but a risk that the PP had apparently been ready to run given its commitment to reasserting its notion of a unitary Spanish nation.

In another effort to assert the values and symbols of Spanish nationalism, the PP government adopted a regulation governing the use of the Spanish national anthem. The first draft stipulated the occasions when the anthem must be played and how people should conduct themselves while this is happening. The regulation also stipulated that the anthem must be played, before any other, at all official events of the ACs.[55] Once again, Catalan and Basque nationalists objected. Beyond that, the PP leadership angered Catalan nationalists with its failure to dissociate the party from public demonstrations of anti-Catalan sentiment.[56]

These actions strengthened the opposition among Catalan nationalists, including leaders of the CiU, to the very idea of CiU-PP coalition. Whereas the two parties shared common views on social and economic questions, making them more natural allies than the CiU and the PSOE, on the national question, which was the raison d'être of the CiU, they were bitterly opposed. During the fall of 1997, pressure built within the CiU against renewing the agreement.[57]

None the less, the CiU leadership, Pujol in particular, was committed to maintaining the coalition.[58] Public opinion in Catalonia, as well as the rest of Spain, clearly appreciated the political stability that came from the coalition and supported the agreement's renewal.[59] Moreover, the impending decision by the European Community as to Spain's eligibility for participation in the new European currency made political stability even more important. Accordingly, after Pujol met with Aznar and some of his cabinet, Aznar announced in January 1998 that he had agreed to maintain the coalition through 'day-to-day' negotiations.[60] With the March 2000 election, Aznar won his parliamentary majority and was finally freed from the need to maintain a coalition with the nationalists.

Assessing the Gains

What overall assessment should be made of the Spanish system, the State of the Autonomies, and Catalonia's success in acquiring autonomy within it?

Some observers argue that over the last two decades Spain has come to approximate a federal system. Clearly, there was no agreement among the drafters of the new constitution that the system should be federal. At most it was a unitary system with some significant areas of decentralization. Yet, according to some it has become an 'imperfect' or 'incomplete' federation.[61]

Of course, the term 'federalism' continues to have little legitimacy in Spanish politics. Neither major party is prepared to conceive of the State of the Autonomies as a federal system.[62] Nor are Catalan nationalists comfortable with the term, because they believe that it implies equal status among all constituent units. Still, the question remains whether the Spanish polity has, in its operations, become a federation—whatever the Spaniards may choose to call it.

Clearly, the State of the Autonomies has become more decentralized than many of its creators had anticipated. In several areas, Catalonia and other ACs can exercise considerable autonomy, even if bound by basic laws, and all the ACs now have a certain fiscal autonomy with the right to 30 per cent of income tax revenue. The growth in the AC governments' activities is reflected in a number of indicators: the proportion of laws passed by the Spanish parliament, as opposed to the ACs, fell from 68 per cent in 1981 to 14 per cent in 1990; the AC proportion of total government spending rose from less than 2 per cent in 1981 to nearly 15 per cent in 1990; and by 1991 the ACs employed an early one-third of all government employees.[63] Also, quite elaborate structures of intergovernmental collaboration have now been built up.

It is not clear, though, that these considerations qualify the system to be a federation, that is, a system in which the constituent units have meaningful and secure autonomy. Many of these forms of autonomy are based upon simple agreements between parties in the Spanish parliament as much as between the ACs and the Spanish government. They might resemble federal-style 'compacts'[64] but they have no guarantee of permanency and no constitutional status.

Beyond that, all the aspects of the Spanish constitution that disqualified it from 'federal' status in the first place are still very much present: the ACs' legislative roles are highly circumscribed; the ACs have no meaningful fiscal autonomy; they have no say in constitutional amendments; there is no effective body for intra-federal regional representation;[65] the ACs have no say in the appointment of justices to the Constitutional Court; and so on.[66] Indeed, one recent study argues that the constitution precludes the most important outcome of the CiU-PP accord, which was the 1996 law establishing new fiscal arrangements with the ACs.[67] By the same token, in 1991 'own-source revenues' accounted for only 13.7 per cent of AC budgets.[68]

Finally, in assessing Catalonia's gains, it must be noted that Spain remains as divided as ever over the national question. Catalan and Basque nationalists have made very little progress in having their idea of a 'multinational Spain' accepted. The signing of a formal agreement between the PP government and the CiU has only heightened the conflict between Catalans and other Spaniards over the nature of Spain.

Relations outside Spain

Over the years, given the continuing limitations on Catalonia's status and autonomy within Spain, many Catalan nationalists have tended to find hope in Catalonia's dealings outside Spain, especially its relationship with Europe. Part of this simply involves making Catalonia known to the world, for until 1980 Catalonia had no existence as a political entity. Conceivably, international sympathy for the Catalan cause might be useful in dealings with Spain. Beyond that, Catalonia might be able to carve out some areas of autonomy. Here the emergence of the European Community has loomed very large.

Beyond these essentially nationalist concerns, the Generalitat shares the motivation for pursuing international activity that is felt by most substates, whether or not they are self-proclaimed nations. With globalization many of them are trying to attract investment and tourism from other countries and to promote exports. Often this has involved maintaining offices in foreign countries. Frequently, heads of government travel to other countries to meet political and economic leaders. In addition, bordering substates of different countries have been increasingly involved in contacts and joint programs to address common problems.[69]

Traditionally, states have viewed foreign policy as their own monopoly and have viewed the growth in international activity of their substates with suspicion. The Spanish government has been no exception, repeatedly complaining about President Pujol's foreign visits, arguing that his declarations about Spanish politics may misinform foreigners, that he is often treated by political and economic leaders as if he were a head of state, and so on.[70] Nor has the Spanish government welcomed the opening of AC offices in foreign countries. When the Basque Country established an office of its own in Brussels, Madrid launched a challenge with the Constitutional Court.

The Constitution does in fact give responsibility for foreign affairs to the Spanish government. Article 149 lists the Spanish state's exclusive jurisdictions, which include 'international relations' although without specifying what that might entail.[71] As for Catalonia's statute of autonomy, it simply states that the Generalitat can call upon the Spanish government to enter into treaties and agreements with foreign jurisdictions with respect to the Catalan language and that the Generalitat must be informed of treaties that affect its responsibilities. Similarly, under the statute the Generalitat is explicitly obliged to undertake whatever measures are necessary for the implementation of treaties.[72]

In its jurisprudence the Constitutional Court has shown some flexibility with respect to international activities by the ACs. It rejected the state's case against the Basque office in Brussels, for example, but it has consistently reserved for the state the 'hard core' of international relations, including the treaty-making power.[73]

As a result, Catalonia has been able to engage in extensive low-level international activity, similar to that of most other substates, and indeed, most of Spain's ACs have done so. But it has made little progress in becoming an international actor in its own right. Even within the institutions of the European Union, Catalonia and the other ACs are restricted to peripheral roles. Unlike the federal member states—Belgium, Germany, and Austria—the Spanish government has joined with the other members, all unitary states, to resist any enhanced role for substates in European Union affairs.

Catalonia's International Activities
It is obvious that the establishment of an international presence, albeit through low-level activities, has been a priority of the Catalonia government. Indeed, it has been a personal priority of Jordi Pujol.[74] In the process, Catalonia has become much more active internationally than most other ACs. More foreign trips are taken by Catalan officials than their counterparts in any other AC. In 1992, they accounted for 31 of 178 trips taken by all the ACs; in 1994, they constituted 50 of 161 trips.[75]

The institutional structure has gone from a secretariat for interdepartmental affairs (Secretariat d'Afers Interdepartamentals), established in 1981 and renamed general directorate for interdepartmental affairs (Direcció General d'Afers

Interdepartamentals) in 1984, to a cabinet for external activity (Gabinet d'Actuacions Exteriors) in 1990, to the present commission for external activity (Comissionat per a Actuacions Exteriors), created in 1992. The law creating the Comissionat gave it a mandate both to co-ordinate the international activity of the Generalitat's departments and to promote it. At the same time, the law was careful to state that co-ordination did not imply concentration of activity within the Comissionat.[76]

Aversion to bureaucratic concentration can also be seen in the network of structures through which the Generalitat has conducted its international relations. By and large, rather than using its own agencies, the Generalitat has preferred to rely upon mixed bodies in which it plays a role, often the leading one, but in which the private sector is also directly involved. In part, this is intended to make Catalonia's international activities less provocative to Madrid.[77] But according to Generalitat officials, this arrangement is also intended to fully involve Catalan civil society in this international effort.[78]

On this basis, two bodies have been created to strengthen Catalonia's economic competitiveness. CIDEM (Centre d'Informació i Desenvolupament Empresarial) was created in 1985 to stimulate industrial development in Catalonia. With offices in New York, Tokyo, and Düsseldorf, as well as six offices in Catalonia,[79] it has tended to focus on securing foreign investment.[80] COPCA (Consorci de Promoció Comercial del Catalunya) was established in 1987 to promote Catalan exports. It claims to have 107 members. Beyond the Generalitat, the members include Catalan chambers of commerce, export and sectoral associations, and institutions dealing with foreign trade. COPCA has two modes of operation: its market analysts help Catalan enterprises to develop export strategies, and it maintains offices ('Business Promotion Centres') in foreign cities around the world.[81]

Another organization, COPEC (Consorci Català de Promoció Exterior de la Cultura) was created in 1991 to promote cultural products. Along with the Generalitat's departments of Culture, Industry, and Energy, COPEC consists of associations representing book publishers, musicians, art galleries, film producers, folklorists, and creators of decorative arts.[82] The Generalitat also finances Catalan cultural centres, which exist in a number of foreign cities to support Catalan communities.

Beyond that, the Generalitat has an aid program for Third World countries. In 1997, it budgeted 1.150 million pesetas for international aid and development.[83]

In addition, the Generalitat has established a large number of joint programs with regions in other states; in some cases these have involved bordering regions. For instance, in 1983 the Communidad de Trabajo de los Pirineos was formed with Andorra and neighbouring regions of France and Spain (including Catalonia). The 'Euroregio' was formed in 1991; it consisted of Languedoc-Rousillon, Midi-Pyrénées, and Catalonia.[84]

In other cases, however, the agreements have involved regions that are not contiguous. The most prominent is the '4 Motors per a Europa', created in 1989 with

Catalonia, Baden-Württemberg, Rhône-Alps, and Lombardy. It has a simple structure consisting mainly of an annual conference, a co-ordinating committee, and working groups. According to Catalan officials, the program has resulted in a large number of bilateral projects. Between Catalonia and Baden-Württemberg, its most comparable region, 25 to 30 co-operative projects are established each year.[85]

Finally, Catalonia has become involved in a large number of bodies and associations grouping together regions in a particular area, including the Pyrenees in 1983, the peripheral maritime regions in 1986, and the Mediterranean basin in 1992. With respect to the Mediterranean, an institute for Mediterranean studies has been established in Barcelona.

Throughout its international activities, the Generalitat has insisted that it has no interest in independence.[86] And its mixed public-private associations are intended in part to make their activities less provocative to Madrid. Indeed, despite the Constitutional Court decision allowing the Basque Country to maintain an office of its own in Brussels, the Generalitat has shown no intention of following suit and abandoning its mixed format.[87] Most important, all these programs fall in the category of the 'low-level international activity' that has become the norm for substates in Europe. None of them involves formal relations, let alone treaty making, with sovereign states. Nor do they entail participation in international bodies, such as the United Nations. In short, they do not directly involve the 'hard core' of international relations.

Nevertheless, many of these activities met with hostility from the Spanish government. The creation of COPCA led to a fierce conflict because Madrid saw it as an intrusion on its own exclusive jurisdiction.[88] In 1989, Joaquín Almunia, the PSOE minister for public administration, in co-operation with the foreign affairs minister, attempted to set conditions on such AC activities: foreign trips would be planned in consultation with Madrid, permission would be needed to open foreign offices, and agreements would be limited to 'comparable' entities.[89] However, the ACs, including Catalonia, refused to comply.[90] With time, the Spanish government became reconciled to these forms of AC international activity.[91] However, Madrid has rejected the demand from the Generalitat that on matters of Catalan language and culture it should be the exclusive international spokesperson and negotiator.[92]

Relations with Europe

In pursuing international connections, the Generalitat's primary focus has been on Europe, which is in keeping with the longstanding Catalan tradition of using the European connection to supplement or qualify their links with Spain. This strategy has been made all the more compelling by the emergence of the European Community and the general belief that European integration is weakening the prerogatives and powers of established states, including Spain. Perhaps by dealing directly with the institutions of the new Europe Catalonia will be able to increase its autonomy.

One of the Generalitat's earliest initatives was to bring about the creation of the Patronat Català Pro-Europa in 1982 in preparation for Spain's entry into the European Community. The Patronat was given a double mandate: to promote and co-ordinate Catalonia's relations with the European Community and to prepare Catalonia's economy and society for Spain's membership in the Community. The first public-private consortium to be created through the initiative of the Generalitat, the Patronat draws together a broad range of public and private organizations. In 1986, the Patronat established an office in Brussels. Despite the Constitutional Court decision allowing the Basque Country's office in Brussels, the Generalitat has continued to rely upon the Patronat rather than establishing an office of its own.[93]

By the same token, Europe has been the primary focus of President Pujol's foreign travels. Of 226 trips, between June 1981 and July 1995, 174 involved EC countries. Another 31 involved non-EC European countries.[94]

Catalonia also has played a leading role in various associations linking together European regions. The Association of European Border Regions (created in 1971) is currently headed by Joan Vallvé, CiU member of the European parliament and the former head of the Generalitat's Direcció General d'Afers Interdepartamentals. The association held its first meeting in Barcelona in 1985. In 1992 Jordi Pujol became president of the organization, which by that time had changed its name to the Assembly of European Regions. Although these are private organizations, a primary function of the assembly has been to persuade the European Community to allow regional representation in its own institutions. This pressure finally resulted in a provision of the 1992 Treaty of Maastricht creating a Committee of Regions. In 1996 the presidency of the committee was assumed by yet another Catalan, the then mayor of Barcelona, Pasqual Maragall.

With the committee, regions have direct representation in the European Union for the first time. The committee is only advisory, however. Moreover, it combines regions with municipalities, resulting in 222 members.[95] Its members are not elected. And its importance is weakened by the fact that the 1992 addition to the EU treaty entrenching the principle of subsidiarity, or devolution of responsibilities to the lowest or most local level possible, does not refer to the regions.[96] For its part, the Spanish state has declared that the principle of subsidiarity applies to the EU's relations with member states, not regions.[97] At the 1997 EU meeting in Amsterdam, Spain joined the unitary member states in defeating a German proposal, supported by Austria and Belgium, for an annex to the Amsterdam Treaty specifying that the application of subsidiarity can affect sub-states.[98]

Under the terms of the CiU-PP pact, the Spanish government must allow AC officials to participate in EU working group meetings that bear on their particular concerns and it began to do so, starting with 55 of the 450 such groups.[99] But that privilege does not extend to meetings of the Council of Ministers. Article 146 of the EU treaty, as modified in 1992, does allow regional ministers to participate in council meetings, and this has happened in the case of Belgium.[100] By the same token, under German law Länder are entitled to have representatives present at pertinent meetings of the EU Council of Ministers.[101] However, the Aznar government has fiercely resisted following suit, despite strong pressure from the Basque Country and Catalonia and even after the main opposition party, the PSOE, had embraced the idea. In March 1998 the PSOE was preparing to vote with the Basque and Catalan nationalists in a resolution calling for AC participation in the Council of Ministers, as part of the Spanish delegation. The minister of foreign affairs declared that the measure would be unworkable, and PP leaders made every effort to persuade the PSOE not to support the proposal.[102] The resolution passed. It remains to be seen whether the PSOE supported the proposal out of simple parliamentary opportunism or whether it had abandoned its historical suspicion of Basque and Catalan nationalism, and the accommodation of it within Spain's political institutions.

Of course, Catalans elect members directly to the European parliament, but their representation is organized by party rather than territory. In response to pressure from the ACs, Madrid in 1988 established the Conferencia Sectorial Estado-CC.AA., (state-autonomous communities sectoral consulting body) through which the government can consult the ACs on Spain's relations with the European Community. However, the Conferencia Sectorial has yet to be properly structured,[103] and, though Catalonia may exercise a disproportionate influence,[104] there are 16 other member ACs, many of which have little interest in foreign affairs. As a result, Catalonia has continued to rely on bilateral dealings with Madrid.[105]

Catalonia has been able to establish a wide variety of 'low-level' relations with other European regions and has been instrumental in the creation of organizations to represent the regions' interests. Yet, it has had much more difficulty acquiring the ability to represent itself in the institutions of the European Union. Even its formal parliamentary partner, the PP, fiercely resisted arrangements that have been made available to the regions of Austria, Germany, and Belgium.

Like the González government, the Aznar government has been quite clear that the State of the Autonomies is not a federal system and that the Spanish state, as the national state, should exercise a monopoly over international relations. This attitude was seen in its alignment with the unitary states in rejecting Germany's Amsterdam proposal. In the last analysis, it is difficult to see how the European connection can offer a way to bypass Madrid and to offset the constraints on Catalonia's autonomy that continue to operate within the Spanish order.

Proposals for a Multinational Spain

By 1997 moderate Catalan nationalism had embraced a new agenda: the transformation of Spain into a multinational state. In part this was provoked by the PP government's regular expression of an especially robust Spanish nationalism,[106] whether in the way it deployed it powers in such areas as education or in its resistance to AC involvement in the institutions of the European Union. As the contradictions in the CiU's continued support of the Aznar government became increasingly evident, so a backlash began to develop among Catalan nationalists. It was apparently from a desire to mollify this frustration that the nationalist leadership heightened its demands. In the process, moderate Catalan nationalism had endorsed a set of ambitious proposals. Rather than simply calling upon the Spanish government to allow Catalonia to assume its functions under the existing statute of autonomy, members of the CiU, the CDC, and the Unió started to argue that the limits of the existing constitutional order had been reached.[107] For the first time, they drew up comprehensive blueprints for a new order; at the heart of these schemes is recognition of Spain's multinational character.

Convergència Democràtica per Catalunya

Entitled 'A new Horizon for Catalonia' ('Per un Nou Horitzó per a Catalunya'), the CDC manifesto set as its primary goal 'the recognition of Catalonia as a nation and the political power which rightfully belongs to it'.[108] To this end, it listed six objectives:

1. Transformation of Spain's political culture to one based on the idea of a plurinational state: 'The State of the Autonomous Communities can be interpreted primarily as involving administrative decentralization while the plurinational state represents the recognition of the distinct cultural and linguistic identities of which it is formed'.[109] The educational effort needed to establish this new conception would require, among other things, 'the creation at the state level of a cultural council of the historic nationalities which would bring together, in particular, academics from these nationalities'.[110]
2. 'Linguistic and cultural sovereignty' within Catalan territory, entailing, among other things, the guarantee of 'a Catalan space' in all forms of communication and the creation of a Council of Catalan Letters, along with equal recognition of language and cultures in the Spanish state.
3. Transformation of Spain's political symbols and institutions to accord with the multinational model: the very name of the Spanish state should be multilingual; all four languages (Catalan, Basque, Galician, and Castilian) should appear on personal identification documents (such as passports) as well as on Spanish currency; elimination of the constitutional impediment to federation of ACs; Catalan veto over all state measures affecting its exclusive competèncias; and elimination of state administrative offices in Catalonia.
4. Finances: the establishment in five years of an arrangement equivalent to that enjoyed by the Basque Country and Navarre, by which Catalonia would receive the taxes of Catalans and transfer part to the central government, with reform of existing arrangements in the meantime.
5. A two-stage process leading to such changes as exclusive jurisdiction over language and culture (especially education), exclusive jurisdiction over public order, total jurisdiction over local administration, sole responsiblity for administration, including functions left with the central government.

6. Institutional representation in the European Union and such international bodies as UNESCO, along with a senate reformed along multinational lines, with senators having vetoes over measures of a national character, and the total independence of the Catalan judiciary and Catalan civil law.[111]

The document is striking both for the breadth of change that it proposes and the extent to which these changes are detailed. It constitutes a major departure for the CiU, and for moderate Catalan nationalism.

Unió Democràtica de Catalunya

The CDC's coalition partner, the Unió Democràtica de Catalunya, adopted a document in 1997 that contained largely the same proposals. Indeed, the document carried the logic of a multinational Spain one step further by reaffirming the notion of a confederal Spain, centred in the monarchy, which Unió had adopted at its foundation in 1931. In the words of Unió leader, Duran Lleida, Catalunya must move from 'self-government' to 'sovereignty'; '[it] must abandon the status of an autonomous community in order to be a nation'.[112]

'La Sobirania de Catalunya i l'Estat Plurinacional' called for the creation of a state that would be based on 'full respect for the different national identities that existed before the State'. This state would have a triple character: it would be 'confederal in all that affects the identity of Catalonia and the other national entities, as well as social cohesion policies; federal in economic, financial, and fiscal matters; and autonomous, but not symmetrical.'[113] None the less, as a sovereign nation Catalonia would still be very much part of Spain, albeit a confederal Spain.

However much partisan interest may have led the PP and the CiU to join together, the two parties cannot help but reflect the profoundly different views of the national question that divide Catalans from other Spaniards. At the same time that the PP government was seeking to establish a 'unitary' curriculum about Spain in the schools and to ensure respect for the established symbols of the Spanish nation, the CDC was calling for a massive educational effort to establish the notion of a multinational Spain, and the Unió was proclaiming a confederal Spain.

The CDC and Unió decisions to adopt a comprehensive program for redefining Catalonia's relationship with the rest of Spain brought the two parties closer to the established positions of two other Catalan parties, the ERC and the IC.

Esquerra Republicana de Catalunya

In 1989 the ERC formally committed itself to independence for Catalonia. In its 1995 electoral platform, 'Stand up! Towards independence', the party reiterated this commitment to independence as the ultimate objective but also outlined a program to expand Catalonia's autonomy within Spain. Beyond exploiting all remaining possibilities under the existing statute of autonomy, the program called for a new statute that would, among other things, give Catalonia socio-economic powers and a new fiscal arrangement and direct representation in the European Union, and would remove the constitutional obstacle to a federalization of the Catalan lands.[114] Indeed, the program contained many of the measures which, two years later, were to form the new position of the CDC.[115]

Initiativa per Catalunya
As part of his effort to rejuvenate the Catalan left, Rafael Ribó attempted to place the Initiativa de Catalunya squarely within Catalan nationalism. These efforts were not well-received by the IC's counterpart at the Spanish level, Izquierda Unida, whose leader, Julio Anguita, has been openly hostile to Catalan nationalism. However, in June 1996, a commission formed of members of the IC and of the IU adopted a policy calling for the replacement of the existing State of the Autonomies with an authentically federal system. The policy recognized that such a process could be facilitated by a variety of reforms within the existing order but that it also required constitutional change: explicit recognition of the multinational character of the Spanish state; expansion of the powers of the federated units; permission for special relations among the units; and recognition of the right to self-determination of units. Like the ERC program, this policy anticipated many of the measures contained in the CiU's program of 1997.[116] In his own explanation of the IC's proposal to recognize Spain's multinational character through a federal regime, Rafael Ribó emphasized that it should be an *asymmetrical* federalism in which Catalonia and the other historic nations can assume powers and responsibilities that the other autonomous communities would not.[117] (In the end, however, the proposal fell victim to a formal split between the IC and the IU.)

By 1997 most of Catalonia's political parties were arguing that the existing State of the Autonomies did not meet Catalonia's needs and must be replaced by a new constitutional regime, clearly federal if not confederal, that explicitly recognized Spain's multinational character and guaranteed Catalonia a far wider autonomy. This was the formal position of the two ruling parties, the CDC and the Unió, and of the IC. And it was the minimum requirement for the ERC which, with its off-shoot Partit per la Independència, wanted independence to be the long-term objective of Catalonia. Between them, the parties could claim to speak for the overwhelming majority of voters in Catalan elections. In the 1995 election, they had received 60.2 per cent of the popular vote and 84 of the 135 seats in the Catalan parliament.

Yet, if Catalan nationalists had concluded that a new constitutional framework rooted in a multinational Spain was needed, competing political forces in Catalonia rejected this conclusion. In particular, the Partit dels Socialistes de Catalunya (PSC) was opposed to asymmetry and multinationalism. Moreover, just as nationalist forces dominate the Catalan parliament, so the PSC has its own bases of power in the Spanish parliament and the city hall of Barcelona, the city where most Catalans live.

Partit del Socialistes de Catalunya

In the statutes that the PSC adopted in 1978, Article 2 gives the national question equal status with class objectives: the PSC 'has as goals the achievement of a class-less society, socialist and self-managing in which every sign of class or national oppression or exploitation will disappear, and the claim of the Catalonia national identity.'[118] But at least two different forces shaping the party have restrained any clear expression of a nationalist perspective.

First, when the larger party to which the PSC is tied, the PSOE, was in power, it was largely unsympathetic to Catalan demands for further decentralization and indeed to Catalan nationalism in general. That can be seen in the González government's resistance to the PSC's proposals for decentralization in 1987.

In principle, the PSC is a fully independent political party[119] without any official relationship with the PSOE. Still in 1987, the PSC general secretary, Raimon Obiols, referred to 'jacobin' tendencies in the González government and observed, 'There exist[s] a dependence relationship [with the PSOE] which implies losing part of the party sovereignty.'[120] Over the years, ideological and structural integration with the PSOE has clearly led to a weakening of the PSC's nationalism.[121]

Second, the PSC draws much of its support from immigrants from other parts of Spain and their descendants, who may be uneasy with Catalan nationalism. In fact, over half of its supporters see themselves as being as much Spanish as Catalan, and a large proportion see themselves as strongly Spanish.[122]

Thus, in 1996, the PSC party congress came out squarely in favour of federalism in Spain but, unlike the IC, which also advocates federalism, insisted that federalism can be achieved within the existing State of the Autonomies: 'The State of the Autonomies created by the constitution has all the attributes of a federal state and all the potential to function as one even though it is not formally designated as such.'[123]

In describing the form of federalism that would be appropriate, the party rejected the terms asymmetrical and symmetrical federalism in favour of 'differential federalism'. A 'federalism of the nationalities and regions' would contain elements of uniformity but would also accommodate 'distinctive facts', largely through bilateral agreements.[124] More concretely, the document called for decentralization, Senate reform, reduction in the size of the state bureaucracy, and reform of fiscal arrangements.[125] Nowhere to be found is the description of a multinational Spain that figures so strongly in the programs of the ERC and CiU, as well as the IC.

A somewhat different approach to these questions can be found in the speeches of Pasqual Maragall, past mayor of Barcelona and PSC candidate for the Catalan presidency in the 1999 election. There, the rationale for Catalan autonomy is more technocratic. Efficiency lies with devolution of control and the principle of subsidiarity. Especially with globalization and European economic integration, there should be an enhancement in the autonomy of all communities, whether cities such as Barcelona or societies such as Catalonia.[126] Here too there is little emphasis on nationalism. Indeed, Maragall has publicly described himself as 'a Catalan who claims to be a Catalanist but does not like nationalism'.[127]

Partido Popular

Not only Catalan nationalism and a multinational Spain but even the concept of federalism are rejected by the Partido Popular. The PP is the most recent in a series of parties seeking to draw together conservative voters, both in Catalonia and in Spain as a whole.

Despite its rejection of Catalan nationalist discourse, the PP was able to win 18 per cent of the Catalan popular vote in the 1996 Spanish election, the highest ever for the PP and its predecessor, the Alianza Popular. And in the 1995 Catalan elections it jumped from its 1992 level of 6 per cent of the popular vote, and seven seats, to 13.1 per cent of the vote, with 17 seats. In 1999 it fell to 9.5 per cent and 12 seats. None the less, in the 2000 Spanish election, the PP had its greatest success ever in Catalonia, with 22.8 per cent of the popular vote and 12 seats.

The continuing impasse over the national question led the two main bearers of Catalan nationalism, the CiU and Unió, to make detailed proposals for a multinational Spain that were very similar to those of two other nationalist parties, the ERC and IC. To that extent a consensus had formed among Catalan nationalists that the Spanish political order must change along multinational lines. Given the preponderance of nationalist parties in the Catalan parliament, that consensus became the dominant point of view.

Yet the Catalan representation in the Cortes and Barcelona city hall continued to be dominated by a party that does not subscribe to this consensus. While the PSC advocates federalism and local autonomy, its attitude to Catalan nationalism is heavily qualified. Moreover, in both the Catalan parliament and among the Catalan representation in the Cortes, a party that openly rejects Catalan nationalism, the Catalan PP, has been making its presence felt.

In the end, nothing came of these schemes for a 'multinational Spain'. By 1998, the CiU, committed as ever to support the Aznar government, made little sustained effort to promote these notions. Moreover, the 1999 Catalan elections further reduced the CiU's ability to advance the cause. In order to retain power, it had to rely on the formal support of the Catalan PP. The 2000 Spanish election, giving the Aznar government a parliamentary majority, seems to have sealed the fate of the ideal of a 'multinational' Spain. Yet it remains part of the formal agenda of moderate Catalan nationalism.

Conclusions

During the last two decades Catalonia has been able to make effective use of the opportunities contained in the new Spanish constitution. The notion that Catalonia and the other autonomous communities should be able to enjoy a certain degree of autonomy seems to be firmly entrenched. Moreover, thanks to skilful bargaining with the Spanish government parties, especially when they lack a parliamentary majority, the CiU, along with the Basque PNV, have been able to expand substantially the autonomy allowed them under the constitution.

None the less, however impressive may be the autonomy that Catalonia enjoys today, compared to just over two decades ago these gains have little constitutional protection. They have been heavily dependent upon bargaining between parties in the Spanish parliament, and upon the need of minority governments to obtain the support of the CiU. Hence they are not based upon agreements between the Spanish and Catalan governments. Spain has not become a federation in any meaningful sense, and all the constitutional provisions precluding that are still intact. Nor has the polity taken on a multinational character, whether in its institutions or in its political culture. Even when linked to the Catalan nationalists in a formal parliamentary alliance, the Spanish government pursues measures tailored to promote unitary Spanish nationalism, with the inevitable reaction among Catalan nationalists. Now that the Aznar government enjoys a parliamentary majority, this nationalism may be given freer rein and Catalonia's new-found autonomy may face a fundamental challenge. Thus, even in terms of the prerogatives and constitutional protections that come with federalism, not to mention formal independence, Catalonia remains a nation without a state.

Chapter 5

Political Economy: Europeanization and the 'Region State'

Whereas changes in Catalonia's political status had to await the death of Franco, its economy was launched on a new path midway through the Franco regime. By the time of the transition to democracy, the structure of the Catalan economy had already changed in fundamental ways. The focus of economic activity had shifted, and the Catalan bourgeoisie had declined beyond the point of return, European and Japanese capital having firmly replaced it. As the Generalitat undertook to lead Catalonia's national reconstruction, it could not hope to restore the past glories of Catalonia's economy; rather, it had simply to cope with ongoing processes of economic change, and could draw upon few resources to do so.

1960–1975: Spain and Catalonia's 'Economic Miracle'

In 1959, under the leadership of a new generation of technocrats linked to the Opus Dei, Franco and his colleagues had reluctantly abandoned the autarchic model they had been faithfully pursuing since coming to power. The new Plan de Estabilización set radically different objectives—promoting international trade at the cost of gradually opening up Spain to exports, actively encouraging foreign investment, cutting state spending, and raising the price of utilities.[1]

The main purpose of this reversal of policies may have been to stave off the popular economic discontent that was threatening the Franco regime, but one effect was to rescue Catalonia from its post-Civil War stagnation. Despite the Franco regime's enduring hostility, Catalonia enjoyed two decades of economic boom, perhaps its greatest boom ever.[2] Given Catalonia's established industrial strength, economic liberalization was bound to be to its advantage.

The timing could not have been better. Western Europe had been enjoying sustained economic growth, thanks to the combined effects of the Marshall Plan (from which Spain had been excluded), trade liberalization, and American investment.

And during the 1960s, Spain was admitted to the major international economic institutions—GATT, the OECD, and the IMF—although not the emerging European Economic Community, which spurned Spain because of its dictatorial regime.

As a result, Spain enjoyed its delayed 'economic miracle', its economy growing faster than all capitalist economies except Japan.[3] And the miracle was especially strong in Catalonia; indeed Catalonia was its 'principal motor'.[4] Catalonia's share of Spain's gross domestic product rose from 18.7 per cent in 1960 to 20.1 per cent in 1973.[5]

Over the period 1955–75, Catalonia's GDP grew by over 400 billion pesetas (in constant pesetas).[6] In fact, between 1960 and 1973 GDP grew by a yearly average of 8 per cent—5.3 per cent in per capita terms.[7] Employment grew by an annual rate of 1.8 per cent over 1955–75, and incomes rose by 6.1 per cent, or 3.6 per cent per capita. (The comparable figures for Spain as a whole were 0.5, 5.5, and 4.4 per cent.)[8]

Especially dramatic was the resurgence of Catalonia's industries. Between 1955 and 1975, the gross composite value of Catalan industrial production grew by 287 per cent. Production increased by at least 300 per cent in all sectors but textiles, wood and cork, and mining. Such growth, which was unprecedented, constituted a sort of 'reindustrialization' of Catalonia.[9]

Foreign investment in Spain soared, and Catalonia received a disproportionate share thanks to its industrial base, strong internal market, and location. The primary beneficiary was manufacturing, especially petrochemicals, pharmaceuticals, electrical machinery and appliances, and transportation equipment.[10] For instance, during the 1950s the SEAT automobile complex was established through the collaboration of Spanish banks, the Franco regime's Instituto Nacional de Industria (INI), and the Italian Fiat corporation. Determined as ever to spread industrial activity beyond Catalonia, INI had tried to have the plant established elsewhere, but Fiat had insisted on Barcelona. Thus the complex was established in Barcelona's Zona Franca—with the head office in Madrid. By 1964, more than half the cars on Spanish roads were products of SEAT. In turn, there developed a large number of small and medium-sized enterprises producing automobile parts. Ultimately, SEAT was joined by Renault.[11]

In some cases, foreign capital linked up with long-established Catalan industrial enterprises. The 200-year old Catalan chemical enterprise, Cros, joined with the British Laport Chemical and others to create another complex at the Barcelona Zona Franca.[12] Similarly, Tarragona became the centre of a petrochemical industry, largely tied to foreign multinationals. During the 1960s, the establishment of an asphalt refinery (Asesa) was followed by the creation of enterprises owned partially or even wholly by major foreign chemical firms, including the German Hoechst, Bayer and BASF, the American Dow, and the British-Dutch Shell. In the mid-1970s a refinery for crude petroleum was established in Tarragona.[13] Other multinationals that established operations in Catalonia included Solvay (based in Belgium) and the Swiss firms Sandoz and Ciba-Geigy.[14]

Table I: Gross Added Value by Sector

	1955	1960	1967	1975
Food	5.0%	7.2%	7.2%	6.2%
Textiles	37.7	29.7	19.7	12.6
Fur and leather	5.9	5.9	8.1	6.0
Wood and cork	5.0	4.6	3.7	2.7
Paper	3.4	3.8	3.7	7.1
Chemicals	10.7	11.3	12.6	13.0
Ceramics and cement	3.4	2.8	3.9	3.5
Metal	10.9	19.7	23.5	28.0
Mining	1.5	1.9	1.2	1.3
Water and energy	4.2	5.1	4.1	5.3
Construction	12.3	8.0	12.3	14.3
Total, industry and construction	100.0	100.0	100.0	100.0

Source: Adapted from Maluquer de Motes, *Història econòmica de Catalunya*, 188.

Some Catalan companies shared in the industrial boom, but the results were mixed. Several manufacturers capitalized on the post-war popularity of motorcycles. In 1967, the recently created Telesincro, S.A. launched a minicomputer that, in 1972, ranked third in Spanish sales, but by the late 1970s, it fell under the control of a French multinational.[15] Several ventures in the manufacture of colour televisions and semiconductors ended in failure.[16] The fact remained that by 1976 close to one-third of Catalonia's largest enterprises were under the control of foreign companies, largely based in the EEC, and they tended to constitute the more dynamic sector of the Catalan economy.[17]

With the Franco regime's new encouragement of tourism, foreign tourists flocked to Catalonia. Costa Brava, their primary destination, rapidly became overdeveloped and environmentally spoiled. Between 1954 and 1965 Catalonia's hotel capacity grew from 20 per cent of Spain's total capacity to almost 31 per cent.[18] This in turn was the basis of extensive foreign investment.[19]

Catalonia's foreign trade also increased dramatically, going from 4.9 per cent of Catalonia's GDP in 1964 to 9.7 per cent in 1977.[20] Nevertheless, Catalonia remained highly dependent on trade with Spain. Indeed, trade with Spain grew from 37.4 per cent to 48.5 per cent of Catalonia's GDP. The proportion of Catalonia's total exports that stayed in Spain had been 88.8 per cent in 1967, and it remained at 85.6 per cent in 1975.[21] And Catalonia's new prosperity attracted, and was in turn reinforced by, an influx of an unprecedented number of migrants from other parts of Spain.

In the course of this remarkable boom, Catalonia's industrial sector changed radically as it became more diversified. Catalonia's historical staple, textiles, continued its slide, falling from 37.7 per cent of industrial gross added value (GAV) in 1955 to 12.6 per cent in 1975, while metals rose from 10.9 per cent to 28 per cent

Table 2: Evolution of Gross Domestic Product by Sector

	1955	1962	1969	1975
Agriculture	7.5%	10.3%	6.2%	3.9%
Industry	42.9	43.2	42.1	41.1
Construction	6.0	5.1	6.2	6.8
Service	43.6	41.4	45.6	48.1

Source: Adapted from Maluquer de Motes, *Història econòmica de Catalunya*, 170.

and chemicals from 10.7 to 13 per cent.[22] The relative weight of other sectors changed as agriculture fell from 7.5 per cent of GDP in 1955 to 3.9 per cent in 1975 and services rose from 43.6 to 48.1 per cent.[23]

At the same time, some historical weaknesses of the Catalan economy persisted. In particular, Catalonia's financial sector remained restricted, with serious consequences for the Catalan economy. During the 1920s, Barcelona, which had several large banks and a dozen local ones, had been the financial capital of Spain.[24] Its stock exchange, La Borsa de Barcelona, had been the most important in Spain and was supplemented by a major private exchange: L'Associació del Mercat Lliure de Valors de Barcelona.[25] However, one of the most important Catalan banks, El Banc de Barcelona, had disappeared in 1931 as the Spanish Republican government settled scores with businesses that had collaborated with the Primo de Rivera dictatorship. Under the Franco regime, the Catalan banking system collapsed entirely.[26] Dominance by Spain's seven largest banks, which included Basque banks but no Catalan banks, was formalized under the Consejo Superior Bancario, which was created by the Spanish regime in 1946 to advise the ministry of finance and which was dominated by the seven big banks. The regime facilitated the concentration of ownership of Spanish banks, and until 1963 new banks could not be formed. Thus, over the period 1940–53, 21 Catalan banks were absorbed by banks elsewhere in Spain.[27] The largest of these, El Banco Hispano Colonial, was absorbed in 1950 by the Banco Central, which was under avowedly anti-Catalanist management.[28]

By the same token, the private stock exchange was closed down during Franco's first year in power,[29] and under Franco's centralism, the Borsa de Barcelona steadily lost ground to the Madrid exchange. The Spanish bourgeoisie had favoured centralization of market activity in Madrid, as did foreign capital. As a result, by 1982 the Borsa de Barcelona was responsible for only 15.5 per cent of values traded; the Madrid exchange was responsible for 68.9 per cent.[30] In the early 1960s, several Catalan nationalists, including Jordi Pujol, established a new Banca Catalana.[31] But it collapsed in 1983.

Another persisting weakness of the Catalan economy was the mediocre productivity in its industrial sector. Despite improvements, by the mid-1970s industrial productivity was still barely above the Spanish average. The two most important industries, chemicals and metal processing, remained below the Spanish average. This may have been due to the relative absence of a basic industry to support them.

In other areas of industrial activity, mediocre productivity was due to another continuing structural weakness of the Catalan economy, the dominance of small and medium-sized enterprises with limited investment in fixed capital goods, heavily reliant on subcontracting, specialized in the local market, and displaying only modest levels of technological innovation.[32] The relative absence of large Catalan-owned enterprises was itself partly a result of the absence of major Catalan banks. Substantial Catalan credits were drained away by Basque- and Madrid-based banks.[33]

Finally, as was to be expected under Franco, the public sector remained under-developed in Catalonia. As a percentage of the GAV for services in all Spain, 'public administration' in Catalonia started at 7.4 per cent in 1955 and had not risen beyond 10.7 per cent by 1975.[34]

The Franco regime was fundamentally hostile to Catalonia's economic interests. It may well have undermined Catalonia's financial sector. Catalonia's underlying industrial strength, and especially its appeal to foreign capital, was such that it could only prosper once the regime had abandoned its dream of autarchy. Indeed, as with the SEAT plant, Catalonia attracted investment that Spanish economic planners had wanted to direct elsewhere. The migration of over one million Spaniards was clear testimony to Catalonia's economic strength. At the same time, Catalonia's remarkable growth had been financed largely by outside economic interests, at the expense of Catalonia's own historical economic leadership:

> As a result of the penetration of European and North American capital, the power of the Catalan bourgeoisie will yield, more and more, to the power of the bourgeoisie of Europe of the Six and, especially, of the West German bour-geoisie. On the other hand, the big Spanish banks (based in Madrid and the Basque Country) and Spanish public capital are steadily increasing their own control over the Catalan economy.[35]

1976–1998: Downturn, Then Recovery

By the time Franco finally died and the transition to democracy was formally underway, Spain's economy—and especially Catalonia's—was in a severe down-turn. Over 1973–85 Catalonia's yearly growth in GDP was 1.7 per cent, even lower than Spain's 2 per cent.[36] Investment declined throughout the period,[37] and for the first time in decades, Catalonia experienced major unemployment as the jobless rate surged from 50,000 in 1975 to over 450,000 in 1985.[38]

In large part, the downturn stemmed from international conditions, most notably the OPEC energy crisis and its negative impact upon foreign tourism in Spain and the ability of Spanish immigrants to send money home. But some argue that it can also be blamed on Spain's political class, which was more interested in designing new political arrangements than attending to the economy.[39]

By the late 1980s, however, the energy crisis had ended and Spain's entry into the European Economic Community (in 1986) was stimulating economic growth. In addition, labour law reforms introduced in 1984 were having their effects. Once again, Catalonia pulled ahead of Spain: over 1985–91, yearly growth in Catalonia's GDP averaged 4.55 per cent, compared to Spain's, which was 4.1 per cent.[40] Investment grew between 1985 and 1990. Job creation exceeded the Spanish average, and unemployment eased.[41] In 1991, Catalonia entered another slump, largely because of international conditions, but it began to recover in 1994. Throughout this period, as before, Catalonia's economy demonstrated greater volatility than the Spanish economy as a whole, exceeding it both in growth rates during periods of upturn and in declines during downturns.[42]

Given the uneven performance of the economy over this period, Catalonia did not receive the massive migration of previous decades. Indeed, over the period 1982–86 it registered a net out-migration of 84,353. From 1987 to 1991 it registered a modest in-migration of 37,287.[43]

Contemporary Catalonia: A Restructured Economy

However complete the recovery, the Catalan economy is now profoundly changed from two decades ago. The restructuring, some of which was already underway in the 1960s and 1970s, has been accelerated by Spain's membership in the European Community, and by globalization in general.

Industrial Restructuring

In terms of economic sectors, the most dramatic change is the decline in the relative importance of industry. To be sure, Catalonia remains Spain's most important industrial region, with 25.1 per cent of Spain's industrial added value (which was what it had been in 1978);[44] indeed, Catalonia is one of the major industrial areas of Europe as a whole. But as a percentage of GDP, industry fell from 41.1 in 1975 to only 28.9 in 1996.

It can be argued that this decline will not continue at the same rate and that industry will remain a large part of the Catalan economy. Allegedly, the decline is due to processes of adjustment also evident in other countries, such as changes in consumption habits, contracting out of services, growth of the public sector, and relocation of plants, which are running their course.[45] Nevertheless, the radical change that has already taken place amounts to no less than a deindustrialization.[46]

At the same time, the structure of industrial specialization changed significantly over the last two decades. In 1992, metal products continued to represent the largest share of GAV; however, energy and water, which had been one of the least important in 1975, rivalled chemicals for second place. And textiles had slipped even farther, though in 1992 it still had the most workers.[47]

Agriculture has continued to decline in importance, slipping from 3.9 per cent of Catalonia's GDP in 1975 to 1.4 per cent in 1995. Just as elsewhere in Spain, Catalan agriculture went into a 'crisis'.[48]

At the same time, as elsewhere, Catalonia's service sector gained in importance, growing from 48.1 per cent of GDP in 1975 to 57.2 per cent in 1996. The largest factor in this growth is the public sector, reflecting directly the emergence of Catalonia as an autonomous community. But also responsible is the contracting out of services previously provided within corporations, along with continued growth in local commerce and tourism.[49] Indeed, tourism is now responsible for close to 20 per cent of Catalonia's GDP, if all its effects are taken into account.[50] Catalonia receives nearly 14 million foreign tourists each year[51] and, arguably, is Europe's premier tourist region.[52]

Finance: Continuing Limitations

The continued weakness of the financial sector is a serious handicap for the Catalan economy. Catalonia still lacks a bank able to play an important role within Spain as a whole. Catalonia itself is dominated by Spanish and Basque banks. Indeed, the banking crisis of the early 1980s consolidated the position of the Madrid-based and Basque banks. In 1980, these banks held 43.9 per cent of commercial bank deposits in Catalonia; by 1983 they held 80.1 per cent.[53]

On the other hand, Catalonia's *savings* banks are prospering. They are far more important in Catalonia itself, compared to commercial banks, than savings banks elsewhere in Spain.[54] In fact, Catalan savings banks play a significant role throughout Spain as a whole. The Caixa d'Estalvis i Pensions de Barcelona (La Caixa), which was created by the merging of two Catalan savings banks in 1990, is the largest savings bank in all of Europe on the basis of its capital, although not investments. On the same basis, it is the largest financial institution in Spain. The Caixa de Catalunya is among the 10 most important Spanish financial institutions, once again on the basis of capital.

Still, as savings banks formally committed to social objectives, the Caixas do not provide the capital needed to build the large enterprises that Catalonia continues to lack. And the largest of the Catalan banks, Banc de Sabadell, invests only in financial enterprises that complement its activities. In recent years, however, La Caixa has begun to invest in highways, real estate, and utilities, as well as in Gas Natural SA.[55]

Just as Catalonia continues to lack major Catalan-owned banks, so it continues to have relatively few large Catalan-owned companies. In 1994, fewer than 1 per cent of Catalan firms had more than 250 employees; only two had more than 10,000.[56] Indeed, whereas Catalonia contained 283 of Spain's 1,000 largest firms in 1973, by 1994 it had only 273. The number in Madrid had risen from 381 to 427.[57] On the other hand, the number of large foreign-owned enterprises has grown dramatically.

Catalonia in the Global Economy

Foreign Investment

Throughout the last two decades, Catalonia has continued to attract a disproportionate share of foreign investment. In the mid-1980s investment started to grow at an unprecedented rate, in response to Spain's entry into the EEC.[58] Between 1985 and 1994 direct foreign investment grew at an annual rate (in real terms) of 23 per cent in Catalonia, compared with 19.5 per cent in Spain. As a result, by 1994 foreign investment as a share of Catalonia's GDP had risen to 4.7 per cent, from 1 per cent in 1985.[59] Over the period as a whole, Catalonia received about a quarter of foreign investment in Spain—27 per cent between 1985 and 1995.[60]

The bulk of this investment went to industry, especially chemicals, but also electronics, automobiles, and railway equipment.[61] However, there was a shift in the sources of this investment. American capital, which was responsible for the largest number of foreign-owned firms in 1973, had produced only two new investments by 1994, and was displaced by France, Germany, and the Netherlands along with Japan and Southeast Asia.[62]

Among the most important instances of new investment was the SEAT automobile plant. SEAT was created jointly by the Italian Fiat and Spanish capital, but in 1981 Fiat sold its shares. Unable to function on its own, SEAT entered into an arrangement with Volkswagen in 1982; by 1990 Volkswagen owned SEAT outright. The most important automobile producer in Spain, SEAT is by far the largest source of Catalonia's exports (16 per cent in 1990).[63] Similarly, during the 1980s, Motor Ibèrica, which had been owned by a series of foreign interests, was taken over jointly by Nissan and several Spanish banks; after the banks withdrew, Nissan became majority owner and the firm became Nissan Motor Ibèrica.[64] In 1990 it exported 34 per cent of its automobile production.[65] Plants were also established by the major Japanese electronics manufacturers—Sony, Sanyo, Matsushita, Sharp, and Pioneer.[66] Indeed, Catalonia is the site of 85 per cent of Japanese industrial investment in Spain.[67]

As a result, by 1990, 14 of Catalonia's 22 largest industrial firms were foreign-controlled.[68] As well as the two automobile assembly plants, foreign capital controlled two of four motorcycle plants, five of twenty-five automobile part plants, virtually all electrical appliance manufacturers, most electrical motor and material plants, and most of the large chemical, pharmaceutical, and plastic manufacturers.[69] The proportion of Catalonia's large enterprises that were held in part by foreign capital had grown from 34.3 per cent in 1973 to 60.4 per cent in 1994. Foreign interests had majority ownership in 51.6 per cent of all companies and owned 109 companies.[70]

Whether and to what degree the Catalan economy was strengthened by this investment is a matter of debate. Some analysts point to the introduction of technology, the training of workers, and the adoption of new methods of production.[71] Others believe that most foreign investment has involved the takeover of existing Catalan firms rather than the creation of new enterprises as happened elsewhere in Spain.[72] Some even argue that foreign capital has become so important as to distort the Catalan economy with its demand for local goods and services.[73]

To be sure, some Catalan firms have themselves established operations in other countries. In 1997, 106 firms had 199 foreign operations, which extend over much of the world: 29.6 per cent were in the EEC, 25.6 per cent in Latin America, 18.1 per cent in the three NAFTA countries, and 12.1 per cent in Asia.[74] In monetary terms, however, Catalan investment is concentrated primarily in the EU countries.[75]

Some of these operations have been in existence for many years and involve Catalonia's largest companies. For instance, in the mid-1960s the publishing house Editorial Planeta set up branches in Mexico, Colombia, and Argentina. Now, with operations in nine countries, it is the eighth-largest publishing complex in the world.[76] Freixenet, one of Spain's leading wine producers, opened its first foreign operation, in the United States, in 1935 but soon abandoned it. However, it set up a new American operation in 1981, and a German one in 1984. With operations in several other countries as well, Freixenet exported 41 per cent of its production in 1996.[77] Finally, Roca Radiadores, Spain's leading producer of sanitation equipment, started opening offices in Europe in the mid-1970s. It now has seven factories in Spain and five in foreign countries.[78]

Still, at least two-thirds of Catalonia's foreign operations are recent developments, dating from the late 1980s and 1990s.[79] And, contrary to expectations, they are not concentrated among the larger Catalan firms: the overwhelming majority are held by small or medium-sized enterprises. Fifty-four per cent belonged to firms with annual billings of 5,000 million pesetas or less.[80]

However, these foreign operations cannot really offset the presumed harmful effects of foreign investment in Catalonia because they are on a much smaller scale: foreign investment in Catalonia represents 5 per cent of Catalonia's GDP, whereas Catalan investment outside Catalonia represents 0.6 per cent.[81] The striking participation of small and medium-sized Catalan enterprises in foreign investment may mean that they have been better able to adjust to the internationalized and much more competitive economy than has been presumed. Indeed, it may raise questions as to whether the development of more large Catalan enterprises is as pressing a need for the Catalan economy as has often been argued. Yet, even if it is not, it appears that Catalonia's competitiveness is still hindered by the absence of large Catalan-owned enterprises in the banking sector. In a 1997 survey of Catalan firms with foreign operations, the most common problem cited was the difficulty of obtaining external financing.[82] Indeed, 77 per cent of the firms rely upon their own resources to finance the initiatives.[83]

Growth in Foreign Trade
As those patterns of foreign investment would suggest, over this period Catalonia's foreign trade grew in significance, from 4.9 per cent of GDP in 1964 to 21.5 per cent in 1995.[84] In the same period Catalonia's share of total Spanish exports rose from 16 per cent to 26.5 per cent.[85]

Not surprisingly, the European Economic Community assumed a greater and greater role in this trade during the 1980s, especially the late 1980s. Exports to EEC countries rose from 51.9 per cent in 1980 to 71.2 per cent in 1992, and imports from EEC countries rose from 40.3 per cent to 62.7 per cent.[86] In 1996 the figures were 70 and 69 per cent.[87] Indeed, over the period 1985–92, EEC countries were responsible for 94 per cent of Catalonia's export growth.[88] Among EEC countries, foreign trade (both exports and imports) has been primarily with Germany, France, and Italy—in that order.[89]

At the same time the relative importance of commodities changed, in part because of the increased integration with the EEC. Exports, which were essentially in industrial products (95.2 per cent in 1996),[90] became increasingly concentrated in transportation equipment, electrical equipment, machinery, and plastics. Throughout, chemical products were important.[91] Imports have displayed a similar structure, reflecting the need of Catalan industries to import capital goods and intermediate goods.[92] By the same token, exports became increasingly concentrated in medium- and high-technology products.[93] Needless to say, these are all industries in which foreign capital is now predominant.

Throughout the period, Catalonia's commercial balance in foreign trade has been negative. In recent years, however, it has improved markedly, with exports as a proportion of imports rising from 49.5 per cent in 1990 to 78.2 per cent in 1997. Although imports have grown over this period, in each year the increase in exports has been substantially higher.[94] While this growth in export speaks well of the competitiveness of Catalan industry, it may also be due to a devalued peseta and low domestic demand.[95]

Continued Role of Tourism

As in the past, Catalonia's foreign trade deficit is partially offset by a strong surplus in tourism. Thus, in 1994 expenditures by foreign tourists in Catalonia reached 704,182.4 (current) million pesetas (MPTA), exceeding by 544,633.2 (current) MPTA spending by Catalans outside Spain. Catalonia's tourism balance with the rest of Spain was negative, but it represented only 48,423.6 (current) MPTA.[96] Constituting 4.5 per cent of Catalonia's 1994 GDP, the balance in foreign tourism partially offset Catalonia's foreign commercial deficit of 8.2 per cent.[97]

Catalonia within Spain

Surplus in Trade

Despite the growth in foreign trade, with its mixed results, Catalonia continues to depend primarily upon the rest of Spain for exports: 39.9 per cent of Catalonia's GDP in 1967, 35.6 per cent in 1987,[98] and 44.4 per cent in 1994. In 1994 trade with Spain represented 69 per cent of Catalonia's total exports and 53.3 per cent of its total imports.[99] Moreover, Catalonia's trade balance with the rest of Spain has been highly positive. Thus, in 1994 Catalonia's commercial balance with the rest of Spain was 1,508,900 MPTA, or 12.4 per cent of its GDP; its foreign balance was -1,004,000 MPTA.[100] By and large, Catalonia continues its historical practice of re-exporting to Spain goods obtained elsewhere and processed in Catalonia.[101]

Just as Catalonia's foreign trade has grown in importance, so has its trade with the rest of Spain. As a percentage of GDP, foreign exports rose from 12.7 per cent in 1987 to 19.8 per cent in 1994, but exports to Spain rose from 35.6 to 44.4 per cent. Foreign imports rose from 21.2 to 28.1 per cent, but imports from Spain rose from 23.3 per cent to 32.1 per cent.[102]

Persisting Fiscal Deficit

However profitable Catalonia's trade relations with the rest of Spain may be, its fiscal relations are quite a different matter. While estimates of the size vary substantially, there can be no doubt that Catalonia does have a 'fiscal deficit'.[103]

Since the Spanish constitution allows little room for autonomous communities to generate their own revenue, in Catalonia's 1996 budget, only 14.5 per cent of revenues came from the Generalitat's own taxation. And of this amount, 91 per cent came from taxes that had been 'ceded' by the Spanish state; only 5.7 per cent came from the taxes (on gambling) that Catalonia was entitled to levy independently. A much larger share of Catalonia's total government revenue (30.6 per cent) came through transfers from the Spanish state. As with the other autonomous communities, part of this transfer (38.1 per cent in Catalonia's case) was linked to the share of personal income tax that the Spanish state collected within Catalonia's territory, but the formula contains floors and ceilings designed to limit variation among the autonomous communities. Another 34.7 per cent came from social security transfers, which depend on the size of each autonomous community's eligible population. Another 12 per cent was based on state transfers to local governments in Catalonia, for which the Generalitat served as an intermediary. Transfers from the European Union accounted for only 1.4 per cent of Catalonia's revenues. This left a deficit of 5.9 per cent to be covered through borrowing by the Generalitat.[104]

In short, the Generalitat's fiscal position is effectively determined by its relationship with the Spanish state, and the terms of that relationship largely ignore the extent to which Catalonia generates higher revenue for the Spanish state than do any other autonomous community. To be sure, like the other autonomous communities, the Generalitat has been able to assume a steadily larger share of total public spending. By 1995, among all autonomous communities, this share had grown to 21 per cent.[105] But Catalan nationalists continue to insist that the Generalitat does not receive its fair share of public revenue.

Charges of 'fiscal discrimination' by the Spanish state against Catalonia have a very long history. The Franco regime was only one of a long line of Spanish governments to resent Catalonia's relative affluence and to try to divert some of this wealth for its own purposes.[106] But fiscal deficit, if not fiscal discrimination, did not end with the transition to democracy. One study found that Catalonia's fiscal deficit has actually grown over the period 1986–94. By 1994, it was estimated to be between 687,000 and 781,000 million pesetas.[107] At 740,000 million pesetas the deficit would represent about 6 per cent of Catalonia's GDP. Catalans not only paid more taxes than other Spaniards, but they received less in the way of state spending. Whereas in all of Spain per capita spending was equivalent to 112.86 per cent of per capita taxation, in Catalonia it was only about 80 per cent of per capita taxation.[108] Put differently, Catalonia generated 19.3 per cent of public revenue but received only 13.7 per cent of public spending.[109]

Arguably, Catalonia's fiscal deficit could be seen as merely offsetting its strong surplus in trade with the rest of Spain or as part of an effort to equalize the well-being of all Spaniards. Yet, according to some analyses this deficit far exceeds any such balancing effects. While the actions of the Spanish state have increased family income in the rest of Spain, in Catalonia they have substantially reduced it. In 1993, Catalan gross per capita income was 22.7 per cent above the Spanish average but disposable family income was only 17.8 per cent above the Spanish average. For the same reason, disposable family income has grown more slowly in Catalonia than in the rest of Spain.[110]

Given Catalonia's relative affluence, however, some fiscal deficit would seem to be in order. What then would be a reasonable deficit? By one calculation Catalonia's share of taxation would depend on its share of Spain's GDP, and its share of spending would depend on the size of its population. On this basis, Catalonia would provide 19.05 per cent of Spain's tax revenue, rather than 19.29 per cent, and would receive 15.56 per cent of total spending, rather than 13.66 per cent. Its 1994 deficit would have fallen from 734,000 million pesetas to 282,617 million, or 2.29 per cent of GDP.[111] But what if the populations of other autonomous communities are in greater need of public spending than Catalonia's? It has also been argued that Catalonia's deficit would have been less if the Spanish state had maintained a balanced budget,[112] though it is not clear why this should be part of any notion of inter-regional equity.

Catalonia's economy has emerged from the last few decades profoundly changed. The path on which it was launched in the late 1950s, long before the transition to democracy, has been followed at an ever increasing pace. From the autarchy of the early Franco period, Catalonia has become increasingly bound up in international trade, especially with the EU, and foreign interests, once again largely from EU countries, control an ever increasing share of its enterprises. In the process, Catalonia's economy has been restructured as industry has yielded in importance to service sectors, especially tourism, and has itself been oriented away from its traditional emphasis on textiles to the manufacture of cars, electrical equipment, and chemical products.

Catalonia continues to enjoy its favoured position within the Spanish economy, as seen in such measures as industrial activity, GDP, and per capita income. Still, it has major weaknesses. For all the strength of its Caixes, it continues to lack strong banks. Madrid has effectively replaced Barcelona as the financial centre of Spain. Important sectors of Catalan industry have fallen under foreign control. The Catalan-owned enterprises, most of which are small and medium-sized, often display mediocre levels of productivity and competitiveness. Levels of research and development are relatively low.

There are signs, however, that the Catalan-owned enterprises are overcoming their historical weaknesses, as shown by their recent forays into foreign operations. And the terms of Catalonia's foreign trade balance are becoming less negative. But difficulties persist, as seen in the inadequate financing for foreign investment by Catalan firms.

The fate of Catalonia's economy may be largely determined by outside forces, whether the EU to which the Spanish state is conceding crucial economic responsibilities, or the international economy in general. However, to the extent that it is shaped by influences within Catalonia, the leading roles will lie with both class forces and the organizations claiming to speak on their behalf, and with the Generalitat. As it happens, in recent years the Generalitat has been drawn into new forms of co-operation both with employers' associations and with unions in an effort to address the structural weaknesses of Catalonia's economy.

Classes and Their Representation

A Transformed Bourgeoisie

In the new, restructured Catalan economy, there are few traces of the bourgeoisie that shaped Catalonia's economy and political life in the nineteenth century and early decades of the twentieth century: 'The great names of the traditional Catalan bourgeoisie have almost totally disappeared and with them the great textile enterprises that they controlled. The descendants of these families are present in Catalan life but not as great entrepreneurs or holders of great concentrations of capital.'[113]

The Franco years were difficult for many of the old firms. In their revulsion from the excesses of the Second Republic, the Catalan bourgeoisie may have turned to Franco and may have recovered much of their property in the process. But in the eyes of the Franco regime they were Catalan none the less and were consequently held in suspicion. With this political marginalization came economic decline.[114] Indeed, there is evidence that, especially in its early years, the Franco regime actively blocked economic development in Catalonia, hindered the functioning of the Barcelona stock exchange, and failed to provide a sufficient supply of electricity.[115]

Beyond that, the old Catalan firms were not well placed to face the accelerated international competition that came with 1970s and 1980s. As a result, large numbers of them were closed or were taken over by foreign interests.[116]

A few old firms have survived, such as the newspaper publisher Grup Godó-La Vanguardia, founded in 1881, the brewery Damm, S.A., founded in 1910 and the wine producer, Miquel Torres, S.A., which dates back to 1860. But most of today's large Catalan firms were founded in the second half of the twentieth century and are led by first- or second-generation entrepreneurs.[117] Large Catalan-owned enterprises are especially prominent in the production of food and chemical products. Otherwise, of course, there are the many large enterprises controlled by foreign capital. At the same time, Catalan ownership remains strong among small and medium-sized enterprises.

Representing Business Interests

As befits its role as one of Spain's earliest sites of industrialization, Catalonia has a longer history of business representation than any other part of Spain. The Fomento del Trebajo Nacional, which is still Catalonia's leading business organization, emerged from associations created in the late eighteenth century to represent the interests of the emerging class of cotton manufacturers.[118] The Fomento was suppressed by the Franco regime, which imposed its own corporatist structures, but with the transition to democracy it regained its historical role and is now clearly established as the primary representative of business in Catalonia.

Rather than speaking for specifically Catalan business, Fomento claims to speak for all business interests that are based in Catalonia, whether they be owned in Catalonia or beyond. This excludes companies with head offices in other parts of Spain; they are members of other regional associations. Functioning mainly within a confederal structure, *Fomento* draws together over 300 associations representing employers in different economic sectors, defined in terms of both territory and industry. The associations themselves range in size from the four-member association of cement producers to the more than 1,000-member association of small-store owners. In addition, Fomento has several hundred individual members, mainly large corporations. On this basis, it can claim to represent in one way or another about 80 per cent of employers in Catalonia.[119]

As in the nineteenth century, when it articulated the Catalan bourgeoisie's project of protecting the Spanish market and catalanizing Spain, the post-Franco Fomento is squarely oriented to Spain as a whole. Indeed, from its re-emergence in the mid-1970s, Fomento focused its energies on campaigning to create a new Spanish-wide employer's organization. In fact, a Catalan was the first president of the Confederación Española de Organizaciones Empresariales (CEOE) (Spanish confederation of business organizations), created in June 1977. At the time, Catalan business leaders argued successfully that the CEOE should have a highly centralized structure, in the process affording little autonomy to Fomento. Generally Fomento has followed the positions taken by the CEOE.[120]

Fomento did not take a formal position on the creation of an Autonomous Community of Catalonia, but apparently was uneasy about extensive autonomy.[121] But in the past it has actively opposed the expansion of the Generalitat's responsibilities in such areas as labour relations, which it sees as threats to the integrity of the Spanish market: 'The other regions of Spain constitute our primary market. We cannot enter into agreements that lead to higher costs than in the rest of Europe.'[122] Also, despite its support for protectionism in the nineteenth century, Fomento is now resolutely Europeanist in its outlook and strongly supports the liberalization of markets and mobility of capital in general.[123]

Fomento defines its mandate broadly. In 1984 its president declared: 'In recent years, acceptance of co-operation between public and private institutions has been a principal objective of Fomento, which defines itself as a civic institution that represents Catalan enterprises in all their aspects, rather than strictly economic ones.'[124] With its claim to speak for the overwhelming majority of Catalan employers, Fomento has been well placed to exercise such influence.

A separate organization claims to speak on behalf of small and medium-sized Catalan firms: Petita i Mitjana Empresa de Catalunya (PIMEC). This organization, which was created in 1978, also has a confederal structure. It claims to bring together 70 associations from industry, commerce, services, and agriculture, representing about 45,000 businesses.[125]

Reflecting its distinctive base, PIMEC has presented a somewhat different public face for employers than has Fomento. It has tended to be more critical of unions. For their part, the union organizations have preferred to deal only with Fomento. PIMEC also promotes Catalan, which it uses for its news magazine and other publications; Fomento regularly uses Spanish. Unlike Fomento, PIMEC collaborates with the Direcció General de política Lingüística in maintaining a Servei Lingüístic to assist its members in strengthening the use of Catalan in their operations.[126] Arguably, it has a closer relationship with the Generalitat.

In principle, Fomento and PIMEC are competitors, and Fomento has sometimes resented PIMEC's demand for equal representation on business-labour bodies, as have the unions.[127] None the less, in 1998 they entered into negotiations over a merger; they ended without an agreement.

Finally, in 1987 a group of dissidents in Fomento created the SEFES. Expelled from Fomento in 1989, SEFES has challenged openly Fomento's claim to speak for Catalan business, just as it has openly attacked the Generalitat and the union organizations.[128] In the late 1990s it merged with PIMEC to form PIMEC-SEFES.

In the representation of employers' interests, the employers' associations, especially Fomento, have provided stiff competition to the 13 chambers of commerce and shipping boards, and despite a modernization program, the Barcelona Chamber of Commerce has had to reduce its spending dramatically in recent years.[129]

A Restructured Working Class

Until the 1970s, most of Catalonia's work force conformed to the classical working-class model of skilled and semi-skilled workers, along with foremen and other supervisory personnel, working primarily in industry and enjoying stable employment. This structure had been reinforced by the spectacular growth of the 1960s. By 1970, these working-class categories, along with associated administrative personnel, accounted for about 70 per cent of Catalonia's working population.[130]

But the economic and political changes of the 1970s led to major changes in Catalonia's labour force. First, various middle-class categories expanded rapidly. In part, this change had to do with development of the public sector and the hiring of teachers, health professionals, and administrators. But it also sprang from the restructuring of Catalonia's economy and consequent growth in service industries and need for various kinds of technicians. Second, in striking contrast with growth of the new middle class, economic restructuring and technological change increased the ranks of the partially employed with low incomes and no job security.[131]

By 1991 'workers' had slipped from 45.6 per cent of the work force to 29.7 per cent, 'technicians' had grown from 6.21 to 26.8 per cent, and 'clerical staff' had grown from 16.01 to 21 per cent.[132] On the other hand, the 1970s saw a radical increase in unemployment resulting from the elimination of jobs. Unemployment in Catalonia and Spain remains markedly higher than elsewhere in Europe, at around 12 per cent, and participation in the work force is substantially lower.[133] According to one analyst, these trends could condemn a considerable part of the population to 'silent marginalization'.[134]

Representing Workers

Though Catalonia's labour force may have become much more complex and diverse, the main instruments for expression of economic and social interests remain two union organizations—Comissió Obrera Nacional de Catalunya (CONC) and Unió General de Treballadors (UGT). The larger of the two, the CONC, was created in 1976 out of the Comissións Obreres that were based in Catalonia. During the last years of the Franco regime, these Comissións had emerged throughout Spain as the major labour force, in close association with the Communist party. The UGT traces its history back to 1888, when it was founded under socialist leadership. It was suppressed by the Franco regime but re-emerged during the 1970s with the support of socialists in Catalonia and elsewhere in Spain. A far less significant role is played by a third union organization, Unión Sindical Obrera (USO), which was founded in 1959. USO enjoyed the support of progressive Catholics and some Catalan socialists in the 1970s but was subsequently undermined by defections to the UGT and by internal factionalism.[135]

In the election of workers' representatives held in Catalonia in 1978, the CONC triumphed over the UGT, 42.31 to 17.33 per cent. Though the UGT improved its position in subsequent elections the CONC has kept its lead, winning 43.4 per cent in 1994–5 to the UGT's 35.5 per cent. The USO had only 2.97 per cent in 1978 and 5.27 per cent in 1994–5.[136]

As in the rest of Spain, membership in unions is low. In 1994, only 12.5 per cent of wage-earners were union members; in Spain as a whole the figure was 17.20 per cent. With unemployed workers excluded, Catalonia's figure rose to 14.12 per cent, but Spain's rose to 20.71 per cent.[137] Moreover, Catalonia's share of all unionized workers in Spain has decreased substantially over the years, owing to the greater intensity of economic restructuring in Catalonia. On the other hand, union membership in Catalonia is higher now than it was in the 1980s. Moreover, in specific economic sectors membership is above average, although not constituting a majority.[138] In any event, under Spanish labour law, union strength is substantially greater than the membership figure would suggest.

Unlike the two other historic nations, Catalonia has been inhospitable to distinctly 'nationalist' unions that do not belong to Spanish nation-wide organizations. In Galicia, nationalist unions grew steadily during the 1980s and 1990s. In the Basque Country, the nationalist ELA is close to being the predominant union, and a second nationalist union, LAB, has significant strength.[139] Yet, several attempts to establish nationalist unions in Catalonia, from the transition onward, have been unsuccessful.

Two factors seem to be at play. First, in Catalonia these initiatives lacked the party support needed for success. At the time of the transition, the nationalist leadership in Catalonia was exercised by the CiU, which had little affinity with unionism and whose working class members, to the extent they existed, were found in small and medium-sized enterprises rather than the large plants more propitious to union organizing. The PSC and PSUC represented a somewhat nationalist point of view but were linked to the two Spanish-nation-wide organizations themselves.[140] Subsequently, the CiU has found itself obliged, as the government party, to come to terms with the existing unions. Beyond that, there is the predominance within the Catalan working class of immigrants and their descendants who would see little reason for an independent Catalan union.

As for the CONC and the UGT, the former has always tried more than the latter to take nationalist positions while at the same time affirming its solidarity with workers elsewhere in Spain. In recent years, however, the UGT has joined the CONC in becoming more outspoken in support of Catalonia's autonomy within Spain. Both unions have supported the creation of a distinctly Catalan labour relations system, which Fomento has opposed, and expansion of the powers of the Generalitat.[141]

The conventional mechanisms of class representation, which had been suppressed during the Franco era, have now been effectively re-established, with all their inherent limitations. This aspect of national reconstruction has been achieved, however ambivalent these organizations may be about the national question.

Moreover, not only the employers' associations but the CONC and UGT have been willing to work with the Generalitat in addressing some of the structural problems of the Catalan economy. Yet, the affect of any such initiatives is necessarily constrained by the limits of the Generalitat's own powers and resources.

The Generalitat and Catalonia's Political Economy

Under Catalonia's statute of autonomy, the Generalitat's economic responsibilities are limited. Beyond matters of local infrastructure, it has responsibility for industry, but only without prejudice to any Spanish laws, and it can supervise credit unions and savings banks and consumer protection as well as agriculture, within the framework of economic planning and monetary policy set by the Spanish state. In addition, the Generalitat can implement state plans for industrial restructuring.[142]

The Generalitat has made important gains with respect to social policy, but in Catalonia, as in the rest of Spain, primary responsibility for industrial and labour policy lies with the central state.[143] This is faithfully reflected in the pattern of the Generalitat's spending. In 1996, only 1.2 per cent of its budget went to 'industry, commerce, and tourism' and only 0.3 per cent to 'economy and finances'.[144]

Without an independent taxing power, the Generalitat is not in a position to encourage new investment through tax concessions, nor does it have the resources for large direct subsidies to industry. In any event, it is subject to the Spanish and European limits on such subsidies.[145] However, it has made some capital available to Catalan enterprises through the Institut Català de Finances.

The Institut's credibility was somewhat damaged during the mid-1990s by a financial scandal,[146] but it has been expanding its activities in recent years, going from 92 loans and loan guarantees, amounting to 12,845 million pesetas, in 1996 to 156 loans and guarantees, for 21.176 million pesetas, in 1998.[147] The Generalitat has also fostered the creation of technology-transfer design centres, which operate at arm's length from the government and are self-supporting.[148]

Infrastructure Development
The Generalitat can attempt to stimulate and guide economic activity through its responsibilities for local infrastructure and transportation. Recently it has achieved full jurisdiction over management of the Port of Barcelona, though the Spanish state continues to be the landowner and to provide the port's budget.[149]

Under the Generalitat's management, a World Trade Centre has been built at the port to house leading hi-tech and logistics firms. Thanks to additional terminals, Barcelona has become the main Mediterranean port for cruise traffic.[150] At the same time, facilities for freight have been improved and expanded, with total traffic exceeding 25 million tonnes in 1997.[151] Indeed, the Port Authority has produced an ambitious plan to establish Barcelona as the primary site for the movement of goods into and out of southern Europe, through the expansion of wharf and container facilities.[152] The plan also calls for improved rail connections with Europe. Construction is well under way to make Barcelona the terminus of a high-speed freight and passenger train by 2003.

As manager of the port, the Generalitat is closely involved in the Delta Plan project, which, at $2 billion (US), is the most important undertaking since the 1992 Olympic Games. The plan is designed to enable the port to double in size over 10 years. Connections with an expanded Barcelona airport, the railways, and highways will create the largest logistic platform in southern Europe. The intention is to secure financing, in almost equal parts, from the port, from the Spanish state, and from the private sector through land leases. Some help from the European Union is also expected.[153]

Tripartism
The Generalitat has also become increasingly involved in co-operative arrangements with business and labour. This tripartite collaboration grew out of ventures that the employers' associations and unions mounted themselves, with the Generalitat's close support. These initiatives are evidence of the generally good relations between labour and business in Catalonia.[154]

In 1992 a labour relations tribunal was set up by the CONC, the UGT, and the Fomento del Treball Nacional (but not PIMEC). Through this body, which has the clear support of both Fomento and the unions, labour disputes are settled without recourse to the courts, and thus at considerably less cost.[155]

In 1993 Fomento, the CONC, and the UGT agreed to adopt an industrial development strategy. Noting the decline in the relative importance of industry in

Catalonia's economy, along with an influx of foreign capital, the agreement recognized that Catalonia was running the risk of a 'deindustrialization' that would compromise its economic development. It set out a wide range of objectives, such as improvements in quality and productivity, increased technological transfers, rationalization, and collaboration among companies. Beyond pursuing these objectives themselves, the parties to the agreement were to propose appropriate policies to the public authorities.[156]

Four years later, the Generalitat formalized its function of guiding economic development through the creation of a Consell de Treball, Econòmic i Social de Catalunya,[157] which has 12 members each named by the unions, the employers, the Generalitat, and other economic sectors. The council advises about projected Generalitat measures, reports on Catalonia's socio-economic conditions, conducts studies, and so on.

Subsequently, the Generalitat joined the employers' associations, both Fomento de Treball and PIMEC, and the two union federations, the UGT and Comissións Obreres, in a new tripartite job-creation strategy.[158] Thanks to concessions by the Aznar regime, the Generalitat now has more authority for implementing employment policies. In addition, new resources are available through the European Union under agreements reached at Luxembourg in November 1997.

The strategy has several components—all of which afford a central role to the Generalitat. Promising new areas of work and employment are to be identified and job-creation projects within them are to be funded through Generalitat grants. The Institut Català de Finances is to receive a special line of credit of 25,000 million pesetas to fund job creation among Catalan small and medium-sized enterprises. The Generalitat is to initiate negotiations with businesses and workers to reorganize and reduce work time so as to free up new work opportunities. Failing an agreement, the Generalitat is to submit a draft decree to the Consell de Treball Econòmic i Social. The Generalitat is to draw upon a variety of European Union programs for grants to help at least 86,000 individuals find work or obtain training or retraining. A tripartite Consell Català de Formació Professional is to be established and charged with producing a Pla General de Formació a Catalunya. A new Observatori del Mercat de Treball is to collect job market data. A tripartite Comissió de Catalunya de control i seguiment de la contractació is to monitor labour contracts. Another tripartite body is to be created to co-ordinate public employment services. Overall, projected Generalitat spending under the program was 74,479 million pesetas for 1998 and 99,802 million pesetas in 1999–2000.[159]

Those various agreements and joint bodies represent an increasingly formal collaboration between the Generalitat on the one hand and business and labour on the other—largely on the initiative of the latter. This collaboration, which goes beyond industrial relations, now entails a comprehensive effort to stimulate and guide Catalonia's economy. Despite the fact that, with the exception of PIMEC, the major actors are themselves closely integrated with Spain-wide organizations, they appear to have taken the lead in creating tripartite structures that are distinctive to Catalonia. At the same time, the job-creation program shows how the European Union's programs may help to offset the Generalitat's limited fiscal resources.

Whether these developments have yet reached the stage of full-fledged tripartite 'corporatism' is perhaps debatable,[160] and in any case their importance is restricted by the limits to the Generalitat's own responsibilities. It is significant, however, that in Catalonia, business and labour themselves seem to have wanted the Generalitat to assume a greater role in guiding Catalonia's economic development. The obstacle lies not with Catalonia's internal political economy but with its place in the Spanish political order.

The Generalitat has also become active in promoting the Catalan economy internationally, by establishing an international network of offices to promote Catalan exports and encourage foreign investment in Catalonia. Moreover, this operation is viewed with favour by Catalan business leaders,[161] who in fact are directly involved in such ventures as the Patronat Català Pro-Europa.

'Four Motors of Europe'
By the same token, the Generalitat has linked Catalonia with three other European regions in the much-touted 'Four Motors of Europe'. The arrangement was created in 1998 in concert with Baden-Württemberg (in Germany), Rhône-Alps (in France), and Lombardy (in Italy). Officially, its purposes were to (1) improve infrastructures, especially in telecommunications and communications; (2) promote collaboration in research and technology; (3) represent common interests in economic and scientific activity outside Europe; (4) collaborate in providing aid to development; and (5) collaborate with respect to art and culture.[162] The underlying purpose was to promote the economic development of these four high-technology regions by exchanging knowledge, pooling experience, and stimulating innovation. In the process, it would offset the European Commission's emphasis on areas in economic decline.[163]

The 'Four Motors' has a simple structure. With no bureaucracy of its own, it depends on the four member governments for logistical and technical support. A co-ordinating committee oversees the activities of several working groups and ad hoc groups. In addition, it arranges annual meetings of the four regional presidents, at which a program for the coming year is approved. The working and ad hoc groups themselves are each supported by one of the regional governments.[164] The groups cover a wide range of topics, including education, agriculture, art and culture, social issues, and youth and sport. Most projects involve the exchange of information among experts and policy makers in a given area or the preparation of common submissions to the European Union, whether for policy changes or for funding under EU grant programs.[165] Despite the original concern of the Four Motors with high-technology industry, most of the projects lie elsewhere. In 1997–8 one committee dealt with the economy and another with telecommunication;

others ranged over such topics as agriculture, the environment, youth and sport, society, and crime prevention.[166]

Clearly, the Four Motors arrangement has led to considerable exchange of information and collaboration among regional governments and public institutions.[167] It has also led to the formulation of common positions vis-à-vis the European Union.[168] It is less clear, though, that the Four Motors has made progress in its initial purpose of promoting knowledge-intensive industries.[169] Indeed, it has proved difficult to establish networks among R&D institutions and private and semi-private organizations in the four regions.[170] More generally, it is difficult to demonstrate that the arrangement has had a direct effect on levels of trade and inter-regional economic links. Conceivably, the mere existence of the agreement has led entrepreneurs in one region who are seeking new opportunities to look to the other regions, although there is no clear-cut empirical evidence to that effect. Otherwise, the economic payoff of the Four Motors will be the long-term benefits of information sharing.

Paralleling the Generalitat's Four Motors project, indeed competing with it, is Barcelona's leadership of a network of six Spanish and French regional capitals known as C-6. Its objective is to promote a multi-city Mediterranean region through the spread of public and private innovation.[171]

Conclusion

Recent decades have seen a transformation of Catalonia's economy. The shift from the traditional reliance on textiles to new industries and the service sector has in fact been part of a larger process of internationalization or, more precisely, Europeanization. Catalonia's trade with other parts of Europe has grown; European (and Japanese) capital now owns many of its leading enterprises.

Catalonia within Europe

This Europeanization of Catalonia's economy is, of course, in keeping with Catalonia's historical tendency to link itself with the rest of Europe, not just economically but culturally and intellectually as well. From the outset, the Generalitat favoured integration with Europe, creating the Patronat Català Pro-Europa in 1982 to prepare the ground for Spain's entry into the European Community. By the same token, surveys regularly show that Catalans are more strongly oriented to Europe than are other Spaniards. A 1996 survey found that among all Spanish autonomous communities, residents of Catalonia (and the Balearic Islands) were the most positive in their attitude toward Europe. Forty-four per cent said that they were 'enthusiastic' about Europe, the highest of all ACs. Catalans also had the highest level of confidence in the European Union's institutions.[172]

None the less the results of this economic Europeanization have been uneven. Catalonia's trade balance with the rest of Europe has been chronically negative; only recently has it begun to post surpluses. Important parts of the Catalan economy remain weakly competitive. In short, there are heavy qualifications to the popular image of Catalonia as a dynamic region standing at the forefront of the new Europe.[173]

To be sure, European economic integration has given Catalonia access to the European Union's Cohesion Funds; between 1994 and 1999 Catalonia received a yearly average of 115 MPTA.[174] But it does not qualify for the most important form of EU support ('objective one'), since its per capita GDP exceeds 75 per cent of the EU average. Nor does it draw much benefit from the EU's agricultural programs. As a result, Catalonia's overall fiscal balance with the EU has been negative. This deficit represented 30,000 MPTA in 1995; for the same year Spain as a whole had a positive balance of between 1 and 1.2 billion pesetas.[175] In countries that are poorer than Spain, such as Greece and Portugal, the relatively wealthy regions fare much better from EU spending.[176]

Beyond that, in most other EU countries, the regions with the same per capita income as Catalonia are not among the wealthiest, and therefore they tend to gain rather than lose in fiscal flows with the central states to which they belong. The regions that do lose in fiscal exchanges and are the wealthiest regions of their respective countries tend to be far wealthier than Catalonia, with about 130 per cent of the European Union mean per capita income as opposed to Catalonia's 93 per cent.[177] Catalonia continues to enjoy strong trade surpluses with the rest of Spain, but they are outweighed by substantially greater deficits in its fiscal exchanges with Spain.[178]

The fact remains that, within the new Europe, Catalonia is not among the more advantaged regions. Its per capita GDP falls slightly below the regional average for Europe as a whole; in fact, it has the lowest per capita GDP among the Four Motors of Europe. Only in Spanish terms is it a prosperous region.

It can be argued that Catalonia has the worst of two worlds by being a wealthy region in a poor country.[179] It lacks the strong commercial balances and high levels of affluence that are enjoyed by the wealthier regions of relatively rich countries, but it suffers from a fiscal deficit with its own central state and is ineligible for much of the EU funding provided to regions in poorer countries. 'Rich in Spain and not sufficiently poor in Europe, Catalonia finds itself in a unique situation.'[180]

Despite the official pronouncements, Europeanization has been as much a challenge as a boon for the Catalan economy. Given the persisting structural weaknesses of its economy, Catalonia has had difficulty profiting from the new trade opportunities. Nor has it received the financial support from the EU that its middle-level status in terms of affluence would warrant.

At the same time, Europeanization (or globalization) has, by definition, meant a loss in the control that Catalan institutions exercise over the Catalan economy. Multinational capital has virtually replaced Catalonia's historically powerful bourgeoisie. The Barcelona stock exchange continues its decline in comparison with Madrid's. Catalan financial institutions remain weak. Nor has this decline in Catalonia's economic institutions been offset by any emergence of the Generalitat as a major economic actor in its own right.

The Economic Role of the Generalitat

Within the terms of the constitution and the political order that has emerged from it, the Generalitat's economic functions are closely circumscribed by the Spanish state. Dealings beyond Spain, both with other regions and with the European Union, have provided some new opportunities for the Generalitat to exchange information and, in the case of the EU Cohesion Fund, even to secure some funding. But the Generalitat has little ability to shape the structure and development of the Catalan economy.

The Generalitat can act as broker or facilitator, bringing private interests together for a project and supporting it through public expenditures (drawing upon its own funds as well as the Spanish state's). The 1992 Olympic Games, in which the city of Barcelona played the lead role, was the most dramatic instance of this. The current Delta plan for expansion of the Barcelona port is another. In addition, we have seen how the Generalitat has entered into formal tripartism, as with its new job-creation strategy that is financed, in part, through the EU Cohesion Fund. But this initiative remains quite limited in scope.

It might be argued that the limitations on the Generalitat's economic role are immaterial. After all, historically Catalonia never has been able to harness state resources on behalf of its economic interests. In the past, they were monopolized by the Spanish state, which was usually indifferent or even hostile to Catalonia's economic interests. Yet, this did not prevent Catalonia from being one of Spain's economic leaders. Indeed, Catalonia enjoyed one of its greatest booms under the Franco regime, which was the most hostile government of all. In the past, however, Catalonia had a strong bourgeoisie to provide economic leadership; that is no longer the case. In fact, the bourgeoisie was itself a victim of the internationalization upon which the Franco-era boom was based.

Catalonia as a 'Region State'

In some analyses, any comparison between Catalonia's overall ties with Spain and those with the rest of Europe obscures what has been most beneficial in recent years, namely, Catalonia's emerging links to specific *regions* (as opposed to countries) outside Spain. It is argued that such links are giving rise to a new phenomenon, found not only in Europe but in Asia and the Americas as well—the 'region state', which ranges far beyond the national economy in its search for economic partners.

Indeed, Catalonia is sometimes viewed as the quintessential region state,[181] having all the characteristics posited by Kenichi Ohmae, one of the leading theoreticians of the concept. To be 'an effective port of entry to the global economy', a region must have a population of between 5 and 20 million, a strong orientation toward the global economy, and the infrastructure necessary to participate in the global economy, including communications, professional services, and transportation. Among other things Catalonia has the international airport and the 'one good harbour with international-class freight-handling facilities' that are required.[182]

Still, despite all the attention to Catalonia as a rising region state, it is difficult to come by precise estimates of the economic significance of these new links, let alone their effect on the Catalan economy. The evidence tends to be anecdotal rather than systematic.[183]

What is clear is that the Generalitat has made a sustained effort to promote such regional economic links by establishing links of its own with regional governments elsewhere in Europe. Here too though, it is difficult to prove that these efforts have had economic effects. Even the Four Motors arrangement has spawned relatively few specifically economic projects. There may still be economic benefits from inter-regional projects in other domains, but they will be felt over the long term.

Within some contemporary notions of the new region state, state structures have in any event a secondary importance. With new technologies and means of communication, private economic actors are now able to roam Europe and beyond in search of partners for creative collaboration. They do not need regional governments to act on their behalf. At most, they need regional governments that will play the kind of broker role or facilitator that the Generalitat, along with the city of Barcelona, has already been doing with such success.

Yet, however powerful and synergetic may be the trans-regional links that the private economic actors of a region are now free to forge with their counterparts elsewhere, does it necessarily follow that the region's governmental structures will remain of minor significance? To put it differently, does not the region state need a state?[184]

In the case of Catalonia, the Generalitat has already been drawn into initiatives that go beyond simply facilitating trans-regional links for the private sector. It has established a comprehensive tripartite strategy to create jobs. It has become concerned with ensuring that the local population has the skills and resources necessary to support the trans-regional projects and to benefit from them. Beyond that, pressures for an enhanced economic role for the Generalitat may arise from the continuing structural weaknesses of Catalonia's economy—low research and development, weak financial institutions, and limited international competitiveness of Catalan enterprises. The question remains as to how firmly the CiU's 'bourgeois regionalism' will be able to withstand such pressures.[185]

Chapter 6

Society: The Challenges of 'National Reconstruction'

During the 1970s, Catalans often used the term 'national reconstruction' to describe the struggle upon which they were embarked. But 'national reconstruction' stood for many processes. Clearly, it meant establishing, or re-establishing, the complex of social institutions needed to support Catalanism and Catalan culture. But, as in any society, it also meant finding the formulas and mechanisms for maintaining cohesion among the classes, social groups, and other entities that make up Catalan society. Moreover, 'national reconstruction' could not mean simply restoring or recovering a kind of society that has existed in the past or was imagined to have existed. Just like Catalonia's political economy, its society had already undergone fundamental changes well before the Franco regime came to an end.

In part, Catalonia had been influenced by the cultural and social liberalization that had affected most of Western Europe. In the 1960s, membership in Catalonia's religious orders began to decline rapidly. Even if this decline was triggered initially by changes and debates that marked the Catholic Church as a whole, it was considerably steeper in Catalonia than elsewhere in Spain. Moreover, it continued unabated after the transition, resulting in the near eclipse of the Church.[1]

Social change had also stemmed from the reorganization of Catalonia's political economy. In particular, the virtual disappearance of the Catalan bourgeoisie meant the loss of what had become a crucial underpinning of Catalan civil society. And both the emergence of a new middle class and the growth in non-established workers had major consequences for the organization of Catalan society.

Finally, the 1950s and 1960s marked the high point of an enormous influx of immigrants, primarily from the south of Spain. As a result, Catalan society was far more complex than it had been before, with close to half its members recent immigrants or their descendants.

Because of these changes, the 'national reconstruction' that began with the late 1970s could not mean simply recovering the society that had existed before the Franco regime. In terms of both class structure and demography, that society was no longer available.

The Importance of the Generalitat

Throughout most of its recent history Catalonia had lacked autonomous political institutions and had instead relied upon civil society to ensure its persistence and development as a culturally distinct entity. Catalan nationalists have often taken pride in this civil society. Jordi Pujol himself declared in 1986: 'Catalunya is a nation without a state. We belong to the Spanish state, but we do not have secessionist ambitions. This must be clearly affirmed. . . . The case of Catalunya is peculiar: we have our own language, and culture; we are a nation without a state.'[2]

Still, as Catalan élites went about seeking to build civil society and social cohesion under the changed circumstances of the late 1970s, they were bound to give a central role to the Generalitat. Not only was it an important new institution, but the Catalan bourgeoisie, which had played such a crucial role in supporting civil society, no longer existed. Moreover, even if the bourgeoisie still had existed, the kind of private institutions it supported would probably have been insufficient to meet the challenge of integrating such an enormous number of immigrants. Nor could they be as effective as the modern welfare state in mitigating the effects of social and economic inequality, especially during a period of economic restructuring such as Catalonia was experiencing. Still, if the Generalitat was front and centre in the process of national reconstruction, its political autonomy and fiscal resources were decidedly limited.

Building Social Institutions

Given the central role of culture in defining the Catalan national identity, any project of national reconstruction was bound to focus on the institutional structure that would support Catalan culture, defined in the broadest of terms: civil society, cultural industries, mass media, and education. In each case, the Generalitat and other Catalan public authorities have been led to assume leading roles. But even with their reinforcement over recent decades, Catalonia's public institutions often lack the capacity and resources needed to meet fully the new responsibilities that have been thrust upon them.

Civil Society

A belief in the ideals of civil society has long been seen as a central trait of Catalonia's culture. Centred on the ideal of citizens participating fully in public affairs, the Catalan notion of civil society in particular has stressed the importance of networks of associations that provide opportunities for participation and of citizens who believe in a civic obligation to participate and who share a commitment to solidarity and mutual support.[3]

Historically, Catalonia has prided itself on having an exceptionally rich network of private institutions of civil society and a strong tradition of citizen participation. It can be agreed that a strong civil society has been the secret to Catalonia's survival as a culture and society, in the face of regularly hostile public authorities. It could persist as 'a nation without a state'.

By the time of the transition, Catalan civil society had been weakened in important respects, especially by the Franco regime. For instance, having no sympathy for the quite elaborate system of agricultural and consumers' co-operatives that had been built up, the Franco regime confiscated more than 200 co-operatives and severely regulated those that remained. And philanthropic foundations ceased to grow in the way that they had for several decades before the Civil War. Many foundations and other social institutions were still able to take a crucial part in the struggle to maintain Catalanism and Catalan culture, but often they could not act as openly and as effectively as in the past. And inevitably, the fading away of the Catalan bourgeoisie deprived Catalan civil society of a central source of support.

Still, many of the institutions of civil society were stronger in Catalonia than elsewhere in Spain. And if Catalan civil society was not as healthy as it had been decades before, the public sector was in far worse shape. Not only had authority always been centralized in Madrid, but public spending was disproportionately low in Spain. Catalonia's new Generalitat had no choice but to work in close co-operation with private institutions. National reconstruction had to involve both. As a result, the 1980s saw growth not only in the public sector but in civil society as well.[4]

This is clearly demonstrated by the case of foundations, which grew in number in Catalonia from 253 in 1983 to 882 in 1995. Growth was especially strong among cultural foundations, going from 54 to 453.[5] In present-day Catalonia, public and private institutions share many functions. In the case of social services, not-for-profit private institutions are more important than public agencies in the provision of services for the handicapped, the treatment of drug addiction, and support for victims of AIDS.[6] And among hospitals, the number of beds is split almost equally between public and private institutions, with not-for-profit organizations predominating among the latter.[7]

None the less, if Catalonia's foundations have maintained and even increased their importance, they have become linked to public authorities in a way they never were before. Ostensibly private institutions are becoming increasingly dependent on public funding, and at a very rapid rate. The Generalitat's data show that within merely three years, between 1990 and 1993, the level of self-financing among Catalan philanthropic foundations fell dramatically from 62.3 to 43.7 per cent. The change occurred primarily among foundations devoted to social services: the Generalitat provided 69 per cent of funding in 1993 (as opposed to 48.4 per cent in 1990). At the same time, however, 80.7 per cent of cultural foundations were able to remain self-financing.[8]

As well as foundations, Catalonia's civil society historically has featured a significant co-operative movement. It too benefited from the transition to democracy; indeed, the Generalitat has taken a special interest in co-operatives, creating several organizations to assist them and providing grants to a good many of them.[9]

At the same time, the Catalan co-operative movement has changed radically. Whereas its historical base was in agrarian and consumers' co-operatives, the movement is now concentrated primarily in worker-run enterprises. By and large, these businesses have been created by workers trying to preserve their jobs in the face of cut-backs and restructuring, and struggling to keep the enterprises economically viable. In the process, the anarchist-syndicalist and socialist principles that originally guided Catalan co-operatism are being challenged by more pragmatic concerns.[10]

Another feature of Catalan civil society has been mutual benefit societies. One form has been societies that deal with workplace accidents and illnesses. Linked to individual companies and responsible for the administration of funds collected under the Spanish government's social security system, they cover 83 per cent of Catalan workers covered under social security, compared to 74 per cent in Spain. A second form of mutual benefit society provides social security itself. In Catalonia, they emerged during the nineteenth century in close association with the union movement and were devoted to workers' solidarity and the reduction of social and economic inequality. While the Catalan Generalitat of the 1930s designed a social security system that would allow these organizations to persist, the Franco regime imposed a public system that effectively reduced them to providing services to liberal professionals, as well as, unlike the rest of Spain, providing private health care. In the post-Franco years, these societies have not regained their working-class clientele and, in the case of health care, have been increasingly displaced by for-profit firms. Despite their origins, the present-day societies have had to focus on areas of market demand.[11]

In Catalonia the notion of civil society has also involved civic associations, special-interest groups, and social movements, which, not surprisingly, have flourished in post-Franco Catalonia. The transition to democracy, combined with a general rise in membership in associations throughout Europe, resulted in a rapid increase in the number of new associations being formed in Catalonia. A yearly average of 1,135 new associations were created between 1977 and 1994, compared with an average of only 198 for the period 1969–76.[12]

With the transition, the type of associations evolved from neighbourhood groups and school parents' associations to new social movements concerned with ecology, feminism, youth, sexual orientation, and physical handicaps.[13] Whereas class has faded as the basis on which associations are formed, nationalism has maintained its central importance.

Nevertheless, the associational life of Catalonia's civil society is no longer as exceptional as it once was. One study found that in 1990 membership in associations and involvement in volunteer work were in fact lower in Catalonia than in the rest of Spain.[14] This may overstate the situation, for other studies have produced higher results for Catalonia, but there is no other comparative study against which this result can be tested. Catalonia may still be stronger in the more modern forms of association.[15]

A similar conclusion emerges when a comparison is made between Barcelona and Madrid (as represented by the Autonomous Community of Madrid). Historically, Madrid civil society had been weaker, owing to its essentially governmental and political base. However, thanks in part to the deliberate efforts of the Franco regime, Madrid has become an economic centre in its own right. Indeed, it is the primary Spanish site of head offices and thus affords ready access to corporate support for foundations and associations. As a result, by some measures civil society is stronger in Madrid than in Barcelona.[16]

Catalan civil society has been generally strengthened with the transition to democracy, precisely as one would expect. Private foundations, associations, and social movements have proliferated. But other types of organization, with working-class roots, such as the co-operative movement and social security societies, have not really recovered from the Franco years. And crucial elements of Catalan civil society that have flourished are for the first time closely linked to public authority. To be sure, this is a formally autonomous Catalan authority—the Generalitat. The same pattern can be seen with cultural institutions.

Cultural Institutions and Industries

The Franco years were especially difficult for newer forms of cultural activity, such as filmmaking, that, unlike music and theatre, did not have established institutions. But even the latter could no longer look to a dynamic Catalan bourgeoisie for support, as it had in the past.

Of course, many creators and artists were suspicious of assistance from the new Generalitat and other Catalan public authorities, and once the common cause of resistance to the Franco regime had ended, they became much more concerned with their individual creative freedom.[17] Political leaders, though, were often only too keen to enlist them in new national struggles. And, especially with inroads of American culture and globalization, the need for public support was inescapable. In the end, most cultural activities have come to depend in one fashion or another on support from the Generalitat and local Catalan authorities. Here too Catalan society has lost its former autonomy.

Upon assuming control of the Generalitat in 1980, the CiU was quick to establish a department of culture, under Max Cahner. But local governments also became involved. Thus, in 1986 the combined cultural spending of the Ajuntament de Barcelona and the Diputació de Barcelona (the Barcelona local government) equalled that of the Generalitat.[18] Cahner's successor, Joan Rigol, tried to arrange for co-ordination among these governments but with little success, given their links to different parties. With time, however, the Generalitat's spending on culture outdistanced by far that of local governments, rising to 29,793,000 pesetas by

1996. (To be sure, this represented only 1.8 per cent of the Generalitat's total spending.)[19]

Despite this new public support, the fate of different forms of Catalan culture has varied greatly. In part, this has to do with how well they had survived under the Franco regime and thus whether they were in a position to take advantage of the new opportunities. The Franco regime had tolerated only cultural forms that had small audiences, especially 'high' culture or ones that were more or less folkloric.[20] But the present-day strength of different cultural forms also has to do with the willingness of the Catalan business class to support culture, as well as the impact of multinational corporations, especially American, that have profoundly affected cultural industries throughout Europe.

Catalan-language book publishing had already made some recovery during the latter years of the Franco regime. During the 1960s and early 1970s, Catalan nationalists were able to create, through exclusively private institutions, the beginnings of an infrastructure for restoring the Catalan language. Established in 1961 with funds from Catalan businessmen, Òmnium cultural, which promoted Catalan language and culture, was closed by the Franco regime in 1963 but was allowed to become active once again in 1967. Over the subsequent years, Òmnium cultural created a network of classes in Catalan, subsidized Catalan publications, supported Catalan cultural institutions, and established literary prizes, including, in 1969, the annual Premi de les Lletres Catalanes.[21] By 1967, the annual production of books in Catalan had reached 650.[22] In 1969, the first of what were to be 15 volumes of the *Gran Enciclopèdia Catalana* was published.

Soon after the transition, the Generalitat made support of book publishing an important priority. In 1982, the new department of culture established a policy of buying 300 copies of every book published in Catalan and distributing them to libraries and other institutions.[23] Spending under the program grew from 21 million pesetas in 1982 to 138.3 million in 1986.[24] By 1993, the Departament de Cultura subsidies of Catalan books had reached 662.4 million pesetas.[25]

The Generalitat's efforts served to reinforce a surge in Catalan publishing that was already underway. Thus, the number of titles in Catalan rose from 1,201 in 1978 to 2,175 in 1982 and 4,145 in 1987.[26] In the early 1990s, owing in part to the economic crisis, the growth levelled off: in 1993, the figure was 4,863.[27]

Still, despite this progress, Catalan remains secondary to Castilian as the language of publishing, even in Catalonia. Although Barcelona has a thriving publishing industry whose yearly production approximates that of Madrid, most of these books are published in Castilian.[28] In 1993, Catalan titles represented only 29.9 per cent of all books published in Catalonia,[29] and Catalan-language books represent only 10 per cent of total invoicing by publishers based in Catalonia.[30]

As for Catalan music, there has been a flourishing in public performances. A popular form of Catalan music, la Nova Cançó, had already achieved prominence in the 1960s. Resolutely Catalan and with strong overtones of resistencialisme, it incorporated influences from current international folk and counter-culture music.

Public performance of la Nova Cançó attracted large audiences in Catalonia and helped to raise national consciousness on a large scale.[31] It even enjoyed some international recognition. Rock català, which emerged in the late 1980s, was sung in Catalan, thus affirming the national identity. Public performances have been popular, although sales of recordings have rarely exceeded 20,000 copies.[32]

Classical music, including Catalan music, is performed regularly at major venues, including two ornate legacies of the Barcelona bourgeoisie: the concert hall el Palau de la Música Catalana and the famous opera house, el Gran Teatre del Liceu. It was a sign of the changed times that when the Liceu was destroyed by fire in 1994, it was rebuilt by the Generalitat rather than the private sector. In the process, the Generalitat assumed ownership. Indeed, most of the Generalitat's funding for music is concentrated on a few prominent opera houses and concert halls.[33]

Theatre and dance companies have also enjoyed public popularity; however, almost all are dependent on public support (sometimes in excess of 50 per cent).[34]

On the other hand, the recording industry did not fare well. At one time Barcelona was an important centre of Spanish recording, but by the 1980s it had lost out to Madrid, where not only Spanish companies but also multinationals have concentrated their operations.[35] Catalan music is a very small part of record sales in Catalonia.[36]

Similarly, film production has not recovered from the Franco era. Despite its promising beginnings, the Catalan film industry was reduced during the Franco years to producing no more than 12 full-length films. In the process, many of Barcelona's studios closed.[37] As a result, lacking a solid tradition and fragmented among undercapitalized enterprises, the industry has remained marginal, producing no more than 20 films a year since the mid-1980s. Nor does it help that film distribution in Spain is dominated by North American companies.[38]

For its part, the Generalitat's department of culture has heavily subsidized the production of full-length and short films, along with television series, spending 588 million pesetas for this purpose in 1993. But the fact remains that of almost 20 million visits to Catalunya's cinemas in 1993, only 1.1 per cent were to films in Catalan.[39] As for videos, Catalan productions are largely absent from video outlets.[40]

It is evident that the recovery of Catalonia's cultural industries from the Franco years has been very uneven. Some industries, such as filmmaking, had been too weakened to re-establish themselves readily, even with sustained support from the Generalitat. In addition, all industries face increasingly strong competition from Spanish and especially North American companies. Finally, Catalonia's cultural industries must contend with an inherently limited market since there are few external markets for Catalan-language publications. Nor have attempts to export dubbed films and television programs been very successful, even in the Spanish market. Beyond that, the domestic Catalonia market is limited by the large proportion of residents whose first language is Castilian. Thus, Catalan books remain less than a third of the titles produced by Barcelona's thriving publishing industry.

In confronting all these obstacles the Generalitat does not have available to it the fiscal and legislative resources that small nations with sovereign states have to support cultural industries.[41] And yet the resources it does have are large enough that most of the cultural industries have become strongly dependent on its support. The traditional Catalan bourgeoisie is no longer there to support cultural activity. Though there has been a proliferation of self-financing foundations with cultural objectives,[42] Catalonia's cultural life is now linked to public authority in a way it never was before.

Mass Media

Catalan nationalists have argued, with reason, that the strength of Catalan culture necessarily depends on the presence of the Catalan language and culture in all the various forms of mass communication that impinge upon people's daily lives. This became an important part of the national reconstruction project. Indeed, partly in recognition of this, the study of mass media has long been an especially developed field among Catalan academics.

Here, the Franco regime had afforded few opportunities at all to Catalan language and culture. During those years, radio stations rarely broadcasted in Catalan. When television was introduced to Catalonia, it was through a public Spain-wide network directly controlled by the Spanish government, although some regular programs in Catalan did begin in the 1970s.[43] And there were no daily newspapers in Catalan. Barcelona's leading newspaper, La Vanguardia, belonged to a family of the old Spanish-speaking bourgeoisie, and its editor was appointed by the Franco government.

Under the statute of autonomy, the Generalitat was given the power to regulate radio and television broadcasting, the press, and media in general, albeit within the state's organic laws. More important perhaps, it was given the authority to create its own television and radio, and even newspapers.

Accordingly, the Generalitat went about creating Catalan-only public radio and television facilities. In 1983, the Generalitat's Corporació Catalana de Ràdio i Televisió launched TV3, which operates wholly in Catalan, and joined two state-run television channels broadcasting primarily in Castilian. In addition, in 1989 it established a second Catalan-language television channel, Canal 33.[44] Barcelona also maintains a television station that broadcasts primarily in Catalan, as do several other localities.

The Spanish state's public system had already established its own Catalan-language station, Radio 4, in 1976. In 1984, the Generalitat established Catalunya Ràdio, the first of four FM stations broadcasting in Catalan throughout Catalonia. And most of the 176 municipally owned radio stations in Catalonia also broadcast in Catalan.[45] In 1995 the Barcelona city government was responsible, as primary shareholder, for the creation of a new station, Com-Ràdio.

Yet, for all the efforts of public authorities to provide television and radio in Catalan, few private interests have been prepared to follow suit. Nor have the

Generalitat's regulatory powers had much effect. A small number of privately owned local radio stations broadcast in Catalan, but there is no privately owned television station broadcasting in Catalan.[46]

By the same token, while the Generalitat can make Catalan radio and television available through public facilities, it cannot guarantee that all Catalan speakers will in fact use them. In the case of television, TV3 did capture a large audience. A 1988 study found that 64 per cent of Catalan-born respondents watched the Catalan-language TV3 more than any other channel. Even among immigrants, 63 per cent watched TV3 'very often', though not most of all.[47] In the same year, however, the largest audience overall was captured by TVE1: 66.3 per cent compared with TV3's 43.6 per cent. TVE1 broadcasted a news program in Catalan, but otherwise its programs were all in Castilian; TVE2 has had some programs in Catalan, but it broadcasts predominantly in Spanish. Finally, with the arrival of private TV, three new exclusively Spanish-language channels came to Catalonia. As a result, by 1994 the combined audience of the two Catalan channels (TV3 and Canal 33) had fallen to 27.7 per cent.[48]

Similarly, Castilian is still the predominant language of radio listening in Catalonia. The large Castilian-language radio networks command three times as large an audience in Catalonia as the two main Catalan-language stations.[49]

In the case of newspapers, the Generalitat could not intervene to establish public corporations and was restricted to making subsidies available to private parties willing to publish newspapers in Catalan.

Outside Barcelona the Generalitat's objectives met with considerable success. After Franco's death there was an explosion of Catalan-language newspapers serving specific localities, although usually not every day.[50] Catalan newspapers now predominate in smaller localities, and most of them no longer need Generalitat support. Some, such as Girona's *El Punt*, have become highly profitable and are spreading beyond their original sites. In effect, these papers have formed the basis of a Catalan press for Catalonia as a whole—outside Barcelona.[51]

However, the story has been very different in Barcelona. The Generalitat did make funding available to *Avui*, which remained the single Catalan-language newspaper in Barcelona and which became heavily dependent on Generalitat subsidies.[52] Yet, *Avui*'s circulation remained modest, even among Catalan-speakers. In 1995 *Avui* had a circulation of only 42,184, compared with the combined circulation of about 480,953 of the three main Castilian-language newspapers: *El Periódico, La Vanguardia*, and *El País*.[53] Clearly, the Castilian-language newspapers were drawing a large number of readers whose first language was Catalan; in fact, a study found in 1989 that a full 37 per cent of Catalan-speakers preferred to read in Castilian.[54] Thus, in the case of the Barcelona newspapers, the limits to the Generalitat's ability to support Catalan language and culture seemed even greater than in radio and television.

None the less, in October of 1997 *El Periódico* began production of a daily Catalan-language edition, identical in content to the Castilian edition. Apparently, it received no Generalitat subsidies specifically for this purpose. Early indications were that about half of its readers opted for the Catalan version. To be sure, *El Periodico*'s initiative primarily involves the translation into Catalan of material written in Castilian, relying heavily upon computer programming to do this. Thus, it is very different from *Avui*, which is written entirely in Catalan.

As for magazines, few are in Catalan.[55] Most of the major magazines produced in Barcelona are geared to the Spanish market as a whole and thus are published in Castilian.[56]

The main components of a Catalan-language mass media system are now in place. This has been due largely to the Generalitat's efforts, whether through public television and radio or through subsidies to local and regional newspapers. By and large, major corporate interests, even those based in Catalonia, have not participated, apparently calculating that Castilian-language media are more profitable since they can attract both Catalan- and Castilian-speakers. Whether the creation of a Catalan version of *El Periódico* represents a major shift remains to be seen. In the case of radio and television, it has been shown that even when Catalan-language media are available, there is no guarantee that Catalan-speakers will prefer them over Castilian media.

Education and Research

Formal education was also bound to play a large part in any project to reconstruct the Catalan nation. If the Catalan language and culture are the essential bases of nationhood, then obviously it is crucial that new generations be able to express themselves in them. The task was all the more important given the large proportion of children in post-Franco Catalonia whose first language was Castilian.

Of course, the Franco regime had taken drastic measures to ensure that education in Catalonia would be exclusively Castilian. Not only were the Catalan language and culture prohibited from schools and universities, but teachers suspected of Catalanist sympathies were sent to other parts of Spain and were replaced by teachers from outside Catalonia with no knowledge of Catalan.[57]

Clearly, the new Generalitat was the key to correcting this state of affairs. Under the statute of autonomy, the Generalitat shares jurisdiction over education with the Spanish state. It has full jurisdiction over the *administration* of all aspects of education but must operate within the terms of the state's organic laws. In addition, the Spanish state has authority to set the conditions for academic degrees and professional qualifications.[58]

Within these constraints, however, the Generalitat has *primary* responsibility for education. The next chapter will examine at length how it has attempted to make Catalan the primary language of education; for present purposes, it can simply be noted that the Generalitat has succeeded in making Catalan the essential language of education at the primary level in public schools and the main language at the secondary level. And the use of Catalan in the universities has increased substantially.

The post-Franco years have seen spectacular growth in the number of students in secondary schools and universities. The number of secondary school students rose from 268,233 in 1980–1 to 403,635 in 1993–4; university students rose from 98,703 to 185,459.[59] Indeed, during this decade the number of universities in Catalonia grew from three to ten.[60] In the process, Catalan education has re-established an emphasis on pedagogical innovation that was already evident at the turn of the century in a variety of progressive and experimental schools that were supported by the Catalan bourgeoisie.[61]

However, the Spanish government's powers in education have sometimes conflicted with the Generalitat's plans, as in the attempts by the Aznar government to define the curriculum of schools so as to require proper treatment of Spanish history and literature.

The Generalitat's role in primary and secondary education is further limited by the large number of Catalan students who attend private schools—43 per cent in 1993–4. While these students are predominantly in Church institutions, in Barcelona province, they are split equally between clerical and secular schools.[62] In fact, this sector is stronger in Catalonia than in the rest of Spain. For instance in 1994–5, 46.2 per cent of Catalonia's primary students were in private schools, as opposed to 34.6 per cent in Spain. While relatively small at the university level, the private sector is growing. At the same time, most of these private institutions are dependent upon grants from the Generalitat.[63]

As one might expect, the use of Catalan is not as great in private schools as in public schools. Thus, among primary schools (for students 3–14 years of age) in Catalonia in 1995–6 Catalan was used exclusively in 73 per cent of public schools but in only 58 per cent of private schools. Indeed, 4 per cent of private schools used Castilian exclusively.[64]

The Generalitat has also tried to support research. In 1980 it established an interdepartmental commission to co-ordinate this support. But though it has exclusive responsibility for research under the statute of autonomy, once again it must function within the constraints of the Spanish state, which has responsibility for the general co-ordination of scientific and technical research. Thus, the state maintains a Spain-wide network of research centres under its Consejo Superior de Investigaciones Científicas and directs research at the university level throughout Spain. About half of the public spending on research in Catalonia comes from Madrid, rather than the Generalitat.[65]

Traditionally, Catalonia did not have centres or networks of scientific research. To remedy this, the Generalitat has pursued three objectives: training researchers, strengthening public research structures, and linking the public and private sectors. It has also produced two research plans, one for 1993–6 and one for 1997–2000.

Since 1980, research in Catalonia has increased sixfold; indeed, it is now at the highest level of all autonomous communities and makes up one-third of all scientific research in Spain.[66]

But for all this progress, scientific research remains precarious. It tends to be heavily weighted toward biomedicine and pharmaceuticals, and there is little basic research. Catalan-owned enterprises have shown little interest in research; this is a major focus of the Generalitat's second research plan.[67] Beyond that, Catalonia's research activity is unable to absorb the numbers of qualified professionals emerging from its universities, who are obliged to look elsewhere for work.[68]

The processes of national reconstruction have created or strengthened a variety of social institutions that support Catalan culture and Catalanism. The range of such institutions is far greater than ever before. But some major weaknesses remain, and, given Catalonia's small population and exposure to international influences, they are likely to remain. Some pre-Franco institutions have never recovered, and most of the institutions that now figure prominently have acquired a close relationship with the Generalitat, if not dependence upon it, whether they are in the media, production and dissemination of culture, education, or even civil society. To that extent, the character of Catalan society has changed fundamentally.

Social Cohesion

Beyond restoring or creating the institutional framework of Catalan society, national reconstruction also meant addressing differences within Catalan society, if only to ensure a minimal cohesion. The traditional divisions of class and wealth have had to be addressed, and the enormous challenge of integrating Castilian-speakers, as well as dealing with the implications of gender and generation, has had to be undertaken. In each case, the new institutions of the Generalitat were to take the leading role.

Social Policy and the Welfare State

As a historical centre of Spain's industrialization, Catalonia was confronted sooner than the rest of the country with the social problems of the industrial economy. During the nineteenth century, while the Spanish state remained largely indifferent, liberal forces in Catalonia were championing public measures to reduce the misery and poverty of workers. In this, they were spurred on by the real threat of social unrest and revolutionary movements.

Some social measures were adopted under the Mancomunitat de Catalunya. Under the Second Republic, the Generalitat assumed exclusive jurisdiction over social assistance. In 1932 Spain's first school for social workers was established in Barcelona. Arguably, Catalonia might have progressed more rapidly in the development of public social reforms if it had enjoyed extended autonomy from the Spanish state.[69]

During the first few decades of the Franco era, the Spanish government developed a largely contributory system of sickness and disability insurance, family allowances, and unemployment insurance. This evolved into a system of universal social security in the 1960s. But, while similar in principle to other European systems of social security, it was not coupled with the political and labour rights that existed elsewhere.[70]

With the transition to democracy, the Generalitat was able to assume responsibility for social policy, though within frameworks established by the Spanish government. Indeed, it was quick to establish a department of health and social assistance in 1977. Especially striking has been the growth in the Generalitat's role in health services. In 1981, Catalonia was the first autonomous community to take responsibility for the provision of health services under the state's social security program. Health care continues to be financed by the Spanish state, which draws upon both general revenues and social security funds. In Catalonia, these state funds are transferred to the Servei Català de la Salut (SCS) which the Generalitat created in 1990 to regulate public health services.

The Generalitat's spending on health services rose to 571,566 million pesetas in 1996, a 228 per cent increase (in constant pesetas) from 1981.[71] This constitutes by far the largest area of social spending by the Generalitat.[72] Overall, the health of Catalans compares well with that of the rest of Europe.[73]

Under the statute of autonomy the Generalitat also assumed responsibility for social assistance and social services. A wide variety of programs have been devolved from the central state. A department of social welfare was established in 1988, and the Generalitat's spending on social services rose to 51,910 million pesetas in 1995 (from 42,208 in 1991).[74]

As is to be expected given the historical importance of civil society in Catalonia, private institutions continue to play an important role in the provision of social services. In fact, social services involved 302 of the 731 private foundations registered in Catalonia in 1993 and accounted for 65 per cent of total spending by foundations. About two-thirds of these are devoted to social assistance, and the rest to health services.[75]

The greatest share of spending on social assistance is made by foundations linked to Catalonia's savings banks; in 1993 it reached 3,286 million pesetas. Thus, reflecting the secondary role of the Church in contemporary Catalonia, spending on social assistance by the main Church organization, Càritas (of the Barcelona diocese), was set much lower—1,189 million pesetas in 1995.[76]

This provision of social assistance through the combined action of public and private institutions has had limited effects. As in so many other areas, when it comes to poverty Catalonia stands midway between the advanced European countries and the European south. There is obviously less poverty in Catalonia than in the rest of Spain: at the end of the 1980s, 15.1 per cent of Catalan families lived below the poverty line, compared to 20 per cent in all of Spain. In Greece it was 19.9 per cent. Still, there is far more poverty in Catalonia than in such countries as Luxembourg (7.6 per cent), Holland (7.2 per cent), and Belgium (6.1 per cent).[77] In short, Catalans are affluent only in southern European terms.

Under the new constitution, the autonomous communities may assume exclusive jurisdiction over housing. The Generalitat established an agency to oversee

the development of new social housing complexes. The complexes are administered by an agency of the social welfare department. As with other social
programs, however, funding is heavily dependent on transfers from the central
state.[78]

In sum, the Generalitat has been able to assume primary responsibility for the
support and provision of health and social services, but generally within frameworks established by the central government, upon which it is highly dependent
for funding. In the end, Catalonia has emerged with a welfare state regime similar
to the more advanced southern European regions.[79]

Whether the Generalitat's entry into social policy has strengthened Catalonia's
social cohesion is far from clear. There may be less poverty than in the rest of
Spain, but there is still far more than in advanced European countries. Catalonia
(like the rest of Spain) has experienced a general increase in crime and delin-
quency since the end of the Franco regime. The precise level may vary with economic conditions, but there is clearly more than before the transition to
democracy.[80]

Advancing Social Groups: The Case of Women
In addition to reducing the effects of economic disadvantage per se, building
social cohesion also means responding to the claims of specific social groups for
enhanced status and opportunity. Here, the most visible development in Catalonia
has been the re-emergence of feminism from the 1930s. This is the primary movement to have obtained a formal response from the Generalitat.

During the 1930s, feminist demands and concerns were voiced by Catalan
worker and republican movements; in fact, the Generalitat legalized abortion in
1936.[81] But under the Franco regime, women were deprived of most rights. In the
late 1970s, the death of Franco, coupled with the ongoing entry of women into the
labour force and the decline in the influence of the Church and traditional values,
produced a new wave of feminism. Indeed, Catalan feminists took the lead in the
creation in 1977 of a Spain-wide co-ordinating body for femininist organizations.[82]

Under Catalonia's statute of autonomy, the Generalitat was granted exclusive
jurisdiction over the advancement of women.[83] There has been some revision of
Catalan family law, which, though more favourable to women than the Spanish
Civil Code, did leave women without economic protection if their marriage broke
down.[84] The Generalitat funds the Institut Català de la Dona (Catalan institute of
women), which was created in 1989. In addition, the Generalitat in 1986 established an interdepartmental commission that has drawn up a series of multi-year
plans to promote equality of opportunity for women.[85]

But while these plans are comprehensive in scope and involve most areas of
the Generalitat, it is far from clear that they have led to important changes in the
condition of Catalan women. Women continue to be disadvantaged in terms of
wages, promotion levels, and occupational segregation.[86] And though women's
participation in the labour force is higher in Catalonia than in the rest of Spain, it

is still significantly lower than in Europe as a whole.[87] Women also continue to play quite marginal roles in the Catalan political élite.[88]

The Generalitat, and Catalan politics in general, seem to have devoted more attention to the status of women than to visible minorities or groups defined by sexual orientation. Yet, by most indicators Catalonia ranks below many European countries even with respect to the status of women.

Integrating Immigrants

The integration of immigrants and their descendants has been the most fundamental challenge for present-day Catalonia. As is to be expected, the Generalitat has played the central role. Catalonia has always attracted large numbers of immigrants, given both its location between Spain and France on the Mediterranean coast and its long history as a site of commerce and then industry. Moreover, the various waves of immigrants have usually been integrated quite smoothly into Catalan society. But the 1950s and 1960s saw immigration of an unprecedented magnitude, and the cohesion of Catalan society was, and still is, challenged in a way it had never been before.

Historical Patterns of Immigration

In the past, immigrants came primarily from the north. Usually, their language was quite close to Catalan, as in the case of Occitan-speakers from southern France.[89] Indeed, at the close of the sixteenth century, French (Occitan) immigrants made up 20 per cent of Catalonia's male population.[90]

By the end of the nineteenth century, the immigrant presence had become relatively minor. In 1897, immigrants represented only 3.33 per cent of Catalonia's population. The percentage was growing, but by 1910 it was still at only 5.44 per cent.[91] At the turn of the century the new immigrants to Catalonia, and more specifically to Barcelona, included large numbers of Catalan-speakers from Valencia, Menorca, and Majorca.[92] Given Catalonia's historical success in integrating immigrants, its leaders continued to see Catalonia in quite pluralist terms. Sporadic efforts to promote a racially defined Catalan identity fell on deaf ears.[93]

But in the 1920s, the numbers of immigrants increased, reaching 14.03 per cent in 1920 and 19.61 per cent in 1930. Even more important, immigrants started to come increasingly from the south of Spain. Thus, by 1930, in Barcelona province Castilian-speaking immigrants were almost as numerous as immigrants who spoke Catalan or a closely related language: 17.49 per cent of the population as opposed to 18.31 per cent.[94]

This in turn provoked considerable discussion among Catalan intellectual and political élites. Many intellectuals, especially on the left, displayed the habitual Catalan optimism about the possibility of assimilation. For that matter, after spending several months in Catalonia in 1912, a French observer concluded that assimilation was extensive among the immigrant children, who spoke Catalan 'as if it were their mother tongue. Catalonia absorbs the immigrants'.[95]

Some Catalan intellectuals, however, began to voice deep concern about the rising numbers of immigrants. A Catalan doctor, Puig i Sais, published a book about the threat of immigrants, in which he proclaimed the need to increase 'the number of racially pure Catalans in order to struggle on all fronts' ('el nombre de catalans de pura raça per a lluitar en tots els terrenys').[96] With the intensified immigration of the 1920s, much of the discussion focused on the susceptibility of immigrants to the appeals of revolutionary ideals and anarchism. There was concern that they might be mobilized by the anti-Catalanism of a renewed *lerrouxisme*.

With the acquisition of autonomy under the Second Republic, some writers, especially on the left, claimed that such possibilities could be forestalled by, as one put it,

> a prudent assimilationist policy of which the primary instruments are the school, the press and spectacles and which destroys the myth that nationality is a racial phenomenon based on purity of blood and establishes that nationality is a cultural phenomenon which can perfectly mould individuals of distinct races . . . that's what would reinforce our assimilationist potential.[97]

Despite such optimistic responses, other intellectuals were alarmed. In particular, Josep A. Vandellós, the author of two large demographic studies, claimed that the magnitude of immigration was such as to make any rapid assimilation very difficult. While eschewing the term 'race', Vandellós argued that the Catalan ethnicity, based on language and culture, was very much in danger. Indeed, the integration of immigrants 'might cause the loss of the distinctive characteristics of the Catalan people'. Immigrants could learn to speak the Catalan language perfectly yet not fully assimilate Catalan culture. Their 'Catalanness' would never be certain.[98] In the end, it was never clear in Vandellós's writings whether the roots of the distinctive Catalan 'mentality' were biological or environmental.[99]

In the 1930s, with economic decline, immigration subsided. The Civil War brought several thousand immigants from Andalusia, while also resulting in a huge exodus from Catalonia. But immigration was halted during the early years of the Franco regime.[100]

The 1950s Wave of Immigrants
None the less, the situation changed dramatically in the 1950s. Between 1950 and 1975, net migration added 1,393,052 to Catalonia's population. More than half of this increase occurred within one decade: 1961–70.[101] Largely because of immigration, Catalonia's population increased by 75 per cent between 1950 and 1975; among the fourteen largest Western European states, the highest increase was 36 per cent. By 1970, 37.7 per cent of Catalonia's population had been born elsewhere.[102]

The new immigrants settled in hastily constructed apartment buildings in the suburbs of Barcelona. In several suburban townships they constituted the overwhelming majority of the population.[103] As a result, in 1975, persons of immigrant descent made up nearly half (49 per cent) the population of the municipality of Barcelona and more than 46 per cent of the rest of Barcelona province.[104]

The arrival of such a large number of immigrants would pose a severe challenge to any society. Even at the height of immigration, foreigners did not represent more than 30 per cent of the population of the United States, Argentina, or New Zealand, according to one estimate.[105] Moreover, this time the immigrants to Catalonia, who came largely from the south of Spain, were overwhelmingly Castilian-speaking. Indeed, Andalusia was the source of 52 per cent of the immigrants to Catalonia between 1962 and 1975.[106]

Catalonia was in no position to integrate these immigrants, having no state structures at its disposal. Indeed, subsumed as it was under the Franco regime, it had no political autonomy at all. And the official position of the governmental authorities was to minimize the extent and impact of immigration to Catalonia, or to ignore it altogether.[107]

At first, some Catalan intellectuals condemned this wave of immigration in ways that were reminiscent of Vandéllos in the 1930s, fearing for Catalonia's survival. Indeed, Vandellós's works were regularly cited by demographers and non-specialists alike. Like Vandellós, many of these writers reacted to the immigrant phenomenon in terms that bordered on racism, even if they rejected racism in theory. Thus they would warn of 'the dangers of crossbreeding' ('els perills del mestissatge') or link language to the 'biology of the people' ('biologia del poble').[108] One such writer, A. Peyrí, went further, denouncing 'this mixing which is clearly undesirable if one wishes to preserve the distinct culture intact'.[109] (He even charged that the massive immigration had been deliberately instigated by Franco and his regime to end the Catalan question.)[110]

But it is generally agreed that this fiercely negative, and exclusivist, reaction to the 1950s and 1960s wave of immigration did not take hold among Catalonia's élites as a whole.[111] Instead, the predominant reaction was inclusive. It effectively constituted a new form of Catalan nationalism that was based on the realistic assessment that, to be viable, any national project would have to win the support of immigrants.[112] It was also informed by a concern with the dangers of segregation and the maintenance of immigrant ghettoes that would be ripe for mobilization by anti-Catalanist forces. The spectre of *lerrouxisme* was very much present.[113]

Jordi Pujol took the lead in articulating a definition of Catalonia that clearly accepted the immigrants. In an oft-cited 1958 statement, he declared:

> Who is a Catalan? A Catalan is any man who lives and works in Catalonia and through his own work, his own effort, helps to build Catalonia. In other words, makes Catalonia his home, that is to say, in one way or another, has been incorporated, admitted, integrated and is not hostile to it.[114] . . . Except for those with anticatalan prejudice, immigrants are in principle Catalan.[115]

At the same time, Pujol insisted that the objective should be not assimilation of immigrants, but their integration. At the centre of this integration would be language: 'Language is the decisive factor in the integration of immigrants to Catalonia. It's the most definitive. A man who speaks Catalan, and speaks Catalan to his children, is a Catalan through and through.'[116] Even then, knowledge of Catalan was not an indispensable requirement to be a Catalan. The essential condition was to be a resident of Catalonia. Beyond that a subjective attachment to Catalonia was the key.[117]

Coupled with Pujol's writings was a best-seller, *Els altres catalans* (the other Catalans), by a journalist, Francisco Candel. Himself a Catalan-speaker of immigrant descent, Candel tried to explain the immigrant experience to native Catalans and to demonstrate that immigrants had a deep love for their new land. The popularity of Candel's book was itself testimony to the concern of native Catalans over the impact of immigration on their society and to their hope that immigrants might indeed be integrated.

Despite its positive message, *Els altres catalans* was followed by *Els no catalans i nosaltres* (the non-Catalans and us), in which Manuel Cruells argued that Candel's book, like Pujol's writings, was sentimental and unrealistic. In point of fact, the immigrant populations did not want to integrate with Catalonia: 'They don't accept Catalonia, nor identify with its problems and its anxieties. They accept neither Catalonia nor the Catalans.'[118]

Despite Cruells's bleak message, other writers continued to express optimism about the prospects of integrating the immigrants. A leftist writer, Marc Aureli Vila, declared in *Les migracions* that:

> It is a serious mistake not to try to incorporate these groups of immigrants. Every effort should be made to ensure that the new arrival feels the country is his and identifies with it. This can be achieved in a minimum amount of time and without coercion. The immigrants' children can be incorporated fully into the nationality before they become young adults.[119]

Similarly, several social scientists published major works arguing that the integration of immigrants was indeed a realistic objective. In 1965, J. Maluquer i Sostres published *Població i societat a l'àrea catalana* (Population and society in the Catalan region), based upon his University of Geneva thesis, in which he identified the factors, such as relative youth, that facilitate assimilation (which he understood as social integration).[120] In the preface Jordi Nadal criticized the 'alarmist' analyses of people like Vandellós and presented as a given a natural process of integration of immigrants.[121] Several years later Nadal distinguished native Catalans' attitudes about immigrants from those held in the 1930s: 'The successes of socialism introduced, above all, a broader, less discriminatory, concept of nation. . . . The social and geographical antecedents have little importance; what counts is the integration of each of them within the same sense of solidarity. . . . Catalans of 1966 have less prejudice that did Vandellós and his contemporaries.'[122] Apparently, Nadal's optimism did weaken somewhat in light of the magnitude of the wave of immigrants.[123]

Similarly, in 1965 a linguist, Antoni M. Badia i Margarit, declared: 'The possibility that the immigrants would escape assimilation is simply nil.'[124]

The Failure of an Ethnic Reaction

With each wave of migration to Catalonia, some of its writers and intellectuals responded in the nativist, exclusivist way that one might expect, defining Catalonia in ethnic, even racial terms, and seeing the immigrants as permanent outsiders and even a threat to Catalonia's survival. Yet, in each instance, the predominant response was to define Catalan identity in terms, such as language or simply residence, that could embrace the newcomers.

The failure of an ethnic reaction to take hold at the turn of the century or in the 1920s might be understood as simply a continuation of a longstanding historical pattern. Even then, it is in striking contrast to many societies, including the Basque Country.[125] Yet, such an explanation seems less compelling for the 1950s and 1960s, when Catalonia's leaders were confronted with a wave of immigrants that in quantitative terms vastly exceeded anything experienced in the past by Catalonia, or indeed most societies. Moreover, this time, few of the immigrants spoke Catalan. And Catalan society was particularly bereft of resources to respond to this challenge, given the Franco regime's proscriptions on Catalan.

To be sure, the Franco regime was also an obstacle to any open mobilization against the influx of immigrants. Not only was it bound to suppress any nationalist activity, but it refused to recognize immigration as a social problem. Yet, this cannot explain why Catalan nationalists themselves tended to adopt an inclusive response to the wave of immigrants.

The Franco regime may, however, have been *indirectly* responsible for this response. Since the new immigrants tended to be mobilized by left-wing organizations, including the Spanish Communist Party, they were allies of the Catalan leadership who shared a common opposition to the Franco regime. Similarly, the influence of Christian democracy among centrist Catalan nationalists, as represented by Jordi Pujol, ensured that these nationalists would make common cause with the immigrants and see them as an underprivileged class deserving of charity and support. An authentically rightist version of Catalan nationalism might have been less likely to see any solidarity with the Castilian-speaking immigrants, but it was largely absent.[126]

Coupled with this ideological disposition of the Catalan leadership to see the immigrants as allies, and even potential members of the Catalan nation, was the patent desire of most immigrants to meet the ostensible requirements for membership in the Catalan nation. Not only did most of them have every intention of remaining in Catalonia for the rest of their lives, but most of them tried actively to learn the Catalan language. The similarity of Catalan and Castilian meant that this was feasible in a way it was not with, for instance, the Basque language. But the fact remained that most immigrants were ready to pursue it, and native Catalans were generally receptive to such efforts.[127]

This point had been clearly established in Maluquer i Sostres's thesis, published in French in 1963 and in Catalan in 1965. There he was careful to distinguish the fate of immigrants in three different settings. In the countryside, he found that young immigrants were 'perfectly assimilated'. Their command of Catalan was such that even a careful observer could not identify them.[128] The same was true in small industrial towns, for immigrants' children who were born there. In a large industrial town, Terrassa, he found that immigrants were quite disposed to learn Catalan; their relative success in doing so was largely a function of whether Catalans had supported their efforts.[129]

The situation in Barcelona was more complicated. There was a small group of Castilian-speaking administrators and professionals. Closely linked with the Franco regime and often in Barcelona only temporarily, they displayed a certain sense of superiority vis-à-vis the Catalans and had no inclination to assimilate.[130] However, the overwhelming majority of immigrants, who were poorly educated and unskilled and who came from the south of Spain, had a marked sense of inferiority vis-à-vis the Catalans and saw knowledge of the Catalan language as a means of social mobility. But the fact that they tended to live in Barcelona's suburban belt, with high concentrations of fellow immigrants, was an obstacle to learning the language.[131] On the other hand, Barcelona was also the site of a high proportion of mixed marriages, which hastened assimilation. In fact, over the period 1950–7, about one-third of the marriages in Barcelona were between a native Catalan and an immigrant.[132]

These findings were confirmed in a series of studies conducted during the early 1970s. A study of Cornellà de Llobregat, a Barcelona suburb that was almost entirely composed of immigrants (only 8 per cent of the population could speak Catalan), found that 97 per cent of respondents wanted their children to learn Catalan. Similarly, another study found that the same proportion, 90 per cent, of immigrants and of native Catalans felt that Catalan should be taught in all of Catalonia's schools; 80 per cent of each group felt that it should be obligatory.[133] Strikingly, these attitudes prevailed among immigrants despite the Franco government's open hostility to the Catalan language.

Intermarriage between immigrants and Catalan natives continued to grow, going from 25.4 per cent of all marriages in 1950 to 34.6 per cent in 1973.[134] And it continued to be an important force for inter-generational adoption of the Catalan language, especially when the husband was the native Catalan.[135]

Still, the willingness of immigrants to learn Catalan did not necessarily result in social mobility. In the late 1970s, immigrants continued to occupy markedly inferior places in Catalonia's economic structure. In 1980 Armand Sàez observed that people from outside Catalonia constituted only 26 per cent of directors and senior personnel and only 25 per cent of middle management, but 60 per cent of Catalonia's skilled workers and 82 per cent of its unskilled workers.[136]

A more detailed study conducted in the same period by Pinilla de las Heras found roughly the same degree of stratification. The study showed that immigrants tended to be concentrated in sectors, such as construction, that were marked by low levels of technology and weak competitiveness and that offered correspondingly low levels of mobility. And they were concentrated in manual occupations, which also provided little mobility.[137] Immigrants in non-manual occupations did experience some mobility. But it was not as great as among native Catalans, and it did not go beyond lower-level, white-collar positions. The children of immigrants enjoyed some mobility, but not if their parents were in manual occupations.

This limited mobility among immigrants is not necessarily a sign of discrimination or any conscious rejection of immigrants; it may simply be due to lower levels of education and job qualifications. Moreover, the economic crisis of the late 1970s limited the extent to which higher levels of education could lead to mobility.[138] None the less, the fact remained that immigrants and their children continued to be concentrated in blue-collar jobs and to have few prospects for escaping them.

Conceivably, this continued economic stratification could have fuelled serious conflict between immigrant and native Catalans. But that danger was largely averted by the fact that the main organizations among immigrant workers were unions, which were themselves organized on class bases that straddled the Catalan-immigrant divide.[139] For that matter, mobility for immigrants and their descendants may well have increased in recent years.[140]

With the economic restructuring of the 1970s, migration to Catalonia fell precipitously, while migration of Catalans to other parts of Spain, notably Madrid and the neighbouring areas of Aragon, Valencia, and the Balearic Islands, increased significantly. As a result, in most years since 1980 outmigration has exceeded migration.[141] The massive waves of immigration from the Spanish south have long since come to an end.

None the less, Catalonia is still struggling with the consequences of these waves of immigration. In 1991 close to one-third (31.6 per cent) of Catalonia's population had been born elsewhere in Spain. In fact, the majority of residents between 45 and 55 years of age had been born outside Catalonia, reflecting the timing of the largest wave of immigration. The impact of this wave of immigration on Catalonia's demographic structure was heightened by the relative youth of the immigrants and the fact that the birth rate among immigrant women was significantly higher than among native-born women.[142]

A graphic demonstration of the demographic impact of past immigration lies in a recent study of the frequency of family names that end with the contraction 'ez', which does not exist in Catalan. Beyond profiles of 400 notable Catalans with such family names, *Els Ez de Catalunya* contains a statistical analysis, prepared by an agency of the Generalitat, showing that 27.9 per cent of Catalonia's population and 30.6 per cent of the population of Barcelona had the 'ez' contraction.[143]

The integration of these immigrants and their descendants from the rest of Spain is a continuing challenge for Catalan society. First, the challenge involves questions of identity. The fact is that most immigrants and their descendants, unlike native Catalans, see themselves as Spaniards first and foremost. The predominant Catalan nationalist discourse may be deliberately inclusive and designed to embrace immigrants and their descendants, but this is no guarantee that they will in fact adopt it. Second, the challenge continues to involve the matter of language. With the transition to democracy and the Generalitat's assumption of responsibility for providing education, immigrant children did receive the instruction in Catalan that their parents desired. But even if most Catalans of immigrant descent have acquired a knowledge of Catalan, they do not necessarily use it in their daily life. Indeed, unless they or their parents have married native Catalans, they are likely to lead their personal lives entirely in Castilian. Thus, in present-day Catalonia, close to half of the population normally uses Castilian at home.

Foreign Immigrants in Contemporary Catalonia

Beyond dealing with the continuing consequences of this past wave of immigrants from elsewhere in Spain, Catalonia is now experiencing a significant influx of immigrants from other countries that currently exceeds migration from within Spain. Foreign immigration is coming predominantly from Third World countries, which now account for the majority of foreign residents in Catalonia.[144] At the head of these countries, by far, is Morocco, which accounted for 42.3 per cent of foreign immigrants over the period 1992–4 (the comparable figure for all Spain is 22.2 per cent) and appears destined to remain the primary source of immigrants in the near future.[145]

In quantitative terms, this Moroccan phase falls far short of the Andalusian phase of the 1950s and 1960s, but it does mean that Catalonia will continue to be marked by immigration.[146] Moreover, the challenges posed by this Moroccan phase involve major differences not just in language but in religion and culture. A 1991 study found that most Catalans were not ready to embrace the notion of a multicultural society: only 15 per cent felt that immigrants should be supported in the maintenance of their own customs, while 46 per cent felt they should be allowed to maintain their customs, but without support, and another 32 per cent felt that immigrants should adapt to local customs.[147] A 1997 study found that 56 per cent of Catalans were concerned about the arrival of immigrants from poor countries and that 68 per cent were concerned about xenophobia and racism.[148]

In addition, learning Catalan may be much more difficult for most foreign immigrants than it was for internal Spanish immigrants, given the similarity of Castilian and Catalan. Not surprisingly, Third World immigrants are less likely to learn Catalan than ones from the First World.[149] Moreover, there is considerable evidence that native Catalans have brought negative stereotypes to bear in confronting racially and culturally different immigrants.[150] These attitudes can extend to second-generation Catalans, as with Catalans of Moroccan origin.[151]

Indeed, during the summer of 1999 there were several racist incidents in areas of Catalonia populated by Catalans of long descent. A mosque in Girona was fire-bombed, as was an apartment building in Banyoles in which several Gambian immigrants were living.[152] In addition, a group of skinheads attacked Moroccans in Vallès Occidental.

In short, Catalans are now being confronted with pressure to accept cultural diversity within Catalan society itself. With the present wave of foreign immigrants, especially from the Third World, Catalonia's historical openness to immigrants may be tested in a way it never has been before.

Conclusions

Catalan society has indeed undergone a process of 'national reconstruction' over the last two decades. Civil society has been restored with a proliferation of private foundations, associations, and social movements. Cultural institutions and industries have been greatly strengthened. Catalan is now used in all types of mass media, at all levels of education, and in scientific research. And Catalonia now has the semblance of a welfare state.

At the same time, the society that has emerged from this process of reconstruction is vastly different from the one of pre-Franco days. First, some elements have not been retrieved. For instance, civil society no longer features the class-based organizations of the past. The fledgling Catalan film industry never recovered from the Franco regime. And the traditional Catalan bourgeoisie has virtually disappeared.

Second, the population of Catalonia is fundamentally different: close to half is now composed of mid-century immigrants and their descendants, most of whom use Castilian as their primary language. This is a radically new situation for Catalonia. In the past immigrants came in much smaller numbers and tended to speak Catalan or a closely related language. The Catalan language may have been suppressed by the Spanish state, as in the Franco years, but never before was it faced with such a strong challenge from residents within Catalonia itself.

Finally, in a radical departure from the past, Catalan public institutions are front and centre in the new Catalonia. One would of course expect the Generalitat to play a central role in maintaining a welfare state and providing education. But the Generalitat has also been pivotal to the development of Catalan media, not just through public television and radio but through subsidies to newspapers, and the Generalitat's largesse has been essential to the re-emergence of Catalan cultural industries. The Generalitat has even become crucial to civil society, as formally private institutions have become dependent on its financial support.

The Generalitat's role in supporting civil society or the cultural industries reflects more than general late twentieth-century trends, with the intermingling of public and private. It reflects a more fundamental change, that is, the virtual disappearance of the Catalan bourgeoisie, which had played such an important role in supporting civil institutions and cultural activity for over two centuries. The Generalitat has been needed to fill a vacuum.

The Generalitat has also been crucial to solving the problems caused by the presence of so many Castilian-speakers. It has been drawn into establishing a comprehensive language regime, not only by supporting Catalan-language media and cultural activities, but also by ensuring that immigrant children are educated in Catalan and, in more recent years, by encouraging greater use of Catalan by residents whose mother tongue is Castilian. There too the process of national reconstruction is a continuing one.

Chapter 7

The Catalan Language:
The Politics of 'Normalization'

For Catalan nationalists, language has always been the most important form of national distinctiveness.[1] Unlike religion, for which some clerics had sought equal status in the Catalan national identity, language serves to distinguish Catalans clearly from other Spaniards. Though many Spaniards may deride it as no more than a vulgar dialect of Spanish, Catalans can point to a rich body of literature in Catalan and to linguists' judgments that Catalan is a distinct language.

In the case of Catalonia, language provides a more credible and reliable basis for claiming nationhood than it does for many stateless nations. In instances such as Scotland or Wales, the national language has largely disappeared; nationalists may be attempting to revive the language, but they cannot afford to link their claims for national recognition too closely to it. Moreover, in some nations, such as the Basque Country, the very possibility of linguistic revival is severely limited by the sheer difficulty of learning the national language, given its distinctiveness from the language that has supplanted it. In the case of Catalonia, about half the residents are brought up in Catalan, and most of those not raised in Catalan are raised in Castilian (Spanish) and can readily learn Catalan, given the similarity of the two. But in the Basque Country, Basque is spoken by only a minority of residents, and, moreover, it is totally unrelated to Castilian or to any other Western European language.

It was inevitable, then, that the preservation and promotion of Catalan would be central to the activities of the Catalan Generalitat, especially given the dominance of the ruling parties, the CDC and the Unió, which regard nation-building as the very reason for their existence. It was also inevitable that the language policies of the Generalitat would be a continuing source of debate not only in Catalonia, but in Spain as a whole.

Linguistic Normalization of Catalonia

Pressures for a Language Policy

In the early 1980s, the new Generalitat's first task was simply to undo the damage inflicted during the Franco regime, whose Spanish nationalism allowed no legitimacy whatsoever for the Catalan language or for any other purported trait of the Catalan nation. As soon as they seized power, the Francoists acted in a concerted fashion to eliminate the public expression of Catalan. After the war, and especially in the 1960s, the regime did relax somewhat its suppression of Catalan, but any revival of the language was largely restricted to the intelligentsia. The Franco regime's suppression of Catalan continued to have a deep effect on Catalan society as a whole. There was no public instruction in Catalan, and Catalan was still prohibited in public institutions.

Coupled with continued state suppression of Catalan was the influx during the 1950s and 1960s of over one million Castilian-speaking immigrants from other parts of Spain, primarily the south. By 1970, immigrants made up close to half the population of Catalonia. As a result, the proportion of Catalan-speakers in Catalonia declined markedly over these years. From 75 per cent in 1930, it fell to 68 per cent in 1960 and 60 per cent in 1975. Thus, in 1975 Catalonia contained 2,265,000 residents who did not speak Catalan;[2] in 1979, only 52 per cent of adults spoke Catalan as their home or habitual language.[3] In the province of Barcelona, a little over half (53.5 per cent) of the residents born outside Catalonia understood Catalan, only 18.9 per cent could speak it, and a minuscule 1.7 per cent could write it. Knowledge of Catalan was limited even among residents born in Catalonia: 79.2 per cent understood it and 69.7 per cent could speak it, but only 19.2 per cent could write it.[4] Beyond that, given the limited knowledge of Catalan among Castilian-speakers and the sheer weight of decades of Francoist suppression of Catalan, Catalan-speakers would automatically switch to Castilian with Castilian-speakers, because they considered it both unrealistic and impolite to use Catalan under these circumstances.[5] And they would automatically use Castilian with political authorities.[6]

During the 1960s and early 1970s Catalan nationalists had already been able to create, through exclusively private institutions, the beginnings of an infrastructure for restoring the Catalan language.[7] With the restoration of the Generalitat, Catalan nationalists could hope to address the situation of the Catalan language in a much more comprehensive and effective fashion. But precisely how was this to be done?

The Generalitat and Linguistic Normalization

For Catalan nationalists, the foundation of the new Generalitat's language policy had to be official status for Catalan. After Franco's death, El Congrés de Cultura Catalana had collected close to 400,000 signatures on a petition requesting that Catalan be made the official language in 'Catalan countries'.[8]

Many Catalan nationalists even thought that official status should be reserved for Catalan alone, for only then could Catalan's manifestly inferior status be raised. This demand became a major topic of debate as Catalan parliamentarians drew up their proposed statute of autonomy for Catalonia. However, the new constitution seemed to make it impossible for Catalan to be the *only* official language.

In stating that at the level of autonomous communities 'other Spanish languages [than Castilian] can *also* be official',[9] the constitution seemed to allow at most for 'co-official' status to other languages.

Nevertheless, during the debate in the Assembly of Parliamentarians of Catalonia over a statute of autonomy, some parliamentarians attempted to contrive formulations that would designate Catalan alone as Catalonia's official language, or appear to do so. For instance CDC parliamentarians proposed the following provision: 'Catalan is the official language of Catalonia. All citizens residing in Catalonia have *the right to express themselves in the Catalan language and the obligation to know it*' (emphasis added).[10]

In effect, the italicized phrases would have applied to Catalan the rights and duties that Article 3(1) of the constitution afforded Castilian in the most unusual of constitutional provisions ('All Spaniards have the duty to know it and the right to use it [Castilian]'). This proposal was defeated. However, another CDC proposal was adopted unanimously, after being rejected in an earlier vote: 'In Catalonia the Catalan language has the same official status that the constitution recognizes for Castilian in the whole Spanish state.'[11]

But the version of Catalonia's statute of autonomy finally approved by the Cortes straightforwardly recognizes Castilian's status as one of two official languages: 'Catalan is the official language of Catalonia, *as is Castilian* the official language of the whole of the Spanish State' (emphasis added).[12] By the same token, the statute commits the Generalitat to guaranteeing 'normal and official use of both languages', ensuring they are both known, and 'creating those conditions that will make possible *their full equality* with regard to the duties and rights of the citizens of Catalonia' (emphasis added).[13] The statute does reserve for Catalan another status: Article 3 begins with the declaration that Catalan is Catalonia's *llengua pròpia*—Catalonia's 'proper' or 'own' language.[14] Still, Catalonia would have two official languages, and any support of Catalan as *la llengua pròpia* would have to be conducted within a framework of linguistic equality.

Even then, some groups in Catalonia, not to mention the rest of Spain, were fearful of what the Generalitat might do. The attitudes of Castilian-speaking residents of Catalonia were tempered at first by the solidarity that they had developed with other Catalans, including nationalists, in their common struggle against the Franco regime. But some categories of public employees soon felt under attack. In June 1978, a year before the statute was passed, the Generalitat had already taken a first step in reinstating Catalan. The *Decret del Català* required a small amount of instruction (three hours a week) in Catalan at the lower grades in all public schools, while also allowing for public schools in which unlimited amounts of instruction would be given in Catalan. At the time, few teachers had any proficiency in Catalan; in fact, most, who had been appointed under the Franco regime, came from other parts of Spain.[15] They obviously felt threatened by the decree. And some Castilian-speaking civil servants also feared the Generalitat's intentions.

As a result, 2,300 Catalonia-based teachers and civil servants signed a manifesto, published in a Madrid newspaper on 12 March 1981, that bore the title 'For equal language rights in Catalonia'. The document defended the integrity of the principle of co-officiality, accused the Generalitat of wanting to make Catalan the *only* official language, and declared that the Generalitat's plans for a law to 'normalize' the use of Catalan did not 'take account of the social and linguistic reality of Catalonia.'[16] Alleging that children of Spanish-speaking immigrants were being discriminated against in Catalan schools, it called for an end to confrontation between the Catalan- and Castilian-speaking communities.

The manifesto had the effect of mobilizing a broad range of Catalan nationalists in defence of the Catalan language. A reaction had also been building against the UCD-PSOE pact to reduce the powers of Catalonia and other ACs by passing the LOAPA. Six days later, a meeting at the University of Barcelona, with the rector presiding, approved a counter manifesto entitled Declaració en defensa de la llengua, la cultura i la nació catalana. It denounced both the Madrid manifesto and the LOAPA as part of an aggressive Spanish nationalism, supported by both right-wing and left-wing forces, which:

> do not accept the existence of our nation and agree to continue oppressing it, including even what is one of the essential bases of our national continuity: linguistic recovery and normalization.[17]

An organization that was named after the manifesto, CRIDA, and which brought together 1,300 different organizations, was created to lead the struggle. On 14 June 1981, 80,000 people gathered at Camp Nou football stadium in Barcelona and chanted, 'we are a nation'.[18] And CRIDA continued to campaign for a vigorous law to support Catalan.

The battle had been joined. Some Castilian speakers, such as professionals whose careers depended upon being able to work in Castilian, could only see a direct threat in any intervention by the Generalitat to support Catalan. They did not trust the Generalitat to remain within what they saw as the proper limits of co-officiality. And they could count on being able to mobilize public opinion in the rest of Spain to support them. Yet this resistance only fuelled the determination of Catalan nationalists to have the Generalitat pass a language law that would stretch the limits of co-officiality to the maximum so as to redress Catalan's historical inferiority. In a pattern that was to be repeated many times, the debate over language policy in Catalonia was fuelled by the struggle between Catalan nationalism and Spanish nationalism. It was as much, if not more, a debate between Catalonia and the rest of Spain as a debate among Catalans.

The Generalitat continued to organize its intervention on behalf of Catalan. In 1980 it established a directorate for language policy in its department of culture. In 1983, the directorate released a white paper that surveyed the status of Catalan and defined the directorate's objectives as follows: 'to generalize knowledge of the language, to encourage and facilitate its use in different social milieux, and to encourage modification of language attitudes and behavioural practices that present obstacles to normalization of Catalan.'[19]

Linguistic attitudes and behaviour had in fact been the focus of a massive public education campaign that the directorate had launched the previous year: Campanya per la normalització lingüística de Catalunya, with the slogan 'Catalan is everyone's affair'. Drawing upon the support of municipal governments and a broad range of associations and social groups, the campaign sought to legitimize the use of Catalan: it is not discourteous to use it with Castilian-speakers, to speak it poorly is better than not to speak it at all, and bilingual conversations would be an important first step to 'normalizing' the status of Catalan. The campaign was personified by a young girl, dubbed 'la Norma', who called upon Catalans to be normal (*sóc la norma*) and use Catalan, and culminated on 23 April 1982, which was declared 'Language Day'. The campaign was highly successful in mobilizing the political and social élites on behalf of the cause of Catalan. In particular, an intense campaign to obtain endorsements by municipalities had dramatic results: the complying municipalities represented close to 98 per cent of the population of Catalonia.[20] The everyday diglossia that the campaign was supposed to elimi- nate remained very much in place,[21] but the mobilization of élites was crucial for the passage of a linguistic law, which was the next stage.

The campaign had helped to legitimize a particular way of conceiving a policy for Catalan—'normalization'. Defined this way, a language law might be generally acceptable and also compatible with co-officiality. The stated objective was not to replace Castilian with Catalan or even subordinate it to Catalan, but to bring Catalan up to an equal status with Castilian after so many decades of suppres- sion. After all, except for a brief interval during the 1930s, Catalan had been offi- cially illegal since 1714.

Not all Castilian-speakers were hostile to enhancing the place of Catalan with a basic linguistic equality. Many immigrants from the rest of Spain considered it in their children's interest to learn Catalan. They tended to see themselves and their children as permanently established in Catalonia and, given the extent to which Catalan-speakers were often owners of economic enterprises, Catalan was the language of social mobility. Thus, they did not necessarily share the aversion of Castilian-speaking professionals to support for the Catalan language.[22]

The Language Normalization Law

After almost three years of negotiations in the Catalan parliament, the Catalan government obtained the support of all Catalan parties for an Act for Linguistic Normalization, which passed in the Catalan parliament on 6 April 1983 with 105 votes in favour, none against and one abstention.

The preamble of the Act proclaims that 'the Catalan language is the funda- mental element of the Catalan entity' and goes on to detail how Catalan has fallen into 'a precarious situation, characterized principally by the limited presence that it exercises in the area of official use, education and the means of social communication'.[23] The preamble notes that the constitution allows autonomous communities to make other languages official and that the terms of the statute of autonomy make Catalan the *llengua pròpia* of Catalonia and commit the Generalitat to establish equality between Catalan and Castilian. On this basis, it sets as the law's purpose 'to overcome the current linguistic inequality by spurring normalization of the use of the Catalan language throughout the territory of Catalonia'.[24] Accordingly, Article 1 declares the objectives of the Act to be:

1. To support and encourage the use of Catalan by all citizens.
2. To bring about the official use of Catalan.
3. To normalize the use of Catalan in all means of social communication.
4. To extend knowledge of Catalan.[25]

The rest of the Act contains specific provisions dealing primarily with the institutions of the Generalitat, the education system, and the means of mass communication. In each case, the Act declares a privileged role for Catalan, thereby heightening the tension between Catalan's status as a language 'proper' to Catalonia and the Act's framework of formal equality between two official languages.

Section I, dealing with 'De l'ús oficial', makes Catalan *la llengua pròpia* of the Generalitat and of all administrations and public bodies that derive from the Generalitat. Most of the subsequent provisions, however, establish a passive form of official bilingualism in parliament and the administration. A significant exception is official toponomy, which 'will have a single Catalan form.'[26]

Section II, dealing with education, once again affirms the essential status of Catalan: 'Catalan, as Catalonia's own language, is also that of instruction at all levels of education'.[27] Here too, however, the subsequent provisions seem to establish a bilingual regime with the right to early education in either language, obligatory instruction in both languages at later levels, requirement of mastery of both languages for graduation, the right of teachers and students to express themselves in either language, a requirement that teachers know both languages, and so on. But the bilingualism is not one of two parallel systems with students choosing one or the other. Rather students are themselves to become bilingual, and the students' right of choice is subordinated to that requirement. One provision, in fact, specifies that students are not themselves to be segregated into different schools because of their language.

Finally, section III, which deals with means of mass communication, focuses exclusively on Catalan. The Generalitat should promote Catalan language and culture in its own means of communication and those it controls. It can subsidize publications that are exclusively or partially in Catalan, should encourage the normalization of Catalan in radio stations it subsidizes, should support production of films in Catalan and dubbing of other films, and should stimulate publishing in Catalan.

The drafters of the normalization law were trying to reconcile the promotion of Catalan with the constitutional requirement for co-officiality of Catalan and

Castilian. The result is not simply an official bilingualism, in which two languages are treated in the same way for all purposes: Catalan is given a slight edge. Two rationales are given for doing this. First, the preamble of the Act discusses at length the fact that Catalan is in an inferior position to Castilian. To that extent, linguistic equality dictates that Catalan be brought up to the same level. The second rationale is that Catalan is the *llengua pròpia* of Catalonia. It is for this reason that the law makes Catalan the language of each of the three main domains with which it is concerned—the Generalitat, education and mass media, and place names.

None the less, Catalan has only a slight edge, constrained by the law's commitment to two official languages. Laws and other important texts are published in both languages, just as citizens can use either in dealing with the Generalitat. The public schools must enable students to master both languages. There are no linguistic obligations imposed on private means of communications, but they may receive subsidies if they use Catalan.

Apparently, the early drafts of the bill constrained official bilingualism more fully. A draft prepared by the Generalitat's department of culture in 1980 established the general principle that only individuals had the right to choose between the two official languages; legal entities, as well as the Generalitat, were obliged to use Catalan for some purposes, although they could also use Castilian. Thus, a section of the draft bill applied to private enterprises, requiring them to use Catalan in their labour relations and their communications with the public, although they could also use Castilian. Another section applied similar provisions to non-governmental organizations, foundations, and professional associations. By the time the bill reached its final form, these two sections had disappeared.[28] Echoing the desire of nationalists with respect to the statute of autonomy, the law did establish an obligation to know Catalan. But that provision was challenged by the González government and determined to be unconstitutional by the Spanish Constitutional Court.

The 1983 linguistic normalization law is in fact quite modest in its scope and its promotion of Catalan and it falls considerably short of Quebec's *Charte de la langue française*, or Bill 101, which has often been cited as its inspiration. Under Bill 101, a single language, French, is formally proclaimed as the official language of Quebec. In public schools, a mastery of French alone is required; there is no requirement regarding English, Canada's other main language. Most important, Bill 101 imposes substantial obligations on private enterprises. Their corporate name must be in French alone. To be able to conduct business in the province they must qualify for *francisation* certificates, which attest to their efforts to make French the effective language of internal communications. And all commercial advertising must be exclusively in French.

Obviously it would have been unconstitutional to make Catalan the *only* official language of Catalonia, but the failure of the normalization law to cover the private sector, other than through subsidies to the media, set clear limits to its ability to raise Catalan from its disadvantaged position in Catalonia's society. This continuing limitation was to become the focus of a renewed language debate years later—one that was to prove much harder to resolve.

Implementing the Law

The provisions regarding the Generalitat and institutions connected with it could be put into effect fairly easily. Though the law declared Catalan to be 'the language of administration', in fact the various provisions amounted to official bilingualism. With some important exceptions, they have been implemented. All Generalitat documents are published either in Catalan alone or in Catalan and Castilian. By and large, citizens can use either language when dealing with the Generalitat or with municipal institutions. Though the law does not require it, the Catalan parliament and most municipal councils function essentially in Catalan.

But there are still some major shortcomings. In the administration of justice, Catalan is used in informal oral communication, but formal oral and written communication remains essentially in Castilian.[29] In part, the Generalitat is to blame for being slow to address the question. But this state of affairs also reflects the fact that judicial administration remains in the hands of the Spanish state, most judicial personnel come from outside Catalonia and for limited periods of time, training in Catalan in Catalonia's law schools is inadequate, and the traditional attitude is that Catalan is not suitable for formal purposes.[30]

Even though the law did not specify it, the Generalitat has interpreted the objective of normalization to mean that within its own institutions Catalan should become the effective language of its internal communications. Under a decree passed in 1985, mastery of Catalan was made a formal requirement for employment in the civil service; existing employees without it were given training in Catalan. None the less, there are still limitations to the use of Catalan. In 1994 a study found that Catalan speakers were indeed able to use Catalan in most of their activities, but when it came to dealing with the minority of colleagues whose first language was Castilian they would tend to opt for Castilian.[31] This was especially the case if the Castilian-speaker was a superior: in that case, Catalan-speakers would use Catalan only 45.3 per cent of the time.[32] Respondents explained that it had long been their practice to switch to Castilian with Castilian-speakers and that their Castilian-speaking colleagues might not speak Catalan. Besides, work materials were not always available in Catalan.[33]

The Generalitat's obligations with respect to the media were similarly straightforward: to regulate the use of Catalan in the media that were under its direct responsibilities and to encourage, essentially through subsidies, the use of Catalan in the other media. The Generalitat's Corporació Catalana de Ràdio i Televisió established TV3 and Canal 33 and four FM radio stations. The Generalitat has maintained an important program of subsidies to Catalan newspapers, and its department of culture has provided extensive support for book publishing. If the effect of these efforts on the overall use of Catalan in the media may be less than the Generalitat might have hoped, the policies themselves have been quite straightforward and have generated relatively little public controversy.

Implementing the provisions about education was quite a different matter. Indeed, the Act seemed to recognize competing principles: Catalan was to be the language of education, children were to be able to choose between Catalan and Castilian for their early education, students could not be segregated according to language, and students were required to graduate with a mastery of both languages.[34] In the words of a leading scholar, the Act called for a 'mixed model of individual and territorial rights.'[35]

This has resulted in a system in which children (or their parents) can choose the language of instruction in nursery school, kindergarten, and the first and second years of primary school.[36] After that, primary education is conducted mainly in Catalan.

Under the Decret del Català of 1978, *all* students were to be exposed to a minimum number of hours of instruction in Catalan every week, even if they were early-education children who had opted for Castilian. At first, the Generalitat concentrated on ensuring that this requirement was met, but it soon became clear that for children whose home language was Castilian this minimal exposure to Catalan was too little to have any real effect. Accordingly, in the mid 1980s the emphasis shifted to Catalan immersion for such children. Although the choice remained with the parents, a large proportion did enrol their children in immersion programs. In one predominantly Castilian-speaking suburb of Barcelona, the proportion of kindergarten children registered in Catalan rose from 13.3 per cent in 1983–4 to 51 per cent in 1986–7.[37] As a result, by 1988–9 in Catalonia as a whole approximately 70 per cent of public school children between the ages of four and seven were being taught in Catalan.[38]

Problems remain in implementing this educational scheme. First, there has been difficulty in finding enough teachers who are qualified to teach in Catalan.[39] Second, at the secondary level Castilian continues to be used extensively, if only because of the lack of textbooks in Catalan.[40]

In addition to this implementation of the various sections of the normalization law the Directorate for Language Policy has undertaken a range of other activities. By 1994 it had 100 employees, most of them language planning specialists.[41] The directorate helps to finance and co-ordinate a network of municipal offices of Catalan that promote the proper use of Catalan. In 1988 there were 41 such municipal offices in the Barcelona area.[42]

The directorate has mounted a series of campaigns to encourage Catalans to use their language more. In 1985–6 it staged a publicity campaign aimed at the general public, which, like the Norma campaign of 1982–3, encouraged the use of Catalan in daily life, including in conversations with Castilian-speakers. A 1986–7 campaign was designed to ensure the proper use of Catalan in restaurants, and in 1987–8 a similar campaign was aimed at shopkeepers. A 1988 campaign encouraged the study of Catalan in adult courses as well as its greater use in daily life. Other campaigns were aimed at supermarkets, the world of sports, and tourism.[43] The directorate also oversees and partly finances Catalan classes for adults. By the mid-1990s yearly enrolment had reached nearly 35,000. Every year about 10,000 participants take examinations supervised by a Junta Permanent de Català.[44]

The directorate maintains a sociolinguistic institute, which conducts research on sociolinguistic questions and maintains an extensive information centre. The Generalitat has created other organizations to facilitate linguistic normalization. A commission for language normalization draws together the Generalitat's general secretaries to co-ordinate normalization within the Generalitat.[45] In 1988 the Generalitat joined with major corporations to form a consortium for language normalization, which employs more than 400 specialists in language planning.[46] The Generalitat also joined with the institute for Catalan studies to form TERMCAT, a centre for terminological research.

The Contemporary State of Catalan

It is obvious that the Generalitat's effort to strengthen the knowledge of Catalan has had an effect. The proportion of Catalonia's population that understands Catalan rose from 80 per cent in 1975 to 95 per cent in 1996.[47] To be sure, fluency in Catalan is lower by other indicators: in 1996, 75.3 per cent could speak it; 72.4 per cent could read it; and only 45.8 per cent could write it.[48] But in the 10–14-year-olds, who were the age group that would have benefited directly from the educational reforms, 99.2 per cent said that they understood Catalan, and 94.5 per cent said they could write it.[49] The improved knowledge of Catalan extends to immigrants, for, according to the 1991 census, among children living with mothers who did not understand Catalan, 86 per cent understood Catalan themselves, 56.7 per cent could read it, 48.2 per cent could speak it, and 35.6 per cent could write it.[50]

But the degree to which people actually *use* Catalan is quite a different matter. As we have already seen, even within the Generalitat itself there are situations in which Catalan speakers feel obliged to use Castilian; the justice system continues to function essentially in Castilian. We have also noted how in the schools, Catalan is not used much at the secondary level.

By the same token, though the Generalitat can increase the availability of Catalan mass media, it cannot guarantee that all Catalan speakers will in fact use them. Indeed, Castilian remains the predominant language in each of the media in which the Generalitat has promoted Catalan: television, radio, books, and newspapers.

In spite of the Generalitat's public education campaigns to make Catalan the norm for conversations between Castilian- and Catalan-speakers, this goal is far from being achieved. This can be seen in a study of consumers' attitudes, conducted in 1992 by the Generalitat's sociolinguistic institute. Among other things, respondents were presented with hypothetical situations in which they had to indicate the language they would use with a shopkeeper.[51] The results demonstrated clearly that Catalan has not become the normal language of exchange. Even when they have the added power of being the customer, most Catalan-speakers will switch to accommodate a Castilian-speaker.

Other studies have shown that Catalan has not become the norm of exchange even among youth—who should have been the most affected by the Generalitat's efforts. The studies do show that among both Catalan-speaking and Castilian-speaking youth there has been some relaxation in attitudes regarding language use. The old norm of using Castilian in exchanges has lost some of its force, although it has not completely disappeared. However, no new norm has replaced it.

Through two applications of a matched guise test, first in 1980 and then in 1987, Kathryn Woolard was able to show that Castilian-speaking youth have become more willing to use Catalan.[52] Significantly, Woolard explained this change not as a result of the Generalitat's programs of public education encouraging Catalans to use Catalan in exchanges with Castilian-speakers, but of the effect upon Castilian-speakers of hearing fellow Castilian-speakers, whether teachers, politicians, or television and radio figures, speaking Catalan.[53]

Still, the relaxation of the disincentives for Castilian-speakers to use Catalan does not in itself ensure that Catalan will predominate. In his study of Barcelona youth in the early 1990s,[54] based upon experiments and participant observation, Emili Boix found that neither language predominated: 'The majority of these youths are basically indifferent as to whether they are addressed in Catalan or Castilian. They accept the two languages as a given, about which they make no deliberate effort, whether individual or, even less, collective, to change the practices of usage.'[55] In short, the Generalitat's efforts may have helped to break down the old norm, but the goal of making Catalan the normal language of exchange is still far from being attained.

Finally, while the normalization law did not address language use in the private sector, at least in its final version, the Generalitat made some efforts to encourage greater use of Catalan. However, as the author of a 1995 study on corporate language practices declared, 'The fact is that the linguistic inertia inherited from the previous era weighs more heavily in the functioning of enterprises than in any other area of our society.'[56] The study found that 82.2 per cent of the managers who were interviewed used Catalan 'most often' in oral communication, but only 21 per cent read most often in Catalan, and only 12 per cent wrote most often in it.[57]

As to the private lives of citizens, where of course the Generalitat has not tried to intervene, Catalonia's population continues to be segregated on the basis of language. A recent study showed that in Barcelona the two linguistic groups live in different districts, which also correspond to their quite different socio-economic positions.[58]

Continuing Obstacles to the Expansion of Catalan

The Generalitat has made enormous progress in its effort to give the residents of Catalonia the ability to use Catalan. Yet, despite the Generalitat's active support of Catalan media, Castilian is still the dominant language in most media. The business world continues to function largely in Castilian. And, despite public campaigns for much of the last 15 years, Catalan is still not the normal language in conversations between Catalan-speakers and Castilian-speakers. At best, the old norm of using Castilian exclusively in such exchanges has broken down, but no new norm has taken its place.

How can this state of affairs be explained? The behaviour of Castilian-speakers is not especially surprising. A variety of factors could be at play—lingering solidarity with their group, insufficient mastery of Catalan, and the simple fact that while Catalan may be the language of prestige in Catalonia, given the greater social and economic status of Catalan-speakers, that is not the case in Spain as a whole. But the behaviour of Catalan-speakers is more puzzling. Why have they not made greater use of their increased ability in Catalan?

As we have seen, there is evidence that Castilian-speaking young people are more willing to use Catalan in these exchanges. But, despite strong encouragement from the Generalitat's public education campaigns, Catalan-speakers still shrink from making Catalan the exclusive language of exchanges. Among older Catalans, the practice of switching to Castilian may be due to habits acquired during the Franco period and a strong desire to be accommodating. But young people, it seems, are simply indifferent to language. Clearly, this does not reflect a lack of solidarity with their linguistic group; in fact Catalan-speaking youth have a strong sense of Catalan identity and are more receptive to nationalist messages than their elders. But they seem unaware of what is at stake, at least as understood by analysts such as Emili Boix, who believes that young Catalans do not understand the linguistic situation and have a false sense of security.[59]

Another factor is Catalan-speakers' choice of media. Here, there may well be less social pressure for solidarity with Catalans, since the choice between Catalan-language and Castilian-language media is individual and private. And in the case of newspapers, *most* Barcelona Catalan-speakers have routinely rejected the Catalan paper, *Avui*, in favour of one of the Castilian-language ones. The usual justification is the higher quality of the Castilian papers. But beyond the obvious fact that low circulation ensures that the Catalan paper will remain inferior, it suggests a marked lack of loyalty to the Catalan language, despite all the promotion of Catalan that has taken placed over the last 15 years.

The arrival of a Catalan version of *El Periódico* may dispel the notion that solidarity has to come at the expense of quality. Even then, it will be interesting to see whether long-time Catalan-language readers of *La Vanguardia* will abandon it in order to read in Catalan. In other media, trading off quality against solidarity may be unavoidable, given the relative size of the markets for cultural products in Catalan and Castilian. And even if the quality is equal, there is bound to be more choice in Castilian. This clearly is true for movies and is likely to remain true for television as well. Even with the Generalitat's two Catalan channels, there are more Castilian-language channels available in Catalonia.

The fact is that not only are Catalan-speakers a small minority in Spain as a whole, but their demographic pre-eminence in Catalonia itself is fragile. Catalan-speakers may be in the majority in Catalonia as whole, but they are a distinct minority in Barcelona, the metropolitan centre of Catalonia and home of about half its residents. According to one study, in 1985–6, 60.8 per cent of Barcelona residents had Castilian as their first language; only 34.2 per cent had Catalan as their first language.[60]

Finally, there are important sectors of life in Catalonia where Catalan-speakers simply to do not have the opportunity to choose between the two languages. Many institutions impose Castilian as the language of work. This can be seen in the data on economic firms, where employees use Catalan extensively in oral communications, but where written work is largely restricted to Castilian. While this aspect of the language question has not been studied as thoroughly, it would seem that such factors as ownership and control outside Catalonia, integration with the Spanish and foreign markets, and the importation of technology all place Catalan at a disadvantage. Of course, this is an area where the Generalitat has been much less vigorous in promoting Catalan. The normalization law does not even address the language practices of private institutions, whatever may have been envisaged in early drafts.

The Generalitat's linguistic program, especially as defined in the 1983 law, could not of itself make Catalan the primary language of Catalonia. It may have done so within the Generalitat's own institutions, but not within Catalonian society as a whole. Indeed, in these terms it could not even bring Catalan up to a position of equality with Castilian.

A New Language Law

By the early 1990s pressure was building for a revision of the normalization law to make it more effective, both by strengthening its existing provisions and by making it applicable to areas that had been covered in the original drafts but then deleted. Many argued that revision of the existing law would not do and that a new law was necessary.

In March 1995, the Generalitat approved a new language normalization plan,[61] which set language targets in seven sectors. These sectors included not only the areas covered by the 1983 law (public institutions, education, and the media), but also the 'socio-economic field', where the plan sought to make Catalan 'the habitual working language' of trade unions and business organizations and, in the case of private businesses, 'a habitual language for work, products and services, and dealing with the public',[62] and 'health and social institutions', where the plan called for guaranteeing 'the normal use of Catalan' in the full range of institutions and associations and for facilitating 'the full incorporation of new immigrants into the Catalan language, culture, and society.'[63]

Finally, in February 1997, the Generalitat produced the outline of a new language law.[64] It was to be a *new* law, not simply a reform of the 1983 law, and rather than linguistic 'normalization', it was to deal with the *use* of language (both Catalan and Castilian). And, unlike the 1983 law, it would define the term *llengua pròpia.*[65] At the same time, Catalan and Castilian would continue to have equal status as official languages.

The law was to cover five different areas. First, with respect to public institutions, existing linguistic measures were to be consolidated and services to the public in both languages were to be strengthened. Second, Catalan was to remain the only official language for place names, and citizens would have the right to use Catalan surnames. Third, in education, existing measures were to be consolidated and there was to be greater promotion of Catalan in specialized education. Fourth, in the case of mass media and cultural industries, existing support for Catalan-language media was to be increased by the establishment of quotas for cable television, future private television stations, and radio stations that fall under the Generalitat's jurisdiction.

Finally, there were provisions regarding 'socio-economic activity', which were to distinguish among different types of enterprises. Public enterprises were to use Catalan for all purposes, internal and external. Enterprises in transportation, communication, and supplies were to use Catalan *de manera generalitzada* ('in a general manner') for external purposes; citizens could demand to be served in either language. Businesses specializing in the sale of products and services must be able to serve the public in either language. Professional offices must respect *disponibilitat lingüística* ('the right to be served in one's own language'). Firms conducting business with the Generalitat or receiving subsidies from it were to use Catalan in the activities involved. In certain cases, labels on products sold in Catalonia were to be in both Catalan and Castilian; labels on all products manufactured in Catalonia had to contain Catalan. Catalan was to be the preferred language for advertising by Catalan institutions and publicly owned enterprises.

But unlike the Generalitat's plan, the treatment of the 'socio-economic field' in the proposed law did not cover business associations or trade unions. Moreover, only in the case of public enterprises did the measures seem likely to affect 'the habitual language of work', to use the plan's term. Otherwise, they concerned essentially the language of dealings with customers and the public. Beyond that, the outline contained no provisions for another area that had been designated in the Generalitat's plan: 'health and social institutions'.

Over the next few months, nationalist forces organized a broad-based coalition of support for a new language law. In March, the Associació per a les Noves Bases de Manresa released a manifesto entitled 'Per a un Nou Estat Social de la Llengua' ('For a new social status for the Catalan language'), signed by 350 prominent intellectuals and cultural figures. According to the manifesto, the Catalan language remained 'a language still not normalized in terms of social use'. A new language law was needed so that Catalan could at last become the common language for all public uses and assume an unqualified official character. Indeed, reviving the objective around which nationalists had rallied in the early 1980s, the manifesto called for Catalan to be the only official language of Catalonia. This was to be reinforced by a 'social dynamic' aimed at making Catalan the normal public language in Catalonia.[66]

In June 1997, the Associació per a les Noves Bases de Manresa organized a dinner to celebrate the theme of 'Llengua i convivència: Per la unitat i pel futur del Català' ('Language and Coexistence: For Unity and the Future of Catalan'). Among the more than one thousand guests were leaders of all parties but the PP, as well as the secretary-generals of the two union federations. By this time, the manifesto had 3,500 signatures.[67]

In September 1997, 140 organizations joined together in calling for a new law designed to greatly expand the social use of Catalan.[68] In October, La Coordinadora d'Associacions per la Llengua Catalana, an association of 150 primarily cultural organizations, expressed apprehension that the proposed law was being weakened in an effort to secure broad support. They referred to 'the concern, shared by broad sectors of society, that the new law departs more and more from the initial projects of the Catalan political parties that were committed to the full recovery of our language.'[69]

In effect, the Coordinadora was referring to the deliberations underway in a parliamentary commission examining the Generalitat's outline for a language law. The commission's deliberations involved leading members of all Catalonia's parties. In October 1997, after six months of often intense debate, the commission produced the draft of a new law. Back in 1983, a parliamentary commission had taken four times as long, 26 months, to produce the language normalization law. Its deliberations had been difficult and confused and frequently broke down,[70] but eventually 105 members of parliament had voted in favour, a single member abstaining. This time, there was no such unanimity, for the language debate had taken a very different turn.

The ERC had rejected the draft outright, voting against or abstaining on 30 of the bill's 39 articles and stating that the bill could not modify Catalan's position of legal inferiority. Josep-Lluís Carod-Rovira declared, 'What was a language normalization law has become a soothing guarantee of the use of Castilian'. Without substantial improvements, no serious national party could support it.[71] In this, the ERC, which had wanted Catalan to be the only official language, was expressing the views of a significant number of Catalan nationalists.

Yet, if some nationalists rejected the bill as being too weak, other Catalan political forces thought it went much too far. Here too the situation was markedly different from 1983.

Leading the opposition was the Partido Popular. In 1983, the PP's predecessor, the Alianza Popular, had had no member in the Catalan parliament. When it did enter the parliament in 1984, the normalization law was already in effect and the AP had no choice but to accept it.[72] In 1997, however, the PP was strongly represented in the Catalan parliament, having gained additional seats in the 1995 election in part by championing the rights of Castilian-speakers. Nor was it prepared to allow the CiU-PP alliance in the Spanish parliament to prevent it from assuming its normal role of champion of Spanish nationalism. Indeed, the Catalan PP had already broken with the long-standing consensus around the 1983 law, seeming to question immersion in Catalan schools.[73]

Denouncing the draft law as a 'pamphlet' that was dividing citizens and was totally unnecessary, the PP declared its unqualified opposition to the bill. In his denunciation of the bill, PP leader Fernández Diaz even challenged a central principle of the existing 1983 law by calling for an end to Catalan immersion in schools.[74]

Also opposing the bill was a coalition of intellectuals, primarily leftist. In 1981 2,300 teachers and civil servants had signed the manifesto Por la igualdad de los derechos lingüísticos en Cataluña (For equality of language rights in Catalonia), but it was eclipsed by a massive counter-mobilization of Catalan nationalists, which gave rise to CRIDA. This time, intellectuals opposed to a new language law conducted a highly visible campaign right up to and even after the adoption of the law.

In April 1997, a group calling itself Foro Babel produced a manifesto signed by a hundred intellectuals. It argued that Catalan 'had achieved a state of normalcy' and that 'a substantial part of the Catalan people' is Castilian-speaking. The group embraced bilingualism as an objective, but one that required 'an adequate timetable'. And it insisted that Catalan's status as *la llengua pròpia* of Catalonia must be understood as 'diferenciadora' (distinctive) or 'específica' (particular), not 'única' (unique) or 'preferente' (preferable). It warned against governmental infringement on citizens' rights to use either language, arguing that a government cannot legitimately impose one language or the other in economic life and the world of work. Similarly, the manifesto contended that promotion of Catalan cultural production should not entail restriction of the free use of languages.[75]

In September 1997, Foro Babel produced a second document, expressing disagreement with the whole of the draft language law. It denounced the law as 'xenophobic and reactionary', reflecting 'un nacionalisme essencialista' (an essentialist nationalism) and contended that the law 'threatens the current constitutional and legal order'. It charged that the draft law was trying to impose Catalan by making the term *la llengua pròpia* equivalent to 'official language'. Moreover, the text 'indicates an interventionist and controlling mentality' toward social, economic, and cultural relations that threatens citizens' liberties and social stability.[76]

The nationalists were quick to respond. La Plataforma per la Llengua, grouping together nationalist youth, discerned in the Foro Babel documented evidence of 'Francoist thinking' in progressive clothing.[77] Indeed, the Foro was behaving like 'the intellectual heirs of those who sought to commit genocide against Catalan during the Franco regime'.[78]

The bill was rejected outright by the primary organization representing Catalans of immigrant descent, Cecrec (la Confederación de Entidades Culturales y Regionales de Cataluña Cecrec), which criticized the designation of Catalan as Catalonia's *llengua pròpia* and argued that the term should apply to Castilian as well. It also rejected each of the bill's main measures—quotas, the right to be served in one's language, sanctions, and school immersion. In the case of immersion, Cecrec said the focus should be on ensuring mastery of both Catalan and Castilian.[79]

With such a polarization of political and social forces, the PSC assumed a pivotal role. Since a large part of its support was among voters of immigrant descent who would be attracted to the PP's militant opposition to the law, the PSC tried to fashion a position that would be acceptable to them while keeping the support of voters of Catalan descent.

At first the PSC took the position that there was no need for a new law, that the 1983 law, with additional regulations, would suffice. It then agreed to take part in the commission's efforts to formulate a new law but insisted that any such law must be based on the broadest possible consensus. And its objections extended to most if not all the new measures under discussion. It was opposed to sanctions for failure to abide by the terms of the law. It opposed quotas for Catalan content on radio and television program. It rejected the notion that a business or government bureaucracy should have to respond to citizens in their own language. It was concerned that the education provisions should clearly delimit the role of Catalan immersion. It even argued that the new law should be called an amendment to the 1983 law rather than a distinctly new law.[80]

The CiU leadership recognized that with the size of the PSC's electorate, PSC consent was indispensable to the legitimacy of any new language law. For that matter, Catalonia's two largest union federations had told the parliamentary commission that while Catalan needed to be granted the same rights as Castilian, and its social use should be generalized, the new law should not contain sanctions.[81]

Accordingly, through much of the commission's proceedings, PSC leaders were involved in bilateral negotiations with the minister of culture, Joan Maria Pujals, over the terms of the draft law. At the same time, the PSC was careful to maintain its links with the the organizations representing Castilian-speakers. Indeed, on some occasions the main PSC representative absented himself from commission sessions to meet with Cecrec leaders.

The commission did take some of the PSC's concerns into account. It removed a reference (also contained in the 1983 law) to 'immigrant flows' in explaining the precariousness of the Catalan language—the PSC (along with Foro Babel) said the phrase stigmatized immigrant groups. By the same token, a reference was added to 'the significant contribution to Catalan culture' that had resulted from immigration.[82] But when the commission's proceedings had drawn to a close, major issues still remained outstanding and the PSC did not endorse the draft.

Negotiations continued in the ensuing weeks, and finally, in early November the CiU and the PSC came to terms. Under the agreement, references to the linguistic availability (*disponibilidad*) of public administrative personnel were changed to linguistic qualifications of the personnel (*habilitación*).[83] The requirement that 50 per cent of radio broadcasts be in Catalan was modified to allow the Generalitat to adjust the percentage in light of a station's particular audience. The requirement that public enterprises and private companies offering public services must use Catalan in 'oral' communications was modified to refer only to broadcasts by loudspeaker. The education provisions were modified to limit the extent of linguistic immersion, raising to the status of law provisions previously passed as government decrees. Provisions for sanctions were modified so that they would not apply to individuals. And reference to sanctions for public employees were removed.[84]

To some observers, these changes involved form more than content,[85] but for the ERC they were a reason to vote against the bill: 'This [CiU-PSC] agreement seeks to water down and tone down the commission's report.' Though the bill was some improvement over the 1983 law: 'at bottom, [it] was not able to meet the two requirements for the future survival of Catalan: juridical equality of Catalan with Castilian in all spheres in Catalonia and a real guarantee of its use in all spheres of life.'[86] In fact, the ERC had proposed 99 amendments to strengthen the bill.[87]

But the Partido Popular remained opposed to the bill, claiming that it was unnecessary and introduced an unacceptable system of sanctions: 'In the Catalonia of the twenty-first century our two languages will have to be used in all spheres in which Catalans are active. From this deep conviction we propose that new language laws are not necessary, that they do not accord with the social majority.'[88] The former leader of the PP, Aleix Vidal-Quadras, even urged that the law be disobeyed. That suggestion was rejected by the party leadership.[89]

'The Catalan Law'
On 30 December 1997, the Catalan parliament approved 'La llei de política lingüística' (An act for language policy), popularly known as 'the Catalan law'.[90] The 110 members of the CiU, PSC, IC, and PI voted in favour; the nine ERC members and 16 PP members voted against, for diametrically opposed reasons.

The first article of the act, which establishes that it concerns the *use* of Catalan, defines the objectives of the law as follows: (1) to encourage the use of Catalan by all citizens; (2) to establish the official use of Catalan and Castilian; (3) to normalize and encourage the use of Catalan in the administration, teaching, mass media, cultural industries, and socio-economic world; and (4) to extend knowledge of Catalan by all citizens.[91] Unlike the 1983 law, the new law defines the meaning of Catalan's status as *la llengua pròpia*: 'the language of all of Catalonia's institutions', especially the Generalitat and local administration, public enterprises, institutional mass media, teaching, and toponomy; and as 'preferred language' for all other institutions, including the Spanish state's administration in Catalonia.[92]

Like the 1983 law, the new law has sections on public administration, toponomy, teaching, and mass media. Most of the provisions of the 1983 law are reiterated, but there are some new ones. For instance, civil servants should have a knowledge of Catalan that is appropriate to their functions; collective agreements are valid in either language.[93] The use of Catalan should be guaranteed and promoted in all university-level activities, and professors should know both languages, as their duties warrant.[94] Catalan-language quotas are to be applied in the mass media: 50 per cent of general programs on cable television and radio and 25 per cent of music programs.[95] And the Generalitat is to support the development of Catalan-language software and linguistic technology.[96]

In addition, the new law has a section on 'L'activitat socioeconòmica'. Public enterprises 'should normally have to use Catalan' in their activities, internal documentation, signs, and so on. Enterprises serving the public must use 'at least' Catalan in signs, loudspeaker communications, and written communication. Enterprises that offer goods or services in Catalonia must be able to communicate with their customers in either official language and must produce signs and posters 'at least' in Catalan. Companies that have contracts with the Generalitat or local administrations or have received grants from them must use 'at least' Catalan in signs and documents addressed to the public, at least when related to the purpose of the contract or grant.[97] Catalan must be used for crucial information in the labelling of Catalan products distributed in Catalonia. The same requirement is to be introduced gradually for products originating elsewhere.[98] Public institutions must use Catalan as a general rule (*de manera general*) in advertising, and the Generalitat will attempt to make it the language used normally (*la llengua d'ús normal*) in advertising in general.[99] Finally, the Generalitat will promote the use of Catalan in labour relations and, with the help of professional bodies, in the professions.[100]

A final set of provisions contains the statement that 'this act does not establish sanctions for citizens.'[101] Nor does it establish sanctions for businesses; rather, it invokes the system of sanctions contained in existing laws to require compliance of license-holders with the law's Catalan content requirements and of businesses with the provisions concerning the use of Catalan.[102] By the same token, transitional provisions allow enterprises periods of two years, five years, or even longer, to comply with the requirements of the act. Universities have two years to comply. Existing radio and television stations will need to comply with the Catalan-language quotas when they renew their licences.[103] Also, the requirements concerning labelling of industrial and commercial products will await new regulations from the Generalitat.

Assessing the New Law

On the face of it, the additional measures introduced with the new language law seem quite limited. The new section on the 'socio-economic world' is not as far-reaching as those adopted in some other countries. This can be seen by comparing them with Quebec's *Charte de la langue française*, which is often said to have been the inspiration for Catalonia's language program.

The *Charte* requires that *all* outdoor advertising be *exclusively* in French; signs identifying a business must feature French more prominently than any other language. The *Llei de Política Lingüística* applies to advertising only by public institutions. The *Charte* requires that *all* enterprises in Quebec, public and private, make French the effective language of internal operations. The *Llei de Política Lingüística* deals with the internal operations only of *public* enterprises; private enterprises simply have to use Catalan (but not exclusively) in dealing with the public. Thus, the *Llei de Política Lingüística* does not meet the objective of the Generalitat's own plan to make Catalan 'a habitual language of work' in private businesses.

The provisions establishing Catalan-content quotas for radio and television are not at all unusual in Europe. And though the Canadian provinces do not have jurisdiction over radio and television, the Canadian federal government has long required Canadian broadcasters to meet quotas for Canadian-produced material. In addition, the Canadian federal government has long required that English and French both appear on all product labels. But European Union regulations prevent the Generalitat from requiring that all product labels be in Catalan.[104]

The *Llei de Política Lingüística* contains no requirements for private organizations, foundations, or associations. In the early 1980s, those had been an important element in early drafts of the first language law. And they had been targeted in the 'health and social institutions' section of the Generalitat's 1995 plan. Nor does the *Llei de Política Lingüística* facilitate 'the full incorporation of new immigrants into the Catalan language, culture and society', as the 1995 plan had proposed. For that reason, the law was denounced by some linguistic nationalists, and the ERC voted against it.

On the other hand, the new law was rejected in some quarters as going much too far. The CiU's concerted efforts to make the bill acceptable to the PSC ultimately succeeded. But other political forces remained bitterly oppposed to the end, and some politicians called for civil disobedience. In 1983, prolonged negotiations had produced a consensus among all political parties around the new language law; in 1997 this proved to be impossible.

One reason that the hostility to the new language law was so strong was that the forces opposed to the promotion of Catalan were themselves stronger. In 1983, there had been no party in the Catalan parliament like the PP, the self-appointed champion of Catalonia's immigrant population and of Spanish nationalism.[105] Intellectuals opposed to Catalan nationalism, especially those on the left, seem to have been better organized in 1997, as were organizations speaking for Catalonia's immigrant population.

But the hostility to the new law is also due to the fact that, however modestly, it does expand the Generalitat's role in promoting, and in some cases imposing, the Catalan language. Thus it heightens the fundamental contradiction between the formal equality of Catalan and Castilian as official languages, and the promotion of one of them, Catalan, as Catalonia's 'proper' language.

Conclusions

Over the last two decades the Generalitat has been able to make substantial progress in restoring the Catalan language. Of course, the progress has been greater on some fronts, such as education and public administration, than others, such as the economy or the cultural industries.

At the same time, the debate surrounding the draft of the second language law and the amendments that had to be made to secure its adoption reveal the obstacles that face any straightforward promotion of the Catalan language. In effect, it must be conducted within a language regime that calls for full equality of Castilian with Catalan. For two reasons, that regime is unlikely to change.

First, the constitution states explicitly that, although an autonomous community may declare a language to be official, this can only be in addition to Castilian.[106] Consequently, when Catalonia's statute of autonomy was being drafted, Catalan nationalists had to give up the hope that Catalan could become Catalonia's sole official language or that all Catalan residents could be required to know Catalan, just as they are required by the constitution to know Castilian.

The weight of this constitutional structure was evident in the Spanish ombudsman's response to the request by Aleix Vidal-Quadras's *Convivència Cívica Catalana* that he submit the *Llei del català* to Spain's Constitutional Tribunal. While refusing to do so, the ombudsman expressed concern that even this law, as it is presently written, does not afford Castilian its proper place as an official language. Certain provisions do not conform sufficiently clearly with the principle of linguistic co-officiality as laid down in the constitution, Catalonia's statute of autonomy, and the ombudsman's own pronouncement. He asked that those sections be amended; at the same time, he warned that he would be monitoring the implementation of the law and might on that basis submit it at some future point to the Constitutional Tribunal.[107]

Second, in the case of Catalonia, Castilian is the first or preferred language of close to half the population and will likely stay that way. The proportion of Catalonia's population using Catalan at home is estimated to have been 51.3 per cent in 1996; obviously, Castilian is the language used by almost all the rest. Not until 2011 will the Catalan-speakers, according to some projections, reach 52 per cent; in 2026, it could reach 54 per cent.[108]

The fact remains that in places which have adopted a single language as official language—whether Quebec, Belgium's regions, or the Swiss cantons—that language is overwhelmingly predominant in demographic terms. For instance, the proportion of Quebec's population that speaks French at home is 83 per cent and, by all demographic projections, will only increase in the coming years.[109] At the same time the case can be readily made that even the new law is insufficient to meet the challenges and dangers facing Catalan. Arguably, Catalan is far more threatened than the different languages of Belgium, Switzerland, or Canada because it is spoken only in Catalonia (along with the Balearic Islands and Valencia). Unlike French or German, it does not have the support of sovereign states and of large communities elsewhere.

Even by the most generous of estimates, it is spoken by fewer than 7 million people.[110] Thus, the range of cultural products available in Catalan is limited, as is the international market for Catalan products. To be sure, other European countries, such as the Scandinavian countries, have been able to maintain languages that also have little use externally and are spoken by only a few million at home. Yet each of those languages has the status and support accorded the 'national' language of a sovereign state. Not only are the Generalitat's powers to support Catalan very limited, but the Spanish government actively supports Castilian in a multitude of ways. To be sure, institutions of the European Union are providing some recognition and support for 'regional languages',[111] but this hardly compares to what is provided to the national language of a sovereign state.

In addition, in Catalonia the national language is threatened by the presence of large numbers of people, indeed about half the population, that prefer to use Castilian and generally do so, however well they may know Catalan. The similarity between Catalan and Castilian can facilitate the integration of immigrants from the rest of Spain, but it also means that Catalans can readily switch out of their national language and conduct their activities in Castilian. Most Catalan speakers regularly do so, and in fact, almost all Catalan-speakers also speak Castilian. While many Catalans use Catalan almost exclusively in their private lives, their public lives are quite a different matter. To that extent, Catalan doesn't envelope the whole range of life experiences and therefore runs the risk of atrophying. Granted, regions such as the Netherlands and Scandinavia have been forced to allow a considerable use of English; in fact, personal bilingualism is very high. But, without a large concentration of anglophones in the country, the sociolinguistic implications of this diglossia are not the same as in Catalonia.

Both the Spanish constitution and Catalonia's own demographic structure prevent the Generalitat from going much further. This was underlined by the strength of the opposition to the 1998 law in Catalonia itself. Most commentators agree that there is little room left for a third law. Yet, by some readings, Catalan faces formidable challenges. To be sure, Catalans tend to be quite relaxed about linguistic matters. Catalan-speakers are still prepared to switch to Castilian, doing it even unconsciously, should the situation seem to make it appropriate. The recent debates were largely restricted to élites, and had little resonance in daily life. Yet, the structural position of the Catalan language is such that Catalan nationalists are bound to remain concerned about the fate of this central element of Catalonia's national distinctiveness.

Chapter 8

Nation and Identity in Contemporary Catalonia

The coherent nationalist ideology that has dominated Catalonia's political life and guided the processes of national reconstruction has been defined and disseminated to the general Catalan public primarily by Jordi Pujol and his Convergencia i Unió. Some of the main ideas of this ideology have also been articulated by other political parties, such as the Partit dels socialistes de Catalunya, Iniciativa per Catalunya, and Esquerra republicana de Catalunya. But we can identify a set of ideas which, taken as a whole, is distinctive to the CiU and which, for our purposes, can be called 'moderate' nationalism.

Catalonia's Political and Intellectual Élite

The Moderate Version of Catalan Nationalism

At the heart of this moderate Catalan nationalism is the premise that Catalonia is a nation and that the personal identity of Catalans should be rooted, first and foremost, in this fact. Though this nation can be located geographically, its physical boundaries are not clearly set since, for some Catalan nationalists, it extends beyond the autonomous community of Catalonia to embrace the Balearic Islands and even Valencia and a tiny section of France in the larger Catalan lands. In any event, the coherence of the idea of a Catalan nation derives less from geography than from culture. Its defining trait or 'core value' is, of course, the Catalan language.[1] Linked to the language are various forms of cultural expression, ranging from folklore and popular dances to literature and music. Beyond a distinctive culture, distinctive world views are ascribed to the nation, such as a tradition of *pactisme*, a spirit of hard work and entrepreneurship, and an outward-looking European sensibility. Binding together all these presumed traits of the Catalan nation is a well-cultivated sense of historical memory rooted in struggles to maintain Catalonia's distinctiveness and autonomy in the face of external threats.

At the same time, membership in the nation is usually defined in inclusive terms. Thus, a Catalan is any person who lives in Catalonia or, in the more limiting version, a Catalan resident who is at least seeking to acquire the Catalan language and culture. Especially within official versions of the nationalist discourse, ethnic descent is explicitly rejected as a criterion for membership in the nation. To that extent, Catalan nationalists can make a credible claim that their nationalism is 'civic' rather than 'ethnic'. While it has a clearly defined national project that is fundamentally cultural, this project is to be available to all comers.

Finally, a defining characteristic of the moderate view of national identity is that it does not exclude other identities. Membership in the Catalan nation is to be the primary basis for individual identity, but Catalans can also legitimately see themselves as Spaniards, as well as Europeans. As one formulation puts it, Catalans are 'the most European of Spaniards'. Indeed, within the moderate discourse the tendency and capacity to maintain multiple identities is presented as yet another distinctive Catalan trait. On this basis, Catalans stand as virtual precursors of post-modernism who, whether by choice or by necessity, have a historically developed capacity to switch among identities and to use them to their personal and collective advantage.

A well-articulated political strategy flows from these defining values and attributes of the Catalan nation. First, the moderate nationalists insist that just as the Catalan national identity does not preclude Spanish and European identities, so the Catalan nation does not need to have a sovereign state. Rather than becoming a nation-state Catalonia is to continue in its traditional path of a stateless nation. Catalonia's right of self-determination should include the right to choose secession. Thus, the CiU was able to support the ERC's 1989 parliamentary resolution declaring that the Catalan people had not renounced their right to self-determination. But, unlike the ERC, the CiU does not propose that Catalans should actually exercise that right and become independent. Instead, Catalonia should continue its struggle to obtain recognition within Spain, which itself is not a nation-state but a multinational state. Within that state, Catalonia, as a historic nation, should be afforded national status. The Spanish state should be not unitary, or even federal, but confederal and, on that basis, Catalonia should be sovereign in key areas. But there is no reason to contemplate Catalonia's taking the ultimate step and assuming the full sovereignty of an independent state.

Second, political action is to be based on democratic institutions and methods. Indeed, it is claimed that Catalonia is a birthplace of parliament. And violence is to be eschewed as a political weapon. There may have been periods of domestic upheaval and violence in the past, even during the first few decades of this century, but they are seen as aberrations that should have no echoes in contemporary Catalonia. Thus, the short-lived Terra Lliure is said, and credibly so, to be of no real consequence.[2]

Third, as the most European part of Spain, Catalonia has every reason to pursue a closer relationship with the rest of Europe. We have seen how the Generalitat has energetically developed links with other European regions and has tried, with much less success, to obtain recognition within the institutions of the European Union.

Finally, given the centrality of language to Catalonia's national identity, a primary focus of political action must be to strengthen the Catalan language. Here, the Generalitat is to play a major role, defending and promoting Catalonia's 'own' language within the terms of two successive statutes.

It is obvious that these various premises and principles constitute a coherent belief system. Moreover, the CiU has actively promoted them throughout its unbroken tenure in the Generalitat, and each of them has been faithfully reflected in actions and policies of the Generalitat. And to varying degrees they have been advocated by such other political parties as the PSC and the IC.

Challenges to the Dominant Nationalism

None the less, this moderate nationalism has also been challenged by other elements of Catalonia's political and intellectual élite. One line of opposition rejects outright the fundamental premise that Catalonia is a nation. In particular, the Catalonia wing of the Partido Popular has articulated a fundamentally Spanish nationalism in which Catalonia is relegated to the status of a 'nationality' or, better still, a region. Though individuals may see themselves as Catalan, their primary identity must be as Spaniards.

In 1989, inspired by the efforts of the Baltic republics to exercise their self-determination, the ERC introduced a resolution in the Catalan parliament stating that 'the observance of the constitution does not imply the Catalan people's renunciation of self-determination';[3] the CiU was able to support it even though Pujol then proceeded to disclaim any desire to exercise that right. But the PP managed to be absent from the parliament at the time of the vote. For its part, the PSC was present and voted against.

Similarly, in 1997 the PP voted against the revised language law. In its opposition to the bill, it was joined by Foro Babel, which developed a sustained critique of Catalan nationalism. Its second manifesto, signed by 500 intellectuals, artists, and professionals, attacked the nationalism of the CiU, claiming that it had led Catalan society 'towards a model that corresponds neither to what the majority wanted at the inception of our democracy nor with what is revealed in the free and public statements of many Catalans today.'[4]

The ability of the PP and Foro Babel to attack central elements of the moderate nationalism is, of course, enhanced by the Spanish constitution itself, which reserves the term 'nation' for Spain as a whole and restricts Catalonia to the status of 'nationality'. Moreover, in declaring the indivisibility of the Spanish nation, the constitution effectively nullifies Catalonia's right to self-determination. Finally, in requiring that Castilian be an official language of all autonomous communities, the constitution seriously limits the ability of the Generalitat to promote Catalan. Constitutional provisions such as these virtually ensure that the dominant Catalan nationalist discourse will be directly contested, not only elsewhere in Spain but within Catalonia itself.

On the other hand, elements of moderate nationalism have also been attacked from precisely the opposite direction, most notably by the ERC and the PI (disbanded in 1999). While sharing the same basic premises regarding Catalonia's nationhood and distinguishing national characteristics, this version of the nationalist ideology draws more radical political conclusions. First, it refuses to recognize any Spanish identity, even if secondary to the Catalan one. Second, it embraces, if only for the long term, the objective of Catalonia's disengagement from Spain to form an independent state. Third, it calls for an aggressive promotion of the Catalan language that breaks openly with the framework of co-officiality. In 1997 the ERC, but not the PI, voted against the new language bill, which it had branded as too timid.

The last two decades of Catalonia's political life have been dominated by a clearly defined nationalism articulated by a political leadership that has held power in the Generalitat virtually from the beginning. But this moderate nationalism has been challenged outright by significant forces within the Catalonia political and intellectual élite, and from opposing directions.

The Catalan Public

In Catalan elections the CiU has always received less than 50 per cent of the popular vote. Moreover, a significant number of Catalans who normally vote in Spanish elections tend not to vote in the Catalan elections, in large part because they feel alien from Catalan political life or consider the elections to be of little importance.[5] Thus, there is good reason to question the extent to which the nationalist world view articulated by the CiU leadership is shared by the general public of Catalonia. To that end, I will turn to analysis of opinion surveys, in particular, one administered by the Centro de Investigaciones Sociológicas throughout Spain in 1996. The survey is especially well-suited to our purposes since it was devised to examine attitudes bearing on national identity. I use the data set from this survey to analyse the responses of 784 respondents living in Catalonia.[6]

Support for Moderate Nationalism

Analysis of the CIS survey suggests that there are real limits to the support for moderate nationalism. Despite the Generalitat's sustained efforts, it apparently remains a minority viewpoint within the Catalan population as a whole.

As Table 1 shows, only a minority of respondents agree with the fundamental premise of all Catalan nationalist discourse, that Catalonia is a 'nation'. In the 1996 survey, only 34 per cent of respondents chose 'nation', whereas 59 per cent considered Catalonia to be a 'region'. This specific question does not appear to have been asked in other surveys, so there are no bases for comparison, but there is reason to believe that these findings may underestimate the actual support for 'nation' among Catalans.[7] Still, once allowance is made for this, they at least

Table 1: Catalonia: Nation versus Region

'What term do you prefer in order to refer to Catalonia? Is it a region or a nation?'[a]

Region	59.3%
Nation	34.1
Neither	4.7
Don't know	1.9
	100.0
N	780

Source: Centro de Investigaciones Sociológicas 1996.

[a] ?Qué término prefiere utilizar Vd. para referirse a Cataluña? ?Es una región o una nación?

Table 2: Catalan versus Spanish Identities

'With which of the following statements do you most closely identify: 'I feel uniquely Spanish'; 'I feel more Spanish than Catalan'; 'I feel as much Spanish as Catalan'; 'I feel more Catalan than Spanish'; 'I feel uniquely Spanish'.[a]

Only Spanish	12.9%
More Spanish than Catalan	11.5
As much Spanish as Catalan	36.5
More Catalan than Spanish	25.7
Only Catalan	11.0
Don't know or no response	2.4
	100.0
N	784

Source: Centro de Investigaciones Sociológicas 1996.

[a] ?Con cuál de las siguientes frases se identifica Vd. en mayor medida? Me siento únicamente español, me siento más español que catalán, me siento tan español como catalán, me siento más catalán que español, me siento únicamente catalán.

establish that this view is not held by the clear *majority* of Catalans. At the same time, 'nation' is chosen by a clear majority of respondents whose mother tongue is Catalan or who were born in Catalonia.

Similarly, when it comes to the relationship between Catalan and Spanish identities (see Table 2), only a quarter of respondents (25.7 per cent) adopted the

Table 3: Characteristics of Catalan Nation

'In your opinion which is the main factor that makes Catalonia a nation? Which is the second? Its language, its ethnic or racial characteristics, its history, its economic characteristics, its culture (customs and traditions), the consciousness and will of the people, the existence of nationalist parties.'[a]

	Most Important	Second Most Important
Language	45.5%	20.6%
Ethnic or racial characteristics	1.2	3.2
History	30.0	31.6
Economic characteristics	3.2	5.9
Culture (customs and traditions)	14.2	32.0
Consciousness or will of the people	5.1	5.1
Existence of nationalist parties	—	0.4
Don't know or no response	0.8	1.2
	100.0	100.0
N	265	265

Source: Centro de Investigaciones Sociológicas 1996.

[a] En su opinión, ?qué factor es el principal que hace que Cataluña sea una nación? ?Y en segundo lugar? Su lengua, sus características étnicas o raciales, su historia, sus características económicas, su cultura (sus costumbres y tradiciones), la conciencia y la voluntad de la gente, la existencia de partidos nacionalistas.

position favoured by the moderate nationalist discourse: 'more Catalan than Spanish'. Here it can be noted that the overall distribution of responses accords with the findings of other surveys.[8] At the same time, this position is adopted by half (50.2 per cent) of the respondents who do subscribe to the underlying premise of the nationalist discourse, that is, that Catalonia is a nation. Only slightly more than a quarter (27.5 per cent) declared themselves to be exclusively Catalan.

By the same token, when asked to describe the distinctive characteristics that make Catalonia a nation (see Table 3), those who saw it as a nation chose precisely the terms preferred by the major forms of nationalist discourse. Close to half (45.5 per cent) selected 'language' as the most important characteristic, and 14.2 per cent selected 'culture'. Another 30 per cent selected history. These three traits also dominated selection of the second-most important characteristic. Also, 'ethnic or racial characteristics' was chosen by very few respondents: 1.2 per cent on the first round and 3.2 per cent on the second. This would suggest that

Table 4: Preferred Option for Catalonia

'Specifically what would you prefer with respect to Catalonia? That it cease to be an autonomous community and form part of the State with a single government, as in the past. That it continue to be an autonomous community as it is now. That it continue to be an autonomous community, but with more powers. That it be able to exercise its right of self-determination so as to become an independent state.'[a]

Spain as a unitary government	9.4%
Autonomous community as now	33.9
Autonomous community with more powers	29.5
Exercise right to self-determination and	
become an independent state	22.6
Don't know or no response	4.7
	100.0
N	(784)

Source: Centro de Investigaciones Sociológicas 1996.

Note: Because of rounding column does not total to 100%.

a ?Y en concreto, pensando en Cataluña, Vd. qué preferiría? Que dejara de ser una Comunidad Autónoma y formara parte de un Estado con un único Gobierno central, como antes. Que siguiera siendo una Comunidad Autónoma como ahora. Que siguiera siendo una Comunidad Autónoma, pero aumentando sus competencias. Que pudiera ejercer el derecho de autodeterminación para llegar a ser un Estado independiente.

Table 5: Preferred Option by Nation versus Region

	Catalonia as Region	Catalonia as Nation
Preferred Option:		
Unitary Spain	14.7%	0.8%
Autonomous community with same powers	48.8	7.5
Autonomous community with more powers	25.9	34.6
Independent state	5.8	56.0
Don't know or no response	4.7	1.2
	99.9	100.1
N	463	266

Source: Centro de Investigaciones Sociológicas 1996.

Note: Because of rounding columns do not total to 100%.

168   *Catalonia*

Table 6: European versus Spanish Citizenship

'As you probably know, there is talk of creating in the future a "European citizenship" for all the citizens of the member states of the European Union. Personally, what would you prefer: to be at the same time a European citizen and a Spanish citizen, to be above all a Spanish citizen, or to be above all a European citizen?'[a]

European and Spanish citizens	34.0%
Spanish citizen above all	37.0
European citizen above all	18.8
Don't know or no response	10.1
	99.9
N	783

Source: Centro de Investigaciones Sociológicas 1996.

Note: Because of rounding column does not total to 100%.

a Como Vd. probablement sabe, se ha hablado de crear en el futuro una 'ciudadanía europea' para todos los ciudadanos de los países miembros de la Unión Europea. ?A Vd., personalmente, le gustaría: ser ciudadano europeo a la vez que español, ser sobre todo ciudadano español, ser sobre todo ciudadano europeo?

Catalans who do see Catalonia as a nation define membership in the nation in inclusive terms, precisely as the dominant discourse does.

Turning to political strategies for Catalonia (see Table 4), the data suggest that the moderate nationalist objective of an autonomous community with additional powers is the preferred objective of only a minority of Catalans (29.5 per cent). This rejection of the CiU option is characteristic even of Catalans who see Catalonia as a nation (see Table 5): only 34.6 per cent opt for securing additional powers but remaining within Spain. Among those who see Catalonia as a nation, the clear majority, 56 per cent, support an independent state.[9] Support for Catalan independence is even higher when it is presented simply on its own, although without reference to an independent *state*, rather than as one of several options. Catalan independence received the support of 71.4 per cent of respondents who see Catalonia as a nation and 58.1 per cent of those whose mother tongue is Catalan. Among all respondents, 33.6 per cent were in approval.[10] In short, despite the emphasis of the centrist nationalist discourse on the notion of Catalonia as a nation without a state, within the Catalan public, nationalists seem prepared to view independence as the logical condition for the Catalan nation. On the other hand, most respondents who see Catalonia as a region rather than a nation draw precisely the opposite conclusion regarding Catalonia's status, favouring either the status quo (48.8 per cent) or a unitary Spain (14.7 per cent).

Table 7: Nation versus Region by Party Identification

'Here is a series of political parties. Please tell me if you feel very close, close, neither close nor distant, distant, or very distant with respect to each of them.'[a]

	Respondent feels 'very close' or 'close'				
	CiU	ERC	IC	PSC	PP
Catalonia as:					
Region	46.4%	20.6%	57.6%	63.6%	81.8%
Nation	47.6	75.7	37.6	29.1	10.0
Neither	5.0	2.9	4.0	5.0	7.6
Don't know	1.0	0.7	0.8	2.3	1.3
	100.0	99.9	100.0	100.0	100.7
N	349	136	125	258	79

Source: Centro de Investigaciones Sociológicas 1996.

Note: Because of rounding columns do not always total to 100%.

a Voy a citarle ahora una serie de partidos políticos. Dígme, por favor, si se encuentra Vd. muy cercano, cercano, ni cercano ni distante, distante o muy distante de cada uno de ellos.

Finally, there appears to be widespread popular support for the nationalist objective of strengthening links with the rest of Europe. When presented with the notion of 'European citizenship', 34 per cent of respondents stated that they would like to be citizens of both Europe and Spain and another 18.8 per cent said that they would like to be European citizens 'above all' (See Table 6).

But, as one might expect, views about Europe are shaped by views about Catalonia itself and about Spain. Thus, the option of 'European citizenship above all' was selected by a large proportion (42.5 per cent) of respondents who see Catalonia as a nation, but only by 5.9 per cent of those who see it as a region. By the same token, almost half (48.7 per cent) of the latter group chose 'Spanish citizen above all'; only 15.4 per cent of the former group did so.

On the basis of available survey data, it appears that the nationalist discourse has been embraced by only a minority of Catalans: fewer than half accept the fundamental premise that Catalonia is a nation rather than a region. Among those who do, there is a general tendency to see as the characteristics of the nation precisely the terms favoured by the nationalist discourse, that is, language and culture but not ethnic origin. They are also prepared to acknowledge a secondary identification with Spain and to favour European citizenship. Yet when it comes to political strategies, they seem inclined to favour independence for Catalonia rather than a continued, albeit enhanced, role within Spain.

Thus, the moderate CiU nationalism faces a double challenge. It is contested by radical forces within the ranks of Catalan nationalism. But also impressive is the apparent influence among Catalans of forces that reject Catalan nationalism outright, seeing Catalonia as no more than a region and rejecting the need for it to have more powers.

Explaining the Limits to Moderate Nationalism

Part of the explanation of the limited popular support for moderate Catalan nationalism seems to lie with the ineffectiveness of the CiU, which is the primary vehicle for disseminating this nationalism. Presumably attraction to the CiU is based at least in part on its brand of Catalan nationalism. By the same token, adherence to the CiU should serve over time to strengthen this nationalism. Surprisingly, Table 7 shows that among CiU adherents, respondents who say that they feel 'close' or 'very close' to the party were almost evenly split over whether Catalonia was a nation or a region.[11] The responses are much more consistent among supporters of the two 'counter-discourse' parties, with ERC supporters overwhelmingly (75.7 per cent) choosing 'nation' and PP supporters overwhelmingly (81.8 per cent) rejecting it. As one would expect, IC and PSC supporters favoured 'region', but some gave the nationalist response.

Perhaps the more limited effectiveness of the CiU is due to the fact that as a long-time government party it has attracted support on many bases other than ideology, whether economic and social policies or specific public benefits. Indeed, some may support the party *despite* its ideology. Normally, one would expect that long-term supporters of a party would eventually adopt the central tenets of party ideology, but apparently this has not happened in the case of the CiU.

Beyond political party affiliation, readiness to view Catalonia in nationalist terms should be heavily influenced by the extent to which Catalans are themselves incorporated into Catalan society. To what extent does the idea of a distinct Catalan nation accord with their own experiences? A first indicator of incorporation would be whether they began their lives in Catalonia. Indeed, as Table 8 demonstrates, 44.4 per cent of respondents born in Catalonia agree that Catalonia is a nation, but only 15.2 per cent born outside Catalonia agree. A second indicator, mother tongue, would tend to exclude native Catalans descended from recent immigrants. This does indeed produce a strong majority (59.3 per cent) agreeing that Catalonia constitutes a nation; among those whose mother tongue is Castilian only 17.0 per cent agree.[12] Since the moderate version of Catalan nationalism presumes neither native birth nor Catalan mother tongue, the full potential clientele for this nationalism perhaps would be better identified in terms of all people who have acquired the Catalan language, whatever their birthplace or mother tongue. Taking as an indicator the ability to write in Catalan, the most stringent measure of linguistic ability, 49.1 per cent see Catalonia as a nation; but among respondents unable to write in Catalan only 23.8 per cent do so. In each case, then, the presence of substantial numbers of people who are not fully incorporated into Catalan society has been an obstacle to the spread of nationalism.

Whether Catalans see Catalonia in nationalist terms may also result from the conditions under which they entered political life. On the basis of theories of

Table 8: Nation versus Region by Birthplace and Language

	Place of Birth		Mother Tongue		Write in Catalan	
	Catalonia	Elsewhere	Catalan	Castilian	Able	Not able
Catalonia as:						
Region	50.0%	76.4%	34.8%	76.2%	44.6%	69.7%
Nation	44.4	15.2	59.3	17.0	49.1	23.8
Neither	4.6	5.1	3.9	5.3	5.1	5.2
Don't know	1.0	3.3	2.0	1.5	1.2	1.3
	100.0	100.0	100.0	100.0	100.0	100.0
N	504	276	305	454	334	383

Source: Centro de Investigaciones Sociológicas 1996.

Table 9: Nation versus Region by Age and Mother Tongue

Catalan as Mother Tongue

	Age				
	18–24	25–34	35–50	51–64	65+
Catalonia as:					
Region	38.6%	26.8%	30.9%	44.6%	35.8%
Nation	56.8	67.9	65.4	50.0	55.2
Neither	4.5	3.6	2.5	5.4	3.0
Don't know	—	1.8	1.2	—	6.0
	99.9	100.1	100.0	100.0	100.0
N	(44)	(56)	(81)	(56)	(67)

Castilian as Mother Tongue

	Age				
	18–24	25–34	35–50	51–64	65+
Catalonia as:					
Region	82.9%	81.4%	67.5%	78.6%	74.6%
Nation	14.3	15.5	20.5	16.5	14.9
Neither	2.9	3.1	12.0	1.9	4.5
Don't know	—	—	—	2.9	6.0
	100.1	100.0	100.0	99.9	100.0
N	(70)	(97)	(117)	(103)	(67)

Source: Centro de Investigaciones Sociológicas 1996.

Note: Because of rounding columns do not always total to 100%.

political socialization, one might expect that Catalans who are disposed to adopt nationalist views would be much more likely to do so if, when they came of age politically, important leaders were expounding such ideas. Thus, one would expect a high proportion of younger Catalans, especially native-born Catalan-speakers, to be imbued with nationalist ideas, since they would have reached their twenties and become politically active during the collapse of the Franco regime or under the influence of the CiU-dominated Generalitat. But one might also expect relatively strong levels of Catalan nationalism among elderly Catalans,[13] who would have come of political age *before* the Franco regime, especially under the influence of the ERC leadership of the Second Republic, or who would at least have learned of this period from their siblings or parents.

The data in Table 9, on whether Catalonia constitutes a nation, seem to confirm these effects. Among respondents whose mother tongue is Catalan, support for 'nation' is indeed related to age but not in a consistent or linear fashion. It is highest among respondents aged 25–34, for whom the Generalitat was well established before they entered political life. But it is also strong in the next group, 35–50 years of age, most of whom would have entered their twenties during the 1970s as the transition to democracy was under way. Support for 'nation' dips substantially in the following age group, 51–64 years, which would have reached its twenties while the Franco regime was well entrenched. But support for 'nation' is somewhat stronger among respondents aged 65 and over, some of whom would have experienced the Second Republic of the 1930s. On this basis, the relationship to age reflects not aging but a cohort effect rooted in formative political experience.[14]

As for respondents of Castilian mother tongue, their resistance to viewing Catalonia as a nation is unaffected by aging or membership in an age cohort. The youngest two age groups, which would have received the Catalan language instruction and political socialization of the Generalitat's schools before entering political life, are just as impervious to the idea of a Catalan nation as are their elders.

Table 10, on Catalan and Spanish identities, shows that among respondents whose mother tongue is Catalan, the 'Catalan only' response is stronger among younger respondents, confirming a pattern found in other studies on identity in Catalonia.[15] On the other hand, it suggests a somewhat more nuanced pattern among respondents whose mother tongue is Castilian when it comes to Catalan and Spanish identities. Younger people are much less likely to identify exclusively with Spain and more likely to profess dual identities in which their Catalan identity is as important as the Spanish one. But there is little tendency to make the Catalan identity the primary one, as the moderate nationalists would have it.

Table 11, on alternative political options for Catalonia, shows that essentially the same pattern of age cohorts exists among respondents whose mother tongue is Catalan when it comes to support for the idea of making Catalonia an independent state, which is the most popular option of all among respondents under

Table 10: Spanish versus Catalan Identities by Mother Tongue and Age

Catalan as Mother Tongue

| | Age | | | | |
Identity:	18–24	25–34	35–50	51–64	65 +
Spanish only	2.3%	1.8%	—	—	—
More Spanish than Catalan	2.3	1.8	—	3.6	—
As much Spanish as Catalan	20.5	18.2	26.8	30.4	25.4
More Catalan than Spanish	45.5	41.8	43.9	53.6	46.3
Catalan only	29.5	34.5	24.4	12.5	26.9
Don't know or no response	—	1.8	4.8	—	1.5
	100.1	99.9	99.9	99.9	99.9
N	(44)	(55)	(82)	(56)	(67)

Castilian as Mother Tongue

| | Age | | | | |
Identity:	18–24	25–34	35–50	51–64	65 +
Spanish only	11.3%	13.4%	23.3%	27.9%	28.6%
More Spanish than Catalan	16.9	17.5	14.7	23.1	22.9
As much Spanish as Catalan	53.5	50.5	45.7	31.7	38.6
More Catalan than Spanish	16.9	12.4	12.1	12.5	8.6
Catalan only	—	2.1	2.6	1.9	1.4
Don't know or no response	1.4	4.1	1.8	2.9	—
	100.0	100.0	100.2	100.0	100.1
N	(71)	(97)	(116)	(104)	(70)

Source: Centro de Investigaciones Sociológicas 1996.

Note: Because of rounding columns do not always total to 100%.

50.[16] At the same time, among respondents whose mother tongue is Castilian, support for more powers for Catalonia as an autonomous community does have a clear and consistent relationship to age. With the youngest age group excepted, support declines in a linear fashion to age. Presumably, the younger groups are more likely to have started their lives in Catalonia, and thus to identify with it as their home—if not their nation. Still, among all age groups, respondents whose mother tongue is Castilian have a clear preference for the status quo. Even younger Castilian speakers show little interest in independence.

The most striking finding in Tables 9, 10, and 11 is that among respondents whose mother tongue is Catalan, the youngest age group, 18–24 years, shows substantially less support for the nationalist position than the next two groups.

Table II: Preferred Option by Mother Tongue and Age

Catalan as Mother Tongue

	Age				
	18–24	25–34	35–50	51–64	65 +
Preferred Option for Catalonia					
Unitary Spain	2.3%	3.6%	1.2%	3.5%	3.0%
Autonomous community as now	20.5	12.7	15.9	29.8	23.9
Autonomous community more powers	34.1	27.3	30.5	31.6	35.8
Independent state	38.6	56.4	48.8	35.1	31.3
Don't know or no answer	4.5	—	3.6	—	—
	100.0	100.0	100.0	100.0	100.0
N	(44)	(55)	(82)	(57)	(67)

Castilian as Mother Tongue

	Age				
	18–24	25–34	35–50	51–64	65 +
Preferred Option for Catalonia					
Unitary Spain	5.7%	7.4%	12.8%	23.3%	21.4%
Autonomous community as now	52.9	46.3	37.6	38.8	48.6
Autonomous community more powers	31.4	32.6	36.8	21.4	10.0
Independent state	10.0	10.5	10.3	6.8	7.1
Don't know or no answer	—	3.2	2.6	9.7	12.8
	100.0	100.0	100.1	100.0	99.9
N	(70)	(95)	(117)	(103)	(70)

Source: Centro de Investigaciones Sociológicas 1996.

Note: Because of rounding columns do not always total to 100%.

This may be due to a recent and incomplete entry into political life. But it could also be due to youthful alienation from the political discourse and general world view of older Catalans.

Finally, one might expect that acquisition of nationalist ideas would be linked to education. Catalans with higher levels of education might well be more likely to follow political debates and, thus, to the extent they are receptive to Catalan nationalism, might be more likely to acquire nationalist ideas. Indeed, Table 12 shows that among Catalan-speakers the likelihood of agreeing that Catalonia constitutes a nation increases substantially if they have pursued post-secondary education. (The first category, 'no education' has too few respondents to warrant consideration.) Table 13 suggests (with the exception of the 'F.P.' category) that

Table 12: Nation versus Region by Mother Tongue and Education

Catalan as Mother Tongue

	None	Primary	Secondary	F.P.	University	Superior
			Education			
Catalonia as:						
Region	30.0%	45.8%	43.9%	34.6%	20.0%	29.2%
Nation	70.0	47.9	45.6	57.7	77.1	66.7
Don't know						
or no response	—	6.3	10.6	7.7	2.9	4.2
	100.0	100.0	100.1	100.0	100.0	100.1
N	(10)	(96)	(57)	(26)	(35)	(24)

Castilian as Mother Tongue

	None	Primary	Secondary	F.P.	University	Superior
			Education			
Catalonia as:						
Region	72.7%	77.0%	85.8%	72.4%	75.0%	87.1%
Nation	18.1	18.0	8.8	27.6	19.2	6.5
Don't know						
or no response	9.1	5.0	5.3	—	5.8	6.5
	99.9	100.0	99.9	100.0	100.0	100.1
N	(11)	(139)	(113)	(29)	(52)	(31)

Source: Centro de Investigaciones Sociológicas 1996.

Note: Because of rounding columns do not always total to 100%.

with post-secondary education Catalan-speakers are also much more likely to declare a personal identity of 'Catalan only'. Post-secondary education does not seem to support the dual-identity formula favoured in moderate nationalism— 'more Catalan than Spanish'. This pattern, moreover, has already been established in other studies.[17]

Among Catalans whose mother tongue is Castilian, education does seem to favour coupling a Spanish identity with a Catalan one. But it does not favour making the Catalan identity primary, let alone exclusive. And it does not seem to have encouraged the adoption of the idea that Catalonia is a nation rather than region.

Conclusions

Several implications flow from these findings. Among the Catalan public there is a system of beliefs and attitudes that corresponds to the official nationalism. Catalans who recognize the existence of a Catalan nation do tend to ascribe to it

**Table 13: Catalan versus Spanish Identities
by Mother Tongue and Education**

| | | | Catalan as Mother Tongue | | | |
| | | | Education | | | |
	None	Primary	Secondary	F.P.	University	Superior
Identity:						
Spanish only	—	—	—	3.8%	—	—
More Spanish than Catalonian	—	1.0%	5.2%	—	—	—
As much Spanish as Catalonian	20.0%	30.2	31.0	19.2	16.7%	26.1%
More Catalonian than Spanish	80.0	43.8	36.2	69.2	44.4	39.1
Catalan only	—	24.0	24.1	7.7	38.9	34.8
Don't know or no reply	—	1.0	1.7	—	—	—
	100.0	100.0	98.2	99.9	100.0	100.0
N	(10)	(96)	(58)	(26)	(36)	(23)

| | | | Castilian as Mother Tongue | | | |
| | | | Education | | | |
	None	Primary	Secondary	F.P.	University	Superior
Identity:						
Spanish only	5.0%	30.7%	19.5%	10.3%	9.8%	6.5%
More Spanish than Catalonian	25.0	21.4	21.2	20.7	17.6	12.9
As much Spanish as Catalonian	33.3	33.6	43.4	48.3	58.8	74.2
More Catalonian than Spanish	16.7	10.7	13.3	20.7	9.8	—
Catalan only	—	3.6	0.9	—	2.0	3.2
Don't know or no reply	—	1.0	1.7	—	—	—
	80.0	100.0	101.0	100.0	98.0	96.8
N	(10)	(96)	(58)	(26)	(36)	(23)

Source: Centro de Investigaciones Sociológicas 1996.

Note: Columns do not always total to 100%.

precisely the character depicted in the official nationalism. They overwhelmingly choose language as the distinguishing feature of the nation, followed closely by 'history' and 'culture', and hardly any of them select 'ethnic or racial character- istics'. Thus, in the eyes of all Catalan nationalists, mass as well as élite, their nationalism is first and foremost linguistic and, on this basis, is inclusive or 'civic'. Beyond that, they are more likely to favour European citizenship as the superior one.

At the same time, the data also suggest that only a minority of Catalans sub- scribe to this nationalism, and that those who do tend to draw different conclu- sions about Catalonia's political future than the CiU version of nationalism. In the 1996 survey, the majority of nationalists appeared to favour independence over remaining in Spain, even with additional powers. And a significant proportion claimed to identify with Catalonia alone. These attitudes were especially promi- nent among Catalan-speakers between 25 and 34, who would have entered polit- ical life after the Generalitat was in existence and the CiU was actively disseminating its moderate nationalist ideology.

More fundamentally, the findings show that beliefs and attitudes are closely related to language. Among all respondents whose mother tongue is Catalan, Catalonia is seen as a nation by 59.3 per cent; among those between 25 and 34, the figure is 67.9 per cent. But among respondents whose mother tongue is Castilian, only 17 per cent are prepared to see Catalonia as a nation and there is no evidence of any movement toward nationalism, even of the moderate variety. Even the Castilian-speaking youth who have undergone the Catalan instruction and political socialization of the Generalitat's schools are as resistant as their elders to the notion that Catalonia constitutes a nation.

As many scholars have stressed over the years, relations between Catalans of Catalan and Castilian mother tongue are generally harmonious. In everyday life there is little of the tension between natives and immigrants that one finds in such places as Flanders or Northern Italy.[18] A 1997 survey found that 95.8 per cent of Catalan citizens feel 'integrated' with Catalonia, up from 94 per cent in 1995.[19] But beneath the surface as it were, Catalans are divided between two fun- damentally different visions of their political community, and the demography of Catalonia is such that neither vision can hope to prevail. From time to time, as in the 1997 debate over revising the language law, these underlying differences can suddenly come to the surface.

There is little evidence that this gulf is narrowing; indeed, the evidence sug- gests the opposite. Among Catalan speakers, younger age groups were more inclined than their elders to see themselves as 'only Catalan'. And higher levels of education seemed to favour the same attitude. The overwhelming majority con- tinue to favour dual identities, especially with Catalan as the more important one, but the exclusive Catalan identity does appear to be gaining ground. This is con- firmed by other studies.[20]

For their part, Castilian-speaking youth do seem be more inclined than their elders to adopt a Catalan identity in combination with their Spanish one. But recognizing Catalan as a *nation* is quite a different story.

Over the last 18 years the Generalitat and its CiU have fashioned a coherent vision of Catalonia and have sought to turn it into reality through a wide variety of policies. In the process, they have tried to rally Catalans around a moderate nationalist vision, rooted in dual identities and the nation without a state. Though this vision may have strong historical roots in Catalonia, the social composition of Catalonia is radically different today, with close to half of the population composed of people whose primary language is Castilian and who have no affinity for the idea of a Catalan nation. Young Catalan-speakers, however, for whom both the Catalan language and the Generalitat have a normalcy not known by previous generations, seem more prepared to contemplate a Catalan nation-state. If the goal is to find a formula by which Catalans can not only live together in relative harmony, but share a common understanding of their country, the process of national reconstruction is far from complete.[21]

Chapter 9

Conclusions

Back in the 1200s, Catalonia may have been closer than any other European society to becoming a nation state. In Pierre Vilar's famous phrase, Catalonia was 'perhaps the European country about which it would be the least inexact, the least risky' to use the term 'nation state'.[1] In these still medieval times Catalonia had acquired the essential elements of a nation state: parliamentary institutions, a dynamic merchant class, an international consular corps, economic and military power sufficient to dominate much of the western Mediterranean, and a strong sense of social solidarity. It possessed 'the fundamental conditions for a nation'.[2]

In the end, of course, Catalonia did not become a nation state. When nation states finally did emerge in Europe, Catalonia remained in the grip of Castile. Indeed, it was not until the end of the nineteenth century that a clear national consciousness finally emerged in Catalonia. However, once established, this national consciousness proved to be inextinguishable. It survived the concerted efforts of the Franco regime to erase not only a Catalan national consciousness but the language and cultural distinctiveness on which this consciousness is based.

Still, this nationalism has never produced a strong movement for political independence. In contemporary Catalonia the dominant nationalist leadership is calling for sovereignty, but this is to be a partial sovereignty within the Spanish state: the CiU has been consistent in its rejection of outright secession. Sovereignty for Catalonia would amount to federalism, even if the CiU and some other Catalan nationalists are uncomfortable with the term. Other Catalan parties, such as the PSC and the IC, have been straightforward in calling for federalism, whether it be 'differential' or 'asymmetrical'. Only the ERC is formally committed to independence, and even there independence is a long-term objective.

But even federalism has yet to be achieved, although the State of the Autonomies does offer Catalonia a substantial degree of autonomy. That represents a remarkable reversal of Catalonia's situation during the Franco years. Indeed, Catalonia's emergence as an autonomous community constitutes the first existence of Catalonia as a distinct political entity in over two-and-a-half centuries, apart from the relatively short periods of the Second Republic and the Mancomunitat. But the State of the Autonomies is not a federal state. Not only are Catalonia's jurisdictions heavily circumscribed by the Spanish state, but Catalonia has neither the independent fiscal base nor the right to participate in constitutional amendments that would come with a full-fledged federation. Even in terms of federalism, let alone independence, Catalonia remains a nation without a state.[3]

Catalonia as a 'Nation Without a State'

Catalonia has had remarkable achievements to its credit and continues to do so, despite the absence of a state, even a federal one. It has long been one of two centres of economic innovation in Spain. It was in Catalonia, as well as the Basque Country, that industrialization came to Spain. For decades, industrialization remained restricted to these two areas. Indeed, Catalonia emerged as an industrial power precisely during the period when it had no political autonomy whatsoever, and the efforts of the Franco regime to steer economic development away from Catalonia had only limited success.

In the current period, Catalonia continues to enjoy a standard of living much higher than most other parts of Spain. Its economic activity far exceeds that of Spain as a whole: on a per capita basis its gross domestic product in 1996 was 122 per cent of the Spanish average, the second highest among the autonomous communities.[4] It continues to be a major exporter—the source of 26.5 per cent of Spain's exports in 1995[5]—and has become a favourite site for foreign investment, receiving 27 per cent of foreign investment in Spain between 1985 and 1995.[6]

Culturally, Catalonia has long been a centre of innovation and creativity. Once again, its period of greatest cultural achievement may well have been toward the end of the nineteenth century and the beginning of the twentieth century, a period when it had no autonomous political structure at all. During those decades it underwent its Renaixença, produced *modernisme*, and innovated boldly in architecture.

In the contemporary period, Catalonia continues to distinguish itself culturally. In opera, Josep Carreras, Victoria de Los Angeles, and Montserrat Caballé are recognized worldwide. The *nova cançó* is known far beyond Catalonia. Not only have new generations of Catalan writers emerged, but their works are increasingly available through translation. The 1992 Olympics in Barcelona was an occasion for new architectural triumphs and highly successful urban renewal.

The Catalan nation survived the systematic attempts of the Franco regime to eliminate it. Not only were Catalonia's political institutions abolished, but the Catalan language was forbidden in public institutions, including schools, and for a time its use was actively discouraged in all public places. Catalans could not even use Catalan names when they registered their newborn children. Officially, the Catalan nation had ceased to exist; yet it survived.

In short, Catalonia appears to be a most compelling demonstration of the ability of nations to achieve greatness without the advantages of a state. Indeed, some observers consider that Catalonia is a model for other nations without states and that it demonstrates the irrelevance of sovereignty and other outmoded political notions. Thus, in *The Power of Identity* Manuel Castells quotes Prat de la Riba's contention that 'the State must be fundamentally differentiated from the Nation' and goes on to argue that

> [Catalonia's] differentiation between cultural identity and the power of the state, between the undisputed sovereignty of apparatuses and the networking of power-sharing institutions, is a historical innovation in relation to most processes of construction of nation states, solidly planted in historically shaky soil. . . . By not searching for a new state but fighting to preserve their nation, Catalans may have come full circle to their origins as people of borderless trade, cultural/linguistic identity, and flexible governmental institutions, all features that seem to characterize the information age.[7]

And advocates of the region state have cited Catalonia's contemporary economic success as proof of the irrelevance of political structures and interventionist governments.

The Continued Viability of 'Statelessness'

Nonetheless, for contemporary Catalonia the formula of 'nation without a state' is increasingly problematic. In the past, Catalonia's remarkable achievements were made possible by the presence of an equally remarkable bourgeoisie, which, largely through its own efforts, led Catalonia into the industrial age and, in conjunction with the Basque Country, led Spain itself into the industrial age. At the same time, this class underwrote much of the cultural achievements of the late nineteenth and early twentieth centuries. Collectively, it built such monuments as the Liceu and the Palau de la música catalana; individually, its members commissioned many of Gaudi's greatest buildings. The same bourgeoisie also made possible the many associations and foundations that produced Catalonia's distinctively rich civil society.

But this bourgeoisie is no more, and the Generalitat has been drawn into filling the void. Indeed, the re-emergence of the Generalitat came none too early. Cultural activities have become increasingly dependent on Generalitat funds. The Generalitat and all other governments had to assume a leading role in financing the rebuilding of the Liceu. And civil society has become steadily more dependent on grants from the Generalitat. Similarly, with the loss of Catalonia's indigenous economic institutions, the Generalitat has been drawn into developing job-creation strategies and orchestrating new forms of collaboration between business and labour.

At the same time, the enormous wave of immigrants that came with the 1950s and 1960s has presented Catalonia with challenges that it never had to face before. This wave differed from the past not only in numbers but in the extent to which the immigrants spoke Castilian. It is difficult to see how this population could have been integrated without the deliberate efforts of public institutions, such as schools. Nor for that matter could native Catalans have recovered full mastery of Catalan after the Franco years without concerted support not only from educational institutions but also from publicly financed mass media.

In short, it would have been impossible to meet the challenges of restoring Catalonia's cultural and linguistic distinctiveness after the Franco years without the institutions of the Generalitat and the development of comprehensive language policies.

Even then, given the limitations on the Generalitat's jurisdictions and such constitutional strictures as co-officiality of languages, it has been difficult to frame an adequate linguistic policy. And the Generalitat's capacity to intervene in the economy is restricted.

To some extent, the fortunes of parliamentary politics have compensated for these limitations on the Generalitat. Thanks to the dependence of minority governments on the CiU and the other nationalist parties, Catalonia has been able to obtain much-needed fiscal resources as well as some additional responsibilities. But, strictly speaking, these various arrangements are the results of agreements among parliamentary parties. They have no formal guarantee of permanency should a future government party enjoy majority status. With time, and continued minority governments, a 'culture' of federalism might well become established. But so far, the actions of both PSOE and PP governments have belied this. And the most recent Spanish election may have signalled an end to the era of minority governments and freed the Spanish government from the need to deal with the CiU and other nationalist parties.

Nor, in the end, has economic integration with the rest of Europe provided Catalonia with new forms of political autonomy. Clearly, Catalonia has become more and more economically linked with the rest of Europe, whether by trade patterns or through the control of the Catalan economy by European capital, and has been able to move beyond the national market. But it is not as clear that it has been able to move beyond the nation state of Spain and establish the kinds of *political* links that would parallel its new economic links.

The Catalan Generalitat has not been able to establish formal reations with sovereign states, though it has been able to do so with 'substates' or regions within sovereign states. Indeed, Catalonia has been conspicuously active in cultivating such inter-regional links. But these links, even in the elaborate form of the Four Motors of Europe, do not seem to go beyond information exchanges and joint projects, and their economic significance is far from clear, even in the case of the Four Motors.

Nor has the Generalitat been able to secure direct representation in the central organs of the new European political institutions. The Spanish state has made sure that the opportunities available to the members of the formally federal states of Germany, Austria, and Belgium, such as participation in some discussions of the Council of Ministers, would not be available to Catalonia and the other autonomous communities.

In fact, Catalonia may well have more political power in Spain's political institutions than it has in the EU institutions. At least in the case of the Spanish parliament, Catalonia is guaranteed formal representation, and under minority governments its influence could be far greater than its quantitative presence would suggest. Yet, power has shifted from the Spanish state to Brussels. Catalonia does receive some new fiscal transfers thanks to the EU, but even these are limited by the fact that Catalonia tends not to qualify for support, given its status as 'a rich region in a poor country'.[8]

The advocates of the region state seem to argue that such relations with a central state or international organizations are of limited importance since political institutions are themselves declining in significance. All that counts are economic links. What matters is that a region have the human capital and the infrastructure necessary to initiate economic links with other regions, whether in the same continent or in other parts of world. From this neo-liberal perspective, the active support of any autonomous government of the region seems to be of little consequence.

Yet, we have seen how the Generalitat has promoted trade by maintaining offices in many parts of the world. More to the point, the Generalitat has been drawn by labour and business into tripartite employment strategies. By the same token, the extent to which Catalonia has the human capital appropriate to its potential as a region state is very much dependent on its educational system, in which the Generalitat plays a central role. At the same time, the Generalitat's ability to act in these areas is limited both by the fiscal resources available to it and the jurisdictions and responsibilities afforded by the statute of autonomy.

The fact remains that, however advanced Catalonia may appear in relation to the rest of Spain, it is considerably behind the leading regions of the other major countries of Europe. This is reflected in its history of trade deficits with the rest of Europe, however profitable its trading within Spain may be. It is difficult to see how Catalonia can, as a region state, correct this disadvantage in its relations with the rest of Europe.[9]

For all these reasons, pressures are bound to continue for the Generalitat to enjoy, if not the status of a sovereign state, at least the status of a 'federal state'. Even if Catalan nationalists may fear that the term federalism implies equality with Spain's various regions, they will continue to seek what amounts to a federal relationship with Madrid such that, for certain purposes but with full constitutional guarantees and fiscal autonomy, the Catalan nation will indeed have a state of its own; Catalonia would at last become a nation state.

Catalonia as a 'Civic Nation'

Beyond its historical success as a nation without a state, Catalonia has another claim to relative distinctiveness, namely, the extent to which its nationalism is 'civic'. Among all the stateless nations, Catalonia may be one of the closest to being a 'civic nation', in other words, one whose nationalism is based not on ethnicity but on a common project, both political and cultural, to which all citizens can subscribe.

To be sure, the notion of a 'civic nation' is an 'ideal type', to which no actual nation will conform entirely.[10] That can be seen in the attempts by some nationalist thinkers to define the Catalan nation in ethnic terms, that is, to stress descent as the basis of membership in the nation. Invariably those attempts have been rejected by most Catalans, including nationalists. This general rejection of 'ethnic nationalism' is all the more remarkable given the exceptional levels of immigration that Catalonia experienced in the 1950s and 1960s. Few societies have had to cope with such large waves of immigrants, and among those that have, such as the United States, some have had strong nativist movements. Unlike the US however, Catalonia had no state apparatus to facilitate the integration of immigrants; nor do the current efforts of the Generalitat to promote the Catalan language necessarily reflect any emphasis on ethnicity, despite some criticism to the contrary. Rather, as in the insistence on a single Catalan-dominated public school system, the Generalitat is eager to integrate Castilian-speaking immigrants into the Catalan nation. For that matter, most scholars agree that Catalan nationalism is largely civic.[11]

Challenges to the Civic Nation

None the less, Catalonia's claim of civic nationalism has increasingly come under strong attack. In particular, Foro Babel has emerged as a platform for opposition forces. Born of opposition to the new Catalan language law, this organization claims that its second manifesto, which is a sweeping attack on the claims of Catalan nationalism, has been signed by 500 intellectuals, artists, and professionals.[12] Although Foro Babel's denunciations of the dominant Catalan nationalism have not resonated with the Catalan public in general, its existence and high visibility in intellectual circles have given Catalan nationalism a much more coherent and articulate opposition within Catalonia than it had in the past.

Moreover, current immigration trends mean that the basic nationalist premise of openness to newcomers will be tested as never before. Catalonia has now become a magnet for immigrants from northern Africa, especially Morocco, who, unlike earlier immigrants, may speak languages that are far removed from Catalan. Moreover, this trend may pose issues of religion and race. Indeed, the new immigrants have already been the object of racist attacks.

Impressive as they may be, Catalonia's achievements as both a nation without a state and a civic nation are now faced with much more rigorous challenges, and only time will tell whether Catalonia's established formulas will survive. That being said, what general lessons might be drawn from Catalonia's past experience?

Lessons from Catalonia

The Formation of Nations

Catalonia is an especially clear demonstration of the extent to which nations, and in particular nationalist movements, do not simply emerge in some spontaneous manner but are created or 'constructed'. Thus, Catalonia has a historical existence as a distinct community extending back to the late 900s. It has long possessed all the preconditions of a nation. But it was only quite recently, at the end of the nineteenth century, that this potential was finally realized and a clear sense of nationhood emerged as leadership articulated the idea that Catalonia constituted a nation.

Still, this nationalist leadership was successful only because its idea of nation was so clearly supported by the social and cultural reality that was experienced by most members of the would-be nation. The idea of a Catalan nation 'took' because most Catalans could recognize themselves within it. For the same reason they consistently rejected the idea of membership in a Spanish nation, both before and after the emergence of Catalan nationalism. Thus, if nations are 'imagined', it is in terms of the possibilities offered by the patterns of cultural, social, and economic relations that are already in existence.[13]

The case of Catalonia also shows that the emergence of a nationalist leadership and the processes through which it manages to construct the idea of a nation are more complex than is sometimes believed. Thus, one school of historical interpretation, linked in particular to Pierre Vilar, assigns the leadership role to the Catalan bourgeoisie and roots its promotion of Catalan nationalism in the failure of the Spanish state to adopt its program of economic protection. Yet, the bourgeoisie was in fact a latecomer to Catalan nationalism. The case for Catalan nationalism was already being made by a range of intellectual and literary leaders. By the time the bourgeoisie came around, the Catalan nation had already been 'constructed'. Even then, its allegiance to Catalan nationalism was tenuous, as was soon revealed by its attitude to the Primo de Rivera dictatorship.

Moreover, once the idea of a Catalan nation had been formulated in intellectual and literary milieux, it spread rapidly to other parts of the Catalan population precisely because they had long had a sense of distinct identity as Catalans. Catalan nationalism gave form to an identity and a way of functioning that had long existed among the Catalan people. The nationalism was not simply imposed on the Catalan population by any class, least of all the Catalan bourgeoisie, however powerful it may have been.

In short, the sense of nationhood does involve active construction on the part of a leadership, but, at least in nations without states, these leaders do not create the nations. Conceivably, in the case of nation states the nations that emerge are the creations of the respective states. However, as states such as France demonstrate, the building of nation states usually entails the generalization throughout the state's population of the cultural traits and ideals of one of the nations within the state, that is, the one that controls the state. In any event, by definition, nations without states are not the creation of a state apparatus. There, at least, the emergence of a sense of nation involves the transformation of a long-standing sense of identity and a historically constituted culture.

Catalonia and the Other Minority Nations
At the same time, if the case of Catalonia conforms to general notions about the processes of construction through which nations and nationalism emerge, it also offers one more demonstration of the infinite variety of forms that nations may

take and the futility of trying to explain the growth and force of nationalism by any simple formula, whether it be based upon language, ethnicity, or economic and political conditions.

Catalonia is often compared with several other nations that can be dubbed minority nations within larger states: the Basque Country, Wales and Scotland, Flanders and Walloonia, and Quebec. Wales and Scotland can best be seen as territorial units to which limited powers have been devolved by the central parliament, whereas Flanders, Walloonia, and Quebec are fully autonomous states within federal systems. The Basque Country is somewhere between the two models since it shares Catalonia's ambiguous status as an autonomous community but enjoys a fiscal independence that is possessed by none of the others.

All these nations are industrialized, located in the First World, and firmly situated within Western civilization. In all these nations, nationalists claim to be outward looking and to favour free trade and continental economic and political integration, and they profess that their nationalism is civic rather than ethnic, although the credibility of these claims may vary. In other respects, however, these nations are fundamentally different; and Catalonia is different from all of them.

For instance, although all these nations are concerned with the status of their 'national' languages, the actual conditions of these languages are remarkably different. In some nations the nationalists' concern with language seems to derive more from their nationalism itself than from the sociology or political economy of language. Thus, in the Basque Country, Wales, and Scotland, few members of the nation still actually speak the national language. The objective for nationalists is more one of reviving a language that has virtually disappeared and that has difficulty functioning within an urban, industrial society.

In the cases of Flanders, Walloonia, and Quebec, as well as Catalonia, the issue is one of saving a commonly used language that is under threat, whether from speakers of another language or from the forces of economic and cultural globalization. But even then, there are important differences. In Quebec, for instance, the national language, French, is in fact the *primary* language in which most members of the nation can express themselves. According to the 1996 census, only one-third (33.7 per cent) of Quebec francophones could also speak English.[14] Thus, in the work world, the requirement to use English can place francophones at a distinct disadvantage. Historically, the desire to eliminate this disadvantage and the economic and social consequences that flow from it was a primary force behind language policy. Similarly, in Belgium historically only a minority of the population has known both French and Flemish, and those have tended to be Flemish.[15] In these cases, the defence of the national language is in fact a defence of individuals' primary means of expression.

In Catalonia, however, virtually all Catalan-speakers are also quite comfortable in Castilian; they can switch quite easily between the two and regularly do so. Indeed, the difference between the two languages is far less than the difference between the languages of Canada or Belgium. Thus, affirmation of the Catalan language has little to do with offsetting any economic or social disadvantage that comes from having to use Castilian. For that matter, Catalan-speakers continue to enjoy a superior economic position to Castilian-speakers. Affirmation of the Catalan language has much more to do with affirming a national identity, of which the Catalan language is an expression.

The dynamic of nationalism is sometimes traced to the struggle against uneven development and economic subordination. Quebec, Scotland, and especially Wales have indeed known such economic disadvantage, whether or not the disadvantage actually explains their nationalism. Flemish nationalism could be understood as a reaction to domination of Belgium's economy and political institutions by French-speaking Walloons.[16] Ultimately, even Walloon nationalism might be explained in these terms given the shift of economic power to Flanders.

Yet, once again, the situation is different in Catalonia, which for centuries has remained economically *superior* to the rest of Spain while politically subordinated to Madrid. It stands at the economic core but on the political periphery.

Catalonia does, of course, share that state of affairs with the Basque Country,[17] which has also long been at the economic centre and the political periphery. Yet, a comparison of Basque nationalism and Catalan nationalism shows that despite this common condition, the two nationalisms historically have followed quite different paths. In the past, if not now, Basque nationalism had a distinctly ethnic character, which is in striking contrast to the general absence of ethnicity within definitions of Catalan nationalism. An even more dramatic difference is the contemporary significance in the Basque Country of political terrorism, represented by ETA, which has been responsible for assassinations, as well as bombings that have resulted in many deaths. ETA is very much a minority movement, whose methods are rejected by the vast majority of Basques. It has no counterpart in contemporary Catalonia. Similarly, the Basque Country, unlike Catalonia, has long had an important secessionist movement; this is not the case in Catalonia.

As one might well imagine, various explanations have been offered as to how the two nationalisms can continue to be so different despite the similarity in economic and political relationships with the rest of Spain. For Juan Díez-Medrano, the answers lies with variations in these very relationships.[18] The Basque Country's industrial development was specialized in capital goods and banking, with a high concentration of ownership. These characteristics led the Basque bourgeoisie to focus on Spain as a whole, and to develop links with Spanish capitalists. Catalonia's industrial development, which was more centred on consumer goods, featured a much larger number of capitalists, and their activities were concentrated primarily in Catalonia. As a result, whereas much of the Catalan bourgeoisie was sympathetic, in varying degrees, to Catalan nationalism, the Basque bourgeoisie was hostile to Basque nationalism. Thus, in the Basque Country the nationalist cause was taken up by pre-industrial élites who, reacting against industralization, imposed a much more radical stance on Basque nationalism, making it both anti-capitalist and separatist.

Others have stressed cultural differences between Catalonia and the Basque Country. One possible explanation lies in Catalonia's long tradition of *pactisme*, which does not have a counterpart in the Basque Country.[19] Another line of argument, developed by Daniele Conversi, stresses differences in the role of language. Unlike Catalonia, the Basque Country did not develop a distinctive 'high culture', its élites were assimilated to Castile, and the Basque language, which survived in only a small part of the population, was marginalized. Lacking language as a 'core value', Conversi argues, Basque culture could not hope to integrate newcomers in the way that Catalan culture could. And during the Franco regime Basque culture did not offer nationalists as effective a route for evading state repression as did Catalan culture: in Catalonia, ostensibly cultural activities such as book publishing and promotion of the Catalan language were actually important forms of national affirmation. This insecurity bred exclusivism, radicalism, and political violence.[20]

Doubtless, no single factor will explain the differences between Catalan and Basque nationalism. The answer probably lies in the interaction between culture and economic and social structure. After all, the fact that in Catalonia the bourgeoisie has been integrated with the national culture and language, whereas in the Basque Country it was assimilated to Castile, itself reflects differences in the predominant activity and economic interests of the two bourgeoisies.

What we can say about 'minority nations', especially on the basis of the Catalan case, is that they tend to emerge on the basis of long-standing identities that are themselves the result of historical processes. The defining characteristics or core values of the nation can vary greatly. The most one can say is that they are rooted in a long-standing culture.[21] Similarly, the social and economic conditions under which a sense of nationhood develops and persists can vary enormously. Nationalism does not result directly from some sort of imperatives in the sociology of language or political economy; these conditions vary far too much to allow for such a straightforward proposition.

By the same token, there is nothing 'new' about the nationalism of minority nations.[22] Sometimes this nationalism is traced to conditions that arose in the middle of the twentieth century, namely, the erosion of the powers of established states through liberalization of trade, regional economic integration, the rise of supranational organizations, the general processes of globalization, and so on. The nationalism of some minority nations may indeed have become more visible in recent decades. As established nation states lose their powers and prerogatives, they are less able to offset or conceal the continued presence of distinct nations within their own territory. We saw how Catalonia has sought to use the institutions of the new Europe to assert its own existence. Clearly, the emergence of global technologies and means of communication has made it easier for Catalan nationalists to make their case known. Yet the Catalan nation itself has been much in evidence throughout this century, as has its struggle for autonomy, whether the adversary be the anti-Catalanism of the Primo de Rivera dictatorship, the Jacobin tendencies of the Second Republic, or the 'cultural genocide' of the Franco regime.

Indeed, on the basis of the Catalan experience, it is not at all clear that the processes of regional integration and globalization actually do give minority nations new leverage and opportunities to expand their autonomy. The Generalitat has been unable to obtain representation in such EU institutions as the Council of Ministers. Even if it had been successful, the Generalitat could have expected no more than what some other EU members have been allowed, namely, the possibility to speak on behalf of all autonomous communities when discussion involves issues that pertain to them. Clearly, the development of the EU has served to transfer powers away from the established nation states, including Spain. By and large, however, the movement has been to the EU institutions in Brussels rather than to Catalonia and the other minority nations.

Federalism and Multinationalism
Finally, Catalonia and Spain demonstrate the difficulties in accommodating minority nations within a larger state. Within Spain, there may be three historic nations but most Spaniards continue to think of Spain as a nation state and the Spanish state itself operates on that basis.

The pressure for Spain to come to terms with its historic nations was greatest at the death of Franco. Clearly, the proponents of democracy could not have succeeded without the active participation of the liberal forces in these nations, especially Catalonia. Yet, even then, the issue was not addressed head on, whether out of deference to the military and other conservative forces or out of a simple refusal to abandon the ideal of Spain as a nation state. Thus, the new constitution recognizes the existence within Spain of 'nationalities' rather than 'nations' and at the same time affirms the indivisibility of the Spanish nation. The autonomous communities are afforded the right to couple another language with Castilian as official languages, but only Castilian has official status within the Spanish state.

The subsequent development of democratic Spain has not really brought any resolution of the question. Minority government, first with the PSOE and then with the PP, has somewhat tempered the actions of the Spanish state, but even so the Aznar government has tried to give full voice to an integral Spanish nationalism, such as through the requirement for uniform teaching of Spanish history and the Castilian language or through regulations about use of the national anthem. And, insisting that Spain is not a federal country, the Aznar government has resisted pressures to allow the autonomous communities to be present at the EU's Council of Ministers.

Nationalists in Catalonia and the other historic nations continue to develop schemes to establish a multinational Spain, but they are largely rejected by Spain's political leadership, whatever its ideological complexion. Catalan nationalists, such as the leaders of Unió, may be quite correct when they claim that Spain's history is rooted in confederal principles, but such appeals have little resonance among Spain's leaders. Not only is there general resistance to any formal recognition of the historic nations and their institutions, but within the Spanish state even the languages of these nations have little status.

Given the general absence of any formal recognition of multinationalism in Spain's political institutions, even through such token measures as official status for national languages, enormous weight is placed on the sole mechanism that remains: bargaining between major parties and the nationalist ones, or 'indirect coalitions'. Like the PP's accords with the CiU and its nationalist counterparts, these bargains are carefully framed in neutral terms that grant most concessions in fiscal resources or responsibilities to all 17 ACs. Yet, these arrangements are very much dependent on whether the major party lacks a majority.

While not recognizing multinationalism, the Spanish constitution did lay the basis for asymmetries in the relations between the ACs and the Spanish state, thereby enabling the historic nations to acquire greater powers than the 14 other ACs. However, it was intended that all 17 ACs would eventually enjoy the same powers. For that matter, one AC, Andalusia, rapidly succeeded in joining the historic nations in their acquisition of additional power. And over the years, other ACs have sought to adopt some of the trappings of the historic nations by declaring themselves to be nationalities as well. Beyond these imitation effects, asymmetry has been weakened by officials in the Spanish state itself, who have tried to reduce any de facto status for the historic nations by encouraging other ACs to assume the same responsibilities. Thus, the Spanish experience would suggest that it is difficult to maintain asymmetrical arrangements if there is no recognition of the underlying multinationalism that makes them appropriate.

At the same time, the continued rejection of full sovereignty by most of Catalonia's nationalist élite gives the lie to the assumption of some scholars that nationalists inevitably aspire to independence, and that there is a slippery slope between nationalism and separatism. Contrary to the claims of some observers, both inside and outside Spain, Catalonia's leadership under the Second Republic was not predominantly separatist. By that time, Francesc Macià had renounced his past tendencies; in his 1931 declaration of Catalan sovereignty he was careful to situate Catalonia within an Iberian federation, and even that declaration was effectively abandoned within a matter of days. And, when it came to the transition to democracy, Catalan nationalists were quite prepared to endorse the new Spanish constitution, however much it fell short of their objectives.

The case of Catalonia demonstrates the viability of multiple identities. Thus, over 70 per cent of Catalans see themselves as both Catalan and Spanish.[23] Even among Catalans whose mother tongue is Catalan, only slightly more than a quarter see themselves as exclusively Catalan.[24] The same is true even among Catalans who see Catalonia as a nation and identify with Catalonia on that basis.[25]

Catalonia's Future

Catalonia has continued to follow its historical path of development as a nation, remaining one of Spain's primary centres of economic activity and a site of cultural innovation that draws attention in Europe and around the world. While it still lacks a sovereign state, that is, one that enjoys either the full sovereignty of independence or the limited sovereignty of federalism, Catalonia's Generalitat has been able to gain autonomy in a wide range of areas. In fact, it is now in the process of implementing a second comprehensive law to strengthen the Catalan language.

Only a few decades ago, Catalonia had no autonomous political institutions. Through policies that amounted to cultural genocide, the Spanish state was effectively seeking to destroy the Catalan nation; now the nation seems to be stronger than ever. Indeed, among Catalonia's CiU leadership there has developed a 'triumphalism' that considers the process of national reconstruction so remarkable and extensive that it cannot be halted.

Yet there are real limitations to this progress and little indication that they will disappear. The Generalitat's gains in its relations with the Spanish state have fallen short of any full-fledged federalism, let alone recognition of Spain's multinationalism. So far, the Generalitat's efforts to reach out to the rest of Europe have had little recognition by the institutions of the European Union. The Generalitat's success in promoting the Catalan language has major shortfalls, such as the language of work in the private sector.

Beyond that, new conditions threaten the accomplishments that have taken place. Catalonia's gains in its relations with the Spanish state have depended largely on minority governments in Madrid. But the March 2000 Spanish election ensured that for the next few years at least Madrid will have a majority government led by the PP, a party that is deeply imbued with Spanish nationalism and instinctively hostile to Catalan nationalism. And, for good measure, the most recent Catalan election made the CiU government dependent on the same party. In addition, the debate over the 1997 language reform gave birth to a new organization, Foro Babel, which has placed in question, in an unprecedented manner, the very assumptions about the role of the Generalitat and its relation to Catalan nationalism which the CiU has tried to established over the last two decades.

With such a state of affairs, it is difficult to see how the continuing ambiguities in Catalonia's political status might be resolved, at least in the direction that Catalan nationalists would wish. Formal independence for Catalonia is clearly not likely. Some young people whose mother tongue is Catalan and who tend to identify primarily with Catalonia might find it attractive, but most native Catalan-speakers continue to couple the Catalan and Spanish identities, and the fact that Castilian is now the mother tongue of close to half the population of Catalonia clearly precludes any possible movement to independence.

Even the limited sovereignty of a formally federal state seems to remain out of Catalonia's reach given the continued strength, if not resurgence, of a Spanish nationalism that rejects the claims of the historic nations within Spain and an endemic suspicion of federalism throughout much of Spain's political leadership.

In short, by all indications Catalonia is fated to continue to struggle with the contradictions of building a nation without a state. So far, it has been remarkably successful in doing so.

Notes

Chapter I

1 Kathryn A. Woolard, *Double Talk: Bilingualism and the Politics of Ethnicity in Catalonia* (Stanford: Stanford University Press, 1989), 13.

2 Robert Hughes, *Barcelona* (New York: Vintage Books, 1993), 58–9.

3 Ibid.

4 See, for instance, Josep M. Nadal and Modest Prats, 'Un bien chèrement défendu', in Joaquim Nadal Ferreras and Philippe Wolff, *Histoire de la Catalogne* (Toulouse, 1982), 91.

5 Jaume Rossinyol, *Le problème national catalan* (Paris: Mouton, 1974), 184.

6 Francesc Vallverdú, 'A Sociolinguistic History of Catalan', *International Journal of the Sociology of Language* 47 (1984), 13.

7 Josep-Maria Puigjaner, *Everything about Catalonia* (Barcelona: Generalitat, 1992), 31.

8 Nadal and Prats, 'Un bien chèrement défendu', 96.

9 Woolard, *Double Talk*, 14.

10 Nadal and Prats, 'Un bien chèrement défendu', 100.

11 Woolard, *Double Talk*, 14.

12 Nadal and Prats, 'Un bien chèrement défendu', 101.

13 Rossinyol, *Le problème national*, 194.

14 Nadal and Prats, 'Un bien chèrement défendu', 109.

15 Nadal and Prats, 'Un bien chèrement défendu', 112, and Daniele Conversi, *The Basques, the Catalans and Spain: Alternative Routes to Nationalist Mobilisation* (London: Hurst, 1997), 13.

16 Nadal and Prats, 'Un bien chèrement défendu', 112-14; and Conversi, *The Basques, the Catalans and Spain*, 14-17.

17 Vallverdú, 'A Sociolinguistic History of Catalan', 23.

18 Nadal and Prats, 'Un bien chèrement défendu', 116.

19 Percentages calculated from Institut d'Estadística de Catalunya, 'El coneixement del català l'any 1996', April 1998, 8. The data are based on the population two years of age and older.

20 The 1986 figures were 2,775,682 for Valencia and 560,995 for Balearic Islands (Generalitat de Catalunya, *The Catalan Language Today* [Barcelona: Generalitat, 1992], Table 1). To be sure, Valencian nationalists insist that the language spoken in Valencia is Valencian rather than Catalan.

21 Generalitat, *The Catalan Language Today*, 19.

22 Institut d'Estadística de Catalunya, 'El coneixement del català l'any 1996', April 1998, 8.

23 In 1993, 5,292,000 people spoke Danish; in 1995 about 9 million spoke Swedish and 5 million spoke Norwegian (Barbara Grimes, *Ethnologue: Languages of the World*, 13 edn (Dallas: Summer Institute of Linguistics, 1996), 474 and 517.

24 Puigjaner, *Everything about Catalonia*, 16.

25 Albert Balcells, *Catalan Nationalism: Past and Present* (London: Macmillan, 1996), 3; and Woolard, *Double Talk*, 16.

26 Salvador Giner, *The Social Structure of Catalonia* (Sheffield: Anglo-Catalan Society, 1984), 4.

27 Balcells, *Catalan Nationalism*, 4.

28 Giner, *The Social Structure of Catalonia*, 8. This discussion of *pactisme* is drawn from Giner's account.

29 'These kings [Jaume I and Pere II 'El Gran'] decided to transform the Corts from a consultative body into an institution with legislative powers, thus making them the first sovereign courts in Europe' (Oriol Vergés and Josep Cruañas, *The Generalitat in the History of Catalonia* [Barcelona: Generalitat, 1991], 5). In the foreword, the Generalitat minister of culture, Joan Guitart i Agell, calls the Corts 'the first sovereign European legislative assembly' (5).

30 Vergés and Cruañas, *The Generalitat in the History of Catalonia*, 13–18; Charles E. Dufourcq, 'Le temps du rayonnement et des crises (1276–1472)' in Farreras and Wolff, *Histoire de la Catalogne*, 3226–7; and Balcells, *Catalan Nationalism*, 8–9.

31 Vilar places the Corts, at the end of the thirteenth century, 'en avance sur l'évolution des organes représentatifs du même genre nés ailleurs en Europe ou dans la Péninsule elle-même' (Pierre Vilar, *La Catalogne dans l'Espagne moderne* [Paris: Flammarion, 1962], 211). Though Castile also had Corts, their powers were less extensive than those of Catalonia (Medrano, *Divided Nations*, 24).

32. Balcells, *Catalan Nationalism*, 4. Indeed, Hughes comments on Catalonia's adoption of St George (*Sant Jordi*): 'Now the desire to be *molt anglès* gave Barcelona a new saint: the patron of Barcelona's perennial Anglophilia'. He also traces this to a new Spanish interest in northern Europe (Hughes, *Barcelona*, 173).

33 Giner, *The Social Structure of Catalonia*, 16.

34 Giner, *The Social Structure of Catalonia*, 5. To be sure, some scholars, such as the French historian Pierre Vilar, do downplay the thesis (Vilar, *La Catalogne dans l'Espagne moderne*, 171.)

35 Vilar, *La Catalogne dans l'Espagne moderne*, 185–6; and Juan Díez Medrano, *Divided Nations: Class, Politics and Nationalism in the Basque Country and Catalonia* (Ithaca: Cornell University Press, 1995), 22.

36 Vilar, *La Catalogne dans l'Espagne moderne*, 181.

37 Ibid., 182.

38 Ibid., 180–1.

39 Ibid., 205.

40 Ibid., 201.

41 Puigjaner, *Everything about Catalonia*, 20.

42 Balcells, *Catalan Nationalism*, 7.

43 Vilar, *La Catalogne dans l'Espagne moderne*, 197.

44 Ibid., 213. Though Vilar is careful to avoid such terms as '*sentiment national*', which is used by Catalan historians but drawn from a later age, he stresses that there was 'a strong feeling of group solidarity, a decline in class rivalry, and an attachment to public power as personified in the count-king' ('un vif sentiment de solidarité de groupe, une atténuation des rivalités de classes, un attachement au pouvoir public dans la personne de comte-roi.') (214).

45 'Peut-être, entre 1250 et 1350, le Principat catalan est-il le pays d'Europe à propos duquel il serait le moins inexact, le moins périlleux, de prononcer des termes anachroniques en apparence: impérialisme politico-économique, ou 'état-nation' (Vilar, *La Catalogne dans l'Espagne moderne*, 220).

46 'Langue, territoire, vie économique, formation psychique, communauté de culture: les conditions fondamentales de la nation y sont déjà, dès le XIIIe siècle, parfaitement réunies: mais il n'y manque même pas cette préoccupation du 'marché', 'école où la bourgeoisie apprend le nationalisme'; dix textes prouveraient que telle est bien la préoccupation dominante qui fait que la classe marchande catalane *veut son Etat*' (Vilar, *La Catalogne dans l'Espagne moderne*, 224). In a subsequent publication, Vilar acknowledged somewhat ruefully that his views had provoked a controversy. But he argues that the position his critics attributed to him, namely, that Catalonia was the first nation in world history, is not his. He insists that he did not say that Catalonia was in fact a nation-state, just that it came remarkably close, and much closer than any other country at the time (Pierre Vilar, 'Introduction: Le 'fait' catalan', in Joaquim Nadal Farreras and Philippe Wolff (eds), *Histoire de la Catalogne* [Toulouse: Privat, 1982], 16).

47 Charles E. Dufourcq, 'Le temps du rayonnement et des crises (1276-1472)', in Farreras and Wolff, *Histoire de la Catalogne*, 316.

48 Vilar notes 10 different points in the fifteenth century at which plagues occurred (Vilae, *La Catalogne dans l'Espagne moderne*, 235).

49 Ibid., 234.

50 Dufourcq, 'Temps du rayonnement et des crises', 338.

51 Vilar, *La Catalogne dans l'Espagne moderne*, 233.

52 Ibid., 235.

53 Balcells, *Catalan Nationalism*, 10.

54 Vilar, *La Catalogne dans l'Espagne moderne*, 235–40.

55 Ibid., 255–8.

56 Dufourcq, 'Temps du rayonnement et des crises', 339.

57 Ibid., 341.

58 Balcells, *Catalan Nationalism*, 13.

59 Dufourcq, 'Temps du rayonnement et des crises', 341–4.

60 Vilar, *La Catalogne dans l'Espagne moderne*, 300; and Giner, *The Social Structure of Catalonia*, 11.

61 Vilar, *La Catalogne dans l'Espagne moderne*, 300–5.

62 Vilar, *La Catalogne dans l'Espagne moderne*, 382–93; and Medrano, *Divided Nations*, 301.

63 The last three paragraphs are drawn from Balcells, *Catalan Nationalism*, 10-15; and Puigjaner, *Everything about Catalonia*, 21–4.

64 Balcells, *Catalan Nationalism*, 16.

65 'se vea el efecto sin que se note el cuidado' as quoted in Roger Masgrau, *Els orígens del catalanisme polític (1870-1931)* (Barcelona: Barcanova, 1992), 8. See also Woolard, *Double Talk*, 21.

66 Masgrau, *Els orígens del catalanisme polític*, 8.

67 Giner, *The Social Structure of Catalonia*, 5–6.

68 Woolard, *Double Talk*, 21.

69 José Alvarez Junco, 'The Nation-Building Process in Nineteenth-Century Spain', in Mar-Molinero and Smith, *Nationalism and the Nation in the Iberian Peninsula*, 99–100.

70 Woolard, *Double Talk*, 21. See also Hughes, *Barcelona*, 189.

71 Pierre Vilar, 'Les élans du 18th Century', in Farreras and Wolff, *Histoire de la Catalogne*, 378.

72 Vilar, 'Les élans du 18th Century', 394–99.

73 Medrano, *Divided Nations*, 45.

74 Giner, *The Social Structure of Catalonia*, 16–17.

75 Balcells, *Catalan Nationalism*, 22.

76 Giner, *The Social Structure of Catalonia*, 16–17.

77 Puigjaner, *Everything about Catalonia*, 26.

78 Medrano, *Divided Nations*, 46–7.

79 Hughes, *Barcelona*, 256.

80 Jordi Maluquer de Motes, 'La grande mutation (1833–1898)', in Ferreras and Wolff, *Histoire de la Catalogne*, 440.

81 Maluquer de Motes, 'La grande mutation', in Ferreras and Wolff, *Histoire de la Catalogne*, 437.

82 Ibid., 437.

83 Ibid., 442.

84 Ibid., 444.

85 Giner, *The Social Structure of Catalonia*, 19. This economic and social élite is analysed in Gary Wray McDonough, *Good Families of Barcelona: A Social History of Power in the Industrial Era* (Princeton: Princeton University Press, 1986).

86 See the account in Hughes, *Barcelona*, 298–306.

87 These points are drawn from Balcells, *Catalan Nationalism*, 25–7.

88 This discussion is drawn from Conversi, *The Basques, the Catalans and Spain*, 15.

89 Conversi develops these points (Conversi, *The Basques, the Catalans and Spain*, 15–16).

90 McDonough, *Good Families of Barcelona*, 189.

91 Hughes, *Barcelona*, 293.

92 Ibid., 191–2.

93 Ibid., 383.

94 Ibid., 449–53.

95 Ibid. 392; and Balcells, *Catalan Nationalism*, 58.

Chapter 2

1 Roser Masgrau, *Els orígens del catalanisme polític (1870–1931)* (Barcelona: Barcanova, 1992), 17–20. In any event, in 1875, works in popular Catalan that Soler submitted anonymously to the Jocs florals won all the major prizes, despite the devotion of the judges to the 'high' literary tradition.

2 Masgrau, *Els orígens del catalanisme polític*, 24–5.

3 Daniele Conversi, *The Basques, the Catalans and Spain: Alternative Routes to Nationalist Mobilisation* (London: Hurst, 1997), 18.

4 For Pi i Margall, Spain was the 'nation', but autonomy should be granted to its 'old provinces' (Angel Smith and Clare Mar-Molinero, 'The Myths and Realities of Nation-Building in the Iberian Peninsula,' in Clare Mar-Molinero and Angel Smith (eds), *Nations, and the Nation in the Iberian Peninsula* [Oxford: Berg, 1996], 5).

5 As Balcells writes, this election 'was the first sign of the appearance of the distinct personality of Catalonia'(Albert Balcells, *Catalan Nationalism: Past and Present* [London: Macmillan, 1996], 28).

6 Masgrau, *Els orígens del catalanisme polític*, 29.

7 Balcells, *Catalan Nationalism*, 32.

8 Conversi, *The Basques, the Catalans and Spain*, 19.

9 Medrano, *Divided Nations*, 47.

10 Pierre Vilar, *La Catalogne dans l'Espagne moderne* (Paris: Flammarion, 1977), 76.

11 Balcells, *Catalan Nationalism*, 22.

12 Oriol Pi-Sunyer, *Nationalism and Societal Integration: A Focus on Catalonia*, Program in Latin-American Studies, Occasional Papers Series No. 15, University of Massachusetts at Amherst, 1983, 32. Vilar, *La Catalogne dans l'Espagne moderne*, 76.

13 Masgrau, *Els orígens del catalanisme polític*, 36-7; and Balcells, *Catalan Nationalism*, 35.

14 Ibid.

15 In the words of his biographer, Antoni Rovira i Virgili, 'For republicans, Almirall was too Catalanist; for Catalanists, he was too republican' ('Pels republicans, Almirall era massa catalanista, pels catalanistes, masa replublicà') (as quoted in Masgrau, *Els orígens del catalanisme polític*, 43).

16 Masgrau, *Els orígens del catalanisme polític*, 42-3; Balcells, *Catalan Nationalism*, 36-7; and Conversi, *The Basques, the Catalans and Spain*, 20.

17 Augustí Colomines i Companys, 'Les Bases de Manresa: approvació i repercussions', in Generalitat de Catalunya, *Les Bases de Manresa, 1892-1992: cent anys de catalanisme* (Barcelona: Generalitat, 1993) 35, 38.

18 Indeed, it went well beyond what Catalonia finally was able to secure in 1932 and 1979 (Jordi Llorens i Vila, 'La unió catalanista: de la fundació fins a Martí Julià (1891-1904)', in Generalitat, *Les Bases de Manresa*, 27.

19 Augustí Colomines i Companys, 'Les Bases de Manresa: Approvació i Repercussions', in Generalitat, *Les Bases de Manresa*, 36.

20 Balcells sees this measure as reflecting an 'organicist' view of society and *pairalisme*, an attachment to tradition and an idealized vision of pre-capitalist structures. Masgrau sees it as slightly *'medievalitzants'* (Masgrau, *Els orígens del catalanisme polític*, 51). But Colomines insists that it is less a reflection of conservatism than a rejection of the falsity and corruption of the Restoration parliament (Colomines, 'Les Bases de Manresa', 36).

21 Unió Catalanista, *Bases pera la Constitució Regional Catalana, Bases 2a* (as reproduced in Josep Termes i Augustí Colomines, *Les Bases de Manresa de 1892 i els orígens del catalanisme* [Barcelona: Generalitat, 1992], 177). Masgrau describes *Base 2a* as 'Defensa el manteniment de la societat tradicional' in Masgrau, *Els orígens del catalanisme polític*, 50. Discussions of the *Bases de Manresa* appear in Termes and Colomines, *Les Bases de Manresa*; Generalitat, *Les Bases de Manresa*; Conversi, *The Basques, the Catalans and Spain*, 21; and Balcells, *Catalan Nationalism*, 38-9.

22 My translation of: 'Catalunya és una nació . . . un esprit col.lectiu, una ànima social catalana, que ha sabut crear una llengua, un dret, un art Catalans' (Masgrau, *Els orígens del catalanisme polític*, 54-7). The term 'Estat compost' had been introduced first by Valenti Almirall.

23 Joan B. Culla, 'El catalanisme polític dels anys 30', in Termes *et al.*, *Bases de Manresa*, 72.

24 Conversi, *The Basques, the Catalans and Spain*, 25.

25 As quoted in Hughes, *Barcelona*, 448.

26 Balcells, *Catalan Nationalism*, 43-4.

27 This is the interpretation of Balcells, *Catalan Nationalism*, 44.

28 Masgrau, *Els orígens del catalanisme polític*, 58.

29 Siobhan Harty, 'Republic and Nation in Interwar Catalonia', unpublished paper, 7.

30 Harty, 'Republic and Nation in Interwar Catalonia', 3.

31 Prat de la Riba refused to publish in *La veu de Catalunya* an article by Joan Maragall calling for the commuting of five death sentences (Balcells, *Catalan Nationalism*, 62).

32 This is the interpretation of Conversi, *The Basques, the Catalans and Spain*, 29.

33 Balcells, *Catalan Nationalism*, 68–9.

34 Susan M. DiGiacomo, 'The Politics of Identity: Nationalism in Catalonia', unpublished doctoral dissertation, University of Massachusetts, Department of Anthropology, 1985.

35 Michel and Marie-Claire Zimmerman, *Histoire de la Catalogne* (Paris: Presses Universitaires de France, 1997), 83–5, 117.

36 Conversi, *The Basques, the Catalans and Spain*, 34.

37 Balcells, *Catalan Nationalism*, Chapt. 7; and Conversi, *The Basques, the Catalans and Spain*, 30–6.

38 Conversi, *The Basques, the Catalans and Spain*, 37.

39 Balcells, *Catalan Nationalism*, 83–5; and Conversi, *The Basques, the Catalans and Spain*, 36.

40 Vilar, *La Catalogne dans l'Espagne moderne*, 63.

41 My translation of: 'C'est seulement parce que, dans sa conquête du marché espagnol, la bourgeoisie industrielle catalane est parvenue ni à s'assurer l'instrument d'État, ni à identifier, dans l'opinion agissante, ses intérêts à ceux de toute l'Espagne, que la Catalogne, petite "patrie", est finalement devenue le point d'appui "national", plus exigu, mais plus sûr, des exigences de cette classe' (Vilar, *La Catalogne dans l'Espagne moderne*, 68).

42 My translation of: 'Les classes moyennes et paysannes, inorganisées, y jouent un rôle politique *subordonné*. La responsabilité du "catalanisme" revient essentiellement à la bourgeoisie aisée, où les groupements patronaux dominent, et poliquement rangée autour d'un parti, celui de Cambó [the Lliga]' (Vilar, *La Catalogne dans l'Espagne moderne*, 63).

43 Jordi Solé Tura, *Catalanismo y revolución burguesa*.

44 Solé Tura's book is discussed in DiGiacomo, 'The Politics of Identity', 32–61.

45 Interview with Josep Termes, 11 March 1996. See the discussion of this debate in Balcells, *Catalan Nationalism*, 23–4. See also Culla, 'El Catalanisme polític dels anys 30', 73.

46 Hughes, *Barcelona*, 452.

47 My translation of: 'es proposa treballar pel reconeixement de la nacionalitat catalana . . . la Unió federal dins l'Estat espanyol' (DiGiacomo, 'The Politics of Identity', 54–5).

48 This is the interpretation of Masgrau, *Els orígens del catalanisme polític*, 65. Balcells contends that the pact was more the result than the cause of the formation's decline (Balcells, *Catalan Nationalism*, 65).

49 Masgrau, *Els origens del catalanisme polític*, 76–7. The electoral history and quotations of the previous paragraph are from pp. 64–75.

50 Balcells, *Catalan Nationalism*, 85.

51 Balcells, *Catalan Nationalism*, 89.

52 Harty, 'Republic and Nation in Interwar Catalonia'.

53 This is based on Siohban Harty's reading of two written accounts by Catalan delegates (Harty, 'Republic and Nation in Interwar Catalonia', 21).

54 For an argument regarding the roots of Catalan republicanism and its importance to the 1932 transition to autonomy, see Harty, 'Republic and Nation in Interwar Catalonia'. See also Siobhan Harty, 'Disputed State, Contested Nation: Republic and Nation in Interwar Catalonia', dissertation, McGill University, Department of Political Science, 1998.

55 Balcells, *Catalan Nationalism*, 94.

56 Seventy-five per cent of Catalan voters participated; among city and town halls, 1,068 were in favour and five abstained (Oriol Vergés and Josep Cruañas, *The Generalitat in the History of Catalonia* [Barcelona: Generalitat, 1991], 75).

57 These developments are detailed in Harty, 'Republic and Nation in Interwar Catalonia', 22–4. According to Paul Preston, the Republican government had expected Catalonia's proposal to be more sweeping. Nonetheless, it was loath to give any real autonomy to Catalonia and did not feel pressured to do so by Macià and the ERC, which it saw as 'a short-lived opportunistic coalition, dependent for its viability on the votes of the CNT rank-and-file. This did not prevent the right from presenting Azaña's cabinet as hell-bent on destroying centuries of Spanish unity' (Paul Preston, *A Concise History of the Spanish Civil War* [London: Fontana, 1996], 39).

58 Vergés and Cruañas, *The Generalitat in the History of Catalonia*, 75–6; and Balcells, *Catalan Nationalism*, 99.

59 Giner, 'The Social Structure of Catalonia', 30.

60 Mary Nash, 'The Changing Status of Women in Contemporary Catalonia', in Milton M. Azevedo (ed.), *Contemporary Catalonia in Spain and Europe* (Berkeley: Gaspar de Portola Catalonian Studies Program, University of California, 1991), 10.

61 Conversi is presumably referring to these experiments when he claims that 'the Catalan school system was transformed into one of the most progressive in Europe' (Conversi, *The Basques, the Catalans and Spain*, 39).

62 Culla, 'El catalanisme polític dels anys 30', 81–2; and Ballcells, *Catalan Nationalism*, 99.

63 Balcells, *Catalan Nationalism*, 99; and Culla, 'El catalanisme polític dels anys 30', 81.

64 Culla, 'El catalanisme polític dels anys 30', 82.

65 This account is based on Balcells, *Catalan Nationalism*, 107–10; and Paul Preston, *A Concise History of the Spanish Civil War* (London: Fontana, 1996), 51–5.

66 Giner, 'The Social Structure of Catalonia', 24–5.

67 Conversi, *The Basques, the Catalans and Spain*, 40.

68 Conversi, *The Basques, the Catalans and Spain*, 41.

69 Hank Johnston, *Tales of Nationalism: Catalonia 1939–1979* (New Brunswick, N.J.: Rutgers, 1991), 37.

70 Giner, 'The Social Structure of Catalonia', 30–4.

71 Balcells, *Catalan Nationalism*, 96, 109.

72 Pelai Pagès, *La guerra civil (1936–1939)* (Barcelona: Barcanova, 1993), 22–3.

73 According to Preston, 'with astonishing candour and not a little cunnning, [Companys] told them [a CNT delegation], "Today you are masters of the city and of Catalonia" and in effect said it was up to them whether he stayed on as president' (Preston, *A Concise History*, 169).

74 Giner, 'The Social Structure of Catalonia', 34.

75 According to Preston, 'the Communists and Prieto [the police commissioner] were delighted to have a chance to break the power of the CNT and limit that of the Generalitat' (Preston, *A Concise History*, 121). Pagès attributes the responsibility for the assault to Eusebi Rodríguez Salas, whom he identifies as a Communist commissioner for public order, and states that Rodríguez justified the measure with a claim that the anarchists were eavesdropping on telephone conversations between the Catalan and Republican presidents (Pagès, *La guerra civil*, 64).

76 Balcells and Pagès say the move to Barcelona took place in October 1937 (Balcells, *Catalan Nationalism*, 121; and Pagès, *La guerra civil*, 67), whereas Preston puts it a year later (Preston, *A Concise History*, 211).

77 Johnston, *Tales of Nationalism*, 38.

78 Pagès, *La guerra civil*, 67.

79 The account in these two paragraphs is from Balcells, *Catalan Nationalism*, 120–4, and Johnston, *Tales of Nationalism*, 38.

80 Culla, 'El catalanisme polític dels anys 30', 82.

81 Balcells, *Catalan Nationalism*, 125–6.

82 Balcells, *Catalan Nationalism*, 128.

83 Josep Benet, *Catalunya sota el règim franquista*, Vol. 1 (Paris: Edicions Catalanes de París), 241–2 (as cited in Conversi, *The Basques, The Catalans and Spain*, 114).

84 Balcells, *Catalan Nationalism*, 125.

85 Prócoro Hernández, 'La diàspora cultural catalana', in Giner, *La societat catalana*, 275.

86 In 1936, Catalonia's population was 2,921,474; by 1940 it had fallen to 2,891,720. This appears to be the only point in the last three centuries that Catalonia's population actually declined. (These data are from Socorro Sancho i Valverde i Carme Ros i Navarro, 'La població de Catalunya en perspectiva històrica', in Giner, *La societat catalana*, Table 1).

87 Jaume Rossinyol, *Le problème national catalan* (Paris: Mouton, 1974), 583.

88 Rossinyol, *Le problème national*, 584.

89 Balcells, *Catalan Nationalism*, 127. Balcells acknowledges that under the Catalan Republic there were 8,360 victims of political repression from 1936 to 1939, but he claims that only 400 were executions, based on normal sentences, as opposed to assassinations (Balcells, *Catalan Nationalism*, 117).

90 Interview with Salvador Giner, 30 April 1998, and Francesc Vallverdú, *L'us del Catala: un futur controvertit* (Barcelona: Edicions 62, 1990), 24.

91 These various examples are from Conversi, *The Basques, the Catalans and Spain*, 111–15; Rossinyol, *Le problème national catalan*, 593–602 and Francesc Ruiz, Rosa Sanz, and Jordi Solé Camardons, Història social i política de la llengua catalana (Barcelona: Climent, 1996), 198–9.

92 Giner, 'The Social Structure of Catalonia, 55, and Balcells, *Catalan Nationalism*, 136.

93 Dalí died in Figueres in 1989. Miró died in Mallorca in 1983.

94 Balcells, *Catalan Nationalism*, 133.

95 Balcells, *Catalan Nationalism*, 139–40; and Conversi, *The Basques, the Catalans and Spain*, 119–20. The editor of *La Vanguardia*, Luis de Galinsoga, had declared upon hearing Catalan used at a Barcelona mass: 'All Catalans are shit' (Todos los catalanes son una mierda). Given the uproar, Franco forced him to resign. Apparently Pujol denied involvement in the second incident (Conversi, *The Basques, the Catalans and Spain*, 120, n. 35).

96 Conversi, *The Basques, the Catalans and Spain*, 128.

97 Culla, 'El catalanisme polític dels anys 30', 73–4.

98 Ibid., 77–8.

Chapter 3

1 Conversi, The Basques, the Catalans and Spain, 191; Gershon Shafir, *Immigrants and Nationalists: Ethnic Conflict and Accommodation in Catalonia, the Basque Country, Latvia and Estonia* (Albany: State University of New York Press, 1995), 42.

2 Maluquer de Motes, *Història econòmica de Catalunya*, 175.

3 According to the *Padrons municipals d'habitants de Catalunya*, 409,570 members of the 1986 population had arrived in Catalonia between 1961 and 1965 (Padrons municipals d'habitants de Catalunya, 1986. Cens lingüístic, Departament de Producció Estadística (Barcelona: CIDC, 1987, Table 3.1). I thank Miquel Strubell for bringing these data to my attention.

4 David D. Laitin and Carlota Solé, 'Catalan Elites and Language Normalisation', *International Journal of Sociology and Social Policy* 9, no. 1, (1989): 7. Another lower estimate is 40 per cent (Armand Sáez, as cited in Wollard, *Double Talk*, 33).

5 Gary Wray McDonough, *Good Families of Barcelona: Social History of Power in the Industrial Era* (Princeton: Princeton University Press, 1986), 29.

6 Jaume Rossinyol, *Le problème national catalan* (Paris: Mouton, 1974), 448.

7 Conversi, *The Basques, the Catalans and Spain*, 115–17; Vallverdú, *L'us del Català*, 30–1.

8 Vallverdú, *L'us del Català*, 31.

9 Ibid., 29.

10 Ibid., 24.

11 The author of the proposal was none other than Juan Antonio Samaranch, then president of the Diputació of the province of Barcelona but later chairman of the International Olympic Committee.

12 Joan B. Culla i Clarà, 'El triomf del president desconegut', in Lluís Bassets, Joan B. Culla, and Bouja de Riquer, *Memòria de Catalunya: del retorn de Tarradellas al pacte Pujol-Aznar* (Barcelona: Tauras, 1997), 30.

13 Culla, 'El triomf del president desconegut', 18.

14 Without consulting the Assembly, Tarradellas travelled from his French residence in exile to Madrid, where he discussed with political leaders and the king the conditions under which he would return to Catalonia as president. The Assembly was left with no choice but to support his initiative (Eugènia Salvador, 'Crònica política', in Lluís Recolon et al. (eds), *Catalunya 77/88* [Barcelona: Fundació Bofill,1989], 210).

15 Carr and Fusi, *Spain*, 234.

16 Kenneth Maxwell, 'Regime Overthrow and the Prospects for Democratic Transition in Spain', in O'Donnell, Schmitter and Whitehead, *Transitions from Autoritarian Rule: Prospects for Democracy* (Baltimore: Johns Hopkins University Press, 1986), 109–37.

17 These points are drawn from José María Maravall and Julián Santamaria, 'Political Change in Spain and the Prospects for Democracy', in Guillermo O'Donnell et al. (eds), *Transitions from Authoritarian Rule*, 80.

18 Raymond Carr and Juan Pablo Fusi Aizpurua, *Spain: Dictatorship to Democracy* (London: George Allen and Unwin, 1979), 222–3.

19 Maravall and Santamaria, 'Political Change in Spain', 80.

20 Gilmour, *The Transformation of Spain*, 140.

21 Suárez was a card-carrying Francoist who had been a member of the Falange and had been minister of the Movimento before his appointment as prime minister (Gilmour, *The Transformation of Spain*, 150–2).

22 Maravall and Santamaria, 'Political Change in Spain', 81. Put differently, Suárez did not want to apply to the political order of Spain as a whole the logic that he ultimately accepted, on essentially partisan grounds, for Catalonia alone when he agreed to restoration of the Second Republic Generalitat.

23 Gilmour, *The Transformation of Spain*, 154.

24 For that matter, the Suárez government effectively marginalized the opposition parties in the referendum campaign (Gilmour, *The Transformation of Spain*, 159).

25 Only 26 per cent abstained (Balcells, *Catalan Nationalism*, 170).

26 Carr and Fusi, *Spain: Dictatorship to Democracy*, 221–5.

27 Analyses of Spain's negotiated transition to democracy are contained in Maravall and Santamaría, 'Political Change in Spain'; and Richard Gunther, 'Spain: The Very Model of the Modern Elite Settlement', in John Higley and Richard Gunther (eds), *Elites and Democratic Consolidation in Latin America and Southern Europe* (Cambridge: Cambridge University Press, 1992), 38–80.

28 Albert Balcells, *Catalan Nationalism: Past and Present* (London: Macmillan, 1996), 169.

29 Juan José Solozábal, 'Spain: A Federation in the Making?' in Joachim Jens Hesse and

Vincen Wright (eds), *Federalizing Europe? The Costs, Benefits and Preconditions of Federal Systems* (Oxford: Oxford University Press, 1996), 244.

30 Population data for 1991 as presented in Luis Moreno, 'Multiple Ethnoterritorial Concurrence in Spain', *Nationalism and Ethnic Politics* 1, no. 1 (Spring 1995), Table 2.

31 These points are made in Enric Company, 'Catalans a la constitució', in Bassets et al., *Memòria de Catalunya*, 62.

32 Ibid., 63.

33 Gilmour, *The Transformation of Spain*, 195–6.

34 This account appears in Companys, 'Catalans a la constitució', 64.

35 Presidencia del Gobierno, *Spanish Constitution*, 1982, Art. 2.

36 Moderne and Bon show how the adoption of the term 'nationality' provoked strong opposition among Spanish academics (Frank Moderne and Pierre Bon, *Les Autonomies régionales dans la constitution espagnole* [Paris: Economica, 1981], 33–36).

37 Soledad Gallego-Díaz and Bonifacio de la Cuadra, *Crónica secreta de la constitución* (Madrid: Tecnos, 1989), 102.

38 My translation of: 'La plurinacionalidad del Estado español' (Manuel Ramirez, *Partidos políticos y constitución* (Madrid: Centre de Studios Constitucionales), 75).

39 Moderne and Bon, *Les autonomies régionales*, 43.

40 Miquel Roca, parliamentary leader of the moderate Catalan nationalists, argued that 'nations' and 'nationalities' were equivalent. He also supported a proposal to refer to Spain as a 'nation of nations' (Modern and Bon, *Les autonomies régionales*, 46).

41 The second transitory provision, the 'fast-track' route, identifies the 'historical nations' indirectly: 'territories which in the past have, by plebiscite, approved draft statutes of autonomy' (Presidencia del Gobierno, *Spanish Constitution*, Transitory Provision Two). This refers to the Second Republic, when Catalonia, the Basque Country, and Galicia had all approved such statutes. But there is no direct naming of the three as the 'nationalities'.

42 'It [the constitution] recognizes and guarantees the right to autonomy of the nationalities and regions of which it is composed, and solidarity among them' (Presidencia del Gobierno, *Spanish Constitution*, Art. 2). It has been argued that this was a serious error since it enabled the other regions to invent a nationalist discourse to advance their own demands for autonomy (Gilmour, *The Transformation of Spain*, 256).

43 Presidencia del Gobierno, *Spanish Constitution*, Art. 3 (1 and 2). At the same time, Section 3 does state: 'The wealth of the different language variations of Spain is a cultural heritage which shall be the object of special respect and protection.'

44 Gallego-Díaz and de la Cuadra, *Crónica secreta de la constitución*, 105–6.

45 It was also aimed at Basque irredentist plans (see Daniele Conversi, *The Basques, the Catalans and Spain: Alternative Routes to Nationalist Mobilisation* (London: Hurst 1997), 144).

46 Presidencia del Gobierno, *Spanish Constitution (1982)*, Art. 145(1).

47 Franck Moderne and Pierre Bon, *Les autonomies régionales dans la constitution espagnole* (Paris: Economia, 1981), 51.

48 President del Gobierno, *Spanish Constitution (1982)*, Art. 145(1).

49 Ibid., Art. 69(1).

50 Ibid., Art. 69(2).

51 Ibid., Art. 69(5).

52 On the inadequacies of the Senate as a forum for representation of the autonomous communities, see Joaquim Tornos, 'L'organisation territoriale de l'Espagne: l'état des autonomies', in Thomas Fleiner-Gerster et al., *Le fédéralisme en Europe* (Barcelona:

ICPS, 1992), 108–9. See also Requejo, 'Cultural Pluralism, Nationalism and Federalism', 25–6.

53 Conversi, *The Basques, the Catalans and Spain*, 144, n. 7.

54 Moreno, *La federalización de España*, 118.

55 Presidencia del Gobierno, *Spanish Constitution*, Art. 146 and 147.

56 Ibid., Art. 152(2).

57 Ibid., Transitory Provision Two.

58 Brassloff, 'Spain: The State of the Autonomies', 31.

59 This is Solé Tura's claim (Companys, 'Catalans a la constitució', 64).

60 Brassloff, 'Spain: The State of the Autonomies', 33.

61 Enric Fossas Espadaler, 'The Autonomy of Catalonia', in Enric Fossas and Gabriel Colomé, *Political Parties and Institutions in Catalonia* (Barcelona: ICPS, 1993) 21.

62 Presidencia del Gobierno, *Spanish Constitution*, Article 133(1).

63 Ibid., Art. 133(2).

64 Ibid., Additional Provision One.

65 In his classic study, *Exploring Federalism*, Daniel Elazar categorizes Spain as a federation, which he defines as 'a polity compounded of strong constituent entities and a strong general government, each possessing powers delegated to it by the people and empowered to deal directly with the citizenry in the exercise of those powers' (Daniel J. Elazar, *Exploring Federalism* [Tuscaloosa: University of Alabama Press, 1987], 7). Yet, at least at the time the constitution was adopted, many of the ACs hardly constituted 'constituent entities'—indeed, they were still being created. More important, the powers available even to Catalonia do not seem to provide a clear constitutional basis to be 'strong'. Ronald L. Watts adopts a similar definition of 'federation' but also specifies that the units deal directly with citizens in the exercise of 'legislative, administrative and taxing powers' (Ronald L. Watts, *Comparing Federal Systems in the 1990s* [Kingston, Ont.: Institute of Intergovernmental Relations, Queen's University, 1997], 8). He contends that on the basis of its constitution, 'Spain is a federation in all but name' (28). However, we have seen that Catalonia (and 14 other ACs) have no meaningful taxation powers of their own; the Basque Country and Navarre are quite a different matter.

66 Presidencia del Gobierno, *Spanish Constitution*, Art. 167. To be sure, the ACs' statutes of autonomy cannot be altered unilaterally by the Cortes Generales; the amendment procedures contained in the statutes must be followed, along with a popular referendum.

67 See Brassloff, 'Spain', 38–9; and Montserrat Guibernau, 'Spain: A Federation in the Making', 248.

68 Guibernau, 'Spain', 248.

69 See the review of the debate among Spanish scholars in Moderne and Bon, *Les autonomies régionales*, 48–54. In the words of one analyst, 'the agreement [the 1978 constitution] consisted of a cocktail of German federalism and Italian and Spanish (Second Republic) regionalism to which had been added a good dose of fiscal federalism designed specifically for the Basque Country and Navarre' ('el acuerdo consistió en un cóctel de federalismo alemán y de regionalismo italiano y español (II República), al que se añadió una buena dosis de confederalismo fiscal pensado específicamente para el País Vasco y Navarra') (Francesc Morata, 'El estado de las autonomías', in M. Alcántara y A. Martínez (eds), *Política y gobierno en España* [Valencia: Ed. Tirant Lo Blanch, 1997], 123). See also the nuanced analysis of the constitution in José Vilas Nogueira, 'La organización territorial del Estado', in Ramon Cotarelo (ed.), *Transición política y consolidación democrática: España (1975-1986)* (Madrid: CIS, 1992), 231–2.

70 Miquel Caminal Badia, *Partits nacionals a Catalunya* (Barcelona: Ed. Empuries, 1998).

71 Salvador, 'Crònica política', 211.

72 The No vote was 4.6 per cent; participation was 68.1 per cent (one point higher than in Spain as a whole) (Salvador, 'Crònica política,' 211).

73 The No vote was 7.8 per cent; 67.1 per cent of voters participated. Salvador, 'Crònica política,' 211.

74 Gilmour, *The Transformation of Spain*, 215; and Companys, 'Catalans a la constitució', 69.

75 Under the terms of the constitution, Tarradellas was (as a non-parliamentarian) excluded from the drafting of the constitution, and the antagonism between him and the parliamentarians deepened (Salvador, 'Crònica política', 211).

76 Membership was proportional to the results of the 15 June election (ibid.).

77 Companys, 'Catalans a la constitució', 65.

78 Ibid., 66–7.

79 Salvador, 'Crònica política', 212 and Companys, 'Catalans a la constitució', 68.

80 Generalitat de Catalunya, *The Catalan Statute of Autonomy* (Departament de la Presidència, 1993), Preamble. These points are made in Montserrat Guibernau, 'Images of Catalonia', in *Nations and Nationalism* 3, no. 1 (March 1997), 94–5.

81 Generalitat, *Catalan Statute of Autonomy*, Art. 1.

82 Ibid., Art. 6.

83 Ibid., Art. 4.

84 Ibid., Art. 3(2).

85 Ibid., Art. 3(3).

86 Ibid., Sec. 1, Art. 9.

87 This is true of responsibility for culture (state cultural institutions), research (state co-ordination of scientific and technical research), land (state environmental protection), and public works (works of general interest to the state) (ibid.). To quote Enric Fossas, '[the statute] assumed exclusive competences (although many are not properly such)' (Fossas, 'The Autonomy of Catalonia', 21).

88 'The jurisdiction of the state consists of establishing the bases or *basic principles to be applied in a specific area*; while the Autonomous Community must limit itself to developing the legislation and is not empowered to intervene in the definition of its basic principles' (Josep Pagès I Rejsek, *Political Autonomy in Catalonia: Origins, Justification and Organisation of the Generalitat* [Generalitat, 1996], 90—italics in original).

89 Generalitat, *The Catalan Statute of Autonomy*, Art. 15. The quotation is from the Spanish constitution, sec. 149, n. 23.

90 Generalitat, *The Catalan Statute of Autonomy*, Art. 17.

91 Ibid., Art. 16. None the less, on this basis the Generalitat is able to control licences for local radio and television as well as to establish its own media organizations.

92 Ibid., Art. 12(1).

93 Ibid., Art. 18(1). Under the Spanish constitution, Catalonia does not possess a distinct judicial power of its own.

94 Ibid., Art. 13 and n. 18.

95 Ibid., Art. 11.

96 Fossas, 'The Autonomy of Catalonia', 22.

97 Generalitat, *Catalan Statute of Autonomy*, Sec. 2.

98 This analysis of presidential tendencies is from Fossas, 'The Autonomy of Catalonia', 26–7.

99 Generalitat, *Catalan Statute of Autonomy*, Art. 35.

100 Ibid., Art. 42.

101 Ibid., Art. 41. See the discussion of the components of the Generalitat in Rejsek, *Political Autonomy in Catalonia*, 53–78.

102 Ibid., Art. 56 and 57.

103 Balcells, *Catalan Nationalism*, 173. Balcells insists that the draft statute 'took into account the terms of the Constitution' (ibid.). In a similar vein, a study published by the Generalitat declares: 'The document suffered further cutbacks [beyond what the constitution imposed on its drafters] when it was passed through the commission of the Madrid *Cortes*. . . . This Statute, although its does not allow for the full recognition of Catalan national rights, marks the beginning of the road to self-government' (Oriol Vergés and Josep Cruañas, *The Generalitat in the History of Catalonia*, trans. Richard Rees [Departament de Culture de la Generalitat de Catalunya, 1991], 96).

104 As quoted in Susan M. DiGiacomo, 'The Politics of Identity: Nationalism in Catalonia', Ph.D. dissertation, University of Massachusetts, Department of Anthropology, 1985), 251.

105 *The Catalan Statue of Autonomy* (Barcelona: Generalitat de Catalunya, 1993), Art. 15. According to DiGiacomo, 'a closer look reveals Article 15 to be almost empty of meaning' (DiGiacomo, 'The Politics of Identity', 253). While this may overstate the case, the final version does represent a very substantial scaling back of the Generalitat's autonomy. The final phrase, 'within the area of its jurisdiction' is redundant, but seems to show a determination to contain the Generalitat's role.

106 This list of amendments is taken from Balcells, *Catalan Nationalism*, 173.

107 Balcells says that, while the new statute is stronger in education and communications media, it is weaker in justice, public order, and local administration (Balcells, *Catalan Nationalism*, 173).

108 *La Vanguardia*, 23 Oct. 1979 (as translated and quoted in DiGiacomo, 'The Politics of Identity', 256).

109 Salvador, 'Crònica política', 212.

110 He declared, 'The Statute will bring us many difficulties, but we will overcome them by our unity' (*Avui*, 24 Oct. 1979, as translated and quoted in DiGiacomo, 'The Politics of Identity', 257).

111 The amendments were not acceptable to Heribert Barrera of ERC and the independent J.M. Xirinachs (ibid.). Balcells believes that these amendments made the statute of 1979 inferior to the statute secured by Catalonia in 1932 (ibid.).

112 The results are from Eugènia Salvador, 'Crònica política,' 212. There has been considerable discussion about the low turnout. Other factors in the low turn-out may have been general fatigue with the long negotiations and with repeated calls to vote (ibid.), along with poor weather and the indifference of immigrants from the rest of Spain (Gilmour, *The Transformation of Spain*, 215). However, while noting that abstention and No votes were greatest in areas that might be most fearful of Catalan autonomy—the well-to-do districts and the immigrant suburbs—DiGiacomo believes that many middle-class Catalans abstained or voted No because they were 'unconvinced that the Statute would bring genuine autonomy' (DiGiacomo, 'The Politics of Identity', 260).

113 The PSC was created through the unification of three Catalan socialist parties (Gabriel Colomé, 'The "Partit dels Socialistes de Catalunya"', in José M. Maravall et al., *Socialist Parties in Europe* (Barcelona: ICPS, 1992), 37.

114 According to a statement attributed to Tarradellas, Pujol had trouble sleeping because he feared he would not be elected president; Roventós had the same problem for fear that he would be elected! Allegedly, Roventós was fearful both of the difficulties in obtaining the support of the opposition party to form a government and of the challenges presented by economic and political crisis in Spain (Sebastián Serrano, 'La victòria per sorpresa de Pujol,' Bassets, *Memòria de Catalunya*, 201).

115 These factors were cited by Ramon Obiols (interview, Barcelona, 6 May 1998).

116 In addition, the *Forment de Treball*, representing employers, waged a vigorous campaign against the socialists (Joseph M. Colomer, 'No era al quió', in Luís Bassets, Joan B.

Culla, and Bouja de Riquer (eds), *Memòria de Catalunya: del retorn de Tarradellas al pacte Pujol-Aznar* (Barcelona: Tauras, 1997), 220.

117 This argument is developed in DiGiacomo, 'The Politics of Identity', 274–5.

118 Pujol had invited the PSC to enter a coalition government but the latter had refused. Arguably, such a coalition would not have lasted (interview with Ramon Obiols, Barcelona, 6 May 1998).

119 There is some speculation that Joseph Tarradellas, who was highly popular, might have been the PSC leader instead. However, this apparently was not a strong possiblity (interview with Ramon Obiols, Barcelona, 6 May 1998).

120 With the IC's three seats and the ERC's 12 seats, the PSC would have been one short of the 68 needed for an absolute majority. For its part, the CiU could have drawn on either the PP or the ERC since they each had the 12 seats that it needed.

121 See Colomé, 'Partit dels Socialistes de Catalunya', 52–7; and Pallarés and Font, *Autonomous Elections in Catalonia*, 30–45.

122 Pallarés and Font, *Autonomous Elections in Catalonia*, 46.

123 Interview with Josep Lluís Carod-Rovira, 6 June 1997. This account draws on Marcet and Argelaguet, 'Nationalist Parties in Catalonia', pp. 9–10.

124 Pallarés and Font, 'The Autonomous Elections in Catalonia', 18.

125 Gilmour, *The Transformation of Spain*, 179.

126 Joan Marcet, 'The Parties of Non-State Ambit: The Case of Catalonia,' in Lieven de Winter (ed.), *Non-State-Wide Parties in Europe* (Barcelona: Institut de Ciències Polítiques i Socials), 172.

127 Pallarés and Font, 'The Autonomous Elections in Catalonia', 14.

Chapter 4

1 My translation of: 'CDC es defineix abans que tot com un partit nacionalista català. CDC fa del reconeixement polític de la personalitat del poble català un punt primordial, bàsic i no negociable del seu programa.' *Què és CDC* (CDC, March 1976), as quoted in Joan B. Culla, 'L'evolució ideològica dels partits', in Lluís Recolons et al. (eds), *Catalunya 77/88* (Barcelona: Fundació Juame Bofill, 1989), 244.

2 Jordi Pujol, *La Personalitat diferenciada de Catalunya* (Barcelona: Generalitat, 1991), 18, as quoted in Montserrat Guibernau, 'Images of Catalonia', *Nations and Nationalism* 3, no. 1 (Mar. 1997), 101.

3 F. Mercade, *Cataluña: intelectuales políticos y cuestión nacional* (Barcelona: Peninsula, 1982), 153, as translated and quoted in Michael Keating: *Nations against the State: The New Politics of Nationalism in Quebec, Catalonia and Scotland* (London: Macmillan, 1996), 127.

4 My translation of: 'Una primera conclusión es la existencia de una realidad catalana basada principalmente en la lengua, en la cultura, en la conciencia histórica, en el sentimiento por supuesto, y también en determinada concepción de España. . . . Pero ni Cataluña ni el catalanismo ni la lengua catalana son una maquinación antiespañola . . . . Segundo hecho permanente. La inserción clara de esta realidad en el conjunto de España y la voluntad de intervenir política, económica, ideológicamente en ella, en España' (Jordi Pujol, *Catalanes en España, Madrid, 30 de noviembre de 1981* [Barcelona: Generalitat de Catalunya, 1994] 35. As for independence, Pujol declared in 1977:

If by radical nationalism one means independentism, then it should be said that although no one can be certain there are independentists within the party, the CDC itself is not independentist. The CDC's program does not contain independentism.

My translation of:

si per nacionalisme radical s'entén l'independentisme, aleshores cal dir que si bé és segur que en el partit hi ha independentistes i n'hi pot haver, CDC no n'és. El programa polític de CDC no inclou la independència (*CDC Informacions*, n. 23, as quoted in Culla, 'L'evolució ideològica dels partits', 244.)

5 As quoted in Caterina Garcia i Segura, *L'activitat exterior de les regions: una dècada de projecció exterior de Catalunya*, Polítiques 12 (Barcelona: Fundació Jaume Bofill, 1995), 57.

6 My translation of: 'contribuir a la reconstrucció d'un espai de centre a Espanya' Salvador, 'Crònica política', 219.

7 Jordi Pujol, *La Personalitat diferenciada de Catalunya*, 1991), 28, as quoted in Montserrat Guibernau, 'Images of Catalonia', 105.

8 As quoted in Garcia i Segura, *L'activitat exterior de les regions*, 80.

9 My translation of:
    'Catalunya va néixer com a poble i com a nació fa 1,200 anys, com una marca fronterera de l'imperi de Carlemany. Nosaltres formàvem la marca Hispànica, l'avançada de l'imperi cap al sud, l'avançada . . . d'Europa cap el sud. . . . D'una certa manera continuem essent fills de Carlemany. . . . I en aquest moment de la incorporació d'Espanya a la CEE he volgut venir, en nom del meu país, a expressar aquí, en la nostra antiga capital, la nostra joia. La nostra joia de tornar a casa' (As quoted in Joaquim Ferrer, 'La projecció exterior de les Terres Catalanes', in Lluís Recolons et al. (eds), *Catalunya 77/88* [Barcelona: Fundació Jaume Bofill, 1989], 223). See also Jordi Pujol, *Penser l'Europe depuis la Catalogne* (Barcelona: Generalitat, 1994).

10 Joan B. Culla, 'Unió democràtica de Catalunya: le parti démocrate-chrétien catalan (1931–1989)', in Mario Caciagli et al., *Christian Democracy in Europe* (Barcelona: ICPS, 1992), 83–110.

11 Trias Fargas, *Programa electoral de 1982*, as cited in Culla, 'L'evolució ideològica dels partits', in Lluís Recolons, *Catalunya 77/88*, 254.

12 Juan Marcet and Jordi Argelaguet, 'Nationalist Parties in Catalonia: Convergència Democràtica de Catalunya and Esquerra Republicana de Catalunya', unpublished paper.

13 In an interview, Rigol acknowledged that he envisaged the construction of such an inter-party coalition but saw it as a second stage whose time had not yet come since it would imply a very different approach to politics from the current one (Interview with Joan Rigol, 27 April 1998).

14 This has also been advocated by IC leader Rafael Ribo (interview, Barcelona, 18 June 1997).

15 On Pujol's reaction see Miquel Caminal Badia, 'Nacionalisme, nacions i partits nacionals: teoria general i aplicació al cas de Catalunya', unpublished manuscript, 138.

16 Cesáreo R. Aguilera de Prat, 'Los socialistas y los pactos de gobernabilidad de 1993 y 1996', unpublished paper.

17 Balcells, *Catalan Nationalism*, 178.

18 Rosa Paz, 'El PSOE plantea que el Estado pueda recuperar las competencias cedidas a las autonomías', *La Vanguardia*, 28 Jan. 1998.

19 After a surge in nationalist voting in Galicia, electoral reform was proposed by both a PP and a PSOE AC president. Aznar and the PSOE leader, Joaquín Almunia rejected the notion (José María Brunet and Rosa Paz, 'Aznar y Almunia excluyen reformar la ley electoral contra los nacionalistas', *La Vanguardia*, 21 Oct. 1997).

20 Against the recommendation and expectation of the Suárez government, voters in all but one province of Andalusia approved the fast track to autonomy in a referendum held under section 51 of the constitution. After reaching an understanding with the province where the vote had fallen short, Andalusia proceeded to assume autonomy on the 'fast track'.

21 Audrey Brassloff, 'Spain: The State of the Autonomies', in Murray Forsyth (ed.), *Federalism and Nationalism* (Leicester: Leicester University Press), 34; and Agranoff, 'Asymmetrical Federalism in Spain: Design and Outcomes', paper presented to International Political Science Association, 21–5 Aug. 1994, 12.

22 Salvador, 'Crònica política', 215.

23 Albert Balcells, *Catalan Nationalism: Past and Present* (London: Macmillan, 1996), 179.

24 The PSC caucus had prepared a set of amendments, but their leader, Ernest Lluch, refused to present them to the parliament.

25 Salvador, 'Crònica política', 215.

26 Josep Ma Valles and Montserrat Cuchillo Fox, 'Decentralisation in Spain: A Review', *European Journal of Political Science* 16 (1988): 401–3. They note that the commission used the example of German and Austrian 'executive federalism' to argue that regional and national governments must work together closely and that sub-units (like the German Länder) should be heavily involved in the administration of the central government's legislation and policies. They contend that these notions, which are clearly set out in the constitution, have been reflected both in Constitutional Court decisions and in the actions of the González government and that they both have served to circumscribe the autonomy of the autonomous communities.

27 They are 'uniform regional elections, term limitation for regional legislators, subjection of regional governments to a constructive no-confidence vote upon petition of fifteen per cent of each assembly; limits on the size of AC governments (ten members); regional supervision of provincial governments; provisions for transfer of national civil servants to ACs; and harmonization of financing mechanisms for the territories' (Agranoff, 'Asymmetrical Federalism in Spain', 13).

28 Brassloff, 'Spain: The State of the Autonomies', 34.

29 Balcells, *Catalan Nationalism*, 192. Catalonia did, however, negotiate an arrangement under which it would jointly supervise financial institutions with Madrid and split a national tax with Madrid (Agranoff, 'Intergovernmental Relations and the Management of Asymmetry', 12).

30 Agranoff, 'Asymmetrical Federalism in Spain', 13.

31 Ibid.

32 Luis Moreno, *La federalización de España: poder político y territorio* (Madrid: Siglo Vientiúno Editores, 1997), 142.

33 Robert Agranoff, 'Intergovernmental Relations and the Management of Asymmetry in Federal Spain' (unpublished paper), 10.

34 Agranoff, 'Federal Evolution in Spain', *International Political Science Review* 17 (1996, no. 4): 388.

35 Francesc Morata, 'El estado de las autonomías', in M. Alcántara and A. Martínez (eds), *Política y gobierno en España* (Valencia: Ed. Tirant Lo Blanch, 1997), 135.

36 Brassloff, 'Spain: The State of the Autonomies', 40.

37 Salvador, 'Crònica política', 221.

38 Agranoff, 'Asymmetrical Federalism in Spain', 16.

39 The material in this paragraph is taken from Agranoff, 'Asymmetrical Federalism in Spain', 16.

40 Morata, 'El estado de las autonomías', 136.

41 Ibid.; and Paul Heywood, *The Government and Politics of Spain* (London: MacMillan, 1995), 152. Heywood notes that the González government had proposed the arrangements the previous year but then shelved them. Loss of majority and reliance on the CiU brought the arrangement to life.

42 Morata, 'El estado de las autonomías', 136–7.

43 Robert Agranoff, 'Intergovernmental Relations and the Management of Asymmetry in Federal Spain', unpublished paper, 10.

44 Agranoff, 'Asymmetrical Federalism in Spain', 17.

45 Anna Grau, 'CiU exigeix a Aznar que reconegui explícitament la nació catalana', *Avui*, 6 Mar. 1996, 11. Pujol called upon his nationalist coalition for 'prudència i discreció'.

46 José Antich, 'Pujol hace frente a los dirigentes de su partido que quieren dejar solo a Aznar', *La Vanguardia*, 6 Mar. 1996, 10; and Anna Grau, 'CiU considera impossible votar a favor de la investidura d'Aznar', *Avui*, 7 Mar. 1996, 13.

47 'Acuerdo de investidura y gobernabilidad', *El País*, 29 Apr. 1996, 18.

48 The Canary Islands obtained a reform of its statute of autonomy, permanent status in the EU, and improved fiscal arrangements. The Basque Country obtained a reinforcement of its distinctive 'confederal-like' fiscal arrangements (Morata, 'El estado de las autonomías', 139).

49 Morata, 'El Estado de las autonomías', 140.

50 Josep Playá Maset, 'La Generalitat exige la retirada del decreto de Geografía e Historia de España por partidista', *La Vanguardia*, 24 Oct. 1997.

51 Óscar Martinez, 'El Congrés tomba el decret d'hmanitats', *Avui*, 17 Dec. 1997.

52 '"Acepto el diálogo pero quiero que el decreto de Humanidades entre en vigor el próximo curso"', *La Vanguardia*, 30 Oct. 1997.

53 'El PP advierte que enviará inspectores a las escuelas y Pujol responde que habrá conflicto', *La Vanguardia*, 31 Oct. 1997.

54 The IU initially tried to spare the PP the defeat through an unsuccessful amendment to the resolution but then the IU rallied to it (Rosa Paz, 'El Gobierno pierde su pulso con CiU y debe retirar el plan de Humanidades', *La Vanguardia*, 17 Dec. 1997). Several days later a PP spokesman announced the government's intention to continue with the project and to amend the requirements so that they would not be 'uniformadores, pero si unitarios', in effect reverting to the government's original position ('El PP cree que el decreto final de Humanidades se parecerá al rechazado', *La Vanguardia*, 28 Dec. 1997).

55 'El PP modifica el uso del himno español y causa malestar entre sus socios nacionalistas', *La Vanguardia*, 10 Oct. 1997.

56 'Pujol exige al PP que condene con más energía las muestras de intolerancia anticatalana', *La Vanguardia*, 17 Sept. 1997; and José María Brunet, 'Aznar desaira a Pujol y considera una "pura anécdota" el abucheo a Raimon', *La Vanguardia*, 18 Sept. 1997.

57 Jordi Juan, 'Pujol constata el progresivo deterioro del pacto con el PP', *La Vanguardia*, 18 Sept. 1997.

58 Ramon Suñé, 'Pujol asegura que no tiene otra opción que apoyar al PP pese a las actitudes anticatalanas', *La Vanguardia*, 16 Sept. 1997.

59 'Apoyo al pacto CiU-PP, pese a todo', *La Vanguardia*, 11 Nov. 1997; and 'El pacto PP-CiU debe seguir sin concesiones', *La Vanguardia*, 17 Dec. 1997.

60 José María Brunet, 'Aznar cree que el voto de CiU en el caso Fungairiño refuerza el pacto', *La Vanguardia*, 21 Jan. 1998.

61 Luis Moreno, 'Ethnoterritorial Concurrence and Imperfect Federalism in Spain', in B. de Villiers (ed.), *Evaluating Federal Sysems* (Cape Town: Juta, 1994), 162–93; and Agranoff, 'Federal Evolution in Spain', 385–401. The central question is whether a political system can become a federation without a formal revision of the constitution.

62 The return to majority government has eliminated any pressure to do so, at least for the PP.

63 Agranoff, 'Federal Evolution in Spain', 388–9.

64 Ibid., 389.

65 On this point see Joan José Solozábal, 'Spain: A Federation in the Making?' in Joachim Jens Hesse and Vincent Wright (eds), *Federalizing Europe? The Costs, Benefits and Preconditions of Federal Political Systems* (Oxford: Oxford University Press, 1996) 246–8.

66 Enric Fossas details each of these points, showing how they disqualify Spain from the status of federation ('Seminari Catalunya-Espanya: el model de l'estat de les autonomies a la llum de les diferents experiències comparades', unpublished paper). While federations can be found that do not allow for representation of sub-units in a legislative body or the participation of sub-units in appointments to a constitutional court, meaningful sub-unit autonomy and participation in constitutional amendment procedures are clearly a *sine qua non* of a federation.

67 Javier Pérez Royo, *El nuevo modelo de financiación autonómica: análisis exclusivamente constitucional*. ICPS Working Paper No. 136 (Barcelona: Institut de Ciències Polítiques i Socials, 1997).

68 Robert Agranoff and Juan Antonio Ramos Gallarin, 'Toward Federal Democracy in Spain: An Examination of Intergovernmental Relations', unpublished paper, 23.

69 See I. Duchacek, *The Territorial Dimension of Politics: within, among and across Nations* (Boulder and London: Westview); Douglas M. Brown and Earl H. Fry (eds), *States and Provinces in the International Economy* (Berkeley, Calif.: University of California, Institute of Governmental Studies, and Kingston: Queen's University, Institute of Intergovernmental Relations); and Ivan Bernier and André Binette, *Les provinces canadiennes et le commerce international* (Quebec: Centre québécois de relations internationales, 1988).

70 Caterina Garcia i Segura, *L'activat exterior de les regions: una dècada de projecció exterior de Catalunya*, Polítiques 12 (Barcelona: Fundació Jaume Bofill, 1995), 88.

71 Presidencia del Gobierno, *Spanish Constitution*, Art. 149(iii).

72 Generalitat de Catalunya, *The Catalan Statute of Autonomy* (Departament de la Presidència, 1993), Art. 27.

73 Javier Cisneros Fernández-Arroyo, 'La actuación exterior de la *Generalitat* de Cataluña: 1980–1996: valoración y perspectivas' (Madrid: Escuela Diplomática).

74 Garcia i Segura, *L'activat exterior de les regions*, 54.

75 Fernández-Arroyo, 'La actuación exterior, 70.

76 Ibid., 22; and Garcia i Segura, *L'activat exterior de les regions*, 61–6. Indeed the organization of Catalonia's international activities remains quite decentralized (interview with Josep Garcia-Reyes, Barcelona, 18 June 1997).

77 Garcia i Segura, *L'activat exterior de les regions*, 66; and interview with Joan Vallvé, Barcelona, 20 June 1997.

78 Fernández-Arroyo, 'La actuación exterior', 24. In the case of the *Patronat Català pro Europe*, which was the first such body, the structure followed logically from its intended role of orienting Catalan society to the EC (interview with Guillem Rovira i Jacquet, Barcelona, 12 June 1997).

79 CIDEM, *Doing Business in Catalonia*, 1995.

80 Fernández-Arroyo, 'La actuación exterior', 59–62; and Garcia i Segura, *L'activat exterior de les regions*, 68.

81 COPCA literature; Fernández-Arroyo, 'La actuación exterior', 54–9; and Garcia i Segura, *L'activat exterior de les regions*, 67–8.

82 Garcia i Segura, *L'activat exterior de les regions*, 69, n. 60.

83 Fernández-Arroyo, 'La actuación exterior', 64.

84 Ibid., 48.

85 Ibid., 50.

86 Garcia i Segura, *L'activat exterior de les regions*, 56–7.

87 According to the past *Comissionat per a Actuaciones Exteriors*, there is no compelling reason to change the practice, especially in light of fiscal constraints (personal interview with Llibert Cuatrecasas, 17 June 1997).

88 Garcia i Segura, *L'activat exterior de les regions*, 90.

89 Fernández-Arroyo, 'La actuación exterior', 8.

90 Ibid., 52.

91 Garcia i Segura, *L'activat exterior de les regions*, 91.

92 Agranoff, 'Intergovernmental Relations and the Management of Asymmetry', 23.

93 Most ACs have now established government offices in Brussels; Catalonia is the only one to maintain a semi-public organization like the Patronat (interview with Guillem Rovira i Jacquet, 12 June 1997). In its literature the Patronat is careful to specify that its representation of Catalan interests in the EU takes place 'in co-operation with the permanent delegation of Spain to the European Union' ('en cooperació amb la Representació Permanent d'Espanya davant la Unió Europea') (Patronat Català Pro Europa, *La primera entitat de Catalunya especialitzada en informació assessorament gestió i formació sobre la Unió Europea*).

94 Garcia i Segura, *L'activat exterior de les regions*, 75, n. 72 and Annex.

95 The committee's own literature makes it clear that the committee is not concerned just with regions. The committee 'recognizes that the public authority closest to the citizens, for example, mayors, municipal councillors, and regional presidents, must be consulted' ('responde a la necesidad de que los poderes públicos más cercanos a los ciudadanos— como, por ejemplo, los alcades, les concejals de ayuntamientos y municipios, y los presidentes regionales—sean consultados') (Unión Europea, Comité de las Regiones, *Introducción al Comité de las Regiones* [Brussels, n.d.]).

96 Fernández-Arroyo, 'La actuación exterior', 37–8; and Garcia i Segura, *L'activat exterior de les regions*, 21–3.

97 Garcia i Segura, *L'activat exterior de les regions*, 21.

98 Ariadna Trillas, 'Espanya refusa reconèixer el poder autonòmic al Tractat d'Amsterdam', *Avui*, 10 Apr. 1997.

99 'Las autonomías españolas tienen vía libre para defender directamente sus intereses en la UE', *La Vanguardia*, 8 Aug. 1997.

100 Personal interview with Joan Vallvé, 20 June 1997.

101 Michael Burgess and Franz Gress, 'The Quest for a Federal Future: German Unity and European Union', Michael Burgess and Alain-G. Gagnon (eds), *Comparative Federalism and Federation: Competing Tradition and Future Directions* (Toronto: University of Toronto Press, 1993), 172.

102 Lluis R. Aizpeolea, 'Las autonomías podrán participar en los Consejos de la Unión Europea', *El País*, 9-15 Mar. 1998.

103 Fernández-Arroyo, 'La actuación exterior', 75–7. It is a far cry from the German case, where the Bundesrat has established a separate EC chamber (Burgess and Gress, 'The Quest for a Federal Future', 172). The inadequacy of existing mechanisms for AC involvement in Spain's relations with the EU is discussed in Solozábal, 'Spain: A Federation in the Making?', 260–3.

104 Interviews with Joan Vallvé, Barcelona, 20 June 1997 and Caterina Garcia i Segura, Barcelona, 11 June 1997.

105 Fernández-Arroyo, 'La actuación exterior', 75–7.

106 On the limits to change under the State of the Autonomies and the resultant resurgence in Catalan nationalism, see Caminal Badia, 'Nacionalisme, nacions i partits nacionals', 139.

107 Interview with Pere Esteve, Barcelona, 13 June 1997. Esteve specified that while most of the measures in the CDC proposal did not require constitutional change some clearly did. He thought that time would be needed to develop a consensus for constitutional change.

108 My translation of: 'el *reconeixement* de Catalunya com a nació i el *poder polític* que de dret, li correspon' (CDC, *Per un nou horitzó per a Catalunya*, Document de Treball, 4 June 1997 [provisional version], 1). The document also reflects the influence of a Catalan political scientist, Ferran Requejo (Ramon Suñé, 'Convergència da un paso a la Esquerra', *La Vanguardia*, 9 June 1997, 16).

109 My translation of: 'l'estat de les autonomies es pot interpretar, principalment, com una descentralització administrativa, mentre que l'Estat plurinacional representa el reconeixement de les distintes identitats culturals i lingüístiques que el formen'.

110 My translation of: 'Creació a nivell d'Estat del *Consell cultural de les nacionalitats històriques*, integrat, especialment, per acadèmics d'aquestes nacionalitats'. (CDC, Per un nou horitzó per a Catalunya, 3).

111 According to Pere Esteve, the fiscal arrangements have the highest priority, given both their inherent importance and the state of Catalonia's public finances, but the change in Spain's political culture, to recognition of multinationalism, is absolutely essential (interview with Pere Esteve, Barcelona, 13 June 1997).

112 Unió, *La sobirania de Catalunya i l'estat plurinacional*, 1997. Despite the term 'confederal', beyond fiscal arrangements patterned after the Basque arrangement, the proposals seem to amount to a federal system in which Catalonia would enjoy special powers and rights in recognition of its national status. Thus 'sobirania' seems to be the limited sovereignty of units in a federal state. At the Unió congress where the document was adopted, a motion from the youth wing calling for secession was supported by only 33 per cent of the delegates (Jordi Juan, 'Unió ve superada la etapa autonómica y aboga por un modelo confederal auspiciado por el Rey', *La Vanguardia*, 1 June 1997, 20).

113 My translation of: 'ple respecte a les diferents identitats nacionals preexistents a l'Estat' and 'confederal en tot allò que afecti a la identitat de Catalunya i d'altres fets nacionals, així com a les polítiques de cohesió social; federal en matèria econòmica, financera i fiscal; i autonòmic, pèro no simètric' in Unió Democràtica de Catalunya (Consell Nacional, 'La sobirania de Catalunya i l'estat plurinacional', 1997, 41).

114 ERC, *Programe de govern: Força! Cap a la independència, 1995*, 86–92.

115 The two documents are compared in Ramon Suñé, 'Convergència da un paso a la Esquerra', *La Vanguardia*, 9 June 1997, 16.

116 *Ponencia sobre modelo de estado de Izquierda Unida—Iniciativa per Catalunya*, Barcelona-Madrid, Barcelona, 13 June 1996.

117 Interview with Rafael Ribó, 18 June 1997. The ideas are developed in Rafael Ribó, 'Nacionalismos, investiduras y partidismos', *Temas Para El Debate* 30 (1997), 34–7; and Rafael Ribó and Ferran Requejo, 'Cap a on va l'esquerra catalana?' *Agora: UPF*, No. 5 (April 1997), 10–15.

118 As translated and quoted in Colomé, 'Partit dels socialistes de Catalunya', 42.

119 Colomé, 'Partit dels Socialistes de Catalunya', 46.

120 Ibid., 48.

121 Culla, 'L'evolució ideològica dels partits', 246.

122 Pallarés and Font, 'The Autonomous Elections in Catalonia', 21.

123 My translation of: 'L'Estat de les Autonomies creat per la Constitució té tots els atributs i totes les potencialitats per funcionar com un Estat federal, encara que formalment no sigui aquesta la seva denominació' (PSC, *8è Congrés: Resolucions*, [October, 1996], 20).

124 Ibid., 20.

125 Ibid., 22–5.

126 Interview with Pasqual Maragall, Barcelona, 20 June 1997.

127 As quoted in Robert Hughes, *Barcelona* (New York: Vintage Books, 1992), 35.

Chapter 5

1 Jean Grugel and Tim Rees, *Franco's Spain* (London: Arnold, 1997), 116. Santiago Quesada, *La industrialització de Catalunya al segle XX* (Barcelona: Barcanova, 1992), 56.

2 Jordi Maluquer de Motes i Bernet, *Història econòmica de Catalunya: segles XIX i XX* (Barcelona: Universitat Oberta/Proa, 1998), 199.

3 Raymond Carr, *Modern Spain, 1875–1980* (Oxford University Press, 1980), 157, as cited by Daniele Conversi, *The Basques, the Catalans and Spain: Alternative Routes to Nationalist Mobilisation* (London: Hurst, 1997), 118.

4 Maluquer de Motes, *Història econòmica de Catalunya*, 163.

5 Juan Díez Medrano, *Divided Nations*: Class, *Politics and Nationalism in the Basque Country and Catalonia* (Ithaca: Cornell University Press), 120.

6 Maluquer de Motes, *Història econòmica de Catalunya*, 169.

7 Medrano, *Divided Nations*, 121.

8 Maluquer de Motes, *Història econòmica de Catalunya*, 169.

9 Ibid., 186.

10 Ibid., 172.

11 'La indústria', in Lluís Recolons et al. (eds), *Catalunya 77/88* (Barcelona: Fundació Jaume Bofill, 1989), 175.

12 Quesada, *La industrialització de Catalunya*, 68.

13 'La indústria', 178.

14 Quesada, *La industrialització de Catalunya*, 69.

15 'La indústria', 176.

16 Ibid.

17 Francesc Roca, 'El poder de la burgesia', in Josep Ma. Rotger (ed.), *Visió de Catalunya: El canvi i la reconstrucció nacional des de la perspectiva sociològica* (Barcelona: Diputació de Barcelona, 1987), 15.

18 Maluquer de Motes, *Història econòmica de Catalunya*, 195.

19 Grugel and Rees, *Franco's Spain*, 116.

20 Maluquer de Motes, *Història econòmica de Catalunya*, 242.

21 Medrano, *Divided Nations*, 124.

22 Maluquer de Motes, *Història econòmica de Catalunya*, 187–8.

23 Ibid., 170.

24 Francesc Cabana, *Espisodis de la burgesia catalana* (Barcelona: Proa, 1998), 192.

25 'El serveis' in Lluís Recolons et al. *Catalunya 77/88* (Barcelona: Fundació Jaume Bofill, 1989), 195.

26 Ibid.

27 These various points are drawn from Medrano, *Divided Nations*, 129. According to Cabana, one of the 12 banks classified as 'national' in 1959 had its head office in Barcelona, but a large proportion of its capital was German. It had been founded by Germans but fell into Catalan hands in 1945 after being expropriated (Cabana, *Espisodis de la burgesia catalana*, 193.).

28 Cabana, *Espisodis de la burgesia catalana*, 176–82.

29 'El serveis', 195.

30 Ibid., 196.

31 Cabana, *Espisodis de la burgesia catalana*, 191–200.

32 Maluquer de Motes, *Història econòmica de Catalunya*, 186–7.

33 Salvador Giner, 'Els orígens de la Catalunya moderna', in Salvador Giner (ed.), *La societat catalana* (Barcelona: Institut d'Estadística de Catalunya, 1998), 68; and Francesc Cabana, 'Els principals grups econòmics a Catalunya', in Giner, *La societat Catalana*, 485.

34 Maluquer de Motes, *Història econòmica de Catalunya*, 193.

35 My translation of: 'la penetració del capital europeu—i nord-americà—tindrà com a resultat el fet que el poder de la burgesia a Catalunya sigui, cada cop més, el poder de la burgesia de l'Europa dels Sis, i, sobretot, el poder de la burgesia de la RFA. . . . Per l'altra banda, la gran banca espanyola (madrilenya i basca) i el capital públic espanyol augmenten progressivament les seves quotes de control sobre l'economia catalana' (Roca, 'El poder de la burgesia', 13).

36 Maluquer de Motes, *Història econòmica de Catalunya*, 206.

37 Ibid., 207.

38 Ibid., 219.

39 Ibid., 203.

40 Àlex Costa i Sáenz de San Padro et al., 'L'economia catalana de 1980 al 1994: aspects bàsics de la seva evolució', *Nota d'economia* 53 (Sept.-Dec. 1995), 81.

41 Maluquer de Motes, *Història econòmica de Catalunya*, 207.

42 Costa et al., 'L'economia catalana de 1980 al 1994', 83.

43 Maluquer de Motes, *Història econòmica de Catalunya*, 217. Maluquer de Motes claims that this may be due to 'cultural and ideological' factors as well as economic ones.

44 Ibid., 227.

45 Costa et al., 'L'economia catalana de 1980 al 1994', 88–91.

46 Maluquer de Motes, *Història econòmica de Catalunya*, 226–7.

47 These comparisons are based on ibid., 228 and 188. For 1992, the fifth to eighth categories have been combined to correspond to the 'metal' category of 1975.

48 Ibid., 221.

49 Ibid., 232–3.

50 Ibid., 236.

51 Pere Lleonart, *Catalunya: un país, una economia* (Barcelona: Cambra Oficial de Comerç Indústria i Navegació de Barcelona, 1992), 15.

52 Àngel Miguelsanz i Arnalot, 'El sector turístic a Catalunya', in *L'economia catalana davant del canvi de segle*, 235.

53 Roca, 'La burgesia en la societat catalana', 16.

54 Ramon Caminal, Lluís Torrents, and Xavier Vives, 'Les entitats financeres a Catalunya (1982–92)', in *L'economia catalana davant del canvi de segle*, 262.

55 Cabana, 'Els principals grups econòmics', 485.

56 Joan-Eugeni Sánchez, 'L'estructura empresarial i productiva de Catalunya', in Giner, *La societat catalana*, 543. Arguing that only 0.2 per cent of Catalonia's firms are large, Quesada offers comparable figures of 0.1 per cent for Italy, 0.6 per cent for Germany, 1.4 per cent for France and 2.5 per cent for Great Britain (Quesada, *La industrialització de Catalunya*, 83).

57 Sánchez, 'L'estructura empresarial i productiva', Table 6.

58 See the data in Jordi Fontrodona and Joan Miquel Hernández, *Les multinacionals industrials catalanes* (Barcelona: Direcció General d'Indústria, 1998), 14.

59 Costa et al., 'L'economia catalana del 1980 al 1994', 100.

60 The figure was 26.97 per cent for 1985–95 (calculated from Anna Tarrach i Colls, 'La inversió estrangera directa a Catalunya durant el 1995', *Nota d'economia* 57 (Jan.–Apr. 1997), Table 1).

61 Maluquer de Motes, *Història econòmica de Catalunya*, 208–9. See also Joan Ortega Galán, 'La indústria catalana en una economia oberta', in *L'economia catalana davant del canvi de segle*, 158–9.

62 Sánchez, 'L'estructura empresarial i productiva', Table 7.

63 Lleonart, *Catalunya: Un país, una economia*, 30.

64 'La indústria', in Récolons et al., *Catalunya 77/88*, 173.

65 Lleonart, *Catalunya: Un país, una economia*, 30.

66 'La indústria', in Récolons et al., *Catalunya 77/88*, 176.

67 Lleonart, *Catalunya: Un país, una economia*, 39.

68 Ibid, 11.

69 This is from Galán, 'La indústria catalana en una economia oberta', 160–70.

70 Sánchez, 'L'estructura empresarial i productiva', 545. See also Quesada, *La industrialització de Catalunya*, 79, 89.

71 Fontrodona and Hernández, *Les multinacionals industrials catalanes*, 14.

72 Cabana, 'Els principals grups econòmics', 484.

73 Sánchez, 'L'estructura empresarial i productiva', 545.

74 Fontrodona and Hernández, *Les multinacionals industrials catalanes*, 47.

75 Costa et al., 'L'economia catalana del 1980 al 1994', 104.

76 Fontrodona and Hernández, *Les multinacionals industrials catalanes*, 69–70; and Cabana, 'Els principals grups econòmics', 489.

77 Fontrodona and Hernández, *Les multinacionals industrials catalanes*, 77–8.

78 Ibid., 90–2.

79 Ibid., 38.

80 Ibid., 39.

81 Ibid., 14.

82 Ibid. 46. The authors acknowledge the contention of consultants that firms tend to provide insufficient guarantees, but they argue that lenders should be prepared to assume more risk.

83 Ibid., 44.

84 Maluquer de Motes, *Història econòmica de Catalunya*, 242.

85 Ibid., 242.

86 Parellada and Garcia, 'Les relacions comercials de Catalunya amb l'exterior', in *L'economia catalana davant del canvi de segle*, 402.

87 Jordi Fontrodona and Joan Miquel Hernández, *Les multinacionals industrials catalanes* (Barcelona: Direcció General d'Indústria, 1998), 13.

88 'Evolució dels intercanvis comercials de productes industrials catalans amb l'exterior, 1985–1996', *Perspectiva econòmica de Catalunya*, Aug. 1977, 39.

89 Gemma Garcia Brosa, 'La balança comercial amb l'estranger', in idem. *La balança de pagaments de Catalunya: una aproximació als fluxos econòmics amb la resta d'Espanya i l'estranger (1993–1994)* (Barcelona: Direcció General de Programació Econòmica, 1997), 92.

90 'Evolució dels intercanvis comercials', 37.

91 Ibid., 40–1.

92 Gemma Garcia and Josep Oliver et al., 'El comerç de mercaderies de Catalunya: una visió de conjunt de les relacions amb la resta d'Espanya i amb l'estranger', in *Brosa, La Balança de pagaments de Catalunya,* 107–111.

93 'Evolució dels intercanvis comercials', 42.

94 'Informe sobre la conjuntura econòmica de març del 1998', Caixa Catalunya, *Econòmica catalana,* 126.

95 'Evolució dels intercanvis', 47.

96 These balances are calculated from Charles Murillo and Ezequiel Baró, 'La balança de turisme', in *Brosa, La balança de pagaments de Catalunya,* Table 6.

97 Martí Paralleda, 'Conclusions', in *Brosa, La balança de pagaments de Catalunya,* Table 1.

98 Parellada and García, 'Les relacions comercials de Catalunya amb l'exterior', 389.

99 Garcia and Oliver, 'El comerç de mercaderies de Catalunya', 106.

100 Martí Paralleda, 'Conclusions', Tables 1 and 3.

101 Garcia and Oliver, 'El comerç de mercaderies de Catalunya', 115.

102 Ibid., 106.

103 Castells lists 10 studies, all of which find a substantial deficit (Antoni Castells, 'Les relacions fiscals de Catalunya amb Espanya: algunes reflexions en el context europeu', in Cabana et al., *Catalunya i Espanya,* 136).

104 These data are all taken from *The Public Sector of the Generalitat de Catalunya,* Chapt. 3.

105 Ibid., 7.

106 See, for instance, Francesc Ferrer i Gironès, 'Història de la discriminació fiscal a Catalunya', in Francesc Cabana, *Catalunya i Espanya: una relació econòmica i fiscal a revisar* (Barcelona: Proa/Omnium cultural), 35–65; and Frederic Ribas, 'Dependència i viabilitat de les relacions entre Catalunya i Espanya a la història recent', in ibid., 67–87.

107 Esther Martínez Garcia, 'La balança fiscal de Catalunya', in Cabana, *Catalunya i Espanya,* 216.

108 Ibid., 203.

109 Castells, 'Les relacions fiscals de Catalunya amb Espanya', 136.

110 Esther Martínez Garcia, 'La balança fiscal de Catalunya', in Cabana, *Catalunya i Espanya,* 201.

111 Castells, 'Les relacions fiscals de Catalunya amb Espanya', 139.

112 Ibid.

113 My translation of: 'Els grans noms de la burgesia tradicional catalana han desaparegut quasi totalment, i amb ells les grans empreses tèxtils que controlaven. Els descendents d'aquelles famílies són presents en la vida catalana, però no com a grans empresaris, ni com a titulars de grans capitals' (Cabana, 'Els principals grups econòmics a Catalunya', 483).

114 Gary Wray McDonough, *Good Families of Barcelona: A Social History of Power in the Industrial Era* (Princeton: Princeton University Press, 1986), 30.

115 Jaume Rossinyol, *Le problème national catalan* (Paris: Mouton, 1974), 590; and David Gilmour, *The Transformation of Spain: from Franco to Constitutional Monarchy* (London: Quartet, 1985), 122.

116 Cabana, 'Els principals grups econòmics', 483.

117 Ibid.

118 Although Fomento officials trace their organization back to that date (interview with Joaquin Trigo Portela and Josep Bertran i Vall, Barcelona, 11 June 1997), others believe the year was 1889 (Jordi Sabater, 'Els sindicats i l'organització patronal', in Recolons et al., *Catalunya 77/88,* 70).

119 This paragraph is based on an interview with Joaquin Trigo Portela and Josep Bertran i Vall, Barcelona, 11 June 1997. The claim of 80 per cent is confirmed by Sabater, 'Els sindicats i l'organització patronal', 72.

120 Jordi Sabater, 'Els sindicats i l'organització patronal' in Recolons, *Catalunya 77/88*, 71.

121 Salvador Aguilar, 'L'empresariat i les seves organitzacions', in Rotger (ed.), *Visió de Catalunya*, 68.

122 The president of Fomento, quoted in *El País*, 25 Jan. 1981 (as cited in Aguiler, 'L'empresariat i les seves organitzacions', 69), my translation. See also Sabater, 'Els sindicats i l'organització patronal', 73.

123 Interview with Joaquin Trigo Portela and Josep Bertran i Vall, Barcelona, 11 June 1997; and 'Són els europeistes més pragmàtics' (Miguélez, 'Divisió social del treball', 560).

124 My translation of: 'La apertura a la cooperación con las instituciones públicas y privadas ha sido un objetivo principal de Fomento en los últimos años, en el cual se define la entidad como institución ciudadana que representa las empresas de Cataluña en todas sus vertientes, no sólo en las estrictamente económicas' (*Memòria Foment del treball nacional*, 1998, as quoted in Alexandre Casademunt and Joaquim Molins, 'Les organitzacions empresarials a Catalunya', in Giner, *La Societat Catalana*, 1026).

125 PIMEC literature and interview with Augustí Contijoch i Mestres and Josep M. Vidal-Barraquer i Cot, Barcelona, 17 June 1997.

126 Interview with Augustí Contijoch i Mestres and Josep M. Vidal-Barraquer i Cot, Barcelona, 17 June, 1997. The May 1997 issue of PIMEC's *Actualitat pimec* featured an interview with Lluís Jou, director general of Política Lingüística.

127 Casademunt and Molins, 'Les organitzacions empresarials a Catalunya', 1027.

128 Ibid, 1027.

129 Ibid., 1035.

130 Oriol Homs, 'Formació i composició de la classe obrera a Catalunya: algunes hipòtesis', in Rotger, *Visió de Catalunya*, 144–5.

131 This argument is made by Faustino Miguélez, 'Divisió social del treball: evolució de l'estructura social a Catalunya', in Giner, *La societat catalana*, 555–60. The growth of a new middle class is discussed in Lluís Carreño et al., 'Per une tipologia de les capes mitjanes', in Rotger, *Visió de Catalunya*, 82–4.

132 These figures are calculated from Miguélez, 'Divisió social del treball', 562. (The Catalan *administratius* has been translated as 'clerical staff'.)

133 Maria Caprile, Clàudia Vallvé, and David Moreno, 'El mercat de treball a Catalunya' in Giner, *La societat catalana*, 565–6.

134 Miguélez, 'Divisió social del treball', 561.

135 Jacint Jordana, 'Les organitzacions sindicals a Catalunya', in Giner, *La societat catalana*, 1005.

136 Ibid., 1014.

137 Ibid., 1010.

138 Ibid., 1011.

139 Jacinte Jordana, 'També són nacionalistes, els sindicats de les autonomies històriques?'

140 Jordana, 'Les organitzacions sindicals', 1016.

141 Jordana, 'També són nacionalistes, els sindicats de les autonomies històriques?' 5–6.

142 Josep Pagès i Rejsek, *Political Autonomy in Catalonia: Origins, Jurisdiction, and Organisation of the Generalitat* (Barcelona: Departament de la Presidència, 1996), 86–92. The Generalitat has 'sole jurisdiction' over territorial and urban planning; public works affecting Catalonia alone; roads internal to Catalonia; and transportation, ports, and airports.

143 This is shown by tables in Quim Brugué, Ricard Gomà, and Joan Subirats, 'Els governs de Catalunya', in Giner, *La societat catalana*, 1090.

144 *The Public Sector of the Generalitat of Catalunya* (Barcelona: Direcció General de Progamació Econòmica, 1997), 31.

145 Keating, *Nations against the State*, 154.

146 In 1994 its former director was convicted and imprisoned for corruption (Keating, *Nations against the State*, 155).

147 The 1997 figures were 65 loans and guarantees for 16.124 million pesetas. (All data from Institut Català de Finances web site.)

148 Michael Keating, 'Rethinking the Region: Culture, Institutions and Economic Development in Catalonia and Galicia', paper presented to conference, Globalization, Regionalism and Governance, Sept. 1998, University of Utah.

149 The Port Act of 1997.

150 Autoritat Portuària de Barcelona, *Annual Report, 1997*, 18.

151 Ibid., 23.

152 Autoritat Portuària de Barcelona, *Actualización del Plan Director: determinación de las necesidades de financiación* (Barcelona, 1998).

153 Interview with Jordi Cisteró Bahima, Cap del Departament de Planificació Estratègica, Port de Barcelona, and Josep Garcia Reyes, Director, Barcelona Linguistics Center, Port de Barcelona, 6 May 1998.

154 Interview with Joaquin Trigo Portela and Josep Bertran i Vall, Barcelona, 11 June 1997.

155 Fundació Tribunal i Laboral de Catalunya, *Tribunal Laboral de Conciliació, Mediació i Arbitratge de Catalunya*, undated.

156 Foment del Treball Nacional, CC.OO. and UGT, *Un nou model industrial: Situació i actuacions a l'àmbit de Catalunya*, signed 3 March 1993.

157 *Diari Oficial de la Generalitat de Catalunya*, No. 2401–29.5.1997, 5839–5843.

158 Text of *Pacte per a l'ocupació a Catalunya, 1998–2000*.

159 Estimates supplied by Generalitat, May 1998.

160 Michael Keating contends that labour and business organization are too integrated with their Spanish counterparts to permit 'regional corporatism' and that the Generalitat has no interest in it (Keating, 'Rethinking the Region').

161 Interview with Joaquin Trigo Portela and Josep Bertran i Vall, Barcelona, 11 June 1997.

162 Text of agreement of a 9 September 1988, as supplied by Generalitat. The agreement also called for common initiatives to support less developed European regions. In addition, the agreement allowed for the addition of other regions. But the only such instance is an agreement with the Province of Ontario, signed on 25 Jan. 1990. This agreement fell into limbo with Ontario citing financial constraints.

163 Michael Keating, *The New Regionalism in Western Europe: Territorial Restructuring and Political Change* (Cheltenham, UK: Edward Elgar, 1988), 180.

164 Documents supplied by Generalitat.

165 Over the period 1997–8, subjects of activities included exchange of university business students, application of multimedia to education, discussions among enterprises in the biotechnology and design industries, development of agriculture policy proposals to the European Union, collaboration in the application for European Union structural grants for economic development, art exhibits, children's theatre, electronic transmission of documents among the member governments, citizens' involvement in the development of social policy, exchange of information and meetings of experts with respect to youth employment, exchanges among environmental experts and policy makers, sports competitions, collaboration among experts and institutions concerned with labour training

and recycling, exchange of information regarding women in the workplace (Quatre Motors per a Europa, *Programa de Treball, 1997–1998*).

166 In 1997–8 it reported four projects: a conference of institutions and enterprises in biotechnology, a conference for the design industry, collaboration among quality control organizations, and co-operation among producers of agricultural and food products. The report stated that the small number of projects resulted from the governments' fiscal constraints (Quatre Motors per a Europa, *Programa de treball, 1997–1998*, 6–8).

167 For instance, the university presidents of the four regions now meet regularly, and a master's degree program in inter-regional business issues has been created (interview with Joaquim Llimona i Balcells, Barcelona, 4 May 1998).

168 For instance, the four governments submitted a common position for the 'Agenda 2000' discussion of reform in the EU's structures and financing (interview with Joaquim Llimona i Balcells, Barcelona, 4 May 1998).

169 John Newhouse, 'Europe's Rising Regionalism', *Foreign Affairs* 76, no. 1, 72; and Michael Keating, *The New Regionalism in Western Europe*, 180.

170 Susana Borras, 'The "Four Motors of Europe" and Its Promotion of R&D Linkages: Beyond Geographical Continuity in Interregional Agreements', *Regional Politics and Policy* 3, no. 3 (Autumn 1993): 170.

171 Francesc Morata and Xavier Muñoz, 'Vying for European Funds: Territorial Restructuring in Spain', in Liesbet Hooghe (ed.), *Cohesion Policy and European Integration: Building Multi-Level Governance* (New York: Oxford University Press, 1996), 204.

172 Marisa Muga, 'La opinión de los Españoles sobre la Unión Europea', (Brussels: Comisión Europea, Direccion General X, July 1996), 4, 7–8. But Catalans were also among the highest when it came to confidence in Spanish institutions as well (ibid., 9).

173 Oriol Homs, 'Distribució de la riquesa i condició socioeconòmica' in Giner, *Societat catalana*, 479.

174 'Cataluña recibirá 1999 115.000 millones al año de fondos de la Unión Europea', *La Vanguardia*, 29 January 1998.

175 Castella i Parellada, 'L'economia Catalana en el context espanyol i europeu' in Giner, *La societat catalana*, 502.

176 Castells i Parellada, 'L'Economia catalana', 502.

177 Antoni Castells, 'Les relacions fiscals de Catalunya amb Espanya: algunes relexions en el context europeu', in Francesc Cabana (ed.), *Catalunya i Espanya: una relació econòmica i fiscal a revisar* (Barcelona: Proa, la mirada, 1998), 145.

178 Castells i Parellada, 'L'economia catalana', 502.

179 This is the thesis of Castells i Parellada (ibid.).

180 Castells, 'Les relacions fiscals', 149.

181 'Most analysts would view Catalonia as the leading exemplar of this type of region state' (Thomas J. Courchene with Colin R. Telmer, *From Heartland to North American Region State: The Social, Fiscal and Federal Evolution of Ontario* [Toronto: University of Toronto Press, 1998], 272).

182 Kenichi Ohmae, *The End of the Nation State: The Rise of Regional Economies* (New York: Free Press, 1995), 89.

183 For instance, in his influential piece on the rising European regionalism, John Newhouse recounts that Toulouse is doing more business with Catalonia than with the rest of France, and he discusses plans for a high-speed train between Barcelona, Montpellier, Lyon, and northern Italy. But he offers no quantitative data on trade or other links between the various European regions, Catalonia included, and other parts of Europe or the global economy (John Newhouse, 'Europe's Rising Regionalism', *Foreign Affairs* 76, no. 1 (Jan.–Feb. 1997): 69–84.

184 Ohmae's work is infused with a criticism of the dead hand of the nation-state that seeks to retain powers of economic intervention which have never produced the desired effects. 'The illusion of control is soothing. Yet hard evidence proves the contrary' (Kenichi Ohmae, 'The Rise of the Region State', *Foreign Affairs* 72, no. 2 (Spring 1993): 83). Region states, on the other hand, are seen to welcome foreign investment and ownership. In effect, they allow the forces of the global economy to act to the benefit of their citizens. 'Region states . . . are economic not political units, and they are anything but local in focus' (Ohmae, *The End of the Nation State*, 88–9). My criticism of this line of analysis is shared by Montserrat Guiberneau, *Nations without States: Political Communities in a Global Age* (Cambridge, UK: Polity Press, 1999), 171.

185 See Michael Keating's distinction between 'bourgeois regionalism', which he associated with the CiU, and the 'social democratic project' in Keating, *The New Regionalism*, 157–9.

Chapter 6

1 Rigol and Jorba, 'La Religió dels Catalans', 845–7. By 1995 only 25.7 per cent of Catalans classified themselves as 'practising Catholics'. Though another 56.5 per cent called themselves 'non-practising Catholics', 14.7 per cent said they were 'non-believers' or 'indifferent'. Just as the first response is less frequent in Catalona than in the rest of Spain, so the second two are higher. On the other hand, these figures don't square with Joan Culla's claim that in 1963 only 15 per cent of Barcelona residents thought of themselves as Catholic and 82 per cent said they were indifferent (as reported by Conversi, *The Basques, the Catalans and Spain*, 126).

2 As quoted in Manual Castells, *The Power of Identity*, Vol. 2 of *The Information Age: Economy, Society and Culture* (Malden, Mass.: Blackwell, 1997), 43.

3 Sebastià Sarasa, 'Prefaci: la societat civil catalana', 981.

4 Sarasa, 'Associacionisme, moviments socials i participació cívica', 1054.

5 Sarasa, 'Mutualisme, cooperació i filantropia', 1050.

6 Ibid., 1053.

7 Ibid., 1051.

8 Ibid., 1050.

9 Ibid., 1045.

10 Ibid., 1044–8.

11 Ibid., 1041–4.

12 Sarasa, 'Associacionisme, moviments socials i participació cívica', 986.

13 Ibid., 989.

14 The figures for membership were 15 per cent and 8 per cent for Catalonia but 22 per cent and 12 per cent for Spain (F. Andrés Orizo and A. Sanchéz, *El sistema de valors dels catalans* (Barcelona: Institut Català d'Estudis Mediterranis, 1991]).

15 These points are made by Sarasa, 'Associacionisme, moviments socials i participació cívica', 994.

16 Interview with Sebastià Sarasa, Barcelona, 1997.

17 Salvador Cardús, 'Els agents culturals', Recolons et al., *Catalunya 77/88*, 359.

18 Cardús, 'Els agents culturals', 360.

19 Direcció General de Programació Econòmica, *The Public Sector of the Generalitat de Catalunya* (Barcelona: Generalitat, 1997), 31.

20 Jordi Busquet, 'Les indústries culturals a Catalunya: nous reptes i velles solucions', in Giner, *La societat catalana*, 891.

21 Rossinyol, *Le probléme national catalan*, 449–50; and Conversi, *The Basques, the Catalans and Spain*, 120–1.

22 Jaume Rossinyol, *Le probléme national catalan* (Paris: Mouton, 1974), 448.

23 Joan M. Corbella, *Social Communication in Catalonia* (Barcelona: Generalitat, 1988), 42; and Busquet, 'Les indústries culturals', 886.

24 Salvador Cardús, 'La creació i producció de cultura', in Recolons et al., *Catalunya 77/88*, 380.

25 Cubeles and Fina, 'La cultura a Catalunya', 71.

26 Cardús, 'La creació i producció de cultura', 381.

27 Busquet, 'Les indústries culturals a Catalunya', 886.

28 Direcció General de Política Lingüística, *The Catalan Language Today*, (Barcelona: Generalitat, 1992) 44.

29 Cubeles i Fina, 'La cultura a Catalunya', 70.

30 Busquet, 'Les indústries culturals a Catalunya', 887.

31 Daniele Conversi, *The Basques, the Catalans and Spain: Alternative Routes to Nationalist Mobilisation* (London: Hurst, 1997), 121.

32 Busquet, 'Les indústries culturals a Catalunya', 887.

33 Ibid., 888.

34 Ibid., 891.

35 Cardús, 'La creació i producció de cultura', 387–9.

36 In 1993, 31.8 per cent of records sold in Catalonia featured Spanish artists, and Catalan music is only a small part of that 31.8 per cent (*'la música en català representa una petita part d'aquest 31.8%'*) (Busquet, 'Les indústries culturals a Catalunya', 887).

37 Cardús, 'La creació i producció de cultura', 394.

38 Busquet, 'Les indústries culturals a Catalunya', 889.

39 Of course, the predominance lay with not Castilian productions but North American ones, which attracted 77.6 per cent of theatre visits in 1993 (Cubeles i Fina, 'La cultura a Catalunya', 81–2).

40 *The Catalan Language Today*, 48.

41 Busquet, 'Les indústries culturals a Catalunya', 883.

42 The number of cultural foundations increased from 54 in 1983 to 453 in 1995 (Sarasa, 'Mutualisme, cooperació i filantropia', Table 2).

43 Salvador Cardús, 'El mitjans de comunicació', in Recolons et al., *Catalunya 77/88*, 345.

44 See Josep M. Baget i Herms, *Història de la televisó a Catalunya* (Barcelona: Generalitat, 1994).

45 Cubeles i Fina, 'La cultura a Catalunya', 85.

46 There are a large number of semi-legal local television stations broadcasting in Catalan (Manuel Parés i Maicas, 'Les communicacions de massa a Catalunya', in Giner, *La societat catalana*, 872–3).

47 *La llengua en el món del comerç: l'actitud dels catalans davant l'ús comercial del català* (Barcelona: Generalitat, 1988), 41.

48 Parés, 'Les comunicacions de massa a Catalunya', Table 5. Subsequently, one of the new stations, *Tele5*, introduced a system that allowed viewers to choose between Catalan or Castilian (Keating, *Nations against the State*, 137). Also, a 1993 CIS survey found that 33 per cent of Catalans preferred television in Catalan, 24 per cent preferred Castilian, and 43 per cent were content with either (ibid.).

49 *The Catalan Language Today*, 41.

50 Mireya Folch-Serra, 'Civil Society and National Identity: the Case of Catalonia', unpublished paper, 11.

51 Ibid,16.

52 Folch-Serra, 'Civil Society and National Identity', 14.

53 Parés, 'Les comunicacions de massa a Catalunya', 869.

54 Vallerdú, *L ús del català*, Table V. The figures held for the younger age groups (which would have been affected by the school reforms) are as follows: 14–17 years: 36 per cent; 18–21 years: 38 per cent. The figures were much higher among older respondents.

55 Cubeles i Fina, 'La cultura a Catalunya', 85.

56 Parés, 'Les comunicacions de massa a Catalunya', 870.

57 See Conversi, *The Basques, the Catalans and Spain*, 109–15; Francesc Vallerdú, *L'ús del Catala: un futur controvertit* (Barcelona: Edicions 62, 1990), 24; and Francesc Ruiz, Rosa Sanz, and Jordi Solé i Camardons, *Història social i política de la llengua catalana* (Barcelona: Climent, 1996), 198–9.

58 *Political Autonomy in Catalonia*, 92; and Guiu, 'Educació i ciència a Catalunya', 938.

59 Guiu, 'Educació i ciència a Catalunya', in Giner, *La societat catalana*, 940.

60 Ibid., 943.

61 Ibid., 938.

62 Serasa, 'Mutualisme, cooperació i filantropia', 1052.

63 Ibid.

64 Joan M. Romaní and Miquel Strubell i Trueta, 'L'ús de la llengua a Catalunya', in Giner, *La societat catalana*, 811.

65 Guiu, 'Educació i ciència a Catalunya', 947.

66 Xavier Martínez Celorrio, 'Capital humà i innovació a Catalunya', in Giner, *La societat catalana*, 973. Martínez's claim that Catalonia has 17 per cent of Spanish researchers (ibid., 973) is difficult to square with his observation that researchers represent only 0.3–0.4 per cent of Catalonia's population but 3.1 per cent of Spain's population (ibid., 974).

67 Ibid., 973.

68 Guiu, 'Educació i ciència a Catalunya', 946.

69 There is, of course, no way to prove this contention, as is noted by both Sebastià Sarasa, 'Prefaci: benestar i polítiques socials a Catalunya', in Giner, *La societat catalana*, 644; and M. Teresa Crespo and Cristina Rimbau, 'Els serveis socials a Catalunya', in Giner, *La societat catalana*,734.

70 Sarasa, 'Prefaci: benestar i polítiques socials', 645.

71 Andreu Segura Benedicto, 'Salut i sanitat a Catalunya', in Giner, *La societat catalana*, 657–60.

72 Crespo and Rimbau, 'Els serveis socials', Table 1.

73 Mediterranean conditions are apparently responsible for the comparatively high life expectancy among women and low death rates due to cancer and circulatory problems. On the other hand, the incidence of AIDS is high (Benedicto, 'Salut i sanitat', 661.)

74 Crespo and Rimbau, 'Els serveis socials', 739–41.

75 Ibid., 742.

76 Ibid., 743.

77 All data are from Jordi Estivill, 'L'estudi de la pobresa a Catalunya', in Giner, *La societat catalana*, 604.

78 Carme Trilla et al., 'Polítiques d'habitatge a Catalunya', in Giner, *La societat catalana*, 679.

79 Sarasa, 'L'Estat de Benestar', 646.

80 Juli Sabaté, 'Víctimes i delinqüents', in Giner, *La societat catalana*, 759.

81 Mary Nash, 'The Changing Status of Women in Contemporary Catalonia', in Milton M. Azevedo (ed.), *Contemporary Catalonia in Spain and Europe* (Berkeley: Gaspar de Portola Catalonian Studies Program, University of California, 1991), 10.

82 This account is drawn from Sarasa, 'Associacionisme, moviments socials i participació cívica', 989.

83 Art. 9.27 Generalitat de Catalunya, *The Catalan Statute of Autonomy* (Departament de la Presidència, 1993).

84 Nash, 'Changing Status of Women', 108–9.

85 Comissió Interdepartamental per a la Igualtat d'Oportunitats per a les Dones, *Pla d'actuació del Govern de la Generalitat de Catalunya per a la igualtat d'oportunitats per a les dones, 1994–1996* (Barcelona, 1994).

86 Nash, 'Changing Status of Women', 112–13.

87 Ibid., 112.

88 In 1988 only 11.11 per cent of members of the Catalan parliament were women (ibid., 120). With the 1999 election it rose to 23.7 per cent (personal communication from Xavier Arbos).

89 Daniele Conversi, *The Basques, the Catalans and Spain: Alternative Routes to Nationalist Mobilisation* (London: Hurst, 1997), 188.

90 Conversi, *The Basques, the Catalans and Spain*, 189.

91 Josep Termes, *La immigració a Catalunya i altres estudis d'història catalan* (Barcelona: Editorial Empúries, 1984), 129.

92 Termes, *La immigració a Catalunya*, 129, 131.

93 Some turn-of-the century writers, such as Pompeu Gener, sought to formulate a racially based definition of Catalan identity, but they were largely ignored (see Conversi, *The Basques, the Catalans and Spain*, 193).

94 Termes, *La immigració a Catalunya*, 131.

95 My translation of: 'comme s'il était leur langue maternelle. La Catalogne nationalise les immigrants' (Jacques Valdour, *L'ouvrier espagnol: observations vécues*, vol. 1: *Catalogne* (1919), 251 [as cited in Termes, *La immigració a Catalunya*, 139]).

96 My translation of: 'el nombre de catalans de pura raça per a lluitar en tots els terrenys' (Puig i Sais, *El problema de la natalitat a Catalunya: un perill gravíssim per a la nostra pàtria* (1915) [as cited in Termes, *La immigració a Catalunya*, 139]).

97 My translation of: 'una prudent política assimilativa, que ha de tenir per instruments primordials l'escola, la premsa i els espectacles, i que destruït el mite de la nacionalitat com un fet d'ordre racial fundat en la unitat de la sang, i establert que la nacionalitat és un fenomen cultural que pot afaiçonar perfectament individus de les races més distintes, . . . el que cal fer és reforçar la nostra potència assimilatòria' (Carles Cardó, 'El murcianisme', *La Veu de Catalunya*, 4 May 1934 [as quoted in Termes, *La immigració a Catalunya*, 145]).

98 My translation of: 'pot fer perdre les característiques pròpies del poble català' (Josep A.Vandellós, *La immigració a Catalunya* (1935), 136 [as cited in Termes, *La immigració a Catalunya*, 148]).

99 Jacqueline Hall, 'Immigration et nationalisme en Catalogne', *Perspectiva Social 14* (Institut catòlic d'estudis socials de Barcelona) (July–Dec. 1979), 100.

100 Conversi, *The Basques, the Catalans and Spain*, 191.

101 Lluís Recolons i Arquer, 'Marc demogràfic dels recents moviments migratoris de Catalunya', *Perspectiva Social 14* (Institut catòlic d'estudis socials de Barcelona), (July–Dec. 1979), 11.

102 Josep Termes, *La immigració a Catalunya* (Barcelona: Empúries, 1984), 132, as cited by Conversi, *The Basques, The Catalans and Spain*, 191.

103 Conversi, *The Basques, The Catalans and Spain*, 191.

104 Salvador Giner, *The Social Structure of Catalonia* (Sheffield: Anglo-Catalan Society, 1984), 43.

105 Juan F. Marsal, 'Sociología de la inmigración', *La Vanguardia*, 24 Apr. 1977 (as cited in Recolons, 'Marc demogràfic', 13).

106 Joaquín Recaño Valverde and A. Miguel Solana Solana, 'Migració residencial entre Catalunya i la resta d'Espanya', in Giner, *La societat catalana*, 224.

107 Hall, 'Immigration et nationalisme', 97–9.

108 Ibid., 101.

109 My translation of: 'Aquesta barreja que cal qualificar d'indesitjable si es vol conservar incòlume la pròpia cultura'. A. Peyrí, *El poder polític: el problema Catalunya-Espanya* (Paris: Colleció SOM de l'Associació Catalonia, 1972), 35 (as quoted in Hall, 'Immigration et nationalisme', 101.

110 Ibid. 153, as quoted in Hall, 'Immigration et nationalisme', 104.

111 Hall, 'Immigration et nationalisme', 132; Conversi, *The Basques, the Catalans and Spain*, 194; and Termes, *La immigració a Catalunya*, 154–7.

112 Hall calls this new realism 'neo-nationalist' (Hall, 'Immigration et nationalisme', 120).

113 Ibid., 121.

114 My translation of: 'Què és un català? . . . Català és tot home que viu i treballa a Catalunya, i que amb el seu treball, amb el seu esforç, ajuda a fer Catalunya. Hem d'afegir-hi només: que de Catalunya en fa casa seva, és a dir, que d'una manera o altra s'hi incorpora, s'hi reconeix, s'hi entrega, no li és hostil' (Jordi Pujol, *Per un doctrina d'integració*, 69–70 [as quoted in Termes, *La immigració a Catalunya*, 155]).

115 My translation of: 'Excepte el que ve amb prejudicis anticatalans, l'immigrat, en principi, és un català' (ibid., 71 [as quoted in Termes, *La immigració a Catalunya*, 155]).

116 My translation of: 'La llengua és un factor decisiu de la integració dels immigrats a Catalunya. És el més definitiu. Un home que parla català i que parla català als seus fills, és un català de soca i arrel' (ibid., 82–3, [as quoted in Termes, *La immigració a Catalunya*, 156]).

117 Jacqueline Hall offers several examples of the notion that attachment to Catalonia was more important than knowledge of Catalan (Hall, 'Immigration et nationalisme', 123). See also Termes's citation of a declaration that knowledge of the language is by no means indispensable by Heribert Berrera, who later became leader of the ERC in the Catalan parliament and who was a firm advocate of Catalan independence (Termes, *La immigració a Catalunya*, 164).

118 My translation of: 'No accepten Catalunya, no senten ni els seus problemes ni les seves inquietuds. . . . No accepten Catalunya ni els catalans' (Manuel Cruells, *Els no catalans i nosaltres* [Edicions d'aportació catalana, 1965], 17 [as quoted in Termes, *La immigració a Catalunya*, 159]).

119 My translation of: 'Constitueix un greu error el no tractar d'incorporar-se els grups d'immigrants. . . . Cal posar tota la voluntat per tal que el nou arribat senti el país com a seu i s'hi identifiqui. . . . La fusió serà portada a cap en un temps mínim i sense forçar les voluntats. La generació infantil dels immigrants es pot incorporar plenament a la nacionalitat abans d'arribar a la joventut' (Marc Aureli Vila, *Les migracions* (Edicions d'aportació catalana, 1965), 18–19 [as quoted in Termes, *La immigració a Catalunya*, 163]).

120 The thesis was originally published in French as Joaquim Maluquer Sostres, *L'assimilation des immigrés en Catalogne* (Geneva: Librairie Droz, 1963).

121 The preface is described in Termes, *La immigració a Catalunya*, 165–7.

122 My translation of: 'Els èxits del socialisme han introduït, sobretot, un concepte més ampli, menys discriminatori, de nació. . . . La procedència geogràfica i social dels seus components té poca importància; el que compta és la integració de cada un d'ells dins d'una mateixa consciència de solidaritat. . . . Els catalans de l'any 1966 tenim menys prejudicis que en Vandellós i els seus contemporanis' (Jordi Nadal, 'En Vandellós, trenta anys després', *Qüestions de vida cristiana*, no. 31 (1966), 113–4 [as cited in Termes, *La immigració a Catalunya*,168]).

123 Termes, *La immigració a Catalunya*, 168.

124 As cited by Conversi, *The Basques, the Catalans and Spain*, 209.

125 See Conversi, *The Basques, the Catalans and Spain*, 196–9; and Shafir, *Immigrants and Nationalists: Ethnic conflict and Accommodation in Catalonia, the Basque Country, Latvia, and Estonia* (Albany: State University of New York, 1995), 79.

126 Hall, 'Nationalisme et immigration', 133.

127 As Shafir points out, linguistic proximity alone does not guarantee that a language will in fact be acquired. It is also a social process, involving the desire to learn the language and a positive response among those who already speak it. See Shafir, *Immigrants and Nationalists*.

128 Malaquer Sostres, *L'Assimilation des immigrés*, 61.

129 Ibid., 111.

130 Ibid., 65.

131 Ibid., 119 and 135.

132 Ibid., 139.

133 Joaquim Torres, 'La immigració i la llengua catalana: documentació sobre coneixements, usos i actituds lingüístics', in *Immigració i reconstrucció nacional a Catalunya* (Barcelona: Fundació Jaume Bofill, 1980), 52–3. See also Shafir, *Immigrants and Nationalists*, 79.

134 Shafir, *Immigrants and Nationalists*, 81.

135 Torres, 'La immigració i la llengua catalana', 51. For his part, Termes sees mixed marriages as likely to produce Castilian speakers, and on this basis predicts that Castilian will become dominant, at least in Barcelona (Termes, *La immigració a Catalunya*, 187).

136 Armand Sàez, 'Catalunya, gresol o explotadora? Notes sobre immigració i creixement', in *Immigració i Reconstrucció Nacional*, 32.

137 Pinilla de las Heras's study is analysed in Faustino Miguélez Lobo, 'Immigració i mobilitat social', in *Visió de Catalunya*, 305–9; and Shafir, *Immigrants and Nationalists*, 74–6.

138 Miguélez, 'Immigració i mobilitat social', 309–10.

139 Ibid., 317.

140 Conversi, *The Basques, the Catalans and Spain*, 212. Apparently there have been no recent studies of mobility comparable to Pinilla de la Heras's work.

141 Joaquín Recaño Valverde and A. Miguel Solana Solana, 'Migració residencial entre Catalunya i la resta d'Espanya', in Giner, *La societat catalana*, 224–30 and Figure 1.

142 Ibid., 236–7.

143 Emma Aixalà i Mateu, *Els ez de Catalunya* (Barcelona: Edicions la Campana, 1997).

144 Colectivo Ioé, *La immigració estrangera a Catalunya: balanç i perspectives* (Barcelona: Institut Català d'Estudis Mediterranis, 1992), 33.

145 Lluís Recolons, 'Migracions entre Catalunya i l'estranger', in Giner, *La societat catalana*, Table 3.

146 Ibid., 263.

147 Colectivo Ioé, *La immigració estrangera*, Table 48. (The frequencies for all Spain were quite similar.)

148 Institut d'Estudis i Professions (EDEP), 'Els Catalans i el civisme (1995–1997): Informe de resultats' (Barcelona, May 1997), 30 and 42.

149 Ibid., 61. See also Gary Wray McDonough, 'Reflections on New Immigration in Catalonia', in Azevedo, *Contemporary Catalonia*, 85.

150 McDonough, 'Reflections on New Immigration', 87–91; Colectivo Ioé, *La immigració estrangera*, 112–13; and idem., *Presencia del sur: Marroguies en Cataluña* (Madrid: Editorial Fondamentos, 1995), 280–1.

151 Collectivo Ioé, *Presencia del sur*, 222–6.

152 Cristina Buesa, 'Dos incendios intencionados en Girona avivan la psicosis racista', *El Periodico*, 22 July 1999; and J. Corachan and J. Tarragona, 'Més detinguts per la violència racista', *El Periodico*, 18 July 1999.

Chapter 7

1 See the quotations from various nationalist writings in Daniele Conversi, *The Basques, the Catalans and Spain: Alternative Routes to Nationalist Mobilization* (London: Hurst, 1997), 169–73.

2 These data are taken from Vallverdú, *L'ús del Català*, Table I.

3 As cited in Woolard, *Double Talk*, 33.

4 Jacqueline Hall, *La connaissance de la langue catalane (1975–1986)*, trans. Marjorie Coup (Barcelona: Generalitat, 1990), Table 16.

5 Ibid., 11.

6 Woolard, *Double Talk*, 83.

7 Rossinyol, *Le problème national catalan*, 449–50; and Conversi, *The Basques, the Catalans and Spain*, 120–1.

8 Ruiz, Sanz, and Camardons, *Història social i política de la llengua*, 202.

9 Presidencia del Gobierno, *Spanish Constitution*, 1982, Article 3(2), emphasis added.

10 My translation of: 'El català és la llengua oficial a Catalunya. Tots els ciutadans residents a Catalunya tenen *el dret d'expressar-se en llengua catalana i l'obligació de saber-la*' (Albert Branchadell, *La normalitat improbable* (Barcelona: Empúries, 1996), 73).

11 My translation of: 'L'idioma català té a Catalunya el mateix tractament oficial que la Constitució reconeix al castellà per a tot l'Estat espanyol' (Branchadell, *La normalitat improbable*, and Joan Colomines, *La llengua nacional de Catalunya* [Barcelona: Generalitat, 1992], 83). Balcells describes the regime proposed in the draft statute as 'exclusive official status' (Albert Balcells, *Catalan Nationalism: Past and Present* [London: Macmillan, 1969], 173).

12 Generalitat de Catalunya, *Catalan Statute of Autonomy,* (Barcelona: Departament de la Presidència, 1993), Art. 3(2).

13 Ibid., Art. 3(3).

14 Ibid., Art. 3(1). Arguably, 'proper' was a prudent choice of terminology, avoiding both 'national', which would have offended many Spaniards, and 'regional', which would have been unacceptable to Catalans (A. Barrera i Vidal, 'La diffusion du catalan', *International Journal of Sociology of Language* 107 [1994]: 52).

15 Laitin and Solé, 'Catalan Elites and Language Normalisation', 9.

16 My translation of: 'No tienen en cuenta la realidad social y lingüística de Cataluña'. Quoted in Salvador Cardus, 'La llengua' in Lluís Recolon et al. (eds), *Catalunya 77/88* (Barcelona: Fundacio Bofill, 1989), 333; Albert Balcells, *Catalan Nationalism: Past and Present* (London: Macmillan, 1969), 179; and Enric Monné and Lluisa Selga, *Història de la Crida a la solidaritat: en defensa de la llengua, la cultura i les Nacions Catalanes* (Barcelona: Balmes, 1991), 22–4.

17 My translation of: 'no accepten l'existència de la nostra nació i es posen d'acord per continuar oprimint-la, fins i tot en allò que es una de les bases essencials de la nostra

continuïtat nacional: la recuperació i la normalització lingüística' (Monné and Selga, *Història de la Crida*, 31).

18 Cardus, 'La llengua', 333.

19 My translation of: 'generalitzar el coneixement de la llengua, impulsar-ne i facilitar-ne l'ús en diferents àmbits socials, i impulsar la modificació de les actituds lingüístiques i les pautes de conducta que obstaculitzen la normalització del català' (Direcció General de Política Lingüística, *Llibre blanc de la Direcció General de Política Lingüística* [Barcelona: Generalitat, 1983], 14).

20 *La campanya per la normalització lingüística de Catalunya, 1982* (Barcelona: Departament de Cultura, 1983), 39–45.

21 Cardus, 'La Llengua', 334.

22 A 1983 survey of the greater Barcelona area found that 96.6 per cent of respondents saw it as very or quite beneficial that children of non-Catalan-speaking parents should be taught Catalan. Moreover, 81.8 per cent (73.3 per cent of immigrants) agreed that Catalan should be a language of instruction. See Ariadna Puiggené i Riera et al., 'Official Language Policies in Contemporary Catalonia', in Milton M. Azevedo (ed.), *Contemporary Catalonia in Spain and Europe* (Berkeley: International and Area Studies, University of California, 1991), 35.

23 My translation of: 'La llengua catalana . . . element fonamental de la formació de Catalunya . . . una situació precària, caracteritzada principalment per l'escassa presència que té en els àmbits d'ús oficial, de l'ensenyament i dels mitjans de comunicació social' (*Llei 7/1983, de 18 d'abril, de normalització lingüística a Catalunya* [Generalitat de Catalunya, 1990], preamble, 3).

24 My translation of: 'superar l'actual desigualtat lingüística impulsant la normalització de l'ús de la llengua catalana en tot el territori de Catalunya' (Ibid., 5).

25 My translation of
    1. Emparar i fomentar l'ús del català per tots els ciutadans.
    2. Donar efectivitat a l'ús oficial del català.
    3. Normalitzar l'ús del català en tots els mitjans comunicació social.
    4. Assegurar l'extensió del coneixement del català.
    (Ibid., 5).

26 My translation of 'Tenen com a única forma oficial la catalana' (Ibid., Art. 12).

27 My translation of: 'El català, com a llengua pròpia de Catalunya, ho és també de l'ensenyament en tots els nivells educatius' (Ibid., Art. 14).

28 Branchadell, *La normalitat improbable*, 75–80.

29 This is acknowledged in the Generalitat's own document, *The Catalan Language Today* (Barcelona: Generalitat, 1992) 23. Indeed Pujol himself has repeatedly expressed personal frustration with the situation (Branchadell, *La normalitat improbable*, 146; and Jordi Juan, 'Pujol no piensa jubilarse', *La Vanguardia*, 5 Mar. 1998).

30 Branchadell, *La normalitat improbable*, 138–47; and Montserrat Solé, 'El català a l'administració de justícia', in Direcció General de Política Lingüística, *Estudis i propostes per a la difusió de l'ús social de la llengua catalana*, 'Situació i evolució recent de la llengua catalana' (Barcelona: Generalitat, 1991), 197.

31 Joan Tudela I Penya, *El Català a l'administració de la Generalitat* (Barcelona: Generalitat, 1994), 22.

32 Ibid., 23.

33 Ibid., 28–9.

34 Michael Keating, 'Nationalism, Nation-Building and Language Policy in Quebec and Catalonia', unpublished paper, 18.

35 Josep Maria Artigal, *The Catalan Immersion Program: A European Point of View*, trans. Jacqueline Hall (Norwood, N.J.: Ablex, 1991), 65.

36 Ibid., 66.

37 Artigal, *The Catalan Immersion Program*, Table 4.6.

38 Ibid., 72.

39 Artigal, *The Catalan Immersion Program*, 83–6. In 1977–8 only 52 per cent of pre-school and primary teachers in Catalonia spoke Catalan. This problem had been only marginally eased by 1981–2. See Puiggené i Riera et al., 'Official Language Policies', 39.

40 Keating, 'Nationalism, Nation-Building and Language', 19.

41 Miquel Renui i Tresserras, *Planificació lingüística; estructures i legislació* (Barcelona: Generalitat, 1994), 6. These activities are also discussed in Puiggené i Riera et al., 'Official Language Policies', 43–5.

42 See Puiggené i Riera et al., 'Official Language Policies', 44.

43 Miquel Strubell, 'L'impuls institucional de l'ús del català, des de la Generalitat de Catalunya', in Direcció General de Política Lingüística, *Estudis i propostes per a la difusió de l'ús social de la llengua catalana*, 204–5.

44 Renui, *Planificació lingüística*, 26.

45 Renui, *Planificació lingüística*, 27.

46 Ibid.

47 The 1975 figure is from Vallverdú, *L'ús del Català*, Table II. The 1991 figure is from Institut d'Estadística de Catalunya, 'El coneixement del català l'any 1996', April 1998, 8.

48 Institut d'Estadística, 'El coneixement del català', 8.

49 Ibid.

50 Among children whose mothers understood Catalan but didn't speak, read, or write it, the figures were much higher (following the same order): 98.8, 75.3, 71.7, and 55.1 per cent. (All figures are taken from Institut d'Estadística de Catalunya, 'Influència del nivell de coneixement del català de la mare en el dels fills', December 1994).

51 M.M. Aguilera I Vilar and J.M. Romaní i Olivé, *Actituds dels consumidors Catalans davant de l'ús comercial del Català* (Generalitat: Barcelona, 1995), 25–6. In the analysis of the results, the respondents were segregated according to whether they had been born in Catalonia of Catalonia-born parents, born in Catalonia of parents born elsewhere, or themselves born elsewhere. Not surprisingly, if the shopkeeper spoke Catalan, 96.6 per cent of the respondents with Catalan-born parents would have used Catalan; only 26.2 per cent of the respondents born elsewhere would have used it. However, if the shopkeeper spoke Castilian, the majority of respondents (58.3 per cent) with Catalan-born parents would have used Castilian, as would 84.3 per cent of the middle group (born in Catalonia of parents born elsewhere), along with 97 per cent of the immigrant group. If the shopkeeper's language was unknown, then 87.3 per cent of those with Catalan-born parents would have used Catalan but 77.9 per cent of those born elsewhere would have used Castilian. In the middle group, 54.4 per cent would have used Catalan.

52 Kathryn A. Woolard and Tae-Joong Gahng, 'Changing Language Policies and Attitudes in Autonomous Catalonia', *Language and Society* 19 (1990): 311–30. In the test, respondents (secondary school students in the Barcelona area) were exposed to recorded statements by speakers with a variety of accents to determine attitudes towards each type of accent, including those of Catalan and Castilian speakers using the other language. In 1980, they found that Castilian-speakers using Catalan were penalized by their fellow Castilian-speakers but were met with relative indifference to their efforts by Catalan speakers. Each group gave higher ratings to people speaking the group's language as native speakers, than when they spoke the language of the other group. Seven years later, they found that Castilian-speakers were less likely to disapprove of their confreres for speaking Catalan and Catalan-speakers were more accepting of the use of Catalan

as a second language. In short, the linguistic boundaries were less clearly drawn and the possibility of Catalan being used in exchanges was correspondingly enhanced.

53 Ibid., 326–7.

54 Emili: *Identitat i llengua en els joves de Barcelona* (Barcelona: Edicions 62, 1993), 203–12. While both Catalan-speakers and Castilian-speakers continued to identify with distinct linguistic groups and to use to their language within that group, they were open to using both languages in inter-group exchanges, they did in fact use both, and they were indifferent as to which language was used. Indeed, there was a sense in both groups that to impose their own language would be to show inflexibility. The old norm of using Castilian had not completely disappeared. In part this is because about one-third of the Castilian-speaking youth of metropolitan Barcelona could not speak Catalan properly, lacking the social circumstances to learn and use it. But to the extent that the norm had disappeared, the result was not adoption of a new norm but the absence of any norm at all.

55 My translation of: 'Per a la majoria d'aquests joves, doncs, és força indiferent que se'ls dirigeixin en català o en castellà. Les dues llengües s'accepten com un comportament de fet, davant del qual no cal plantejar cap intent voluntari, ni individual ni encara menys de grup, de modificació de les normes d'ús' (Boix, *Triar no és trair*, 211).

56 My translations of: 'el fet és que la inèrcia lingüística heretada de l'època anterior pesa més en la vida de les empreses que no pas en altres àmbits de la nostra societat' (Joan Tudela, L'ús de la llengua Catalana a les empreses de Catalunya [Barcelona: Generalitat de Catalunya, n.d.], 5).

57 Ibid., 9. A detailed breakdown of different forms of communication showed that for external relations virtually all forms of written communication were 60 per cent or more in Castilian and languages other than Catalan. Only spoken communications (by telephone and in person) were mostly in Catalan. The same pattern held for relations within the enterprise: all forms of written communication were overwhelmingly in Castilian and languages other than Catalan. Catalan figured heavily only in oral communications (ibid., 16–17). Overall, use of Catalan was greater in banks and financial institutions and least in industrial enterprises (ibid., 22–3). And it was considerably greater in parts of Catalonia beyond the province of Barcelona and in enterprises whose president or CEO was born in Catalonia (ibid., 28).

58 Francesc Xavier Rambla, *Factors de la distribució territorial de l'ús del Català a la conurbació de Barcelona* (Barcelona: Generalitat, 1993).

59 Boix, *Triar no és trair*, 211.

60 Vallverdú, *L'ús del Català*, Table III(a).

61 *General Language Normalisation Plan* (Barcelona: Generalitat, 7 March 1995).

62 Ibid., 44.

63 Ibid., 53.

64 'Criteris del Govern per a l'elaboració d'una llei d'ús de les llengües oficials a Catalunya', Barcelona, 18 February 1997.

65 Proceeding on the basis of the principle of territoriality, Catalan was to be 'la llengua de totes les institucions de Catalunya', at least of a wide range of public and semi-public institutions, and 'la llengua preferentment emprada per les altres institucions i per les empreses i entitats estatals i privades que ofereixen serveis al públic' (ibid., 2).

66 My translation of: 'una llengua encara no normalitzada des del punt de vista del seu ús social' (Associació per a les Noves Bases de Manresa, 'Per a un nou estat social de la llengua Catalana', 1997).

67 L'Hospitalet de Llobregat, 'La festa de la llengua esdevé un clam perquè Catalunya sigui un país normal', *Avui*, 14 June 1997; and 'Todos los partidos, salvo al PP, acudirán a un acto multitudinario en favor del catalán', *La Vanguardia*, 12 June 1997. Of course, as Rafael Ribó pointed out in an interview (18 June 1997) the guests did not by their presence endorse the notion of Catalan becoming the only official language.

68 Lluis Bon, 'Cent quaranta entitats s'agrupen per demanar més suport al català', *Avui*, 17 Sept. 1997.

69 My translation of: 'la seva preocupació, compartida per amplis sectors de la societat, pel contingut del nou text, com més va més allunyat dels plantejaments incials dels partits polítics catalans compromesos amb la plena recuperació de la nostra llengua' (Marta Lasalas, 'Més de cent entitats critiquen la rebaixa de la llei del català', *Avui*, 8 Oct. 1997).

70 Ramon Suñé, 'Un consenso que se retrasó dos años y medio', *La Vanguardia*, 2 Oct. 1997.

71 My translation of: 'ha deixat de ser una llei de normalització lingüística per passar a ser de tranquil-.lització i garanties de l'ús del castellà' (Mayka Fernández, 'Le llei del català supera la primera votació amb el support de CiU, PSC, IC i PI', *Avui*, 26 Nov. 1997).

72 Suñé, 'Un consenso que se retrasó dos años y medio'.

73 Francesc Ruiz et al., *Història social i política de la lengua catalana* (Barcelona: Contextos 3i4, 1996), 205.

74 Lluís Bou and Marka Fernández, 'El PP critica la immersió però vota que el català sigui l'idioma escolar', *Avui*, 7 May 1997. The PP spokesman in the Commission, Josep Curto, dissociated himself from the position (ibid.). However, Curto allegedly placed the principle in question himself at a closed commission hearing (Lluís Bou and Anna Grau, 'Reventós entrega a Ribó una cinta de la ponència del català i obre una crisi institucional', *Avui*, 10 May 1997).

75 'Documento sobre el uso de las lenguas oficials de Cataluña', *El País*, 30 Apr. 1997.

76 'El Foro Babel extrema el seu rebuig a la llei del català i en reclama la retirada', *Avui*, 29 Sept. 1997. Foro reiterated its position in late December, as the bill was about to be passed ('Carbón para las izquierdas y para CiU', *La Vanguardia*, 30 Dec. 1997).

77 'Los nacionalistas consideran franquistas las críticas de intelectuales de izquierda a la ley', *La Vanguardia*, 1 Oct. 1997.

78 'La Plataforma per la Llengua veu ànim "genocida" en el Foro Babel', *Avui*, 1 Oct. 1997.

79 'Las casas regionales creen que la ley vulnera la convivencia pacífica de catalán y castellano', *La Vanguardia*, 3 Oct. 1997; and 'La Cecrec denuncia que el nou text del català no respecta el principi de coexistència pacífica', *Avui*, 3 Oct. 1997.

80 'El PSC se plantea acotar la inmersión', *La Vanguardia*, 30 Sept. 1997; Marta Lasalas, 'El PSC acceptarà per responsabilitat la llei del català si té màxim consens', *Avui*, 7 Oct. 1997; and Ramon Suñé Cristina Sen, 'La ponencia del catalán concluye seis meses de trabajo sin consensuar la ley', *La Vanguardia*, 1 Oct. 1997.

81 Lluís Bou and Marta Lasalas, 'CCOO i UGT donaran avui el suport sindical al català', *Avui*, 26 Sept. 1997.

82 'Los nacionalistas consideran franquistas las críticas de intelectuales de izquierda a la ley', *La Vanguardia*, 1 Oct. 1997.

83 For the director general of language policy, substitution of the term 'habilidad' does not relieve civil servants of the obligation to respond in the language of citizens (interview with Luis Jou i Mirabent, Barcelona, 4 May 1998).

84 Ramon Suñé, 'Un pacto con mucho retoque y alguna cesión', *La Vanguardia*, 10 Nov. 1997.

85 In the opinion of journalist Ramon Suñé, the negotiations 'ha afectado más a la forma, al detalle y al matiz que al contenido esencial de la nueva normativa' (ibid.).

86 My translation of: 'Aquest pacte [CiU-PSC] el que fa és aigualir, descafeïnar, rebaixar el text de la Ponència . . . en el fons no acabava de resoldre els dos reptes bàsics per a la pervivència del català en el futur, la igualtat jurídica del català amb el castellà a Catalunya en tots els àmbits i la guarantia real del seu ús també en tots els àmbits Esquerra Republicana de Catalunya' ('Anàlisi de la nova llei de política lingüística', n.d.).

87 Esquerra Republicana de Catalunya, 'Les 99 esmenes d'ERC a la llei refusades pel pacte Serra-Pujol', n.d.

88 My translation of: 'La Catalunya del segle XXI necessita que les nostres dues llengües es puguin utilitzar en tots els àmbits en què es desenvolupa l'activitat dels catalans. Des d'aquesta profunda convicció propugnem que no són necessàries noves lleis lingüístiques, que estan allunyades de la majoria social' (Partit Popular de Catalunya, 'Llibertat i convivència', Barcelona, 29 Dec. 1997).

89 Oriol Domingo and Ramon Suñé, 'El PP se compromete a respetar la ley y ERC recalca que persiste la inferioridad del catalán', *La Vanguardia,* 31 Dec. 1997.

90 The proper title is *Llei 1/1998 de 7 de Gener, de Política Lingüística.*

91 *Llei 1/1998 de 7 de Gener, de Política Lingüística,* Art. 1.

92 Ibid., Art. 2.

93 Ibid., Art. 11 and 17.

94 Ibid., Art. 22(2) and 24(3).

95 Ibid., Art. 26. In the case of radio, the percentage can be modified in light of a station's audience; the Generalitat can ask for higher percentages when awarding licenses. To be sure, these provisions apply only to television and radio broadcasting that falls under the Generalitat's jurisdiction.

96 Ibid., Art. 29.

97 Ibid., Chap. V.

98 Ibid., Art. 34.

99 Ibid., Art. 35.

100 Ibid., Art. 36.

101 Ibid., 'Disposicions addicionals', Cinquena.

102 Ibid.

103 Ibid., 'Disposicions transitòries'.

104 Interview with Miquel Strubell i Trueta, Barcelona, 28 Apr. 1998.

105 There were two members of the Partido Socialista Andaluz.

106 This is also the view of the Director General, Dirrecció General de Política Lingüística (interview, Barcelona, 16 June 1997).

107 José María Brunet, 'El Defensor del Pueblo no recurre la ley del catalán pero pide que se cambie', *La Vanguardia,* 9 Apr. 1998. In particular, the ombudsman cited provisions requiring that public enterprises 'normally' use Catalan in dealing with fiscal or judicial persons in the Catalan linguistic sphere and that the signs and documentation of firms serving the public must be written 'at least' in Catalan. He also warned against pursuing any notion of Catalonia's residents having a 'duty' to learn Catalan.

108 The 2011 estimate is 52.4 per cent; the 2026 estimate is 54.3 per cent (René Houle and Miquel Strubell, 'La projecció demolingüística a Catalunya', unpublished paper prepared for conference 'Jornades tècniques sobre projeccions demogràfiques de Catalunya', 26–7 May 1997, Barcelona, Table 10).

109 M. Termote, 'L'Évolution démolinguistique du Québec et du Canada', in Commission sur l'avenir politique et constitutionnel du Québec, *Élements d'analyse institutionnnelle, juridique et démolinguistique pertinents à la révision du statut politique et constitutionnel du Québec,* Document de travail, numéro 2 (Quebec City, 1991).

110 Even with the inclusion of Catalan-speakers not only in other parts of Spain but throughout the world, the total number of Catalan speakers comes to about 6.5 million according to Dirrecció General de Política Lingüística, *The Catalan Language Today* (Barcelona: Generalitat, 1992), 17–19. The number that understand Catalan is just over 9 million.

111 David D. Laitin, 'The Cultural Identities of a European State', *Politics and Society* 25, no. 3 (Sept. 1997), 290.

Chapter 8

1 Conversi uses the term 'core value' to describe the relationship of language to Catalan nationalism (Daniele Conversi, *The Basques, the Catalans and Spain: Alternative Routes to Nationalist Mobilisation* (London: Hurst, 1997), Chapt. 7).

2 A small terrorist group, it conducted some small-scale bombings of property before renouncing violence in 1991.

3 As quoted in Albert Balcells, *Catalan Nationalism: Past and Present* (London: Macmillan, 1996), 193.

4 My translation of: 'hacia un modelo que no se corresponde ni con lo que mayoritaria-mente se deseaba en los inicios de nuestra democracia, ni con lo que ponen de manifiesto las expresiones libres y públicas de muchos catalanes de hoy' ('Por un nuevo modelo de Cataluña', as reproduced in Antonio Santamaría, *Foro Babel: el nacionalismo y las lenguas de Cataluña* (Barcelona: Ediciones Áltera, 1999), 290).

5 Joan Botella, 'El comportament electoral', Giner, *La societat catalana*, 11112.

6 Centro de Investigaciones Sociológicas, *Conciencia nacional y regional*, Estudio No. 2.228, Nov.–Dec. 1996. This analysis is based upon the Catalonia subsample of this study, which consisted of 784 respondents. I thank Jordi Sanchez, of Fundació Jaume Bofill, for making the data set available to me.

7 The sample appears to have a disproportionately large number of respondents whose mother tongue is Castilian: 457, or 58.28 per cent of the full sample. Obviously, this could affect the distribution of responses to the questions we are examining. However, our analysis will focus not on the distribution of responses within the full sample, but on the extent of association among responses and, in particular, the *comparative* responses of Catalan and Castilian speakers.

8 In his time analysis of surveys over 1984-6, Jordi Sanchez found roughly the same distribution of responses: Spanish only, 11 per cent; more Spanish than Catalan, 7.4 per cent; equal, 43.3 per cent; more Catalan than Spanish, 22.5 per cent; and Catalan only, 13 per cent (Jordi Sanchez, 'Identitats collectives i cultura cívica dels Catalans', Giner, *Societat catalana*, Table 1).

9 One might presume that including the phrase 'exercise its right to self-determination' might encourage selection of this option. The 1996 annual survey by the *Institut de Ciències Polítiques i Socials* posed a similar question but without referring to any such right. The result was only 16 per cent (*1996: Sondeig d'Opinió—Catalunya* (ICPS: Barcelona, 1997), 88). However, the previous year it was virtually identical to the CIS result: 22 per cent (*1995: Sondeig d'opinió—Catalunya* (ICPS: Barcelona, 1996), 88).

10 CIS, Study No. 228, question 33: 'Are you, personally, in favour of or against the autonomous community becoming independent?' (*Personalmente, estaría Vd. a favor o en contra de que su Comunidad Autónoma fuera independiente?*) Among all respondents, 52.9 per cent were opposed; among those with Catalan as their mother tongue, 27.9 per cent were opposed. The 1996 ICPS annual survey produced 29 per cent in favour of the independence of Catalonia (*1996: Sondeig d'opinió*, 1997, 98). Conceivably, the phrase 'the independence of Catalonia' might be seen by some to imply simply greater autonomy rather than full sovereignty. This would explain why the percentages agreeing are higher than when, as in the previous question, the reference is to 'independent state' and this is presented as one of several alternatives.

11 Among respondents stating that they felt 'very close' to the CiU ($N = 107$), the proportion choosing 'nation' was higher: 57.9 per cent. Still 36.4 per cent opted for 'region'.

12 A similar analysis of the same data set, using as a dependent variable the question on Catalan and Spanish identities, can be found in Sanchez, 'Identitats collectives i cultura cívica dels Catalans', 1073-4.

13 ERC leader Josep-Luis Carod-Rovira claims that his party following, at least until recently, has had precisely this profile (interview, 8 June 1997).

14 See the analysis in ibid., 1072.

15 In an analysis by DEP, an opinion research firm in Barcelona, respondents were offered just three choices: 'only Catalan', 'only Spanish', and Catalan and Spanish. (A fourth response, 'neither Spanish nor Catalan' had few takers.) The 'Catalan only' was strongest (34.7 per cent) among the 16–24 age group and second-strongest (27.9 per cent) among the 25–34 group (Institut DEP, 'Els catalans i el civisme (1995–1997): Informe de resultats', May 1997, 54). This relationship is also shown in Sanchez's 1989–97 time-line data (Sanchez, 'Identitats collectives i cultura cívica dels Catalans', Table 3).

16 A relationship between age and support for Catalan independence regularly appears in the annual analyses of opinion published by the Institut de Ciències Polítiques i Socials. See *1996: Sondeig d'opinió: Catalunya* (Barcelona: ICPS, 1997), 88, 98.

17 See Luis Moreno, Ana Arriba, and Araceli Serrano, 'Multiple Identities in Decentralized Spain: The Case of Catalonia', *Regional and Federal Studies* 8, no. 3 (Autumn 1998): 80. A relationship between education and exclusive identification with Catalonia is also confirmed in Institut DEP, 'Els catalans i el civisme (1995–1997): Informe de resultats', May 1997, 55.

18 'Catalonia offers an example of high social integration between both natives and immigrants. Both collectives seem to be interwoven in various degrees and manifestations. Integration and tolerance are among the main features present in Catalonia's social life'. (Moreno et al., 'Multiple Identities in Decentralized Spain', 78.)

19 Institut DEP, 'Els catalans i el civisme (1995–1997): Informe de resultats', May 1997, 59. The authors believe that with such a high percentage one is justified 'in saying that Catalonia has a very strong capacity to involve all its residents in the Catalan project, whether or not they are native to the country.' (My translation of: 'parlar d'una molt elevada capacitat catalana d'implicació dels seus habitants-hagin nascut al país o no-en el projecte català').

20 Sanchez, 'Identitats collectives i cultura cívica dels Catalans', 1072.

21 To cite Sanchez: 'Even so, this reality [the predominance of dual identities] should not lead one to underestimate the importance to Catalan political life of the existence of sectors with exclusive identities, especially if the dynamic of age cohorts increases such attitudes' (ibid., 1072–3). My translation of 'Tot i així, aquesta realitat no ens pot portar a menystenir la importància que en la vida política catalana pot tenir l'existència de sectors amb percepcions identitàries excloents, especialment si les dinàmiques de cohorts incrementen aquestes actituds.'

Chapter 9

1 Pierre Vilar, *La Catalogne dans l'Espagne moderne* (Paris: Flammarion, 1961), 220.

2 Ibid., 224.

3 In this I differ with Guiberneau, who in her systematic study of 'nations without states' sees nations as lacking a state unless they have full political independence or sovereignty. She excludes federal status since federations 'tend to exclude foreign and economic policy, defense and constitutional matters' (Montserat Guibernau, *States without Nations: Political Communities in a Global Age* (Cambridge, U.K: Polity Press, 1999), 17. Yet it is not clear why a nation should be judged to be without a state if it has a state structure that can exercise effective and constitutionally guaranteed control over matters central to the nation's survival and development, such as education, cultural affairs, linguistic matters, regional development, social policy, and so on. By definition, this is a qualitatively different situation from arrangements such as devolution or decentralization which can be unilaterally terminated by the central state. At the same time, if federalism is to be conceived in terms of the autonomy needs of *nations*, as opposed

to regions, then it must be a robust form of federalism with full constitutional guarantees, independent fiscal sources, and effective control over exclusive jurisdictions. I believe this warrants a rigorous scrutiny of claims that Spain is effectively a federation, and justifies my rejection of them.

4 Antoni Castelle i Martí Parellada, 'L'economia catalana en el context espanyol i europeu', in Giner, *La societat catalana*, 496.

5 Jordi Malaquer de Motes i Bernet, *Història econòmica de Catalunya: segles XIX i XX* (Barcelona: Universitat Oberta/Proa, 1998), 242.

6 Anna Tarrach i Colls, 'La inversió estrangera directa a Catalunya durant el 1995', *Nota d'economia* 57 (Jan.–Apr. 1997), Table 1.

7 Manuel Castells, *The Power of Identity*, Vol. 2 of *the Information Age: Economy, Society and Culture* (Malden, Mass.: Blackwell, 1997), 50. In the end, Castells places Catalonia in the category of a 'national quasi-state (52).

8 A sceptical assessment of the progress to date in the emergence of a 'Europe of the Regions' appears in Guibernau, *Nationalisms*, 113.

9 Montserrat Guiberneau, who offers a similar critique of the 'region state' thesis, claims that '"region states" will inevitably become political units' (Guiberneau, *States without Nations*, 171).

10 See the critique of the ethnic/civic distinction in Rogers Brubaker, 'Myths and Misconceptions in the Study of Nationalism', in John A. Hall, ed., *The State of the Nation* (Cambridge: Cambridge University Press, 1998), 298–300.

11 See, for instance, Michael Keating, *Nations against the State: The New Politics of Nationalism in Quebec, Catalonia and Scotland* (London: Macmillan, 1996), 218.

12 Antonio Santamaría, *Foro Babel: el nacionalismo y les lenguas de Cataluña* (Barcelona: Ediciones Áltera, 1999), 290.

13 The idea that nations are 'imagined' is, of course, associated with Benedict Anderson, *Imagined Communities: Reflections on the Origin and Spread of Nationalism* (London: Verso, 1983). The thesis is strongly criticized by Manuel Castells, who uses the case of Catalonia to make his point (Manuel Castells, *The Power of Identity* (Malden, Mass.: Blackwell, 1997), 27–51. The importance of a historically constituted community to the success of a nationalist leadership is well argued by Miroslav Hroch, 'Real and Constructed: The Nature of the Nation', in John A. Hall (ed.), *The State of the Nation: Ernest Gellner and the Theory of Nationalism* (Cambridge, U.K.: Cambridge University Press, 1998), 99.

14 '1996 Census: Mother Tongue, Home Language and Knowledge of Languages', *The Daily: Statistics Canada*, 2 Dec. 1997. Francophones were identified on the basis of French mother tongue. Among Quebec anglophones, 61.7 per cent reported that they knew French; 11.2 per cent of Quebec residents of neither mother tongue said they knew both English and French.

15 Kenneth D. McRae, *Conflict and Compromise in Multilingual Societies: Belgium* (Waterloo: Wilfrid Laurier University Press, 1986), 35–8.

16 Alexander Murphy, 'Belgium's Regional Divergence: Along the Road to Federation', in Graham Smith, ed., *Federalism: The Multiethnic Challenge* (London: Longman, 1995), 78–80.

17 Peter A. Gourevitch, 'The Reemergence of "Peripheral Nationalisms": Some Comparative Speculations on the Spatial Distribution of Political Leadership and Economic Growth', *Comparative Studies in Society and History* 21 no. 3 (1979): 303–22.

18 Juan Díez Medrano, *Divided Nations: Class, Politics and Nationalism in the Basque Country and Catalonia* (Ithaca: Cornell University Press, 1995).

19 See John Hargreaves' review of Conversi, *The Basques, the Catalans and Spain* in *Nations and Nationalism* 4, no. 3 (1998): 425.

20 Conversi, *The Basques, the Catalans and Spain,* 257–63.

21 Montserrat Guibernau, *Nationalisms: The Nation-state and Nationalism in the Twentieth Century* (Cambridge, U.K.: Polity Press, 1996), 76.

22 See the exchange between John Hargreaves and Michael Keating in 'Ethno-nationalist Movements in Europe: A Debate', *Nations and Nationalism* 4, no. 4 (1998): 569–77.

23 Table 2 in Chapter 8. See the discussion in Alfred Stepan, 'Modern Multinational Democracies: Transcending a Gellnerian oxymoron', in Hall, *The State of the Nation,* 231.

24 This can be inferred from Table 10 in Chapter 8.

25 As reported in Chapter 8.

Interviews

Alemany i Roca, Joaquina, president, Institut Català de la Dona—Barcelona, 16 June 1997.

Alonso i Perelló, Lluís, secretary, l'Institut d'Estudis Autonòmics—Barcelona, 11 June 1997.

Álvarez i Suárez, secretary-general, Unió General de Treballadors de Catalunya—Barcelona, 18 June 1997.

Argelaguet i Argemí, Jordi, graduate student, Universitat Autònoma de Barcelona—Bellaterra, Catalonia, 13 June 1997.

Arbos, Xavier, law professor, Departament de Dret Public, Universitat de Girona—Barcelona, 4 March 1996, 4 June 1997 and 1 May 1998.

Armet, Lluís i Coma, senator, Partit des Socialistes de Catalunya—Barcelona, 24 April 1998.

Babot Gutiérrez, Ana Maria, researcher, Partit dels Socialistes de Catalunya—Barcelona, 6 March 1996.

Bacaria, Jordi, director, Institut Universitari d'Estudis Europeus, Universitat Autònoma de Barcelona—Barcelona, 5 May 1998.

Balcells, Albert, historian, Universitat Autònoma de Barcelona—Bellaterra, Catalonia, 11 March 1996.

Bargalló, Josep, parliamentarian, Esquerra Republicana de Catalunya—Barcelona, 29 April 1998.

Bartomejus, Oriol, researcher, Institut de Ciències Polítiques i Socials—Barcelona, 22 April 1998.

Batalla, Xavier, journalist, *La Vanguardia*—Barcelona, 11 March 1996 and 19 June 1997.

Berbel, Joan Josep, official, Centre d'Informació i Desenvolupament Empresarial (CIDEM)—Barcelona, 12 March 1996.

Bertran i Vall, Josep, promotor de Grupos de Exportadores, Fomento del Trabajo Nacional—Barcelona, 11 June 1997.

Bonet, Luis, professor of political economy and public finance, Universitat de Barcelona—Barcelona, 4 June 1997.

Caminal Badia, Miquel, political scientist, Universitat de Barcelona—Barcelona, 9 June 1997 and 4 May 1998.

Cardús, Salvador, sociologist, Universitat Autònoma de Barcelona—Barcelona, 10 June 1997.

Carod-Rovira, Josep-Lluís, leader, Esquerra Republicana de Catalunya—Barcelona, March 12 1996 and 6 June 1997.

Carreras Serra, Francesc, member, Consell Consultiu de la Generalitat de Catalunya—Barcelona, 28 April, 1998

Cisteró Bahima, Jordi, official, Cap del Departament de Planificació Estratègica, Port de Barcelona—Barcelona, 6 May 1998.

Colom Gonzalez, Francisco, researcher, Consejo Superior de Investigaciones Científicas—Madrid, 17 March 1996.

Contijoch i Mestres, Augustí, president, PIMEC—Barcelona, 17 June 1997.

Cuatrecasas, Llibert, Comissari per a Actuacions Exteriors, Generalitat—Barcelona, 17 June 2000.

Esteve, Pere, secretary-general, Convergencia i Unió—Barcelona, 13 June 1997.

Ferrer i Roca, Joaquim, former senator, Convergencia i Unió—Barcelona, 7 March 1996.

Folch-Serra, Mireya, geographer, University of Western Ontario—London, Ontario, 7 November 1997.

Flaquer, Lluís, sociologist, Universitat Autònoma de Barcelona—Barcelona, 4 May 1998.

Fontana, Josep, historian, Institut de Història, Universitat Pompeu Fabra—Barcelona, 19 June 1997.

Fossas i Espadaler, Enric, political scientist, Universitat Autònoma de Barcelona—Barcelona, 13 June 1997 and 30 April 1998.

Fusi, Juan-Pablo, historian—Madrid, 14 March 1996.

Garcia Reyes, Josep, Public Relations, Corporate Communications Department, Port de Barcelona (formerly Head, North American Affairs, Generalitat)—Barcelona, 11 March 1996, 18 June 1997 and 6 May 1998.

Garcia Segura, Caterina, professor of law, Universitat Pompeu Fabra—Barcelona, 11 June 1997.

Garcia-Delgado i Segués, Rosa Maria, official, Direcció General de Promoció Comercial (COPCA)—Barcelona, 12 March 1996.

Gausa, Salvador, official, Institut de Ciències Polítiques i Socials—Barcelona, 5 March 1996.

Gil i Miró, Carme, CiU member of Cortes—Barcelona, 18 June 1997.

Giner, Salvador, sociologist, Instituto de Estudios Sociales Avanzados, Universitat de Barcelona—Barcelona, 30 April 1998.

Guri i Fernàndez, Diego, official, COPCA—Barcelona, 12 March 1996.

Jou i Mirabent, Lluís, director general, Direcció General de Política Lingüística—Barcelona, 16 June 1997 and 4 May 1998

Jürgen-Nagel, Klaus, political scientist, Universitat Pompeu Fabra—Barcelona, 19 June 1997 and 4 May 1998.

Keating, Michael, political scientist, University of Aberdeen and Florence Institute—London, Ontario, 7 November 1997 and Barcelona, 25 April 1998.

Llimona i Balcells, Joaquim, director general, Direcció General de Relacions Exteriors, Generalitat—Barcelona, 28 April 1998.

López Búlla, José Luis, director of studies, Comissió Obrera Nacional de Catalunya—Barcelona, 28 April 1998.

López i Casasnovas, economist, Universitat Pompeu Fabra—Barcelona, 11 March 1996 and 5 May 1998.

López i Cobo, Germán, Assumptes transregionals, Secretaria General, Departament de Treball,—Barcelona, 5 May 1998.

Maestro, Jesús, researcher, Institut de Ciències Polítiques i Socials—Barcelona, 22 April 1998

Maragall, Pasqual, mayor, Barcelona—Barcelona, 20 June 1997.

Millàs i Estany, Josep, president, Òmnium Cultural—Barcelona, 4 March 1996, 3 June 1997, and 20 April 1998.

Miró i Ardèvol, politician, Convergencia i Unió—Barcelona, 10 June 1997.

Mitjans, Esther, vice-dean, Facultat de Dret, Universitat de Barcelona—23 April 1998.

Molas, Isidro, director, Institut de Ciències Polítiques i Socials—Barcelona, 10 June 1997.

Molins López-Rodó, Joaquim M., dean, Facultat de Ciències Polítiques i de Sociologia, Universitat Autònoma de Barcelona—Bellaterra, Catalonia, 13 June 1997.

Morata, Francesc, political scientist, Departament de Ciència Política i de Dret Públic, Universitat Autònoma de Barcelona—Barcelona, 22 April 1998.

Moreno Fernández, Luis, political acientist, Consejo Superior de Investigaciones Científicas—Madrid, 15 March 1996.

Morera i Balada, Josep-Ramon, director, Comitè Director per a l'Organització de l'Administració, Generalitat—Barcelona, 12 June 1997.

Niubó i Casellas, Josep M., Departament Relacions Internacionals, Unió General de Treballadors de Catalunya—Barcelona, 20 June 1997.

Nadal, Joaquim, Partit del Socialistes de Catalunya—Barcelona, 5 May 1998.

Obiols, Raimon, Partit dels Socialistes de Catalunya—Barcelona, 6 May 1998.

Oliveras i Prats, Jordi, director, Institut d'Estadística de Catalunya—Barcelona, 5 June 1997.

Ortiz i Cervelló, Rafael, director general de Relacions Laborals, Generalitat—Barcelona, 5 May 1998.

Pardo, José J. Sanmartin, Gabinete de la Presidencia del Gobierno—Madrid, 17 March 1996.

Pascual, Margot, assessora del Gabinet de la Presidència, Iniciativa per Catalunya—Barcelona, 5 May 1998.

Porta, Jordi, President, Fundació Jaume Bofill—Barcelona, March 12 1996.

Pujals, Josep Ma, conseller de Cultura, Generalitat de Catalunya—Barcelona, 20 June 1997.

Pujol, Jordi, president de la Generalitat de Catalunya—Barcelona, 4 May 1998.

R. Aguilera de Prat, Cesáreo, political scientist, Universidad de Barcelona—Barcelona, 10 June 1997.

Ràfols-Casamada, painter—Barcelona, 8 March 1996.

Renau i Permanyer, Enric, director, Institut d'Estudis i Professions—Barcelona, 6 May 1998.

Reniu i Tresserras, Miquel, director general de Política Lingüística, Generalitat—Barcelona, 8 March 1996.

Requejo Coll, Ferran, director, Departament de Ciències Polítiques i Socials, Universitat Pompeu Fabra—Barcelona, 8 June 1997 and 21 April 1998.

Ribó, Rafael, secretari general, Iniciativa per Catalunya—Barcelona, 18 June 1997 and 5 May 1998.

Rigol i Roig, Joan, president, Unió Democràtica de Catalunya—Barcelona, 27 April 1998.

Romani i Olivé, Joan, researcher, Institut de Sociolingüística Catalana—Barcelona, 8 March 1996, 28 April 1997, and 28 April 1998.

Rovira i Jacquet, Guillem, subdirector, Patronat Català Pro Europa—12 June 1997.

Rull, Josep, Joventuts Nacionalistes de Catalunya—Barcelona, 20 June 1997.

Salamero i Salas, Antoni, director general, Direcció General de Programació Econòmica, Generalitat—Barcelona, 5 May 1998.

Sanchez, Jordi, researcher, Fundació Jaume Bofill—Barcelona, 9 June 1997 and 30 April 1998.

Sena i Calabuig, Ernest, director general, Institut Català de Finances—Barcelona, 12 June 1997.

Serase, Sebastià, sociologist, Universitat Pompeu Fabra—Barcelona, 19 June 1997.

Serret i Berniz, Jordi, director, COPCA—Barcelona, 12 March 1996.

Soler Alberti, Josep, secretary-general, Institut d'Estudis Financers—8 March 1996, 17 June 1997, and 21 April 1998.

Sort i Jané, Josep, political scientist, Universitat Ramon Llull—Barcelona, 16 June 1997 and 26 April 1998.

Strubell i Trueta, Miquel, director, Institut de Sociolingüística Catalana—Barcelona, 28 April 1998.

Termes, Josep, historian—Barcelona, 11 March 1996.

Trigo Portela, Joaquin, executive-director, Fomento del Trabajo Nacional—Barcelona, 11 June 1997

Vallvé i Ribera, Joan M., Member of European Parliament—Barcelona, 20 June 1997 and 24 April 1998.

Vidal-Barraquer i Cot, Josep M., director, PIMEC—Barcelona, 17 June 1997.

Willox, Paul, first secretary, Canadian Embassy—Madrid, 5 November 1995 and 15 March 1996.

Wright, David, ambassador, Canadian Embassy—Madrid, 15 March 1996.

Bibliography

Agranoff, R. 1994. 'Asymmetrical Federalism in Spain: Design and Outcomes'. Paper presented to International Political Science Association, 21–25 Aug.

———. 1996. 'Federal Evolution in Spain'. *International Political Science Review* 17, no. 4, 385–401.

———. n.d. 'Intergovernmental Relations and the Management of Asymmetry'.

Agranoff, R., and J.A. Ramos Gallarin. n.d. 'Toward Federal Democracy in Spain: An Examination of Intergovernmental Relations'. Photocopy.

Aguilera de Prat, C.R. 1993. *Nacionalismos y autonomías*. Barcelona: Promociones y Publicaciones Universitarias.

———. n.d. 'Los socialistas y los pactos de gobernabilidad de 1993 y 1996'. Photocopy.

Aguilera i Vilar, M.M., and J.M. Romaní i Olivé. 1995. *Actituds dels consumidors Catalans davant de l'us comercial del Català*. Barcelona: Generalitat.

Ainaud, J., et al. 1980. *Immigració i reconstrucció nacional a Catalunya*. Barcelona: Fundació Jaume Bofill.

Aixala i Mateu, E. 1997. *Els Ez de Catalunya*. Barcelona: Campana.

Aizpeolea, L.R. 1998. 'Las autonomías podrán participar en los Consejos de la Unión Europea'. *El País*, 9–5 Mar.

Alvarez-Junco, J. 1996. 'The Nation-Building Process in Nineteenth-Century Spain'. In Mar-Molinero and Smith (eds), *Nationalism and the Nation in the Iberian Peninsula*, 89–106. Oxford: Oxford University Press.

Anitch, J. 1996. 'Pujol hace frente a los dirigentes de su partido que quieren dejar solo a Aznar'. *La Vanguardia*, 6 Mar.

Artigal, J.M. 1991. *The Catalan Immersion Program: A European Point of View*. Trans. Jacqueline Hall. Norwood, N.J.: Ablex.

Associació per a les Noves Bases de Manresa. 1997. *Per a un nou estat social de la llengua Catalana*. Barcelona: Autoritat Portuária de Barcelona.

———. 1997 *Annual Report*. Barcelona.

———. 1998 *Actualización del plan director: determinación de las necesidades de financiación*. Barcelona.

Avui. 1997. 'La Plataforma per la Llengua veu ànim "genocida" en el Foro Babel'. 1 Oct.

———. 1997. 'La Crecec denuncia que el nou text del català no respecta el principi de coexistència pacífica'. 3 Oct.

Azevedo, M.M. (ed.). 1991 *Contemporary Catalonia in Spain and Europe*. Berkeley, Calif.: Gaspar de Portolà Catalonian Studies Program, University of California.

Baget i Herms, J.M. 1994. *Història de la televisió a Catalunya*. Barcelona: Generalitat.

Balcells, A. 1995. *Catalan Nationalism: Past and Present*. London: Macmillan.

Barrera i Vidal, A. 1994. 'La diffusion du catalan'. *International Journal of Sociology of Language* 107, 41–65.

Benet, J. 1973. *Catalunya sota el règim franquista*. Vol. 1. Paris: Ediciones Catalanas de París.

Bernier I., and A. Binette. 1988. *Les provinces canadiennes et le commerce international*. Quebec City: Centre québécois de relations internationales.

Boix, E. 1993. *Triar no és trair: identitat i llengua en els joves de Barcelona.* Barcelona: Edicions 62.

Bon, L. 1997. 'Cent quaranta entitats s'agrupen per demanar més suport al català'. *Avui,* 7 Sept.

Borras, S. 1993. 'The "Four Motors of Europe" and Its Promotion of R&D Linkages: Beyond Geographical Continuity in Interregional Agreements'. *Regional Politics and Policy* 3, no. 3 (Autumn), 163–76.

Botella, J. 1998. 'El comportament electoral'. In S. Giner (ed.), *La societat catalana,* 111–19.

Bou, L., and A. Grau. 1997. 'Reventós entrega a Ribó una cinta de la ponència del català i obre una crisis institucional'. *Avui,* 10 May.

Bou, L., and M. Lasalas. 1997. 'CCOO i UGT donaran avui el suport sindical al català'. *Avui,* 26 Sept.

Bou, L. and M. Fernández. 1997. 'El PP critica la inmersió però vota que el català sigui l'idioma escolar'. *Avui,* 7 May.

Branchadell, A. 1996. *La normalitat improbable.* Barcelona: Empúries.

Brassloff, A. 1989. 'Spain: The State of the Autonomies'. In Murray Forsyth (ed.), *Federalism and Nationalism,* 24–50. Leicester: Leicester University Press.

Brown, M.D., and E.H. Fry. 1993. *States and Provinces in the International Economy.* Berkeley, Calif.: University of California, Institute of Governmental Studies; and Kingston: Queen's Univesity, Institute of Intergovernmental Relations.

Brugué, Q., R. Gomá, and J. Subirats. 1998. 'Els governs de Catalunya'. In S. Giner (ed.), *La societat catalana,* 1081–98.

Brunet, J.M. 1997. 'Aznar desaira a Pujol y considera "puro anécdota" el abucheo a Raimon'. *La Vanguardia,* 18 Sept.

———. 1998. 'Aznar cree que el voto de CiU en el caso Fungairiño refuerza el pacto'. *La Vanguardia,* 21 Jan.

———. 1998 'El Defensor del Pueblo no recurre la ley del catalán pero pide que se cambie', *La Vanguardia,* 9 Apr.

Brunet, J.M., and R. Paz. 1997. 'Aznar y Almunia excluyen reformar la ley electoral contra los nacionalistas'. *La Vanguardia.*

Buesa, C. 1999. 'Dos incendios intencionados en Girona avivan la psicosis racista'. *El Periódico,* 18 July.

Burgess M., and F. Gress. 1993. 'The Quest for a Federal Future: German Unity and European Union'. In M. Burgess and A.G. Gagnon (eds), *Comparative Federalism and Federation: Competing Tradition and Future Directions,* 168–86. Toronto: University of Toronto Press.

Busquet, J. 1998. 'Les indústries culturals a Catalunya: nous reptes i velles solucions'. In S. Giner (ed.), *La societat catalana,* 881–96.

Cabana, F. 1997. 'Els principals grups econòmics a Catalunya'. In S. Giner (ed.), *La societat catalana,* 483–92.

———. 1998. *Espisodis de la burguesia catalana.* Barcelona: Proa.

Caminal, R., L. Torrents, and X. Vives. 1994. 'Les entitas financeres a Catalunya (1982–92)'. In *L'economia catalana davant del canvi de segle,* 257–91.

Caminal Badia, M. 1998. *Partits nacionals a Catalunya.* Barcelona: Empuries.

———. n.d. 'Nacionalisme, nacions i partits nacionals: teoria general i aplicació al cas de Catalunya'. Unpublished manuscript.

Caprile, M., C. Vallvé, and D. Moreno. 1998. 'El mercat de treball a Catalunya'. In S. Giner (ed.), *La societat catalana,* 565–96.

Cardus, S. 1989. 'La Llengua'. In L. Recolons et al. (eds), *Catalunya 77/88,* 331–43.

———. 1989. 'Els agents culturals'. In L. Recolons et al. (eds), *Catalunya 77/88*, 359–70.

———. 1989. 'El mitjans de comunicació'. In L. Recolons et al. (eds), *Catalunya 77/88*, 345–56.

Carr, R. 1980. *Modern Spain, 1875–1980*. London: Oxford University Press.

Carr, R., and Fusi-Aizpurua, J.P. 1979. *Spain: Dictatorship to Democracy*. London: George Allen and Unwin.

Carreño, L. 1987. 'Per una tipologia de les capes mitjanes'. In J.M. Rotger (ed.), *Visió de Catalunya*, 73–86.

Casademunt, A., and J. Molins. 1998. 'Les organitzacions empresarials a Catalunya'. In S. Giner (ed.), *La societat catalana*, 1025–40.

Castells, A. 1997. 'Les relacions fiscals de Catalunya amb Espanya: algunes reflexions en el context europeu'. In F. Cabana et al., *Catalunya i Espanya*, 127–50.

Castells, A., and M. Parellada. 1998. 'L'economia catalana en el context espanyol i europeu'. In S. Giner (ed.), *La societat catalana*, 493–506.

Castells, M. 1997. *The Power of Identity*. Vol. II of *The Information Age: Economy, Society and Culture*. Malden, Mass.: Blackwell.

Centro de Investigaciones Sociológicas. 1996. *Conciencia nacional y regional*. Estudio no. 2,228. Nov.–Dec. Barcelona.

CIDEM. 1995. *Doing Business in Catalonia*. Barcelona.

Colectivo Ioé. 1995. *Presencia del Sur: Marroquíes en Cataluña*. Madrid: Fondamentos.

Colomé, G. 1992. 'The "Partit dels Socialistes de Catalunya"'. In J.M. Maravall et al., *Socialist Parties in Europe*. Barcelona: ICPS.

Colomer, J.M. 1997. 'No era al guió'. In Culla et al., *Memòria de Catalunya*, 220–2.

Colomines, A. 1978. 'Les Bases de Manresa: Aprovació i Repercussions'. In Generalitat de Catalunya, *Les Bases de Manresa, 1892–1992: Cent anys de catalanisme*. Barcelona: Generalitat, 35–48.

Colomines, J. 1992. *La llengua nacional de Catalunya*. Barcelona: Generalitat.

Comissió Interdepartamental per a la Igualtat d'Oportunitats per a les Dones. 1981. *Pla d'actuació del govern de la Generalitat de Catalunya per a la igualtat*. Barcelona.

Conversi, D. 1997. *The Basques, the Catalans and Spain: Alternative Routes to Nationalist Mobilisation*. London: Hurst.

Corachan, J., and J. Tarragona. 1999. 'Més detinguts per la violencia racista'. *El Periódico*, 18 July.

Corbella, J.M. 1988. *Social Communication in Catalonia*. Barcelona: Generalitat.

Costa i Sáenz, d.Á. 1995. 'L'economia catalana de 1980 al 1994: aspectes bàsics de la seva evolució'. *Nota d'economia* 53, Sept.–Dec.

Courchene, T.J., and C.R. Telmer. 1998. *From Heartland to North American Region State: The Social, Fiscal and Federal Evolution of Ontario*, Toronto: University of Toronto Press.

Crespo, M.T., and Rimbau, C. 1998. 'Els serveis socials a Catalunya'. In S. Giner (ed.), *La societat catalana*, 733–56.

Cubeles, X., and X. Fina. 1995. *La cultura a Catalunya*. Barcelona: Fundació Jaume Bofill.

Culla, J.B. 1989. 'L'evolució ideològica dels partits'. In L. Recolons et al. (eds), *Catalunya 77/88*, 243–246.

———, 1993. 'El catalanisme polític dels anys 30'. In J. Termes, *Les Bases de Manresa de 1892 i els orígens del catalanisme*, 71–84.

———. 1996. 'Unió Democratica de Catalunya: le parti democrate-chrétien català (1931–1989)'. In M. Caciagli et al., *Christian Democracy in Europe*, 83–110. Barcelona: ICPS.

————. 1997. 'El triomf del president desconegut'. In Culla et al., *Memòria de Catalunya*, 30–3.

Culla, J.B., L. Bassets, and B. De Riquer. *Memòria de Catalunya: del retorn de 1997 Tarradellas al pacte Pujol-Aznar*. Barcelona: Tauras.

Departament de Cultura. 1991. *La campanya per la normalització lingüística de Catalunya 1982*. Barcelona: Departament de Cultura.

Departament de la Presidència. 1993. *The Catalan Statute of Autonomy*. Barcelona: Generalitat.

Departament de Producció Estadística. 1991. *Padrons municipals d'habitants de Catalunya 1986: cens lingüístic*. Barcelona: CIDC.

Díez-Medrano, J. 1982. *Divided Nations: Class, Politics and Nationalism in the Basque Country and Catalonia*. Ithaca, NY: Cornell University Press.

DiGiacomo, S. 1985. 'The Politics of Identity: Nationalism in Catalonia'. Doctoral dissertation, University of Massachusetts, Department of Anthropology.

Direcció General de Política Lingüística. 1992. *The Catalan Language Today*. Barcelona: Generalitat.

————. 1983. *Llibre Blanc de la Direcció General de Política Lingüística*. Barcelona: Generalitat.

Direcció General de Programació Econòmica. 1997. *The Public Sector of the Generalitat de Catalunya*. Barcelona: Generalitat.

Duchacek, I. 1986. *The Territorial Dimension of Politics: Within, Among and Across Nations*. Boulder and London: Westview Press.

Dufourcq, C.E. 1982. 'Le temps du rayonnement et des crises (1276–1472)'. In Nadal Farreras and P. Wolff, *Histoire de la Catalogne*, 315–45.

Elazar, D.J. 1987. *Exploring Federalism*. Tuscaloosa, Ala.: University of Alabama Press.

Esquerra Republicana Catalana. 1995. *Programe de govern: Força! Cap a la independència*.

————. n.d. 'Les 99 esmenes d'ERC a la llei refusades pel pacte Serra-Pujol'. Photocopy.

————. n.d. 'Anàlisi de la nova llei de política lingüística'. Photocopy.

Estivill, J. 1998. 'L'estudi de la pobresa a Catalunya'. In S. Giner (ed.), *La societat catalana*, 597–612.

Fernández, M. 1997. 'El Foro Babel extrema el seu rebuig a la llei del català i en reclama la retirada'. *Avui*, 29 Sept.

————. 1997. 'Le llei del català supera la primera votació amb el support de CiU, PSC, IC i PI'. *Avui*, 26 Nov.

Fernández-Arroyo, J. 1997. 'La actuación exterior de la Generalitat de Cataluña: 1980–1996: Valoración y perspectivas'. C.E.I. Madrid: Escuela Diplomática.

Ferrer, J. 1989. 'La projecció exterior de les Terres Catalanes'. In L. Recolons et al. (eds), *Catalunya 77/88*, 223–5.

Ferrer i Gironès, F. 1998. 'Història de la discriminació fiscal a Catalunya'. In F. Cabana et al., *Catalunya i Espanya*, 35–65.

Folch-Serra, M. n.d. 'Civil Society and National Identity: The Case of Catalonia'. Photocopy.

Foment del Treball Nacional, CC.OO., and UGT. 1993. 'Un nou model industrial: situació i actuacions a l'àmbit de Catalunya'. March.

Fontrodona, J., and J.M. Hernández. 1998. *Les multinacionals industrials catalanes*. Barcelona: Direcció General d'Indústria.

Fossas Espadaler, E. n.d. 'Seminari Catalunya-Espanya: el model de l'Estat de les autonomies a la llum de les diferents experiències comparades'. Photocopy.

————. 'The Autonomy of Catalonia'. In E. Fossas and G. C. Colomé, *Political Parties and Institutions in Catalonia*, 5–35. Barcelona: ICPS.

Fundació Tribunal i Laboral de Catalunya. n.d. 'Tribunal Laboral de Conciliació Mediació i Arbitrage de Catalunya'. Barcelona.

Gallego-Díaz, S., and B. De la Cuadra. 1989. *Crónica Secreta de la Constitución*. Madrid: Tecnos.

Garcia Brosa, G. 1997. 'La balança comercial amb l'estranger: una aproximació als fluxos economics amb la resta d'Espanya i amb l'estranger (1993–1994)'. In *La balança de pagaments de Catalunya*, 77–100.

Garcia Brosa, G., and Josep Oliver. 1997. 'El comerç de mercaderies de Catalunya: una visió de conjunt de les relacions amb la resta d'Espanya i amb l'estranger'. In *La Balança de pagaments de Catalunya*, 101–19.

Garcia i Segura, C. 1993. *L'activitat exterior de les regions: una dècada de projecció exterior de Catalunya*. Polítiques 12. Barcelona: Fundació Juame Bofill.

Generalitat de Catalunya. 1988. *La llengua en el món del comerç: l'actitud dels catalans davant l'ús comercial del català*. Barcelona: Generalitat.

——. 1990. *Llei 7–1983, de 18 d'abril, de normalització lingüística a Catalunya*. Barcelona: Generalitat.

——. 1992. *The Catalan Language Today*. Barcelona: Generalitat.

——. 1993. *The Catalan Statute of Autonomy*. Barcelona: Generalitat. Departament de la Presidència.

——. 1994. *General Languages Normalisation Plan*. Barcelona: Generalitat.

——. 1997. 'Criteris del govern per a l'elaboració d'una llei d'ús de les llengües oficials a Catalunya. Barcelona: Generalitat.

——. 1997 *Diari oficial de la Generalitat de Catalunya*, no. 2401-29.5., 5839–5843. Barcelona: Generalitat.

——. 1997. *The Public Sector of the Generalitat of Catalunya*. Barcelona: Direcció General de Programació Econòmica.

Gilmour, D. 1991. *The Transformation of Spain: From Franco to Constitutional Monarchy*. London: Quartet.

Giner, S. 1984. *The Social Structure of Catalonia*. Sheffield, UK: Anglo-Catalan Society.

——. 1997. 'Els orígens de la Catalunya moderna'. In S. Giner (ed.), *La societat catalana*, 43–84.

Giner, S. ed. 1998. *La societat catalana*. Barcelona: Institut d'Estadística de Catalunya.

Grau, A. 1996. 'CiU exigeix a Aznar que reconegui explícitament la nació catalana'. *Avui*, 6 Mar.

——. 1996. 'CiU considera imposible votar a favor de la investidura de Aznar'. *Avui*, 7 Mar.

Grimes, B. 1996. *Ethnologue: Languages of the World,* 13th ed. Dallas: Summer Institute of Linguistics.

Grugel, J. and T. Rees. 1995. *Franco's Spain*. London: Arnold.

Guibernau, M. 1993. 'Spain: A Federation in the Making'. In Graham Smith (ed.), *Federalism: The Multiethnic Challenge*, 239–54. London: Longman.

Guiu, J. 1995. 'Educació i ciència a Catalunya'. In S. Giner (ed.), *La societat catalana*, 937–49.

Gunther, R. 1992. 'Spain: the very model of the modern elite settlement'. In J. Higley and R. Gunther (eds), *Elites and Democratic Consolidation in Latin America and Southern Europe*. Cambridge: Cambridge University Press, 38–80.

Hall, J. 'Immigration et Nationalisme en Catalogne'. *Perspectiva Social* 14, July–Dec.

——. 1990. *La connaissance de la langue catalane (1975–1986)*. Trans. Marjorie Coup. Barcelona: Generalitat.

Harty, S. 1978. 'Disputed State, Contested Nation: Republic and Nation in Interwar Catalonia'. Doctoral dissertation, McGill University, Department of Political Science.

———. n.d. 'Republic and Nation in Interwar Catalonia'. Photocopy.

Hernández, P. 1984. 'La diáspora cultural catalana'. In Giner, S., *La Societat catalana*, 273–82.

Homs, O. 1987. 'Formació i composició de la classe obrera a Catalunya: algunes hipótesis'. In J.M. Rotger (ed,), *Visió de Catalunya*, 141–50.

———. 1998. 'Distribució de la riquesa i condició socioeconòmica'. In S. Giner (ed.), *La societat catalana*, 479–82.

Houle, R., and M. Strubell. 1997. 'La projecció demolingüística a Catalunya'. Photocopy.

Hughes, R. *Barcelona*. New York: Vintage.

Institut de Ciències Polítiques i Socials. 1996. *1995: Sondeig d'opinió—Catalunya*. Barcelona: ICPS.

———. 1997. *1996: Sondeig d'opinió—Catalunya*. Barcelona: ICPS.

Institut DEP. 1992. 'Els catalans i el civisme (1995–1997): informe de resultats'. Barcelona, May.

Institut d'Estadística de Catalunya. 1994. 'Influència del nivell de coneixement del català de la mare en el dels fills'. Barcelona: Generalitat.

———. 1998. 'El coneixement del català l'any 1996'. Barcelona: Generalitat.

Institut d'Estadística de Catalunya. 1998. *El coneixement del català l'any 1996*.

Ioé, C. 1992. *La immigració estrangera a Catalunya: balanç i perspectives*. Barcelona: Institut Català d'Estudis Mediterranis.

Izquierda Unida—Iniciativa per Catalunya. 1996. 'Ponencia sobre modelo de estado de Izquierda Unida—iniciativa per Catalunya'. Photocopy. Barcelona-Madrid, 13 June.

Rotger, J.M. (ed.). 1987. *Visió de Catalunya: el canvi i la reconstrucció nacional des de la perspectiva sociològica*. Barcelona: Diputació de Barcelona.

Johnston, H. 1991. *Tales of Nationalism, Catalonia 1939–1979*. New Brunswick, N.J.: Rutgers.

Jordana, J. 1998. 'Les organitzacions sindicals a Catalunya'. In S. Giner (ed.), *La societat catalana*, 1003–24.

———. n.d. 'També són nacionalistes, els sindicats de les Autonomies històriques?'. Photocopy.

Juan, J. 1997. 'Unió ve superada la etapa autonómica y aboga por un modelo confederal auspiciado por el Rey'. *La Vanguardia*, 1 June.

———. 1997. 'Pujol constata el progresivo deterioro del pacto con el PP'. *La Vanguardia*, 18 Sept.

———. 1998. 'Pujol no piensa jubilarse'. *La Vanguardia*, 5 Mar.

Keating, M. 1996. *Nations against the State: The New Politics of Nationalism in Quebec, Catalonia and Scotland*. London: Macmillan.

———. 1998. 'Rethinking the Region: Culture, Institutions and Economic Development in Catalonia and Galicia'. Photocopy.

———. 1998. *The New Regionalism in Western Europe: Territorial Restructuring and Political Change*. Cheltenham, UK: Edward Elgar.

———. n.d. 'Nationalism, Nation-Building and Language Policy in Quebec and Catalonia'. Photocopy.

Laitin, D. 1997. 'The Cultural Identities of a European State', *Politics and Society* 25, no. 3 (Sept.), 277–302.

Laitin, D., and C. Solé. 1989. 'Catalan Elites and Language Normalisation'. *International Journal of Sociology and Social Policy* 9, no. 1, 1–26.

Lasalas, M. 1997. 'El PSC acceptarà per responsabilitat la llei del català si té màxim consens'. *Avui*, 7 Oct.

──────. 1997. 'Més de cent entitats critiquen la rebaixa de la llei de català'. *Avui*, 8 Oct.

Lleonart, P. 1992. *Catalunya: un país, una economia*. Barcelona: Cambra Oficial de Comerç Indústria i Navegació de Barcelona.

Llorens i Vila, J. 'La unió catalanista: de la fundació fins a Martí Julià (1891–1904)'. In Generalitat de Catalunya, *Les Bases de Manresa*, 19–34.

L'Hospitalet de Llobregat. 1997. 'La festa de la llengua esdevé un clam perquè Catalunya sigui un país normal'. *Avui*, 14 June.

McDonough, G.W. 1985. *Good Families of Barcelona: A Social History of Power in the Industrial Era*. Princeton, N.J.: Princeton University Press.

──────. 1991. 'Terra de Pas: Reflections on New Immigration in Catalonia'. In M.M. Azevedo (ed.), *Contemporary Catalonia in Spain and Europe*, 70–97.

Maluquer de Motes, B.J. 1988. 'La grande mutation (1833–1898)'. In J. Nadal-Farreras and P. Wolff, *Histoire de la Catalogne*, 423–53.

──────. 1998. *Història econòmica de Catalunya: segles XIX i XX*. Barcelona: Universitat Oberta-Proa.

Maluquer Sostres, J. 1963. *L'assimilation des immigrés en Catalogne*. Geneva: Droz.

Maravall, J.M., and J. Santamaria. 1986. 'Political Change in Spain and the Prospects for Democracy'. In G. O´Donell, Schmitter, and Whitehead, *Transitions from Authoritarian Rule: Prospects for Democracy*, xxxx. Baltimore: Johns Hopkins University Press.

Marcet, J. 1994. 'The Parties of Non-State Ambit: The case of Catalonia'. In L. de Winter (ed.), *Non-State Wide Parties in Europe*, 163–78. Barcelona: Institut de Ciències Polítiques i Socials.

Marcet, J., and J. Argelaguet. n.d. 'Nationalist Parties in Catalonia: Convergència Democràtica de Catalunya'. Photocopy.

──────. n.d. 'Esquerra Republicana de Catalunya'. Photocopy.

Marsal, J.F. 1977. 'Sociología de la imigración'. *La Vanguardia*, 24 Apr.

Martínez Celorrio, X. 1981. 'Capital humà i innovació a Catalunya'. In S. Giner (ed.), *La societat catalana*, 965–77.

Martínez García, E. 1998. 'La balança fiscal de Catalunya'. In F. Cabana et al., *Catalunya i Espanya*, 193–215.

Masgrau, R. 1984. *Els orígens del catalanisme polític (1870–1931)*. Barcelona: Barcanova.

Maxwell, K. 1986. 'Regime Overthrown and the Prospects for Democratic Transition in Spain'. In O´Donell, Schmitter, and Whitehead, *Transitions from Authoritarian Rule: Prospects for Democracy*, xxxx. Baltimore: Johns Hopkins University Press.

Mercade, F. 1982. *Cataluña: intelectuales políticos y cuestión nacional*. Barcelona: Peninsula.

Miguélez, F. 1987. 'Immigració i mobilitat social'. In J.M. Rotger (ed.), *Visió de Catalunya*, 303–20.

──────. 1998. 'Divisió Social del Treball: Evolució de l'Estructura Social a Catalunya'. In S. Giner (ed.), *La societat catalana*, 553–65.

Miguelsanz i Arnalot, A. 1994. 'El sector turístic a Catalunya'. In *L'economia catalana davant del canvi de segle*, 231–52.

Moderne, F. and P. Bon 1981. *Les Autonomies régionales dans la constitution espagnole*. Paris: Econòmica.

Monné, E., and L. Selga. 1991, *Història de la Crida a la solidaritat: en defensa de la llengua, la cultura i les nacions catalanes*. Barcelona: Balmes.

Morata, F. 1997. 'El Estado de las Autonomías'. In M. Alcántara and A. Martínez (eds), *Política y Gobierno en España*, 121–50. Valencia: Torant Lo Blanch.

Morata, F., and X. Muñoz. 1996. 'Vying for European Funds: Territorial Restructuring in Spain'. In L. Hooghe (ed.), *Cohesion Policy and European Integration: Building Multi-Level Governance*, 195–218. London: Oxford University Press.

Moreno, L. 1994. 'Ethnoterritorial Concurrence and Imperfect Federalism in Spain'. In B. de Villiers (ed.), *Evaluating Federal Systems*, 163–93. Cape Town: Juta.

———. 1995. 'Multiple Ethnoterritorial Concurrence in Spain'. *Nationalism and Ethnic Politics* 1, no. 1 (Spring), 11–32.

———. 1996. La Federalización de España: poder político y territorio. Madrid: Siglo Veintiúno.

Moreno, L., A. Arriba, and A. Serrano. 1998. 'Multiple Identities in Decentralized Spain: The Case of Catalonia'. *Regional and Federal Studies* 8, no. 3 (Autumn).

Muga, M. 1996. 'La opinión de los Españoles sobre la Unión Europea'. Brussels: Comisión Europea, Dirección General X.

Murillo, C., and E. Baró. 1997. 'La balança de turisme'. In *La Balança de pagaments de Catalunya*, 143–79.

Nadal-Farreras, J. and M. Prats. 1982. 'Un bien chèrement défendu la langue'. In J. Nadal-Ferreras and P. Wolff, *Histoire de la Catalogne*, 91–120.

Nadal-Farreras, J., and P. Wolff. (eds) 1982. *Histoire de la Catalogne*. Toulouse: Privat.

Nash, M. 1981. 'The Changing Studies of Women in Contemporary Catalonia'. In M.M. Azevedo (ed.), *Contemporary Catalonia in Spain and Europe*, 107–27.

Negre i Rigol, P., and J.M. García Jorba. 1998. 'La religió dels Catalans'. In S. Giner (ed.), *La societat catalana*, 839–63.

Newhouse, J. 1997. 'Europe's Rising Regionalism'. *Foreign Affairs* 76, no. 1 (Jan.–Feb.), 67–84.

Ohmae, K. 1993. 'The Rise of the Region State'. *Foreign Affairs* 72, no. 2 (Spring), 78–86.

———. 1995. *The End of the Nation State: The Rise of Regional Economies*. New York: Free Press.

Oriol, D., and R. Suñé. 1997. 'El PP se compromete a respetar la ley y ERC recalca que persiste la inferioridad del catalán'. *La Vanguardia*, 31 Dec.

Orizo, F.A., and A. Sánchez. 1991. *El sistema de valors dels catalans*. Barcelona: Institut Català d'Estudis Mediterranis.

Ortega, G.J. 1994. 'La indústria catalana en una economia oberta'. In *L'economia catalana davant del canvi de segle*, 155–75.

Pagès, P. 1984. *La guerra civil (1936–1939)*. Barcelona: Barcanova.

Pagès i Rejsek, J. 1996. *Political Autonomy in Catalonia: Origins, Jurisdiction, and Organisation of the Generalitat*. Barcelona: Departament de la Presidència.

El País. 1996. 'Acuerdo de investidura y gobernabilidad'. 29 Apr.

———. 1997. 'Documento sobre el uso de las lenguas oficiales de Cataluña'. 30 Apr.

Pallarés, F., and J. Font. 1995. *The Autonomous Elections in Catalonia (1980–1992)*. Barcelona: ICPS.

Paralleda, M. 1997. 'Conclusions'. In *La balança de pagaments de Catalunya*, 295–314.

Parellada, M., and G. Garcia. 1994. 'Les relacions comercials de Catalunya amb l'exterior'. In *L'economia catalana davant del canvi de segle*, 387–418.

Parés, i Maicas, M. 1998. 'Les comunicacions de massa a Catalunya'. In S. Giner (ed.), *La societat catalana*, 865–80.

Partit popular de Catalunya. 1997. 'Llibertat i convivència'. Barcelona.

Paz, Rosa. 1996. 'El Gobierno pierde su pulso con CiU y debe retirar el plan de humanidades'. *La Vanguardia*, 17 Dec.

——— —. 1998. 'El PSOE plantea que el Estado pueda recuperar las competencias cedidas a las autonomías'. *La Vanguardia*, 28 Jan.

Pérez Royo, J. 1997. *El nuevo modelo de financiación autonómica: análisis exclusivamente constitucional.* ICPS Working Paper No. 136. Barcelona: Institut de Ciències Polítiques i Socials.

Perspectiva econòmica de Catalunya. 1997. 'Evolució dels intercanvis comercials de productes industrials catalans amb l'exterior (1985–1996)'.

Pi-Sunyer, O. 1986. *Nationalism and Societal Integration: A Focus on Catalonia.* Program in Latin-American Studies, Occasional Papers Series No. 15. University of Massachusetts at Amherst.

Playá Maset, J. 1997. 'La Generalitat exige la retirada del decreto de Geografía e Historia de España por partidista'. *La Vanguardia*, 24 Oct.

Presidencia del Gobierno Español. 1982. *Spanish Constitution.*

Preston, P. 1996. *A Concise History of the Spanish Civil War.* London: Fontana.

PSC. 1996. '8è Congrés: Resolucions'. October.

Puiggené i Riera, A., et al. 1992. 'Official Language Policies in Contemporary Catalonia'. In M.M. Azevedo (ed.), *Contemporary Catalonia in Spain and Europe*, 30–49.

Puigjaner, J.-M. 1995. *Everything about Catalonia.* Barcelona: Generalitat.

Pujol, J. 1994. *Catalanes en España, Madrid, 30 de noviembre de 1981.* Barcelona: Generalitat de Catalunya.

———. 1994. *Penser l'Europe depuis la Catalogne.* Barcelona: Generalitat de Catalunya.

Quatre Motors per a Europa. n.d. *Programa de Treball, 1997–1998.* n.p.

Quesada, S. 1992. *La industrialització de Catalunya al segle XX.* Barcelona: Barcanova.

Rambla, F.X. 1993. *Factors de la distribució territorial de l'ús del Català a la conurbació de Barcelona.* Barcelona: Generalitat.

Recaño Valverde, J., and A.M. Solana Solana. 1998. 'Migració residencial entre Catalunya i la resta d'Espanya'. In S. Giner (ed.), *La societat catalana*, 221–42.

Recolons, L. 1997. 'Migracions entre Catalunya i l'estranger'. In S. Giner (ed.), *La societat catalana*, 243–72.

Recolons. L. et al. (eds). 1989. *Catalunya 77/88.* Barcelona: Fundació Jaume Bofill.

Recolons i Arquer, L. 1979. 'Marc demogràfic dels recents moviments migratoris de Catalunya'. *Perspectiva Social*, 14. July–December, 9–33.

Renui i Tresserras, M. 1994. *Planificació lingüística; estructures i legislació.* Barcelona: Generalitat.

Requejo, F. 1998. *Federalisme, per a què: l'acomodació de la diversitat en democràcies plurinacionals.* Barcelona: Eliseu Climent.

———. n.d. 'Cultural Pluralism, Nationalism and Federalism'. Photocopy.

Ribas, F. 1998. 'Dependència i viabilitat de les relacions entre Catalunya i Espanya a la història recent'. In F. Cabana et al., *Catalunya i Espanya*, 67–87.

Ribó, R. 1997. 'Nacionalismos, investiduras y partidismos'. *Temas Para el Debate*, 30.

Ribó, R., and F. Requejo. 1997. 'Cap a on va l'esquerra catalana?' *Agora*, no. 5 (April).

Roca, F. 1987. 'El poder de la burguesia'. In J.M. Rotger (ed.), *Visió de Catalunya*, 11–19.

Romaní, J.M., and M. Strubell i Trueta. 1998. 'L'ús de la llengua a Catalunya'. In S. Giner (ed.), *La societat catalana*, 805–20.

Rossinyol, J. 1991. *Le problème national catalan.* Paris: Mouton.

Rotger, J.M. (ed.). 1987. *Visió de Catalunya: el canvi i la reconstrucció nacional des de la perspectiva sociològica.* Barcelona: Diputació de Barcelona.

Ruíz, F. 1994. *Història social i política de la lleugua catalana*. Barcelona: Contextos 3i4.

Ruiz F., R. Sanz, and S.J. Camardons. 1973. *Història social i política de la llengua catalàna*. Barcelona: Climent.

Sabaté, J. 1999. 'Víctimes i delinquents'. In S. Giner (ed.), *La societat catalana*, 757–70.

Sabater, J. 1989. 'Els sindicats i l'organització patronal'. In L. Recolons et al. (eds), *Catalunya 77/88*, 61–74.

Saez, A. 1980. 'Catalunya, gresol o explotadora? Notes sobre immigració i creixement'. In J. Ainaud et al., *Immigració i reconstrucció nacional a Catalunya*, 23–35.

Salvador, E. 1989. 'Crònica Política'. In L. Recolon, *Catalunya 77/88*, 207–22.

Sanchez, J. 1997. 'Identitat Collectives i cultura cívica dels Catalans'. In S. Giner (ed.), *La societat catalana*, 1067–80.

———. 1998. 'L'estructura empresarial i productiva de Catalunya'. In S. Giner (ed.), *La societat catalana*, 535–52.

Sancho i Valverde, S. and C. Ros i Navarro. 1984. 'La població de Catalunya en perspectiva històrica'. In S. Giner, *La societat catalana*, 91–116.

Shafir, G. 1995. *Immigrants and Nationalists: Ethnic Conflict and Accommodation in Catalonia, the Basque Country, Latvia and Estonia*. Albany: State University of New York Press.

Santamaría, A. 1999. *Foro Babel: el nacionalismo y las lenguas de Cataluña*. Barcelona: Áltera.

Sarasa, S. 1998. 'Prefaci: la societat civil catalana'. In S. Giner (ed.), *La societat catalana*, 981–4.

———. 1998. 'Associacionisme, moviments socials i participació cívica'. In S. Giner (ed.), *La societat catalana*, 985–1002.

———. 1998. 'Mutualisme, cooperació i filantropia'. In S. Giner (ed.), *La societat catalana*, 1041–55.

Segura Benedicto, A. 1998. 'Salut i sanitat a Catalunya'. In S. Giner (ed.), *La societat catalana*, 655–70.

Serrano, S. 1997. 'La victoria per sorpresa de Pujol'. In L. Bassets, *Memòria de Catalunya*, 201–13.

Smith, A., and C. Mar-Molinero. 1998. *Nations and the Nationalism in the Iberian Peninsula*. Oxford: Oxford University Press.

Solé, M. 1991. 'El català a l'Administració de Justícia'. In Direcció General de Política Lingüística, *Estudis i propostes per a la difusió de l'ús social de la llengua catalana*. Vol. 2, *Situació i evolució recent de la llengua catalana*, 197–200. Barcelona: Generalitat.

Solozábal, J.J. 1996. 'Spain, A Federation in the Making?' In J. Jens Hesse and V. Wright (eds), *Federalizing Europe? The Costs, Benefits and Preconditions of Federal Systems*, 240–65. Oxford: Oxford University Press.

Strubell, M. 1991. 'L'impuls institucional de l'ús del català, des de la Generalitat de Catalunya'. In Direcció General de Política Lingüística, *Estudis i propostes per a la difusió de l'ús social de la llengua catalana*. Vol. 2, *Situació i evolució recent de la llengua catalana*, 203–6. Barcelona: Generalitat.

Suñé, R. 1997. 'Convergència da un paso a la Esquerra'. *La Vanguardia*, 9 June.

———. 1997. 'Pujol asegura que no tiene otra opción que apoyar al PP pese a las actitudes anticatalanas'. *La Vanguardia*, 26 Sept.

———, 1997. 'Un consenso que se retrasó dos años y medio'. *La Vanguardia*, 2 Oct.

———. 1997. 'Un pacto con mucho retoque y alguna cesión'. *La Vanguardia*, 10 Nov.

Suñé, R., and C. Sen. 1997. 'La ponencia del catalán concluye seis meses de trabajo sin consensuar la ley'. *La Vanguardia*, 1 Oct.

Tarrach i Colls, A. 1997. 'La inversió estrangera directa a Catalunya durant el 1995'. *Nota d'economia* 57, Jan., Apr.

Termes, J. 1984. *La immigració a Catalunya i altres.* Estudis d'Història Catalana, Barcelona: Empúries.

———. 1993. *Les Bases de Manresa de 1892 i els orígens del catalanisme.* Barcelona: Generalitat.

Termote, M. n.d. 'L'évolution démolinguistique du Québec et du Canada'. In Commission sur l'avenir politique et constitutionnel du Québec, *Éléments d'analyse institutionnelle, juridique et démolinguistique pertinents à la révision du statut politique et constitutionnel du Québec.* Photocophy. Quebec City.

Tornos, J. 1992. 'L'organisation territoriale de l'Espagne: l'État des autonomies'. In T. Fleiner-Gerster et al., *Le Fédéralisme en Europe,* 103–18. Barcelona: ICPS.

Torres, J. 1979. 'La immigració i la llengua catalana: documentació sobre coneixements, usos i actituds lingüístics'. In J. Ainaud et al., *Immigració i Reconstrucció Nacional a Catalunya,* 43–58.

Trilla, C., et al. 1994. 'Polítiques d'habitatge a Catalunya'. In S. Giner (ed.), *La societat catalana,* 671–94.

Trillas, A. 1997. 'Espanya refusa reconèixer el poder autonòmic al Tractat d'Amsterdam', *Avui,* 10 Apr.

Tudela i Penya, J. 1994. *El Català a l'administració de la Generalitat.* Barcelona: Generalitat.

———. n.d. *L'ús de la llengua catalana a les empreses de Catalunya.* Barcelona: Generalitat.

Tura, S.J. 1974. *Catalanismo y revolución burguesa.* Madrid: Cuadernos Para el Diálogo.

Unió Democratica de Catalunya. 1991. *La sobirania de Catalunya i l'estat plurinacional.* Barcelona.

Unión Europa, Comité de las Regiones. n.d. *Introducción al Comité de las Regiones.* Brussels.

Vallverdú, F. 1984. 'A Sociolinguistic History of Catalan'. In *International Journal of the Sociology of Language* 47, 13–28.

———. 1990. *L'ús del Català: un futur controvertit.* Barcelona: Edicions 62.

La Vanguardia. 1988. 'Cataluña recibirá 1999 115,000 millones al año de fondos de la Unión Europea'. 20 Jan.

———. 1997.'Las autonomías españolas tienen vía libre para defender directamente sus intereses en la UE'. Aug.

———. 1997. 'Pujol exige al PP que condene con más energía las muestras de intolerancia anticatalana'. 17 Sept.

———. 1997. 'El PSC se plantea acotar la inmersión'. 30 Sept.

———. 1997. 'Los nacionalistas consideran franquistas las críticas de intelectuales de izquierda a la ley'. 1 Oct.

———. 1997. 'Las casas regionales creen que la ley vulnera la convivencia pacífica del catalán y castellano'. 3 Oct.

———. 1997. 'El PP modifica el uso del himno español y causa malestar entre sus socios nacionalistas'. 10 Oct.

———. 1997. 'La Generalitat exige la retirada del decreto de Geografía e Historia de España por partidista'. 24 Oct.

———. 1997. 'Acepto el diálogo pero quiero que el decreto de Humanidades entre en vigor el próximo curso'. 30 Oct.

———. 1997. 'El PP advierte que enviará inspectores a las escuelas y Pujol responde que habrá conflicto'. 31 Oct.

———. 1997. 'Apoyo al pacto CiU-PP, pese a todo'. 11 Nov.

——. 1997. 'El pacto PP-CiU debe seguir sin concesiones'. 17 Dec.

——. 1997. 'El PP cree que el decreto final de Humanidades se parecerá al rechazado'. 28 Dec.

Vergés, O., and J. Cruañas. 1991. *The Generalitat in the History of Catalonia*. Barcelona: Departament de Cultura de la Generalitat de Catalunya.

Vilar, P. 1977. *La Catalogne dans l'Espagne moderne*. Paris: Flammarion.

——. 1982. 'Les élans du 18th Century'. In J. Nadal-Farreras and P. Wolff, *Histoire de la Catalogne*, 377–409.

Vilas Nogueira, J. 1992. 'La organización territorial del Estado'. In R. Cotarelo (ed.), *Transición política y consolidación democrática: España (1975–1989)*, xxx. Madrid: CIS.

Watts, R.L. 1996. *Comparing Federal Systems in the 1990s*. Kingston, Ont.: Queen's University, Institute of Intergovernmental Relations.

Woolard, K.A. 1976. *Double Talk: Bilingualism and the Politics of Ethnicity in Catalonia*. Stanford, Calif.: Stanford University Press.

Woolard, K.A., and T.-J.Gahng. 1990. 'Changing Language Policies and Attitudes in Autonomous Catalonia', *Language and Society* 19, no. 3 (Sept.), 311–30.

Zimmerman M., and M.C. 1988. *Histoire de la Catalogne*. Paris: Presses Universitaires de France.

Index